Hunting Game

North-eastern Central African Republic – a vast space bordering Chad, Darfur, and South Sudan – is a quintessential 'stateless' space, where the government has little presence and armed actors operate freely. In this first ethnographic and historical study of Central African raiding, Louisa Lombard investigates practices of forceful acquisition, a distinctive political repertoire in which claims to social status are linked to the ability to take (from wild spaces or from others) and are frequently overturned. People have developed raiding skills to survive and live in a stateless borderland for over 150 years. From the trans-Saharan slave trade and colonial forced labour regimes, to big-game hunting and coercive conservation, and to rebellion, raiding has flourished where people's status in relation to each other is unclear and where institutional guidance is absent. *Hunting Game* offers rich comparative insights into the vibrant, if not always salutary, role that forceful acquisition plays in the world today.

LOUISA LOMBARD is Associate Professor of Anthropology at Yale University. Her research focuses on African borderlands, politics, violence, sovereignty, peace building, and conservation. She is the author of *State of Rebellion: Violence and Intervention in the Central African Republic* (2016) and articles in journals such as *Comparative Studies in Society and History*, *Journal of the Royal Anthropological Institute*, *African Affairs*, and the *Political and Legal Anthropology Review*.

THE INTERNATIONAL AFRICAN LIBRARY

The International African Library is a major monograph series from the International African Institute. Theoretically informed ethnographies, and studies of social relations 'on the ground' which are sensitive to local cultural forms, have long been central to the Institute's publications programme. The IAL maintains this strength and extends it into new areas of contemporary concern, both practical and intellectual. It includes works focused on the linkages between local, national, and global levels of society; writings on political economy and power; studies at the interface of the socio-cultural and the environmental; analyses of the roles of religion, cosmology, and ritual in social organisation; and historical studies, especially those of a social, cultural, or interdisciplinary character.

For a list of titles published in the series, please see the end of the book.

Hunting Game

Raiding Politics in the Central African Republic

Louisa Lombard
Yale University

CAMBRIDGE
UNIVERSITY PRESS

CAMBRIDGE
UNIVERSITY PRESS

University Printing House, Cambridge CB2 8BS, United Kingdom

One Liberty Plaza, 20th Floor, New York, NY 10006, USA

477 Williamstown Road, Port Melbourne, VIC 3207, Australia

314-321, 3rd Floor, Plot 3, Splendor Forum, Jasola District Centre, New Delhi - 110025, India

103 Penang Road, #05-06/07, Visioncrest Commercial, Singapore 238467

Cambridge University Press is part of the University of Cambridge.

It furthers the University's mission by disseminating knowledge in the pursuit of education, learning and research at the highest international levels of excellence.

www.cambridge.org
Information on this title: www.cambridge.org/9781108746182
DOI: 10.1017/9781108778794

Some of the material in this book was previously published in Lombard 2016b, 2016d, 2017, 2018.

First published 2020
First paperback edition 2022

A catalogue record for this publication is available from the British Library

Library of Congress Cataloging in Publication data
Names: Lombard, Louisa, author.
Title: Hunting game : raiding politics in the Central African Republic / Louisa Lombard.
Other titles: International African library.
Description: Cambridge, United Kingdom ; New York, NY : Cambridge University Press, 2020. | Series: The international African library | Includes bibliographical references and index.
Identifiers: LCCN 2019037647 (print) | LCCN 2019037648 (ebook) | ISBN 9781108478779 (hardback) | ISBN 9781108746182 (paperback) | ISBN 9781108778794 (epub)
Subjects: LCSH: Borderlands–Central African Republic. | Poaching–Central African Republic. | Theft–Central African Republic. | Raids (Military science) | Central African Republic–Social conditions. | Central African Republic–Politics and government.
Classification: LCC DT546.375 .L66 2020 (print) | LCC DT546.375 (ebook) | DDC 967.4105–dc23
LC record available at https://lccn.loc.gov/2019037647
LC ebook record available at https://lccn.loc.gov/2019037648

ISBN 978-1-108-47877-9 Hardback
ISBN 978-1-108-74618-2 Paperback

Contents

Figures

Maps

Acknowledgements

Sovereignty is a term used often by academics but much more rarely by others. Yet it is the answer to the most basic of questions: who gets to decide how people live? I came to north-eastern Central African Republic (CAR) interested in exploring sovereignty as experienced in the world. I saw something different from the vision offered by Thomas Hobbes in *Leviathan*, who wrote of the sovereign as someone whom everyone held in awe. In north-eastern CAR, no sovereign consistently set the terms for social life. Instead, people claimed liberties for themselves while also intermittently lamenting the absence of a sovereign, and wishing for one. But in the sovereign's absence, life in the region was not 'nasty and brutish', as Hobbes predicted, but something different altogether, with political modalities not prophesised by classical theorists.

Here were multiple aspirants to sovereign prerogatives. I went into this project equipped with the personal and disciplinary conviction that Hobbes' account of life outside the sovereign state is more bogeyman than description of actual experience in the world. Anthropologists of old sought to collect accounts from the precolonial past, which they, and their interlocutors, could represent as morally coherent, in contrast to the kinds of distortions, discontent, and injustice that accompanied colonial regimes. That is no longer defensible. Instead, contradictions and inconsistencies are obvious, and it is necessary to account for the resilience, creativity, and joys of people in these places, and their particular struggles.

While life in a controlling state has its discontents, following rules and norms under the *threat* of force rather than its exercise usually has advantages, including for interpersonal relations and especially in the context of widespread armament. For instance, consider the travails of Marcel, the operational chief at the Ministry of Water and Forests in Ndele, a town beside north-eastern CAR's parklands. I saw one subordinate physically attack Marcel when Marcel tried to tell him how to do his job. Marcel's plight was similar to that of a colonial official in the town some 70 years earlier, who had no officers to carry out his directives. The hunting inspector 'lent' him an ungovernable corporal described as 'incapable of doing anything good' (Lignier 1936b). Then as now, officials complained about their inability to address their associates' armed mischief. Marcel appreciated having someone to listen to him. He said with understatement, 'It's a little bit difficult when you recruit someone [for arms-carrying work] without knowing if he's got a good moral compass. It's very difficult.'

Yet it is not right to put all the onus on individuals. They participate in social situations, and in those situations moral precepts can be expressed, re-made, or brought into conflict. There are particular kinds of social situations when one lives in a place such as north-eastern CAR, where there are few people and little institutional and material infrastructure, and where the surrounding region has seen pervasive violent conflict. In this book I describe the contested sovereignty of CAR while avoiding both the demonising stereotypes about stateless spaces and the rosy ones put forth by anarchists and their supporters. Each new version of the manuscript that became this book has been a process of discovery.

My register of debts is long. First are the Central Africans – by nationality or by attachment – who shared time and knowledge with me. Among them: Faouzi Kilembe, Martine Kessy-Ekomo, Sylvain Batianga-Kinzi, Patrick Bonazoui, Boris-Harding Ndovou, Charlotte Mararv, Aziza Kassara, Habiba Mohammed, al-Habib Sanusi, Aminata Gaye, Moussa Fofana, Louis Bainilago, Guy-Florent Ankogui, Florent Zowoya, Gisèle Willybiro, Hippolyte Donossio, Fortune Kinguelewa, Jean-Baptiste Mamang-Kanga, Magloire Kolisso, Sylvain Yakara, Soumaine Ndodeba, Joseph Zoundeiko, Damane Zakaria, Pierre-Armand Roulet, Aleksandra Cimpric, Pierre-Marie David, Philippe Bouché, Stephane Gregoire, Wendy Rice, John Hanson, David Tchouinou, and Meike van Ginneken.

As a PhD adviser, Charles Piot mentored through his generous example. The rest of my committee – Orin Starn, William O'Barr, Peter Redfield, and Janet Roitman – contributed excellent questions and suggestions. Rebecca Hardin and Tamara Giles-Vernick's insightful and ethical engagement with Central Africa inspired me.

Others whose comments helped keep me excited about this project through its countless iterations include Kalyanakrishnan Sivaramakrishnan, James Scott, Marcia Inhorn, Catherine Panter-Brick, Erik Harms, Doug Rogers, Helen Siu, David Watts, Mariane Ferme, Donald Donham, Monica Eppinger, Michael Watts, Nancy Peluso, Joshua Craze, Julie Kleinman, Matthew Ellis, Alice B. Kelly, Karen Hebert, Guntra Aistara, Mike McGovern, Henrik Vigh, Nefissa Naguib, Kevin Sobel-Read, Brian Goldstone, Jatin Dua, Kristina Jacobsen, Jeffrey Schauer, Kinch Hoekstra, Nathan Sayre, Hannah Appel, Ilmari Käihkö,

Henri-Michel Yéré, Aaron de Grassi, Jennifer Devine, Bram Büscher, Marielle Debos, Roland Marchal, Enrica Picco, Lotje de Vries, Matthew Ellis, Andreas Mehler, Rebecca Woods, Claudio Sopranzetti, Jonathan Echeverri Zuluaga, Jennifer Johnson, Pierre Englebert, Mats Utas, Peter Little, Dan Magaziner, Libby Wood, Jonathan Wyrtzen, Crystal Feimster, Eddie Thomas, Alex de Waal, Roy Grinker, Sarah Wagner, Jonny Steinberg, Robert Gordon, Luise White, Stuart Marks, Joseph Hellweg, Mirjam de Bruijn, Esther Marijnen, Rosalind Duffy, Erica Bornstein, and Gino Vlavonou.

At Yale, I have worked with stimulating graduate students, among them Aalyia Sadruddin, Kristen McLean, Jacob Rinck, Amy Johnson, Manon LeFevre, Chandana Anusha, Meredith McLaughlin, Rundong Ning, Wen Zhou, and Scott Ross.

Once this project headed towards the IAL monograph series, Stephanie Kitchen, Adeline Masquelier, and reviewers all helped me make more of it than I could have done on my own. Florence Grant, Priscilla Jensen, and Judith Forshaw clarified and cleaned up the prose and ideas it expresses.

I first landed in CAR 16 years ago due to some combination of luck, ignorance, and hubris. I had completed my undergraduate studies about three weeks earlier and served as a research assistant to Eric Berman, then working on a study of small arms and light weapons in CAR for the Small Arms Survey. My ignorance was deep, but so was my curiosity. Each time I go to CAR, and in many of my remote conversations with Central African friends, I am confronted with the knowledge of how much I don't know, and how impossible it is to know a people or a place comprehensively.

But nor am I wholly in the dark. I have come to see patterns in the dilemmas and opportunities people in Central Africa – whether born there or more recently arrived – face and how they deal with them. These patterns are only a few among many others in the lives of Central Africans, and they are not even necessarily the most prevalent (only a subset of people are directly involved in raiding, those most directly almost all men), but they show both something important about what life here has been like and something about the human condition.

I have tried to convey some of the simultaneous freedom and constraint that marks the processes through which people in a hunting zone strive to acquire some measure of status, liberty, and the ability to make their lives as they desire. I look forward to Central Africans, and others, discussing with me in what ways mine has been a worthwhile endeavour, and what remains to be done.

Abbreviations and acronyms

AEF	Afrique Équatoriale Française/French Equatorial Africa
ARRC	Africa Rainforest and River Conservation
AT	*assistant technique*/technical assistant
BBC	British Broadcasting Corporation
CAMPFIRE	Communal Areas Management Programme for Indigenous Resources
CAR	Central African Republic
CFA	Central African franc
DDR	disarmament, demobilisation, and reintegration
DRC	Democratic Republic of the Congo
ECOFAC	Ecosystèmes Forestiers d'Afrique Centrale/Forest Ecosystems in Central Africa
ECOFAUNE	Ecosystèmes Fauni du nord RCA et du Sud-est de la RCA ques/ Faunal Ecosystems of North and Southeast CAR
EU	European Union
FAO	Food and Agriculture Organization of the United Nations
FPRC	Front Populaire pour la Renaissance de la Centrafrique/Popular Front for the Renaissance of the Central African Republic
ICRC	International Committee of the Red Cross
LAB	*lutte anti-braconnage*/fight against poaching
MINUSCA	United Nations Multidimensional Integrated Stabilization Mission in the Central African Republic
MSF	Médecins Sans Frontières/Doctors Without Borders
NGO	non-governmental organisation
PDRN	Programme pour le Développement de la Région Nord/Programme for the Development of the Northern Region

PDZCV	Programme pour le Développement des Zones Cynégétiques Villageoises/Programme for the Development of Community Hunting Zones
RFI	Radio France Internationale/French International Radio
RPRC	Rassemblement Patriotique pour le Renouveau de la Centrafrique/Union for the Patriotic Renewal of the Central African Republic
UFDR	Union des Forces Démocratiques pour le Rassemblement/Union of Democratic Forces for Unity
UNICEF	United Nations Children's Fund
UPC	Union pour la paix en Centrafrique/Union for Peace in the CAR
ZCV	zone cynégétique villageoise/community hunting zone
ZIC	zone d'intérêt cynégétique/zone of hunting interest

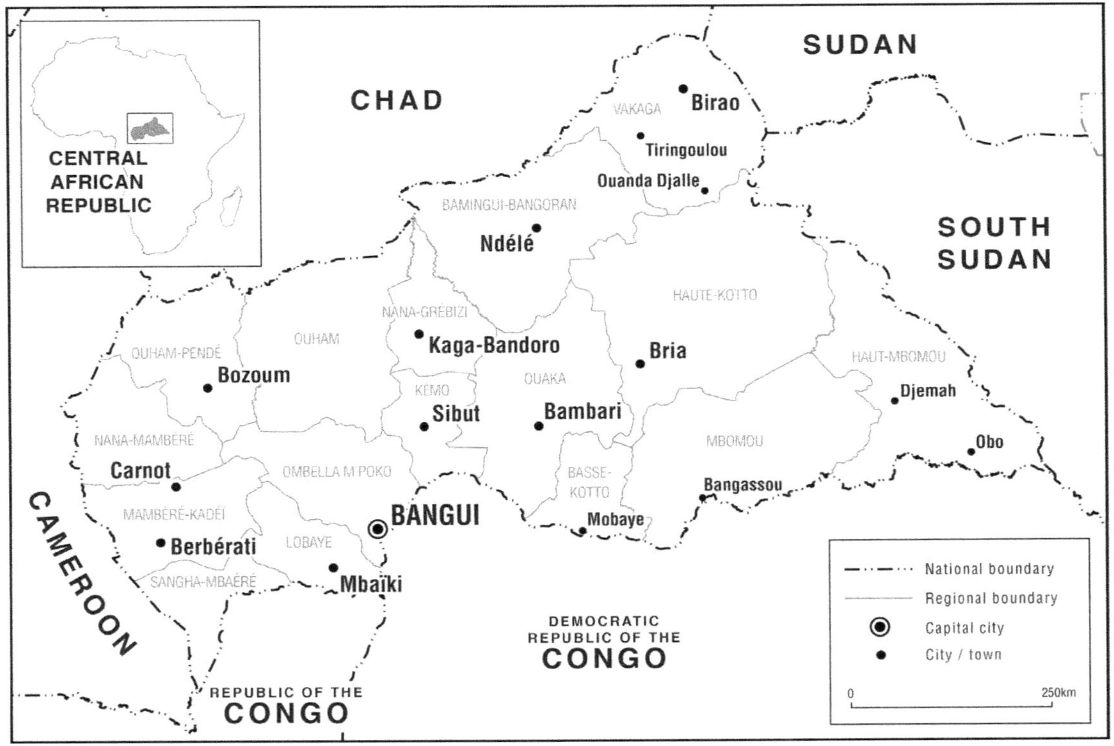

Figure 0.1 Map of the Central African Republic

1 Force, status, and uncertainty in the arts of acquisition

A hunting raid

In the vast parklands of north-eastern Central African Republic (CAR), at a place called Tata, a pathway crosses the road. The built to allow motorised vehicles to travel between the small towns of Ouanda Djallé and Sam Ouandja, appears on maps. The path, which does not show up on the maps, is for hunters, herders, and trackers, people who travel on foot, or on the back of an animal when they are in luck. Neither road nor path is much more than a rutted dirt track; both are constantly encroached upon by trees and scrub. Herds of hundreds of cows are the only force that can effectively blaze an opening.

In the dry early months of 2009, a group of *pisteurs* (tracker-guards employed by an aid project to counter poachers) led by a former French special forces mercenary was tracking the movements of humans and livestock through Tata. The taking of anything from the parklands is 'strictly prohibited'; this does not refer only to hunting – it is 'taking' when livestock are allowed to graze on the wild grasses. To the *pisteurs*, Tata seemed like a promising spot for a blind. They could lie in wait for transgressors who had been spotted in the area and would likely pass this crossroads.

The *pisteurs* set themselves up on either side of the intersection so that it would be harder for their prey to escape. They lay in wait for two hours. Eventually, five or six men dressed in military uniforms (in this region, not always a marker of serving in the armed forces), carrying automatic weapons, and leading pack donkeys came into view. Their appearance and manner of travel made them recognisable as a foreign species: *Janjaweed*[1] come to CAR to collect all the wild goods they could. The

[1] In the words of one of the *pisteurs* who participated in this hunt, 'Those people the Sudanese hired in Darfur, and they don't have work now so they come down here and poach.' The *pisteurs* do not generally verify these kinds of details, however – it is a working assumption. Their choice of terminology makes use of their knowledge that *Janjaweed* are known and vilified internationally.

pisteurs took aim and shot. They killed four men but the fifth managed to shoot one of the *pisteurs* before he ran. The French mercenary pursued and killed him too.

With the most dangerous targets eliminated, the *pisteurs* turned to the donkeys and killed all 36. A rapid inventory of what the donkeys had been carrying provided evidence of a fruitful hunting and gathering mission: many kilos of smoked meat; honey; *mazindi*, a tree seed used in sauces; wild *gumbo* (okra). This they left, although they collected the guns and ammunition, including a G3 battle rifle with 19 rounds. They moved quickly, knowing that associates of the dead men would be roused by news of the raid. The *pisteurs* jumped into their Land Cruiser – a few in the cab, most into the bed – and sped off towards Sam Ouandja.

At that time, Sam Ouandja was home to a few thousand Darfuri refugees; a contingent from the Union des Forces Démocratiques pour le Rassemblement (UFDR, or Union of Democratic Forces for Unity), a CAR rebel group; a few dozen government troops; several thousand residents; some fortune seekers labouring nearby to dig up a diamond or two; and a few middlemen who financed and bought from them. When the Land Cruiser arrived and some former *pisteurs*, now in the UFDR, heard about the loot left behind at Tata, several in the group headed out to retrieve what they could.

'Vengeance,' explained one of the *pisteurs*, summing up their mission in this raid. That word came up a lot; we will return to it later in the book. The *pisteurs* also recognised that they benefited from these operations because they got first dibs on the loot they could capture and received monetary bonuses for items seized. 'When we find someone who has been hunting or fishing in the park, it is us, the *pisteurs*, who benefit from that,' summarised one.[2] At least some of the time, they also distribute to those they consider fellows by alerting them when goods are left behind.

The *pisteurs* spoke of their job as a struggle to stamp out hunting. But the eventful parts of their work consisted of tracking and a particularly violent mode of hunting other hunters. Besides that, they waited, and they told stories. The more I immersed myself in the history of the region, the more I saw the centrality of violent hunting to the projects of coercion and profit pursued there over the last 150 years. State building, in the form of establishing dominant authority and control and managing populations in a stable manner, has been far less significant.

I wanted to explore politics as they are, rather than in terms of what is missing. To do so, I have set aside the usual political frameworks and

[2] This statement came after the reflection that 'the locals are just trying to feed their families, but unfortunately it [hunting or fishing in the parks] is strictly prohibited'.

metaphors, instead trying to understand what skills, capacities, and objectives accompany the more violent forms of hunting, which I refer to for simplicity's sake as raiding. Raiding is due serious consideration as a fundamental element in the constitution of politics, arising as it does in times and places of disputed status, uncertain ownership, and fragile accord.

Limit cases of state and sovereignty

The globe in my university library, benignly round, large, and smooth, divides the earth's surface into a jigsaw puzzle, each coloured piece corresponding to a country. It is such a comfortingly neat portrayal, yet so misleading. Vast spaces that are formally assigned to states remain outside their interest or effective authority. Many terms are pressed into service to describe such remote recesses. Are they frontiers, borderlands, hinterlands, or margins? Most studies focus on what these areas do for state power and/or capitalist modes of production, or how their resources are taken, sometimes violently, to profit actors who are closer to the centre of the state, whether national or foreign, and are bent on accumulation. North-eastern CAR is a quintessential example of such state recesses, and cursory treatments of the area usually tell a version of the accumulation story. Current versions list the region's rebels among the chief profiteers. Such accounts have not discerned what is interesting and illuminating about the difficult history of places such as Tata: namely, that if acquisition is attempted where infrastructure and institutions are ineffective, certain interpersonal repertoires and ethical possibilities – modes of practical power – are likely to develop. A look at Tata and its environs and the encounters that take place there shows that people develop improvisational skills that let them acquire goods and assert their own status. These skills are markedly different from those associated with state building and steady accumulation, and yet this space is not fully outside state logics, either.

Above all, this area has been a site of encounter, innovation, and moral conflict. Although many people in north-eastern CAR claim entitlements and privileges, and the right to distribute to their kin, sovereignty is deeply contested, rather than residing in one leader or institution. Take the 'strict prohibition' against claiming goods from parkland spaces. In fact, *de jure* prohibitions are not as extensive as the *pisteurs* aver, nor are the *pisteurs* legally authorised to ambush as they did at Tata. But nor do the non-*pisteur* acquisitors see the laws as a form of colonial repression, or their own acts as morally defiant poaching. In other words, this is neither a situation in which there exist a number of fairly distinct legal and/or moral orders in competition, nor one in which people see their technically illegal actions as somehow licit. To a great extent, people involved in these kinds of hunting and raiding are more concerned with specific situations. Who, in *this* instance, on this Thursday morning hunting trip, is a fellow? What can we get away with, knowing that rivals are in the vicinity? Abstractions have little weight; people might state that they support a principle and later rally others to denounce its application to those who join in protest. State laws have power – in particular, they can be a kind of scaffolding for collaboration with people outside the space – but they are not hegemonic. Instead, they are negotiable, deeply and continually.

Acquisition, especially raiding, in north-eastern CAR provides an opportunity to revisit classic anthropological discussions of 'statelessness' from a fresh vantage point and to call into question teleological assumptions attached to histories of states and economic development. Statelessness used to be studied as a mode of organisation of a people – the Tiv (Bohannan and Bohannan 1953), the Tallensi (Fortes 1940), and the Nuer (Evans-Pritchard 1940), for example. But while north-eastern CAR is a place where state institutions have little presence, it is not home to 'peoples' organised 'against the state', in Clastres' famous phrasing (1977). Instead, it is a place where legal and cosmological orders are fundamentally plural and contested, as is the content of the terms 'we' and 'they', which change depending on the particular circumstances in which they are employed. Contentious circumstances greatly affect social relations here and raiding encounters are one particularly prominent form of contentious circumstance.

In focusing on raiding encounters and how people go about them, I am reviving the 'situational analysis' promulgated by Max Gluckman (1958), who argued against the analysis of complexes of people and cultures as if they were stable entities in favour of focusing on:

> everyday events of crisis in which ordinary expectations for action were thrown into question and taken-for-granted values opened to interpretation with potentially system-changing effects. Gluckman's method stressed the heterogeneities of value in practice and the conflicts and tensions in interpretation and judgment. (Kapferer and Gold 2018: 7)

These conflictual situations in which values and practice must be argued for or negotiated, Gluckman posited, are how norms are tentatively produced and changed. The insight that process and encounter are more important than 'people and their culture' explanations allows an understanding of the interplay among people with competing world views, operating in the same space or reacting to the same problems. It helps make sense of how people with greatly differing explanations about what they are doing or why (for example, sultans as opposed to colonial officials) nevertheless often engage in similar practices.

The result is not an emic, or ontological, account. 'Raider' is not an identity proudly claimed by people in north-eastern CAR; raiding is instead a complex of practices and encounters that I argue are enacted by a range of people – from European Union (EU) bureaucrats looking for ways to fund conservation, to *pisteurs*-turned-rebels, to itinerant cattle herders. In other words, this raiding analytic is not a 'local' category that I am endeavouring to interpret. The various people I describe as engaging in raiding and hunting do not necessarily see themselves as 'raiders' or 'hunters' in the sense of either assumed or innate identity. 'Raiding' is a framework I have developed to draw out the capabilities, know-how, tactics, and frustrations of the various people who encounter each other in this area as they seek regard and respect from audiences there and elsewhere. Raiding shows similarities among people with disparate qualities and origins who use the area to further their careers,[3] and it shows how their lives have been shaped by 'everyday events of crisis' and 'heterogeneities of value in practice' (Kapferer and Gold 2018: 7). This is not the story of a group with a shared vocabulary for the dynamics I describe, with a coherent, shared moral framework. I have chosen terms of raiding and acquisition as a meta-language to communicate the findings of my situational-analytical project. The utility of these terms in describing a political repertoire – the practices and orientations of those who raid to further their careers – passed a significant test when I shared them with my interlocutors in CAR and they recognised themselves and others working in the zone.

After more than 15 years of familiarity with CAR, I have invested myself in the worth of this place and what life there contributes to understanding the world and the diversity of ways in which people inhabit it. Understanding the trajectory of politics in north-eastern CAR can enrich and alter how we think about politico-economic processes much more broadly. This area disproves accounts that portray 'stateness' as the inevitable direction of politics, if only enough time is allowed. It also demonstrates the limitations of frameworks such as 'modes of production', since raiding encounters are primarily 'modes of acquisition', which has consequences for the political formations that follow. An understanding of CAR's 'hunting zone' also reminds us of the many ways beyond war and conquest in which violence can be part of

[3] As sociologist Erving Goffman explained, 'The concept of the career … allows one to move back and forth between the self and its significant society, without having overly to rely for data upon what the person says he thinks he imagines himself to be' (1959: 123).

governance and extraction, illuminating the point that, while raiding and acquisition have usually been understood as a phase of historical development (e.g. Ling, Earle, and Kristiansen 2018), they remain a fundamental part of the modern world, and can be persistent. In north-eastern CAR, raiding has taken the form of a kind of turbocharged hunting – including, notably, hunts for humans. But the features that I identify as pushing in the direction of raiding, such as uncertainty around status and property, also obtain in contexts far beyond Central Africa.

Many have posited that 'precarity' – in Anna Tsing's (2015) clear and concise phrasing, life without the promise of stability – has become the condition of our times. In the terrains this book covers, most people do indeed live without the promise of political, economic, or social stability. But this is not a recent development; it has persisted for generations. This has been a '*disturbance-based ecology in which many species sometimes live together without either harmony or conquest*' (Tsing 2015: 5, emphasis in original) ever since it became integrated into long-distance trades and political projects some 150 years ago. Certainly, precarity did not happen here first, but the area's prolonged exposure to uncertainty and its mixing of people and species amid dynamics of acquisition offer rich lessons about the vagaries of collaboration, force, ethics, and law when stability cannot be assumed. Self-consistency in ethical striving, identified as the goal of many in fascinating recent anthropological accounts of ethics (Laidlaw 2013; Mahmood 2004; Zigon 2007), becomes possible only when facilitated by infrastructures and institutions. When, in contrast, raiding and acquisition are more prevalent, a different kind of relational ethical person emerges.

But first, we must situate ourselves. Please travel with me to north-eastern Central African Republic (CAR), this book's heart. Once upon a time, not so long ago, places like this were the lifeblood of my discipline, anthropology. The more remote they were the better, for fieldwork bragging rights and for generating anthropological theory. But with the decline of the impetus of 'butterfly-collecting' cultural preservation, over the last few decades remoteness has lost its cachet. The rural, the remote, the village: all came to seem reserves of gossip and tradition and outdated anthropological questions in comparison to those generated from gleaming, congested, rough-and-tumble cities where people went to seek their fortunes and new ways of life and connection. But these rural–urban contrasts, explicit or implicit, are misguided. The 'bush' – places where there are few humans stably resident – has been as much a site of social and economic innovation as anywhere else. It has also been a site where relationships between people and other creatures have been particularly unstable, a site of both quite a lot of violence and unexpected situational collaboration.

Even in the context of a figurative, book-generated journey, it can be difficult to convince people to make the trek to north-eastern CAR. Where is it exactly? 'Central African Republic' conveys a vague sense of location, but rarely clear pictures of the place or its history. In this introductory chapter, let me situate the places, people, and relational dynamics that make it such an important, and neglected, part of social histories of the world and ideas about the future. Throughout the book I show that the area has been a crucible for the development of processes of acquisition and the personal and political repertoires that allow them, and that ignoring the lessons these dynamics confer makes our understanding incomplete. First, though, let me show you around.

A hunting zone

The lands that today form CAR lie at the geographic centre of the African continent. This was the last 'great blank space' (Boulvert 1996) on geographers' maps, drawn as empty space as late as 1890 (Kalck 1971: 1). CAR covers an area about the size of Texas (or France and Benelux combined) and encompasses a range of equatorial geographic zones: the tropical rainforests and rushing rivers of the south give way to forested savannah and the dry savannah of the north-east – marshy during the rainy season and near-desert during the dry. People are known to have lived in these lands for millennia, and indeed the savannah itself – far from a natural or wild condition – is the product of their use of fire for farming and settlement (Cordell 1983: 35–6). The area is well endowed with water, with space, and with other resources such as salt, all of which have supported flourishing settlements for many centuries. Although there has been a strong degree of linguistic continuity, the makeup of communities and networks of solidarity have shifted repeatedly, in part because, for centuries, people have moved around constantly (Cordell 1983; Sikainga 1991). Empires and states in the broader region have formed and disbanded; the Central African expanses were places where those seeking refuge from these upheavals could flee. The area is punctuated by rocky plateaus pockmarked with caves, or *kagas*, which were especially defensible and were good places to live and hide.

By the late eighteenth century, Muslim traders had established a network throughout these lands, both for business opportunities and to lay a pilgrimage route for their fellow believers. Over the course of the nineteenth century, the Muslim presence increased. So did the demand for slaves in the long-booming and transforming Muslim polities to the north and west, such as Darfur and Bornu. The prosperous farmer-hunters of Central Africa became prime targets for raiding.

Occasional slave-hunting missions ramped up and gained intensity just when European colonial explorers started making forays into the area, as the 1800s were drawing to a close. The early (nineteenth-century) written accounts of the people living in this area, by both Arabs and Europeans, describe them as hierarchical only in limited ways. They note instead 'polycellular' modes of organisation characterised by a 'mobile equilibrium' that was a major source of resilience (Prioul 1981: 166). When Europeans passed through small agglomerations of residents, one man would usually come forward to act as interlocutor. The interlopers referred to these people as chiefs, but their authority consisted more of persuasion than command (Prioul 1981).

France had been allotted the area that became Afrique Équatoriale Française (AEF) at the Berlin Conference in 1884–5, but by the 1890s only a handful of French people were staffing Bangui, the recently proclaimed capital of the interior equatorial zone known as Oubangui-Chari, which later became CAR. There was only feeble support in France for the colonisation of Equatorial Africa. A colonial officer wrote dryly of the colony of Oubangui-Chari in 1903 that earlier 'reports, overly pompous, presented [this area] as rich and fertile, which is far from the precise truth' (Colonie du Congo 1903: 32).[4] One attempted solution – the granting of concessions to private companies – was expected by the French government to bring in useful short-term revenue and help establish European profit-oriented rule, in a manner similar to tax farming. But the companies had no lasting interest in the region; rather than investing in infrastructure they sought to extract concrete value – in ivory and rubber, for example – as quickly as they could, although only a few made a profit. The privatisation of governance is often assumed to be a contemporary phenomenon, but that assumption can be sustained only by presentist bias, and in particular by ignorance of the concessionary history of Equatorial Africa.

One of the key historical developments shaping this region was the coincidence of Muslim and European interests. Although their leaders were in some ways antagonistic, they also complemented each other, providing their counterparts with needed resources such as arms or labourers, and the 30 years from the 1890s to the First World War became the most intense period of raiding – forceful and armed (for instance, for people to be made slaves and forced labourers) as well as more negotiated – the region had ever seen. A well-populated, spacious home to people who lived with relative abundance became depopulated, with villages left smouldering and abandoned. Foreign diseases that had

[4] Unless otherwise noted, all translations from the French are my own.

begun to spread some hundred years before intensified, killing many. And the brutal forced labour and other policies of the French administration further decreased the population.

The area, then known as the Oubangui-Chari Division of the Federation of French Equatorial Africa, became a place with a 'disastrous demography' (Kalck 1959: 313). Because it had been such an important site for raiding and refuge, for flight and mobility, any so-called 'ethnic' group was in fact an amalgam, its organisation difficult to ascertain (Cordell 1983; Sikainga 1991: 53). If even French colonisers had been interested in co-opting African 'tradition' for their own despotic rule, as Mamdani (1996) has identified as the key colonial dynamic in Africa, they would have found little to work with. But they were not. The defining feature of French involvement in this part of the world was penury and cheapness, which meant that their rule – to the extent that they were indeed ruling – became an odd pattern of neglect punctuated by outbursts of arbitrary brutality when they needed to acquire people's labour for some project such as road clearing or the relocation of villages.

The only things that French administrators saw as valuable in these lands were the wild animals. In the aftermath of the intense elephant hunting of the raiding apogee of the 1890s to the 1910s, animal populations had dropped, but they began to rise again by the 1920s. The area appeared to be a wild paradise: Africa as it had always been. This was not true, of course, but it was a way for the French to salvage interest, financial and otherwise, in such a vast space at the centre of the continent, with so few people, so little infrastructure, and no straightforward path to industrial or plantation development or institutionalised capitalist rule. The few humans present were joined by a panoply of other creatures: elephants, lions, rhinos, hippos, and massive Lord Derby elands. Colonial administrators never commented on the charms of the 'natives' or the beauty of the landscape, except in the ways in which they both related to hunting. A. Boucher, an administrator in Birao, the north-easternmost outpost of Oubangui-Chari, wrote in a monograph on the area that it 'is without a doubt one of the most beautiful hunting regions in the world' (1934: 49). Colonial officials frequently noted how many animals they encountered, and, clearly captivated, they told verbose hunting stories (Brégeon 1998: 21). In my perusal of the French colonial and military archives, I frequently came across snapshots of proud hunters beside their prey: '*souvenirs de chasse*', or 'memories/keepsakes of hunting'.

The furthest interior corner of the colony, the north-east, was known as the area with the best big-game hunting. Very nearly the entirety of the north-east received the joint designations of *district autonome* (autonomous district, an area too far from the capital and of too limited value to administer directly) and *zone d'intérêt cynégétique* (ZIC, or zone of hunting interest), or, in my shorthand, a hunting zone. Game reserves were created and hunting regulations adopted in an attempt to monetise and control the hunting of big game in the area. The regulations were, however, wholly out of touch with the vicissitudes of life in the area and were never very effective in controlling hunting, even as they became part of how people played hunting games.

In 1960, with the independence of France's West and Equatorial African colonies, Oubangui-Chari became the Central African Republic. The country's main independence visionary, Barthélémy Boganda, had been killed in a plane crash the year before, and in his absence the new leaders struggled to establish a vision for their country. French officials admitted that, of their former colonies, Oubangui-Chari was the least prepared for independence, due to the extremely limited institutional infrastructure built during the colonial period and the minimal formal economy. There were few schools or clinics, and in some parts of the country illegal forced labour persisted (Brégeon 1998).

What little infrastructural or institutional development had occurred was largely concentrated in the southern, riverine area near Bangui. In that area, during the colonial era, many people had converted to Christianity and had learned to speak the trading language Sango, promoted by the French as a lingua franca because teaching French would have been prohibitively difficult and expensive. The north-east, home mostly to Muslims, had been left largely to its own devices, except for the demarcation of the national parks, game reserves, and safari-hunting concessions. Both the French officials of AEF and the British in Anglo-Egyptian Sudan found their half-hearted attempts at indirect rule frustrated by the fluidity of social relations in the area, which 'defied' their notions of 'tribalism' and 'ethnicity' (Sikainga 1991: 53) when, on occasion, they tried to map out groups and lineages.

Neglected and overlooked, CAR gained international notoriety due to the flamboyant Jean-Bédel Bokassa, who seized power in a coup on New Year's Day 1966. Outside CAR, Bokassa is remembered largely for his megalomaniacal tendencies, which became more pronounced towards the end of his rule. In a lavish ceremony in 1977, he had himself crowned emperor. The following year, his troops brutally repressed an uprising by schoolchildren upset over rising costs for school fees and uniforms. Rumour had it he ate humans, including some of the recalcitrant schoolchildren.[5] But Central Africans today remember Bokassa as their sole leader with a

[5] This rumour was started by a former French mercenary, who admitted that it was a fabrication; it has persuaded many, non-Central Africans and Central Africans alike, but it has not been substantiated.

nation-building impulse. He inaugurated the annual *Fête des mères* (Mothers' Day), a day with expectations of gift giving and revelry as major as Christmas; and he built the university and the modernist ministerial edifices that dot the capital. He also had the benefit of leading during a period when foreign aid was relatively lavish and the regional security situation calmer than it would later become.

In the wake of the incident with the students and other signs of what the French government took to be intransigence, French forces removed Bokassa from power in 1979, one of many times when they have played a decisive role in installing Central African leadership. In the decades that followed, most of the countries in the region were wracked by war, the Central African economy plummeted, and outside donors that had paid government salaries and otherwise kept things afloat reduced or ended their assistance. Violent upheaval increasingly became part of Central African politics, as did intervention – by forces from the region and by international coalitions of peacekeepers. I explore the dynamics of rebellion and international intervention in CAR at length in my book *State of Rebellion* (2016d).[6] Here, my focus is on the country's north-east – the hunting zone – and on exploring the improvised politico-economic repertoires of action that have developed out of people's raiding and acquisitive practices in the area.

The north-eastern expanses of CAR cover an area about the size of Switzerland, although this is something of an artificial demarcation because the neighbouring areas in Chad, Darfur, and South Sudan bear many of the same features: not a lot of humans and very little built infrastructure. The three north-easternmost prefectures of CAR make up nearly a third of the country's territory but hold less than 4 per cent of its human population.[7] The area is hard to get to. During the rainy

[6] In *State of Rebellion* I explored the consequences of rigid thinking about nation states as the only proper container for politics that has become dominant in the contemporary world, particularly in relation to the kinds of international interventions that have become widespread in 'fragile' states such as CAR in the post–Cold War world. Here, my interest lies in the mode of relations, the theatres of encounter, and the ways of being that have shaped life in this zone. The fact that the state is primarily understood to be 'absent' plays into all of that, but logics of state-like behaviour have a much smaller role in organising the ways in which people engage with others. Moreover, focusing on 'the state' would risk overshadowing the range of people and scales involved in these political-economic processes – for example, the ways in which humanitarian concern in Europe and beyond has played into the dynamics of raiding in Central Africa for more than a century. It would also prescribe categories of belonging and thereby would group people in ways that are more rigid than what has been seen in the hunting zone.

[7] According to the 2003 census, Vakaga, the north-easternmost prefecture, had a population of 37,595 and an area of 46,500 square kilometres; in Bamingui-Bangoran, that ratio was 38,437/58,200, and in Haute-Kotto it was 69,514/86,650.

season, it becomes a marshy island, impassable to trucks and frequently to small aircraft as well. There are no paved roads unless one journeys hundreds of kilometres to the south, although to the north, in oil-boom Chad, tarmac is more easily accessible (but, for the last decade or so, several rebel groups based on or near the road on the Central African side of the border have made it harder to pass that way). In CAR, an increase in the cross-regional hunting of large animals and cattle herding became the impetus for coercive conservation initiatives, many funded by the EU, beginning at the end of the 1980s and continuing to the present. The tracker-guards employed by these projects hunt people in the vast parklands, and some also participate in processes of acquiring the profitable wild goods this area is known for. Since 2006, rebel groups have also emerged in the area, using shows of force to acquire symbolically important assets in their claim to status and regard.

One way of speaking of this area – a favourite of journalists – is to describe it as 'potentially rich' thanks to its endowments of natural resources. Oil, diamonds, gold, uranium, and water – CAR's licit resources alone make it sound like a treasure chest. However, these resources are all difficult to exploit on an industrial scale, or otherwise less promising than they first sound. The oil is near the village of Boromata, one of the hardest-to-reach points possible, in the middle of an area that the rainy season turns impassable. The diamonds are high quality but spread widely rather than amenable to efficient mining. The gold is mostly in dust form, not chunks. And although the French firm Areva began a uranium-mining project at Bakouma in 2007, its profitability depended on high global prices, which dropped after the Fukushima disaster in 2011. Areva suspended prospecting, and the war in CAR since 2013 has continued to discourage investment. Therefore, although the area is not inherently benighted or desolate, and is indeed well endowed with life-giving features including water, space, and rich forage for livestock and other herbivores, it has never been a resource frontier. That is, it has never been a site for an intensive, overpowering kind of exploitation that allows certain people or classes to accumulate wealth at the expense of others and over time instantiates intensified capitalist relations of domination and effective administration and control of people and other resources. In this vein, resource frontiers are usually understood to be a phase in a process of exploitation, but even in studies of places that get 'stuck' in the frontier phase (such as the Niger Delta as described by Porter and Watts 2017; Watts 2012), their status as sites for accumulation by some at the cost of dispossession of others is never questioned.

The tallies of accumulation and state power in north-eastern CAR are less easily calculated. Instead of accumulation – the amassing of wealth by certain actors, sometimes with regulatory support – this has been a site for projects of forceful acquisition, many of which have been challenged, overturned, or ultimately negotiated. Identifying distinctions between accumulation and acquisition – although, of course, they can overlap – shifts the analytical focus away from what these kinds of spaces do for capitalist processes of accumulation and political domination, which are not pre-eminent here, and towards the interpersonal and political repertoires that develop out of acquisition and uncertainty. While CAR is a 'limiting case' (Rutherford 2003: 229) of state and sovereignty, it shows that assumptions about the range of political-economic repertoires at play in the world today are marked by unwarranted blind spots. There is a tendency to assume that people can be described according to stable categories of status and associated roles or positions (both physical and moral). The story of north-eastern CAR, in contrast, unspools a long historical narrative in which the status that people and other creatures can claim in relation to one another is frequently mutable. And despite the fact that it is not really on the road to anywhere, and is home to very few humans, this has long been a zone of encounter through its long-distance networks of circulation and trade. Raiding as a central mode of action for the zone's would-be leaders was inextricably intertwined with the uncertainties – or exploitable differences – regarding people's social status or claims to property. Must I regard this person as a fellow, equal, or peer? Can they be claimed as property? On what physical and moral grounds? Who can challenge me or my actions, and how?

Raiding calls attention to a crucial set of political-economic dynamics that are often overlooked. James Ferguson (2015) has argued that many contemporary political-economic theories take production – the making of goods and services – as the norm, at the expense of equally important systems of distribution. In north-eastern CAR there is another mode neglected by the norm: raiding and acquisition. Acquisition is different from production, as Plato long ago noted in *The Sophist*. The productive arts 'create their object' whereas the 'arts of acquisition' 'do not fabricate their object but instead appropriate existing things' (Chamayou 2012: 5, footnote 5).[8] Acquisition involves taking something, the status of which is uncertain or at least contested by the taker. Acquisition can be surreptitious; it can include crucial rituals to account for what is taken, as occur

[8] Of course, people must produce and invent tools and technologies that they then put to use in acquiring, as Mavhunga shows in his discussion of the 'professoriate of the hunt' (2014). Dichotomies always have connections too. The distinction between production and acquisition remains important, nevertheless, in terms of the kinds of relationship each fosters.

in many 'traditional' hunting practices; or it can be perpetrated by force. The last of these comes the closest to describing the Tata ambush that opened this book, but the lines between modes of acquisition are not often neatly drawn. For Aristotle, everything from fishing to usury to war was a form of acquisition, often in combination – the fisherman might also be a maritime brigand, for instance (Loos 1899).

As states, with their systems of law and national economies, have become the norm, acquisition has tended to be conflated with production (for example, bioprospecting as a mode of 'drug development' rather than, say, negotiated theft, or 'diamond production', when in reality diamonds are taken, not made); rendered an outlier or otherwise an outlaw; or overlooked. Acquisition has more often been regarded as a matter of accumulation. The problem with that is that projects of acquisition do not always end in the amassing of goods or wealth. 'Accumulation' suggests that taking is the inexorable, cumulative feat of powerful capitalist agents. Acquisition, by contrast, emphasises the attempt to take – the process of taking – and the conditions that facilitate it, but it makes no claim about what happens next: the thing acquired can later be taken by someone else, or traded, or discarded. Therefore, where 'accumulation' is an apt term to describe how government-led coercion and private profiteers frequently work together (Reyna 1999), 'acquisition' tends to happen in the recesses of both state and profit, where authority is plural, status uncertain, and people turn ambiguity into opportunity.

Production is, of course, present in north-eastern CAR as well (particularly in the form of agriculture – groundnuts, manioc, millet – for familial consumption), but acquisition – including forceful acquisition – has been prevalent in a way that is impossible to ignore, unlike, perhaps, in places where the state's reach is more institutionalised and managerial. Here, it is associated with the uncertain status relations that must be negotiated in the absence of the imposition of other rules. Who, or what, may be ignored or disregarded? Who is a danger and must be taken seriously? Who is so dangerous that they must be eliminated? From whom can things – including labour – be seized? Who can contest such a seizure? In addition, there can be a desire to make a name for oneself, in the particular ways that are possible in a place where oversight and surveillance or policing are nearly impossible. It is also gendered: forceful acquisition here has been claimed by men, with women pushed into other roles.

North-eastern CAR offers an opportunity to set aside default political-economic concepts such as accumulation, alienation, production, and investment – none of which help explain the encounters, orientations, and processes at play – and instead consider acquisition, status instability, force, and identification, which do. North-eastern CAR is fully part of the capitalist world; it just reminds us that the world of capitalism is broader than is usually acknowledged. The lost expectation of stability (in Tsing's word, precarity) has recently emerged as a crucial node for understanding the predicaments and possibilities of capitalism. However, looking at CAR shows that precarity is nothing new – here, it has a rich, interesting, and sometimes tragic history, one lacking the luxury of the industrial or state-welfare nostalgia sometimes present in imperial hubs. This long-standing precarity is one reason why the journey this book takes is not to a place or a people but to the situational encounters among insiders and outsiders and people in between as they try to work out claims to status and acquisition in the wooded savannahs of north-eastern CAR, a site where some have claimed renown, status, and profit.

Hunting, raiding, and innovation

When I arrived in north-eastern CAR in October 2009 and began investigating town policies relating to the management of people, I found that domain to be relatively empty. Any attempts to establish control over or 'administer' other people were continually renegotiated or otherwise unsuccessful. Everyone – bureaucrats and citizens alike – agreed that establishing unitary control was the writ of 'the state', an absence so frequently invoked as to become its own presence. Instead, the contests and collaborations in the area were precipitated and sustained by the struggle for privileges and entitlements that could bring renown, status, wealth, and the ability to operate across scales, for example by working with people from elsewhere. Most people do not participate in these processes, and women are rarely able to. They are either prevented from doing so by bureaucratic rules passed by men (for instance, conservation project designers dictated that only men could be *pisteurs*) or kept busy with productive rather than acquisitive work (farming or minding households). But only a few men dare take advantage of opportunities to acquire – to seize from others, to lay claim – and in doing so they become notables, if not leaders. Perhaps attempts to acquire come first, and opportunities are made as much as taken. These men are the focus of this book. And what they do is raid and cultivate flexibility towards the end of freedom to operate.

In Ndele (Figure 1.1), a town at the confluence of several national parks and conservation spaces, dynamics of hunting, raiding, and acquisition were simultaneously obvious and overlooked, for locals and incomers alike. The anti-poaching guards working for an EU-funded

Figure 1.1 'N'délé – pas loin'/'Ndele – not far' sign on the outskirts of town welcomes those who have made the journey

conservation project blasted into town every few days in their well-worn Land Cruiser to do errands. But the guards did not work in town or go after the illicit game meat so obviously on display at the market. As the Ministry of Water and Forests guards put it, 'We work in the town' (what they did, mostly, was to hang out and draw a salary). 'The LAB [*lutte anti-braconnage* or anti-poaching guards],' they said, 'work in the bush.' (What they did, mostly, was to hang out and wait, but they also raided people who aimed to make a living from hunting in the region's vast protected areas, hunted animals, or organised others' hunting and mining, and, when their expatriate supervisors were around, they did some calisthenics and training exercises.)

The international humanitarians, who had been present for a couple of years at this point (2009–10), seemed steadfast in their lack of curiosity about 'bush work', preferring to keep as much distance – social and territorial – as possible between themselves and the anti-poaching commandos. I came to see their lack of interest in the goings-on in the bush not just as practical (for instance, because it let them spend more time on their own 'wat-san' – water and sanitation – projects) but as symptomatic of the usual ways of thinking about spaces like this one, which focus on what they lack (a functioning state, a robust licit economy) rather than on what they have. Many Ndele residents frame their comments using this framework as well, complaining of their own poverty, abandonment, and exclusion from the benefits they associate with modern citizenship.

To be sure, there is plenty of evidence to support the 'undeveloped' lens through which this area and its people are usually seen. One neighbourhood leader (*chef de quartier*) in Ndele showed me his 'modern' agricultural technique, one that none of his neighbours used. It was a form of irrigation employed by the Ancient Egyptians. An international non-governmental organisation (NGO) was working to organise people into collectives that might help them increase yields, but change was slow. Improving crop yields seems unobjectionable,[9] but it also misses a fundamental point: while people might be 'undeveloped' or poor in certain respects, and might live in a state that does not do what states are 'supposed' to do, they do not necessarily occupy some negative space, marked only by what it does not have. North-eastern CAR is rich in opportunities for acquiring the goods that can be claimed from vast spaces uninhabited by humans, or by seizing from people who cannot contest it. 'Everyone' in the area – that is, everyone not of the developmentalist/humanitarian mindset – 'agrees the profits to be earned from gathering [and hunting] are superior to those from agriculture' (Piermay 1977: 347). Farming is for family and necessity, for living and reproducing. Gathering, hunting, and seizing – these are the ways one gains wealth, and, more importantly, status: that is, to be recognised as holding a special position, with that 'specialness' marked more by socially acknowledged privilege than by fulfilling responsibilities in relation to others.

Perhaps acquisition as described here seems too broad a category, including everything from the hunting of non-human animals for consumption to raiding as a mode of war. Yet attempts to definitively separate or fence off modes of acquisition create bigger problems. Aristotle long ago thought that it came down to a straightforward distinction: the art of acquisition could be either 'natural', in other words practised in order to achieve the healthy sustenance of a family or community, or 'unnatural', aimed at making money and hoarding for their own sakes. This distinction and its moral valences remain. Many anthropological studies of hunting have described it as central to reciprocal modes of organising life (e.g. Kohn 2013; Marks 2016; Willerslev 2007), claiming, implicitly or explicitly, a bit of the moral implication found in Aristotle's descriptor 'natural'. The writers would not use that term, but they share in its sense that these are cases of a little-contested, sustainable moral order oriented towards reproduction rather than profit. In contrast, acquiring for status, wealth, renown, adventure, or a show of cunning is harder to value as a coherent moral order – even if Aristotle's descriptor 'unnatural' sounds old-fashioned.[10] Dynamics in north-eastern CAR suggest a different understanding: acquisitive practices

[9] However, elsewhere in CAR this has been quite contentious: members of agricultural co-ops have been killed for their alleged use of *ngbin* – occult means to capture labour power – in order to illicitly increase their yields.

[10] A notable exception is those Marxist accounts that see bandits as valiant Robin Hoods, thieving for the sake of more equitable distribution; Hobsbawm (1969) is an excellent example.

and their objectives are inherently morally complicated, and understanding them requires attention to the tensions that surround any attempt at instituting norms.

While in recounting these tales of north-eastern CAR over the last 150 years I sometimes refer to hunting and sometimes to raiding (and it would be wrong to conflate them entirely), they share a crucial element: people are making claims about their own status and the status of others (human and other creatures), and those claims are frequently contested, rather than largely settled and accepted. For those practices I refer to as 'hunting', there tends to be a general understanding about the status of the being that is tracked, killed, or otherwise acquired. Often, special practices or rituals must be observed in order to account for the injustice of taking the life of a creature. But, of course, the line between hunting and raiding is not clear. Few, animal or human, willingly present themselves to be hunted. The hunter is the one who tells the story – the one whose fellows have concocted the practices they describe as ensuring 'balance' and 'reciprocity', but which ultimately place their own needs above those of the hunted.[11] For those practices I designate as raiding, the status of the tracked being is less settled. Indeed, abrogating its status is central to the practice of acquiring from it; it is accompanied by a claim to raider status; and the accompanying violence is often more obvious or evident. Ultimately, though, hunting and raiding practices overlap, and the difference between them is often a matter of interpretation.

Acquisition, of which hunting and raiding are prominent examples, has always been a locus of innovation. Historically, '[i]n order to procure rifles and ammunition, and to repair rifles, hunters and blacksmiths have always been, among the members of their societies, the most outward-looking and most dedicated to experimentation – not to say the most modern' (Ferme 2001b: 124).[12] Innovation and experimentation frequently – even mostly – require the breaching of norms or status.[13]

11 I largely avoid the term 'poaching' because it designates a contrast with a hegemonic order, which poaching then breaches – whether for reasons of justice or lawbreaking. In contrast, here I weave together the practices and perspectives of a wide range of people involved in acquisition in north-eastern CAR, which requires considering that values and status are contested and are often personalised or determined situationally, rather than perpetrated according to stable principles.

12 'Afin de se procurer fusils et munitions, et de réparer les fusils, les chasseurs et les forgerons ont toujours été, parmi les membres de leurs sociétés, les plus tournés vers l'extérieur et les plus voués à l'expérimentation – pour ne pas dire les plus modernes.'

13 Sven Lindqvist's *A History of Bombing* (2001) shows brilliantly the dystopian futures that arise from trying new things, although he is careful never to draw straight lines, instead showing the variety of impulses at play.

Consider game meat in CAR. Most Central Africans love wild meat – the rich taste, the texture, the many varieties – and it is necessary for nutrition, but people generally do not get to eat it as much as they would like. It is central to the area's gift economies, and in the last few decades it has also become a booming commercial enterprise, with thousands of tons of meat for sale in the Bangui market every year. Meat from the north-east, prohibited by parkland hunting restrictions, is especially sought after for its rich taste. The organisation of this newly expanded traffic is varied, but a common model has developed. City-based entrepreneurs (many of whom are also state civil servants or otherwise close to power) contract with someone living in a rural area. They provide this hunter with ammunition. He gets to keep some of what he kills and turns the rest over to his sponsor via the *waligara*, market women who travel to rural areas to collect meat they transport on an arduous journey to the capital and then sell for vastly higher prices. Along the way the *waligara* may be subject to various sorts of seizure and extortion but they are also protected by their reputations as masters of invisible, occult, or spiritual powers (Tubiana 2018).[14] If CAR's formal economy is woefully moribund, game meat is an example of steady profit and innovation.

Yet game meat has also become a form of 'self-devouring growth' (Livingston 2019). The industry (for it is one) has gone beyond any scale where it could be considered 'natural' hunting and has shifted into a more intensively acquisitive, wealth-oriented mode in which the uncertain status of people and other animals is exploited for gain. Because the extensive prohibitions encoded in state law are so out of tune with what people actually need, the prohibitions do not become a hegemonic order to be enforced or resisted. Instead, they are alternately ignored, contravened, or misused as a pretext for seizure or extortion, thereby increasing the uncertainty around status and property. Is acquisition inherently innovative, as Ferme (2001b) and Mavhunga (2014) have argued in their studies of hunting? Perhaps. But in that case it is also inherently morally turbulent, since such innovation requires seizing opportunities in the midst of unclear status.[15]

[14] No single term quite captures the kind of power or action at play.

[15] Perhaps in places where state laws around hunting are more clearly hegemonic and repressive, such as in Mavhunga's (2014) description of colonial Zimbabwe, the moral turbulence is less apparent, since there appears instead to be a dichotomy between repressive colonisers and resistant, righteous Africans. An element of that is at play in CAR too, of course, but the state laws' dominance has never been so total, and their subversion – perhaps especially by 'agents of law' – is frequent, and with a variety of ends,

Relations beyond state/statelessness and frontiers

This book, while focusing on a little-studied region, follows in the tradition of a node of anthropological interest – one might even call it a paradigmatic interest – in understanding the politics of statelessness in their positivity, rather than as 'lacking' forms of state ideals. E. E. Evans-Pritchard's (1940) description of Nuer life as 'ordered anarchy', rather than, as Hobbes would have had it, 'nasty, brutish, and short', is an early and well-known example of a fecund genre of anthropological making sense of 'ungoverned' spaces.[16] Today, one must account for something Evans-Pritchard and his contemporaries mostly ignored or glossed over: today, at least legally, everyone lives in a state or is otherwise subject to state or sovereign power. (That was true of Evans-Pritchard's time as well, but he was trying to represent what things had been like before.) As James Scott has diagnosed, the contemporary era is one 'in which virtually the entire globe is "administered space" and the periphery is not much more than a folkloric remnant' (2009: 324). Even radical critiques of the state describe the 'stated' nature of the world as an accomplished fact; their accounts of an earlier radical antagonism towards the state are tinged with nostalgia (Clastres 1977; Graeber 2011).

Yet effective government action – for example in making populations and spaces 'legible' (Scott 1998) through surveillance, control, policing, and administration – is not so widespread. What is it like to live in a place where governing action by state entities or their proxies is limited and occasional? The usual answers – from journalists, say, or from humanitarian PR specialists, or certain scholars of international relations theory – include tales of privation and woe that validate Hobbes' pessimism.[17]

many of them more personal than organised around abstract principles of justice or hegemony.

[16] For a particularly stimulating contemporary project, see Scheele (2015), who makes sense of northern Chad's 'anarchy' by jettisoning the concept of order altogether.

[17] The idea of 'stateless' places as no man's lands of brutality has found analytical justification in Thomas Hobbes' *Leviathan* and *De Cive*, which have played central roles in the formation of the Western idea of the state. Hobbes was interested in proto-ethnographic sources, such as accounts of the native peoples of the New World (his 'relationship to an incipient "authority of experience" was not pure rejection, but a complex and surreptitious attitude' [Aravamudan 2009: 43–4]), but his writing actively ignored what he learned from the peoples of the Americas. The 'state of nature' – his term for spaces not subject to unitary sovereign authority – was a thought experiment designed to logically prove the need for a particular kind of state and a sovereign, as well as a means to justify imperial projects. In doing this, Hobbes' writings 'recast' the 'phylogeny of cultural plurality' as an 'ontogeny of political universality' (Aravamudan 2009: 55). Life in the state of nature, then, *had to be* 'nasty, brutish, and

They speak of 'state failures' where people are perhaps not quite in Hobbes' category but are nevertheless too close to the state of nature, bereft of the protection and services bestowed by the state and its culture. In some such places, government is carried out by non-state actors, who tend to assume that their aid will ultimately bolster governmental capacity, when in fact it ends up replacing it indefinitely.[18] Such places are subject to government, but, to all intents and purposes, they are still stateless in a world of states.

Alternatively, spaces such as north-eastern CAR have been described as the 'outside' that is necessary for the 'inside' to function. This, for instance, is the crux of Hannah Arendt's (1973) account of European imperialism and the rise of the nation state. It also resonates with many contemporary accounts of sovereignty, which describe the sovereign's paradigmatic power as differentiating 'inside' the polity from 'outside' (Graeber 2011), or as deciding on who will be cast out to the periphery while yet not being definitively outside (Agamben 1998; Schmitt 2005 [1922]). Such accounts perform a neat trick: those people and places that are generally seen as marginal, extraneous, or otherwise unimportant are revealed as 'what is most politically important to the State idea' (Taussig 1992: 132). That the 'margins of the state' exist as a privileged locus of anthropological inquiry into political power has been demonstrated (Das and Poole 2004; Roitman 2005). Along the way, the idea of margins as centre becomes another way of explaining the paradox of statelessness in the state: it says, effectively, that there is no such thing as a stateless space; even privatising the state is a means of strengthening it (Hibou 2004). Still, this otherwise useful approach tends to elide the disjunction many experience between the state as ideal and the state as experience or institution, and the moral claims that arise from this. Instead, even experiences of being 'outside' become part of the 'inside'.

Analogous to the insight that 'margins' are key to the 'centre' is the idea that 'frontiers' are key to capitalist accumulation. And, indeed, spaces such as north-eastern CAR are often portrayed as frontiers. The problem is that, although there has been much exploitation and extraction in the hunting zone, it is a bit more difficult to identify accumulation

short'; it required a 'war of all against all' to prove Hobbes' point that self-preservation requires submission to an all-powerful sovereign whose shadow awes all into peace. Anthropologists have always considered Hobbes' state of nature a constructivist thought experiment helpful to understanding the genealogy of Western political theory but actively unhelpful for any empirical understanding of places where 'the state' (at least in its Western ideal form) is functionally absent.

18 For a nuanced and useful account along these lines, see Mann (2014).

(amassing and hoarding wealth) as opposed to contested processes of acquisition. Additionally, the hunting zone has not been the site of major 'rushes' (gold rushes, land rushes) – its acquisitive tendencies have been more niche than that. For the 150 years of its intensive incorporation into trade and other relationships, the hunting zone has all too often been ignored by outsiders, although it has been fruitful for those who have positioned themselves to acquire, chiefly through hunting and raiding, in the midst of the uncertain status associated with the fact that the area is in statehood limbo.

My analysis does not, therefore, contend that hunting zone spaces have a functional relationship either to states or to capitalist production. These spaces, and the practices within them, are important because they allow us to rethink the assumption that politics is about state management and administration only, or that economics must consider production alone; instead, we can consider the political-economic forms associated with taking – sometimes violently – goods with contested status or ownership. The area and the interactional dynamics among its wealth seekers force us to reconsider the scope of the political as usually presented, with its antagonistic poles: at one end, the state; at the other, its rejection or antithesis. This is a story neither of frustrated attempts at state-directed government nor of escaping from it.[19] It is the story of the particular dynamics of a space outside government control yet integrated into broader arenas, including those of international bureaucratic actors State–no state and production–poverty dichotomies do a poor job of evoking this history. Raiding and acquisition do justice to the complexity of this space: a zone of abandonment at the same time as it can be a site of adventure, renown (people want to be the kind of person others tell stories about), and profit. It is neither utterly benighted nor emancipated; neither necessary to the state or capitalism nor separable from the world in which we have come to live over the past hundred years.[20] Raiding is not, as it is often considered, archaic. It is a way of being in the modern world.

[19] As philosopher Achille Mbembe has suggested, 'research must go beyond institutions, beyond formal positions of power, and beyond the written rules, and examine how the implicit and the explicit are interwoven, and how the practices of those who command and those who are assumed to obey are so entangled as to render both powerless' (Mbembe 2001: 133) – powerless, that is, in the sense that entanglement dominates rather than stable relations of command and obeisance.

[20] The French, in less guarded moments, called this a *colonie poubelle* – their 'trash-can colony' (Brégeon 1998). Anthropologists know as well as archaeologists that much can be learned from looking at the trash: that is, from looking at what and who has been cast out and does not fit into the usual frameworks of political, economic, and social organisation (Douglas 1966).

Raiding is not, however, necessarily lauded – even by people who do it. People in the area are much more likely to lament that there is no single 'state' that cares for them and protects them. The state they seem to desire sounds like a kind of welfare-providing leviathan, yet, at the same time, when someone tries to enforce a constricting state law, people are likely to denounce it. They do so through displays of force, which, though in part bluff, seem intended to cow those who attempt objectionable interventions. But much of the time, it is preferable to develop forms of camouflage – ways of blending in, hiding in plain sight, and otherwise collaborating without conceding any sort of subordination or limiting oneself to a rigid identity or belief system. From these broad tendencies, it is also possible to identify a recurring orientation towards working in the space: a way of skirting between secretiveness and showmanship, particularly when describing one's activities to those not as immersed in the hunting/raiding milieu. All of this contributes to the volatile mix in the hunting zone, where status and property are frequently fought over.

In other words, insecurity is both a resource and a constraint in the area's productive life. In her study of commerce throughout Central Africa's borderlands, Karine Bennafla (2002) emphasised that they are places of risk, and that the management of risk is therefore a crucial skill for people making their livings in such borderlands.[21] Even highly skilled managers of risk can never guarantee that they will succeed in keeping threats at bay, but they can develop qualifications and practices that seem to help. Raiding and hunting are not just about livelihood but involve flexible self-making in insecure and hard-to-reach areas. As an 'art', raiding entails the meeting and spread of new ideas, fuelled not just by market demands but by the curiosity of the people involved. The demographically and agriculturally prosperous inhabitants of Central Africa who encountered Muslim traders and European explorers in their area at the end of the nineteenth century had other aims besides obtaining the currencies these new arrivals brought with them, which held little interest. But curiosity about new technologies and ways of thinking and acting in the world were shared by all of the parties to these meetings.

In the Lake Chad Basin more broadly, seizure and spoils, and the intertwining of military and commercial interests, have been described as long-standing and intimate aspects of the way in which regulation is enacted (Bennafla 2002; Roitman 1998, 2005). The garrison-entrepôt, a 'material effect' of the area's history over the past several hundred years

[21] Her analysis centred on Cameroon, and so did not directly concern the hunting zone.

(and a term Janet Roitman discovered in the colonial archives), was also a point from which state officials could enrich and empower themselves and the state more widely through militarised commerce in the bush (Roitman 1998). Roitman's is an important reminder that seizure serves both to create wealth and to convey power, and that those in state power have been leaders in seizure since states began. 'Seizure' may be too polemical a way of putting things, however; the term includes many claims, the legitimacy of which is a matter of perspective.

Study of north-eastern CAR reveals an important set of dynamics around hiding, abandonment, and wanting to be seen that are prevalent elsewhere but often overlooked. In the Lake Chad Basin region Roitman studied (northern Cameroon and the abutting part of Chad, including its capital, N'Djamena), commerce and its regulation (including by seizure) proliferate. While people there might experience their region as ungoverned bush (Kelly 2015), it is nevertheless thickly populated by humans and boasts several booming market towns (Mbaiboum, Garoua, Maroua, Kousseri). Roitman noted that 'young men trading along the borders are never lacking in several national currencies and two or three national identity cards, which can either be purchased or procured using family members' birth certificates' (2006: 310).

The hunting zone, in contrast, is not a place of such commercial-political proliferation. Most of the people in the area lack a national identity card. Many have no birth certificate either. Some make the trek to the capital to procure one, but travel to Bangui is arduous, expensive, and time-consuming, with no guarantee that one can navigate the bureaucracy on arrival. People in the capital assume that people from the north-east are foreigners (and dangerous to boot), so they might summarily reject an application from someone from there. Rather than the garrison-entrepôt's profusion – excess, even – of recognised nationalities and entrepreneurial undertakings, people in the hunting zone frequently find themselves with none. Their lives and careers may draw them from one place to another and they may cross national boundaries, but they experience themselves as being nationless in important ways. They aspire to be Central African, but they know that Central Africans in the capital see them as something else. This is true of people born and raised in the area and of many adventurers who arrive here from further afield. Among other things, this context makes the often used term 'mercenary' a misleading one. Arms-carrying jobs are not organised around formal nationality (Debos 2013); they can't be, since many people literally have no official nationality and popular conceptions of nationality and citizenship are quite different from little-applied legal ones. Even if one obtained a national ID card, opponents could always claim that it had been acquired through fraud.

After the Seleka rebel alliance[22] made its presence known in north-eastern CAR in late 2012 and took the capital in March 2013, the opponents to their rule who emerged were inspired by a range of sentiments and discourses of autochthony – that rule should be by those who can position themselves as being 'of the soil'. Recent scholarly attention to struggles over autochthony describe it as a process emerging from straitened economic circumstances and the 'dialectic of flow and closure' (Geschiere and Meyer 1998) that characterise the kinds of global connection that are possible in the contemporary world. The hunting zone, in contrast, is marked not by having been included and then excluded, but by having been largely left to its own devices as a site of acquisition and raiding, until some of its residents rose up in rebellion, making a show of force to demonstrate that they were dangerous and should not be ignored, and claiming entitlement to meaningful, material rights of citizenship. Although being 'overlookable' until one makes a show of force, of dangerousness, is especially pronounced in the hunting zone, it is not unique to it.

North-eastern CAR is far from being the world's only area like this: abandoned by state largesse, imagined as dangerous, and used for raiding and acquisition. The African continent is full of them. Northern Kenya comes to mind, as do the remoter reaches of Ethiopia and large swathes of Namibia. Globally, given the rise of utilitarian administrative calculations (cost per person is very high in remote areas) and urbanisation, the number of areas that are left behind – the 'buffer zones' (Mbembe 2000)[23] – seems likely to be on the rise.

People living in buffer zones also find themselves in a particularly difficult position vis-à-vis the rest of the country they officially belong to and the rest of the world. Despite the fact that they are born within the territory of a state, their provenance is sufficient to suggest that they are 'not national enough' to be full citizens. Even though inhabitants of such areas might be intermittently useful to leaders in the far-off capitals, they remain in a precarious position. Two of the world's latest 'looming genocides' – one in western Myanmar, the other against Muslims in CAR in retaliation for Seleka members' brutality – have targeted people from abandoned, yet not disconnected, zones, areas that have

[22] *Seleka* means alliance in Sango, one of CAR's official languages. Seleka is usually described as having emerged out of north-eastern CAR, but in fact its fighters came from many places, and the plan for alliance and rebellion was hatched abroad.

[23] In his meditation on space and boundaries in Africa, Achille Mbembe noted that, historically on the continent, '[v]ast areas might lie between distinct polities, veritable buffer zones not subject to direct control, exclusive domination, or close supervision' (2000: 263). In this conception, buffer zones remain present today.

simultaneously served as sites of conflict and refuge. The gap between *de jure* legal inclusion and a de facto state of suspension creates enclaves in which people speak of 'the state' and its proper role but no one category of actor dominates.

There is much to lament in such a status. During one discussion with armed group members in Tiringoulou, a small town in CAR's far northeast, the men started talking about their hopes for a potential oil industry there. Look at Chad, they said, how modern and booming it is because of oil. When I countered that oil had brought the most benefit to the Chadian president and much less to the people, one of the armed group members became a bit impatient, saying sharply that if oil were exploited near them 'at least we would have a road'. It was a reminder that abstract discussions of fair allocation of revenue, while important to some, were dwarfed by preoccupations with even the most basic infrastructure.

But the features of the hunting zone also present advantages. Not only Central Africans but also those drawn here from elsewhere appreciate many aspects of what they find, such as the sort of autonomy in increasingly short supply elsewhere. The commercial elephant hunters of the early decades of the twentieth century, for instance, wrote that they sought out eastern Oubangui-Chari not just because it was full of elephants but because it was the 'last place' where regulation of hunting was minimal and they could kill as many as they were able. Today, the commercial elephant hunters tend to come from Sudan and South Sudan, but they share in their predecessors' sense that the region's attractiveness lies in it being 'unclaimed land', as Joseph Kony of the Lord's Resistance Army is said to have described it (Cakaj 2015).[24] Meanwhile, Western funders of conservation often complain about the lack of 'local ownership' of governance initiatives in CAR but also appreciate that its absence makes it easier for them to do as they like. They sometimes compare CAR to West Africa, where government officials are more likely to stake a claim to determining policy. In CAR, people tend to look to international donors to organise things; they will go along with even stringent policies and projects, perhaps because many expect to be able to keep on doing as they wish regardless.

Although many profess frustration at the absence of the state, this absence can be a reason to step in in the name of the state while avoiding presenting oneself as being in charge. This is a way to avoid taking responsibility for others while claiming considerable authority for

[24] Unclaimed or not, Kony was able to evade Ugandan and US forces' technologically robust efforts to track him and the remnants of his group down for eight years here (2009–17).

oneself, a potentially enviable position. There remains a concessionary dynamic at play: the president and ministers in the capital do not see it as their job to govern or regulate the hinterland. Instead, they sell or otherwise grant concessions – for safari-hunting outfits, for instance – to foreign actors who then can play at being sovereign in their domains (Hardin 2000, 2011; Smith 2015b). (People in rural CAR are often quite sophisticated in playing different concessionaires off against each other, challenging their sovereign aspirations [Hardin 2002].)

Raiding challenges more commonly assumed political practices and motivations. Those challenges can take the form of shocking violence (often even shocking to the perpetrators), or of closeness or identification arising from shared experiences of danger, a mode of temporary connection that those who refuse on principle to be involved in raiding find hard to experience. Consider a contrast: international humanitarian NGOs pride themselves on – even define themselves by – their solidarity with the poor and otherwise unfortunate and their refusal to do things they define as corrupt, but the same bureaucratic procedures delineate status and privilege in rigid ways that distance these NGOs from the responsibilities local social relations might be said to require of them (Lombard 2016d; see also Appel 2012 on similar dynamics among foreign oil workers in Equatorial Guinea). 'You want a ride to Bangui in our Land Cruiser because your sister is sick? Sorry, it's against the rules.'[25] In the world of the 'good intentions crowd' (Lombard 2016d), people are divided into stable status categories – local, national, expatriate – that carry with them fundamentally different entitlements. In contrast, the European 'technical assistants' leading raids in the name of conservation, or those involved in the big game-hunting industry, may still speak and think in ways that are thoroughly saturated with colonial tropes. It would be easy, at least for the equality-minded reader, to dismiss them as retrograde. However, these not always savoury characters rely on their fellow raiders, and experience to a higher degree than most humanitarians an intensity of entrainment – a 'process in which participants develop a mutual focus of attention and become entrained [i.e. no longer freestanding bodies but rhythmically intertwined] in each other's bodily micro-rhythms and emotions' (Collins 2004: 47). Raiding social relations are also marked by this.

[25] Some among the humanitarian crowd struggle with how to behave ethically in these situations. In general, the more one is insulated by bureaucratic entitlement (expatriate employees of international organisations generally have the most; volunteer ethical humanitarians the least), the less apparent the struggles.

Doing justice to entrainment can productively jostle the contemporary biases that tend to see humanitarianism as more 'evolved' and as a form of solidarity with the locals involved, and hunting/raiding as less evolved and more colonial. Of course, one must not take this line of reasoning too far. Over a period of about 150 years, the story of the hunting zone includes tragedy as well as adventure and autonomy (particularly freedom from self-consistency). Ultimately, the fact that raiding has been so central to the ways of working in the area is the result of the interplay of a number of factors; among the most important are the relation between a 'stateless-state' place and the people and political-economic processes that extend towards other hubs.

A raiding analytic

This book spans the period of raiding and political entanglement driven by trans-Saharan trading and political networks from the late nineteenth century, through the period of French colonialism, and into the era of the Central African Republic. In many ways, it presents a deluge of woes, seen by many Central Africans as a story of dispossession of both material and spiritual power (Ceriana Mayneri 2014). At every stage the region has been shaped by attempts to acquire. The status of people and goods has generally been open to question (Exclusive property? Free and self-determining? Valuable or not?), and force has often entered into situational determinations. Because the features of raiding depart in certain respects from the incentives and desires of production- and management-oriented politics, which frequently rely on explicit or implicit teleologies of development/accumulation and centralisation, and/or of states and citizens/subjects, it is useful to set them out. They are present elsewhere, too, of course, but they tend to be overlooked.

In the hunting zone, the focus is on acquisition (extracting and taxing), not on conquest (of people or of land) or administration. To the extent that care and control are part of the political repertoire, they tend to take the form of distribution (the allotment of quarry, for example, as an indicator of status). Men claim a privileged, if not wholly exclusive, role in acquisition, through a combination of claims about culture and gender divisions of labour and men's control of the distribution of salaried posts. Rather than making claims to being in charge and controlling other people (so as to ensure order and hierarchical command, for instance), these men search for status: that is, recognition, by audiences close or far, of their value and privileged or otherwise positively marked position. One way to claim status is by making a show of force, a display meant to communicate that one could acquire from or otherwise cow the audience if one so desired.

Displays of force are just one of the ways in which violence is a normal part of the range of interactions in raiding work, rather than being scandalous or surprising. Another is the tracking and capturing or killing that comprise the acquisitive process itself. But while people removed from violent encounters often assume that such emotional repertoires centre on hatred, raiding and hunting processes offer an opportunity to consider instead the role played by confrontational entrainment, which can itself give rise to hostility but also to other kinds of social knowledge akin to a sense of fellow feeling. This is in part because hunting and raiding are full of danger, risk, and fear for the people involved. Even those who seem most dominant know that they can themselves be raided. The distinction between raider and raided is not as clearly differentiated as it might seem to people, far from these areas, who see raiding and hunting as immoral and archaic rather than as accompanying, as they do, the same liberal forms they assume constitute progress.

Hunting and raiding are not only about violence and confrontation. They are also about cultivating a certain mode of stealth that lets people collaborate with others, including with people with quite different interests from their own, without losing autonomy. This requires skills of strategic self-positioning – showing certain aspects of oneself – rather than seeking to be recognised for every aspect of their identity. Self-positioning often requires learning the skill of camouflage: arranging oneself in relation to social and bureaucratic landscapes (from those of colonial governments and the associated humanitarian concerns in Europe, to the more recent involvement and priorities of international aid donors) so as not to stand out, despite being a raider/hunter in a world of normative state-led pastoral (shepherd-like) politics – that is, of states and managed populations.[26]

A few things emerge from this overview. In such a context, the reciprocal duties and obligations enumerated by law – whether defined by the state or determined more locally – have little purchase. Whether the absence of law drives raiding or the presence of raiding drives out law is difficult to say. (Given the violent history of the region – violence that people here have both augmented and decried – it is difficult to say whether people value law and order less than other things, or rather that they are doing their best in difficult circumstances.) But it means that, to

[26] In fact, normative pastoralism sustains raiding politics, because raiding is fostered by the particular limbo of statehood to which the hunting zone – formally a state, but effectively beyond state concern – defaults. This will emerge more fully in subsequent chapters.

a greater extent than elsewhere, people involved in raiding must figure out their own actions and their justifications for them. They tend to do so in relation to the people involved and in relation to their own situations and projects, rather than in terms of abstract principle, not because of some kind of cultural inclination to inconsistency but because of the moral conflicts that arise from their state of limbo and the competing claims made by the needs of the past, present, and future. This suggests that the kind of consistent striving for coherence in one's ethical practice and principles that has been identified as central to ethical personhood elsewhere (e.g. Laidlaw 2013; Mahmood 2004) has institutional and infrastructural prerequisites – it draws on a range of 'affordances' (Keane 2016) that are not present in hunting games. Improvisation, entrainment, and conflicting values/solidarities give rise to a different kind of relational ethical subject, one who aspires to status and privilege.

A note on methods

I first visited CAR in June 2003. Over breakfast one morning at the Hôtel du Centre in Bangui, I spied a young man whose short, shaggy blond hair and age rather resembled my own. He was talking intently with a Central African peer.[27] I introduced myself, and it turned out that he was an American college graduate who had recently arrived to help set up a private conservation militia, Africa Rainforest and River Conservation (ARRC), an organisation founded and funded by a doctor from Wyoming. In the end, ARRC never put its planned anti-hunting militia into operation. The main employees – Central Africans in the office and a couple of South African mercenaries – hurled allegations of murder and theft at each other. Using diamond mining to finance operations proved far from straightforward as well. On that first trip I also met another anti-hunting hunter, someone from France, whose CV was far longer. Employed by an EU-funded conservation project, he had spent the just concluded dry season in the north-eastern parklands, partly leading a group of *pisteurs* combating anyone who wanted to claim wild goods, and partly participating in the back-and-forth raids that had followed the previous year's killing of the region's main spiritual leader – himself an anti-hunting hunter – Yaya Ramadan.

[27] When I met the Central African co-worker a few days later, he showed me photographs of the aftermath of attacks by *hommes caimans* – crocodile men – and I knew he was someone with whom I wanted to keep in touch. I long knew him as a person who seemed always to be at the centre of some drama, but lately he has become one of the country's most successful NGO entrepreneurs.

I returned repeatedly to CAR in the following years while working as a consultant for the Small Arms Survey, a Geneva-based research institute. In designing my thesis research I wanted to show what an effectively stateless borderland, home to plural authorities and a militarised political economy, could contribute to understandings of sovereignty, and I knew that conservation and hunting had been important there for decades. Rebel groups and international humanitarian organisations were setting up in the area as well. I began in mid-2009 by spending two months in the French military archives (the Service Historique de l'Armée de la Terre at Vincennes) and colonial archives (the Archives Nationales d'Outre-mer at Aix-en-Provence), as well as the French National Library in Paris. The moth-eaten and rather disorganised documents presented a range of characters. An eager young officer describing a trip to Anglo-Egyptian Sudan remarked on British progress at state building ('Is that to say that everything is better over there? Certainly not!' [Modat 1910c: 111]). A plaintive and complaining junior staffer at Ndele begged for some chains for the prisoners who kept threatening him (Lignier 1936a, 1936b); another officer was sent out to 'mark our sovereignty' by hunting Arab hunters and herders on the eve of independence in the late 1950s (Bertin 1959). I also drew extensively on an esoteric French-language secondary literature about Equatorial Africa. The quality of English-language ethnographies of Equatorial Africa is high,[28] but the quantity small, and all focus on the country's south-western tropical forest region. The insights from the region's history of granting concessions and privatised, brutal, and neglectful government have thus not been as well known as they should be.[29]

I arrived in CAR for a longer stay in September 2009, and after several weeks in the capital polishing my Sango I headed to the far north-eastern town of Tiringoulou and then on to Ndele. Both towns had rebel groups present or close by, and both towns were surrounded by national parks and other kinds of protected areas. Initially I had quite generous access to the anti-poaching bases and their staffs. I had met one of the expatriate 'technical assistants' when he stopped by the Catholic mission in Ndele, where I was staying, and he invited me to spend time living on the base. I lost access in 2010 when he was summarily fired and his replacement – someone who embraced and even flaunted his mercenary status in a way most in his position avoided – accused me of being a spy and 'warned'

[28] An entirely non-exhaustive but evocative list would include Giles-Vernick (2002), Hardin (2011), Daspit 2011, Rupp (2011), and Robinson and Remis (2014).

[29] For instance, Catherine Coquery-Vidrovitch's (1972) masterful study of the concessionary experiment in Equatorial Africa (1890–1930) is a treasure trove for those considering contemporary experiments in privatisation, but few are aware of its riches and even fewer wade through its 600 richly packed pages.

Figure 1.2 A Friday feast at the compound of Habiba's family

me about voyeuristic rumours circulating about me. At various points attacks by armed groups also affected where I could carry out my research, although I was fortunate to miss being caught in the crossfire, often by just a day or two (perhaps I *was* a spy…). In Ndele and Tiringoulou, I spent time with rebel group members, diamond miners, Water and Forests Ministry employees, *pisteurs*, and others. In the afternoons in Ndele, worn out from all the time spent with men, I would walk half a mile down the road to the compound of Habiba, a Chadian woman I had befriended who was in the process of leaving the abusive husband she had come to CAR to marry. She was waiting for the sultan-mayor to provide written acknowledgement of her mistreatment so that she could return home with her honour intact. But the sultan-mayor never returned from Bangui, where he was convalescing from chronic illness and later died. Habiba kept waiting, and the rebels kept attacking. Sometimes, I would find her at the town's simple hospital, where she went when anxiety caused her heart to race. She and the many women and children who surrounded her were always the most generous hosts, and patient teachers of Chadian Arabic, with which I struggled (Figure 1.2).

I left CAR in July 2010 but returned in October and stayed until the end of the year. That time, I gained access to the European Commission's voluminous archives on the conservation projects it had financed from the 1980s onwards. These became an invaluable resource, particularly when combined with what I gleaned from interviews with people – both Central Africans and expatriates – involved with the projects throughout that period. I have returned to CAR every year since except 2013 and 2019, usually multiple times per year. I have also had the privilege of being able to access great Africa libraries at the University of California at Berkeley and at Yale University, both of which house fascinating primary source material and nearly all the secondary literature about the region. In particular, I filled in the gaps in my understanding of historical and political processes of hunting by reading explorers' – or, as I prefer, adventurists' – accounts of their journeys through what is now CAR, as well as those of safari hunters.

In the stories I recount in this book, I limit my discussion of the personalities involved to those with a public presence, and in many cases I use pseudonyms or do not name the people involved to protect my interlocutors' confidentiality. Perhaps the account will seem short of 'ethnographic characters', but I made that decision consciously. One reason was to avoid projecting the norms or views of individuals as if they were the dominant norms and not as contested and situational as they in fact are. This was a particularly keen concern given that there were certain perspectives to which my access was limited (for example, those of cattle herders, with whom I was able to speak only briefly). Another reason was that I could easily have populated the text with sensational characters (mercenaries), but I realised that they were generally a distraction from the bigger stories my research compelled me to tell.

Plan of the book

I tell the story of acquisition in north-eastern CAR approximately chronologically to capture the troubling tenacity of projects of taking in the midst of the changing interests, networks, and participants.

Chapter 2, 'Zariba contests and collaborations', takes place in the late nineteenth century, when the region was becoming increasingly entangled in political and economic processes far beyond its terrains. The region was where the Islamic and the European colonial frontier processes met, strengthening each other as well as clashing. The crucial variable was exploitation, not conquest; mobility and freedom from being accosted while collecting valuable goods (if necessary, forcefully) were key to personal advancement and to the political-economic mode of life. '*Zaribas*' is the Arabic term for the enclosures built to contain the goods (slaves, ivory, food, etc.) that the raiders were able to amass. Some *zaribas* were temporary, while others became more established, morphing into cities. The chapter focuses on some of the key people involved in these raiding projects to show the personal orientation and skills they developed and the kinds of encounters and confrontations they navigated as they attempted to claim privileged status, or to undermine the status of another.

By the early twentieth century, French colonial officials had become leaders in forceful acquisition, either co-opting or eliminating most of their challengers. While the French colonial government saw itself as replacing the acquisition-oriented polities with one geared towards production and the management of people, the French operated in a context of penury, and as a result their imposition of a bureaucratic state form ironically entrenched forceful acquisition as a tactic of rule and profit. Raiding and acquisition retained their prominence less because they expressed values than because they were an improvised response to conflicts of values between people with competing claims and interests.

Although colonial officials had very little money, their superiors nevertheless demanded that certain tasks be accomplished. In particular, they required labour. And since most Africans were uninterested in exchanging their labour for the special-use currencies the French were offering, labour had to be acquired through force. Chapter 3 delves into how manhunting therefore became the major undertaking of colonial officials during the colony's early decades, particularly in the hunting zone. The cruelty of manhunting and of the way labour was squeezed from the captured comes across as scandalous today; it did to many at the time as well. Many Europeans involved with manhunting experienced the tensions between the future-oriented goals justifying their presence and the actual practices they engaged in (or allowed, or did not punish) as conflicts of values. These conflicts stemmed in part from the multiple arenas in which they sought to be effective actors: how happenings in the Central African interior were perceived by imperial institutions and audiences, and the unfolding of interpersonal relations in the interior where manhunting was necessary for acquisition and exploitation. In neither arena was law much of a guide to action. Instead, ambitious colonial officials learned the skill of camouflage: managing the faces they showed to different audiences so that their practices would not stand out as questionable. Along the way, manhunts entrenched a simultaneously acquisitive and neglectful way of thinking about the value and status of other people.

Manhunts for forced labour led to thousands of deaths. Foreign diseases and slave raiding also dramatically reduced the number of people living in the area. With so few people, the prevalence of big game was all the more striking. The colonial government thought that big-game hunting could thus become a way to profit from this otherwise neglected colony. Professional hunters flocked to the region in search of the numerous and unafraid elephants. Ivory prices fell, and elephants became harder to find. By the 1930s, large expanses of the north-east were consecrated hunting reserves, and safari hunting became the official development plan for the area, which was officially designated an 'autonomous district' because it was too remote and too sparsely populated to warrant the resources of direct administration. Chapter 4 shows that, throughout these shifts in Oubangui-Chari, as the colony was known, passing hunting regulations and dispatching people to implement them required the would-be enforcers to become raiders themselves, tracking and taking from people whose status was precarious but who could also prove dangerous or well resourced. Hunting regulations written in faraway capitals were neither irrelevant nor a blueprint for ethical (licit) behaviour. They were, instead, a kind of scaffolding added to the landscape, a bare-bones structure that could be climbed and manipulated to afford new opportunities for camouflage and for taking. Violence, particularly in the form of forceful acquisition amid status uncertainty, has been an important part of repertoires of meaningful action in the hunting zone, but clear determinations regarding its morality are most easily made at a remove – spatial or temporal – from the encounters themselves. This is because the encounters are marked by entrainment, which diminishes the importance of deontological principle to the conduct of action. Regulation and avoidance, rather than being based on rules and principles, are based on more proximate, interactional moves, in which there are possibilities for both identification with another and violence.

In the wake of ramped-up forceful acquisition in CAR's vast parklands in the 1970s and 1980s, the conservation agenda that had been a minor part of the big-game hunting system also became more forceful. By the late 1980s, an EU-funded conservation project had been deployed. It included a militia of some hundred men whose job it was to patrol the parklands and apprehend anyone they found. Although they were supposed to kill or injure only when necessary for their self-defence, they were able to exercise considerable latitude in their determination. The second half of the book focuses on the transformations wrought by entanglements around forceful conservation. Rather than using this as an example of armed, even militarised, conservation among other cases of militarised conservation, these chapters use conservation as a way to explore the interpersonal repertoires developed in situations where neither law nor identity provides much of a guide. The simultaneous overpresence and powerlessness of law is due in part to the fact that so much of daily life and practice in the region is illegalised, as Chapter 5 demonstrates. When life is illegal all the way down, and the means of enforcement are both constrained and violent, camouflage and denunciation are two key modes of action, and each one forms the heart of a subsequent chapter.

E. P. Thompson wisely noted that those who feel disenfranchised or otherwise disconnected from the law must defend their claims 'by force or stealth' (1975: 240), but he leaves less explored what makes stealth work. For an insight into this, Chapter 6 investigates the plural, situational, and interpersonal ways in which people understand legitimate, or at least reasonable, access to taking in the hunting zone. Stealth, I argue, is less a matter of efficient hiding than of cultivating skills that allow people to blend in across different social and bureaucratic landscapes and that give them greater access to their own acquisitive and status-related projects. I call these skills camouflage, in a nod to their hunter-like, non-pastoral tendencies. Camouflage is not just something state actors do in order to paper over the inconvenient or anomalous cases that might call attention to the limits of state ways of seeing. It is a skill that people develop in order to move in and out of institutional structures, a way to use those structures for their own gymnastic endeavours without drawing attention to the ways in which their practices cause the bars to creak or bend.

Nor is force itself as straightforward as it might at first appear. Stealth proved to be a communicative endeavour, and Chapter 7 shows that force is too. What does force in the context of armed conservation and acquisitive politics intend to communicate? Who is the intended audience? What values underlie the actors' moves? *Pisteurs* often use the idiom of vengeance to answer those questions, or the question of why they pursue manhunts. But vengeance invites further exploration, too. It has often been thought of as a mode of law, a balancing mechanism. Vengeance, in the way *pisteurs*, hunters, and herders enact it, in contrast, is a means of communicating a claim of status. Who is not to be messed with? Who can be subjected to seizure or other insults? How does one respond if attacked? Recourse to vengeance is particularly valuable to people who do not have reliable access to institutional means of protection; it is a mode of denunciation, and a claim to sovereignty, oriented not towards control but towards liberty. Denunciation, like vengeance, is conversational – only in rare cases is it so definitive as to become a Parthian shot; instead, it often becomes a continuing cycle. Few are happy that denunciation is so prevalent, but many see their own denunciations as necessary. By denouncing, they claim an exception from violence that would demean but not include them, as well as from associated rules and norms, and as such it is a process of solidarity and of claiming liberty.

Though forceful, militia-led conservation continues in north-eastern CAR, it has been joined and at times supplanted by rebellions, some led by former *pisteurs* who have turned their martial skills to this new end. Rebellions and interventions by outsiders have long histories in Central Africa, but the particular forms these practices have taken in the last 15 years are new. Among other changes, men consciously self-style as rebels, and there has been an enormous influx of the people I have elsewhere called the 'good intentions crowd' (international organisation officials, aid organisation employees, diplomats, and others who understand themselves as 'external' and altruistic and yet become central, jostling, and interested participants in rebellion in Africa post–Cold War). In Chapter 8 I focus on how the new rebels relate to and transform the serious games surrounding forceful acquisition and status that are the book's main focus. This project provides an opportunity to sit with four adventurous men who have been involved in these shifts around force, acquisition, and status over the last several decades. All had previously been involved in different kinds of shows of force, such as the denunciations for the sake of liberty that made up such a big part of conservation work. Now, by using the symbolic register of rebellion, they wanted their shows of force to communicate something else: namely their status as meriting regard, a status they imagined would take the form of a salaried or otherwise entitled relationship to the state. They hoped that the good intentions crowd's involvement would help them leverage their demands for distribution. In this respect, the rebels have largely failed, or at least been disappointed. But while they have not achieved the kind of entitled status they hoped for, they have also enjoyed certain adventurous aspects of their careers and the new lifestyles and ideas they have encountered.

I use Chapter 9, the conclusion, as an opportunity to consider the consequences of forceful acquisition – what it allows for, and what it makes more difficult – and pose comparative questions. I highlight how important it is to remember the importance of acquisition rather than assuming that production and management (normative pastoralism in politics and economy) are the only ways in which political-economic processes and relationships play out in the world. Precarity – uncertainty, instability – has rightly become a recent area of attention. But the tendency to focus on post-Fordist/post-industrial and/or urban locales, where precarity is often thought of as a recent invention, reveals a troubling blind spot. In the bush, status instability and forceful acquisition have long gone together, and, while the details have changed, they have persisted for more than a century. The history this book recounts has much to offer in understanding the lived experience of precarity, and the adventures and constraints when acquisition fractures sovereignty and distribution.

Conclusion

This book is motivated by a conviction. However out of the way it may seem, the hunting zone and the people who use it are fully part of the modern world (Piot 1999). Acquisition in the form of hunting and raiding is not an archaic, roundabout means to political centralisation and a state; it is not, in other words, a historical mode of political expansion. Hunting and raiding may be that too, but they are fundamental to the political-economic repertoires that exist in the world, their effects are not preordained, and they are certainly not always the work of states in a predatory mode of expansion. Nor are hunting and raiding geographically delimited 'release valves' that account for people with outlaw mentalities in some neat structural-functional way. They are a means to innovate and self-make through acquisition, with uncertain outcomes, and, moreover, they are best thought of as a particular kind of 'serious game':

> The idea of the game – the serious game – in turn is meant to resolve a number of problems in a broader theory of practice, problems that arise particularly from concerns that animate feminist, minority, postcolonial, and subaltern theorizing. One is the necessity for retaining an active intentional subject without falling into some form of free agency and voluntarism. Here I have argued that, if we take the methodological unit of practice as the game, rather than the 'agent,' we can never lose sight of the mutual determination of agents and structures: of the fact that players are 'agents,' skilled and intense strategizers who constantly stretch the game even as they enact it, and the simultaneous fact that players are defined and constructed (though never wholly contained) by the game. (Ortner 1996: 19–20)

The serious game refers to how people, in a place where the control and management of people and territory are limited, participate in political-economic processes that reach far beyond their location, and how they turn the centrality of encounters with potentially dangerous others to their acquisitive advantage. My shorthand for this is the hunting game. It is a game in which violence is important, but not in a manner that requires obliterating enemies. Instead, the violence is part of a process of getting to know one's targets and extracting from them, a process that can result in death but does not always have that as its goal. It is, moreover, a serious game often played amid confrontationally tense entrainment (Collins 2009).

In short, I am expanding on Mariane Ferme's (2001b) contention that hunters are often those most turned towards the world beyond 'home', the ones who first seek, encounter, and experiment with new ways of doing things. This kind of extraversion (Bayart 2000) is an enduring trait of hunting and raiding, even as the targets and objectives change. Focusing on acquisition foregrounds the conflicts of values that arise as people with competing interests meet, sometimes coming into conflict and sometimes cooperating. Therefore, when I speak of hunting games I am not translating a local category used by a particular group, but drawing a range of practices and people into one frame – and in so doing showing that, while they see themselves as different, they can have similar ways of interacting with each other and representing themselves, both to others resident in the area and to those far away.

It is a particularly apt time to focus on acquisition as a mode of both governance and accumulation. Different forms of raiding seem to be growing in prominence, including as a mode of war. Not only is the hunting of 'poachers' on the rise in the world (Duffy 2014), insurgents are being targeted through explicit practices of hunting. In Northern Nigeria, animal hunters have been deputised to track down members of Boko Haram (Collyer 2018). Drones, too, expand the importance of raiding and hunting as a mode of governance and warfare (Chamayou 2015; Gusterson 2017). On the hunting side of the spectrum, wealth through acquisition (rather than production – or at least preceding production) is also growing in prevalence. Bioprospecting (Hayden 2003a, 2003b) is just one way in which modes of claiming value from goods in the global South have continued to intensify over the last several centuries. If anything, these ways of operating have expanded as new players (in Africa, state-affiliated firms from China or Russia, for example) enter the hunt to acquire valuables with ambiguous property status. Not everywhere is state law as compromised as it is in CAR, but in many places prospecting is associated with plural, competing conceptions of property, status, and proper access. While control, discipline, and the management of populations and production remain the ethos of many political projects, they should not be the starting point for understanding the dynamics of acquisition. Nor should one assume that it's always clear who accumulates – indeed there have been a lot of losses for all involved. When acquisition is a main goal, other ways of operating are necessary: displaying force to claim status as one who should not be obstructed by dangerous others while avoiding any responsibility for others; self-positioning through camouflage (finding ways to be where the action is without standing out, across various social, physical, and institutional landscapes); gaining wealth and renown from taking and storytelling. Raiding, as a sometimes violent mode of acquisition, is not a strange anachronism but a game that became possible through imperialism and continues to draw people in, sometimes despite themselves.

2 *Zariba* contests and collaborations

In the last decades of the nineteenth century and in the early twentieth, increasingly powerful and numerous Muslim politico-economic personalities, actors, and innovators encountered European imperialists throughout North-Central Africa. What relational dynamics of wealth and rule were fostered by their meetings, collaborations, and conflicts? Raiding remained absolutely crucial to all who sought power there, and through it larger relationships of influence, alliance, and hostility – all more changeable than those of friends and enemies – were established. Other factors came into play, too, of course, for example social and political arrangements among and between Muslims, African non-Muslims, and Europeans. Such distinctions were important not so much because they provided group identity to united blocs but because uncertainty about the status of people newly coming into sustained contact with one another created fluidity of opportunity as well as of threat. If someone stopped paying their tribute, what could be taken from them – their life? Their liberty? What would happen if someone was a newcomer without relations? Or if someone was of another religion or race?

North-central Africa offers a dramatic cast of actors in this interplay: Sultan Muhammad al-Sanusi, Paul Crampel, Sultan Rabih b. Fadlallah, Émile Gentil, Djellab, Captain Jean Modat. Raiders there are usually described in terms of their origins – national, racial, religious – with the connotations each implies. The first Europeans to arrive are usually called 'explorers', and the Muslim leaders 'sultans' or raiders. The problem with these terms is that they hide a substantial overlap in the way all the players proceeded. Europeans, for instance, spent much energy taking from the people they encountered, claiming not only goods in their possession but their labour power. Central Africans probably did not experience the behaviour of the 'explorers' and the 'slave raiders' as fundamentally different (Prioul 1981: 158).

In French, the word '*raid*' captures a murky area between forcible acquisition and exploring; it refers both to an armed operation of capture and a long-distance trek. This double sense is lost in English, but is perhaps reclaimed in 'adventurism', which places the focus on 'adventurists' – people who sought to acquire (goods or renown) in spaces not considered 'home', and who took on what others saw as dangerous and arguably foolhardy risk in order to do so. *Aventurier*, moreover, has become a Central African term to describe people who have socially transgressive ambitions (particularly for wealth) beyond their place of birth. Encounters among prominent adventurists show raiding acquisition most often as an improvised response to opportunities that arise from occasions when stores of wealth or advantage are present together with potential danger and mutual capacities for force. Raiding acquisition is less the expression of the values of any individual than a mode of action in the absence of clear relationships, and the presence of perceived needs. Many such dynamics still hold true despite our inclination to entrust all such occasions to the oversight of the nation state and the niceties of diplomats.

The adventurists and their raiding encounters

On the morning of 12 January 1911, Sultan Muhammad al-Sanusi[1] awoke in his compound at the top of a rocky plateau. He was just over 50 years old. Around him on the plateau spread the city, Ndele, he had built. Only a few people were living in the area when he and his followers had arrived, just over 15 years previously. Now, some 20,000 did. To find a city of comparable size you would have had to trek a thousand kilometres north to Abeche, in what is now eastern Chad. Al-Sanusi's many wives lived in rock-and-daub houses spread around his, as did other members of his family and his close advisers. Smooth, indented rock faces made elegant chairs and benches. One could lounge there, in the morning enjoying the cool that set in overnight, and in the evening the warmth gathered over the course of the day. From here, one could see for many kilometres into the lowlands all around, although the heat and smoke from fires set to drive game or clear fields for planting sometimes threw a haze over the view.

In the bustling market, one could find all the area's specialities: ivory, herbs and aromatic plants used by people to the north for their incense and perfumes, and slaves. One might pay for them with cloth, the coarse

[1] Al-Sanusi had been born Ahmad Abbakar but while a child got the new name, al-Sanusi, as a tribute to the brotherhood of the same name, far to the north, and as a way of marking a connection to them.

indigo-dyed cotton woven in the area, or the finer, whiter varieties imported from the far north. Interspersed among the houses, markets, and stables[2] were guardhouses and militia outposts. A wall encircled the perimeter of the plateau as well, with guard posts at every opening. The walls were nearly three times as tall as an adult, topped with thorn branches as tough as barbed wire (Modat 1910c: unpaginated photo annex). Ndele was a cosmopolitan city, but of a particular kind: it was built on raiding, and especially on the hunting and capture of people. While most people in Ndele worked, indentured, on the plantations that kept everyone fed, the route to wealth and regard, and maybe even to renown, was clear: work as a *bazingir*.

Bazingir is a term from Chadic Arabic that means 'slave soldier' (Cordell 1985: 18). But while *bazingirs* would sometimes carry out joint operations in an army mode – al-Sanusi's forces came to number several thousand (Mordrelle 1910) – their purpose was not conquest[3] so much as slave hunting. Raiding parties would decamp from Ndele and build a temporary stockade, called a *zariba*, fortified with thorn branches, in the area where they planned to 'hunt'. Then, attacking at daybreak, *bazingirs* would shock a nearby hamlet or small settlement awake with shots from their rifles. (As they were not repeaters, the rifles' frightening noises were more useful than their capacity for close-range combat.) Some village defenders were likely to be killed during this onslaught, while other locals were captured and still others fled into the surrounding bush. Raiders would sometimes camp in the now abandoned villages for 'several days to hunt for refugees' and 'strip the settlement of stored food and items of value, such as ivory' (Cordell 1985: 104) before transporting the spoils to their *zariba* and preparing for the next hunt. When the *zariba* was full, the people and goods assembled there were taken back to Ndele, where al-Sanusi claimed his share, one-third of the captives, and the

2 Al-Sanusi kept some horses but they had to be replaced frequently because of their susceptibility to trypanosomiasis. The horses marked his connection to people and points north, where horses were more widespread; here, they were rare and could inspire awe and fear.

3 A French commander wrote in 1910 that 'the *bazingirs* are vigorous, trained to endure hard fatigue, but their military instruction appears to be basically nil. They are divided into companies themselves composed of subdivisions, but they seem to have no idea of tactics' (Mordrelle 1910: unpaginated). The French officer saw armed men and assumed a *military*, with the norm being the professional militaries that had developed in Europe over the previous century (Huntington 1957). But the *bazingirs*' purpose was different; their skill lay in hunting. ['Les Bazinguers sont vigoreux, entraînées durs à la fatigue, mais leur instruction militaire paraît à peu près nulle. Ils sont répartis en compagnies comprenant elles-mêmes des subdivisions plus faibles, mais ils ne semblent avoir aucune idée de tactique.']

Figure 2.1 Al-Sanusi outside his *zariba* walls in 1910
Source: Mordrelle (1910)

bazingirs arranged to sell the others for their own profit.[4] Ndele was itself a kind of overgrown *zariba* (Figure 2.1).

Al-Sanusi's polity, known as Dar al-Kuti or the 'place of forests',[5] depended on the innovations of those working the temporary *zaribas* (*zara'ib* in the Arabic plural). The political structure of the region at the time has been called a '*zariba* system' (Cordell 1979), but 'structure' and 'system' make things sound far more fixed than they were in a period of massive upheaval and social change. And while the people subjected to raids experienced these as years of terror, they were not passive. They, too, could kill – and their victims could include *bazingirs* – and they could also flee to their own fortified settlements, such as the comfortable homes they

4 Al-Sanusi kept one-third, or sometimes half, of the captives collected through a raid, and the hunter kept or sold the rest. Some of the captives remained in the area to work al-Sanusi's plantations, to be wives or concubines, or to become *bazingirs* themselves. The rest – especially those who had most resisted capture – were sold and exported (Cordell 1985: 121–2), with captives from the region known in the Tunis markets in around 1900 (Kalck 1974: 277).

5 The story of hunting adventurism centres on an area known as Dar al-Kuti ('*dar*' meaning home or place in Arabic, and '*kuti*' being the term used by the area's earliest inhabitants, the Ndoka, for the dense, tsetse-filled forest they called home). In terms of geographical position, what constitutes Dar al-Kuti can be interpreted in different ways. Most frequently, people use it to describe the Aouk River's floodplain area (between Ndele and Chad today), but, during the height of slave raiding in the area, the raiders' influence extended south to the Oubangui River and east to the area that eventually became Sudan, and for that reason contemporary French documents sometimes used this broader sense (Cordell: 1985: 32–3).

built in the area's extensive caves (Cordell 2003; Prins 1909). Whereas in the raiding polities to the north, the raiders could attack with the advantage of being on horseback, in Dar al-Kuti and the hunting zone, the *bazingirs* mostly arrived on foot. The *bazingirs* enjoyed certain technological and organisational advantages, but the roles of hunter and hunted could quickly shift (Cordell 1985: 109). The Central African novelist Étienne Goyémidé's book *The Last Survivor of the Caravan* (1985) portrays one such reversal, whereby the survivors from a village brutally raided by *bazingirs* turned the same tactics against their captors. Although the book is a novel, Goyémidé explains that the story was substantially built from oral histories he collected. As one of the protagonists explained:

> Despite our state of weakness, hunger, and destitution, we had to get vengeance, to get vengeance for our relatives so cowardly assassinated, our village and our happiness that were destroyed. We had to fight, to kill, or to die. At this price alone, the freedom that we had tasted for a few minutes would be perfect. All the men were perfectly in agreement on this point. They were ready to prove to these ghosts [the *bazingirs*] that we belonged to the race of fearless warriors. (Goyémidé 1985: 120)[6]

Early January nights are cold, almost freezing, in Ndele, but as soon as the sun rises the heat arrives. On that twelfth day in 1911, the local French resident, Captain Jean Julien Vincent Modat, had asked al-Sanusi to present himself and his men at 8 a.m. to greet a passing French military convoy, a gesture of respect expected by such important visitors. By eight, the light would have been sharp and bright, and al-Sanusi already up for hours, for he rose just before dawn to pray. Although he permitted and even occasionally attended ceremonies held by the non-Muslim Nduka people who had preceded him in Ndele, al-Sanusi was an observant Muslim. Islam helped assign or denote status, not least justifying who could be raided and enslaved – specifically, non-Muslims. A distinction sometimes more honoured in its breach than its observance, it was nevertheless important to the area's Muslim leaders.

About two kilometres away from where al-Sanusi awoke on that January morning stood a house occupied by the local French *résident* or lead officer, Captain Jean Modat. His house was on a hill, too, but it was a small hump of a rise compared with al-Sanusi's city. Modat had spent nearly three years in Ndele. With him were a few dozen soldiers – some

6 'Malgré notre état de faiblesse, de sous-alimentation et de dénuement, nous nous devions de nous venger, de venger nos parents lâchement assassinés, notre village et notre bonheur détruits. Nous nous devions de combattre, de tuer ou de mourir. A ce prix seul, la liberté à laquelle nous goûtions depuis quelques instants serait parfaite. Tous les hommes étaient absolument d'accord sur ce point. Ils étaient prêts à prouver à ces fantômes notre appartenance à la race des guerriers intrépides.'

French, but mostly African regional guards drawn from closer to the coast. Few in France supported colonisation of this hinterland – all that expense, and for what? So French agents in the interior had established next to no administration and survived mainly on the material and human resources al-Sanusi provided them with.

They still needed to transport goods to and from the coast, however, and the labour needed for both import and export was causing massive upheaval as the French sent the regional guards to hunt porters for the heavy loads. Over the last 15 years these loads had included such behemoths as a disassembled steamship, the *Léon Blot*, to be used in the war against the raiding sultan to the north, Rabih b. Fadlallah, as well as massive iron cauldrons the Europeans used for bathing. (Some also used these cauldrons for boiling the flesh off heads they had collected, so as to leave only the skulls that were so prized by the era's phrenologists [Harrison 2012; Schweinfurth 1873].) One colonial officer, writing in 1902, described the upheaval caused by these hunts to make people into porters: 'Villages fall apart, families split up, each abandoning tribe, village, family, fields to live in the bush like a hunted animal to avoid recruitment. The result is famine, and it is by the hundreds that the Manza [the name used for people living in the area] have died these past months' (cited in Cordell 1994: 143). Even contemporary observers keen to present colonisation positively could not help but admit that what the colonisers were doing was mostly a manhunt ('*chasse à l'homme*'). As one colonial officer stated: '[W]e track them in the bush where they prefer to seek refuge and die of hunger rather than carry our loads' (cited in Kalck 1974: 124).[7] The *bazingir*-led enslavement raids and French-led raids for forced labour mirrored each other, and they defined the processes through which this part of Central Africa became part of larger networks of transport, communication, and exchange.

Paul Crampel was among the first French adventurists in the area. Born in 1864 to a petty bureaucrat father who failed to force his son into a practical profession like his own, Crampel read first philosophy and then theatre at university. While still a student, Crampel went to hear his 'hero' Pierre Savorgnan de Brazza (Kalck 1993: 7), the public face of French ambitions for Equatorial Africa and the person from whom the French Congolese capital, Brazzaville, got its name. Crampel convinced Brazza to employ him, and in this capacity he made his way to the Gabonese interior together with a contingent of *tirailleurs* (African riflemen) and African porters. Crampel described this mission as 'my hunts, my explorations',

[7] '[O]n les traque dans la brousse où ils préfèrent se réfugier et mourir de faim, plutôt que de porter nos charges.'

and indeed he spent much of his time amassing what he could (plants, animals, and other goods) for examination and valuation in France.

Crampel needed a worthy project to make his name as a great adventurist, and he hit on a plan to rouse French interest in Equatorial Africa by trekking from the Atlantic coast into the interior, stopping briefly at the lean-to that had been erected in 1888 to demarcate the capital in name only, Bangui. Turning north, he would sign treaties with the leaders he met along the way, in the process, he hoped, claiming a sphere of French influence that would extend all the way to the Mediterranean (Kalck 1993: 44). It was not the French government but a variety of private actors (media executives, barons, and bankers) (Soulages 1901: 22) who, thanks to Crampel's careful presentation of himself as a well-known, accomplished adventurist, saw in him a worthy figurehead for the greater glory of imperial France.[8]

Crampel, along with a few French subordinates working with him and the dozens of Gabonese porters and *tirailleurs* they had hired at the coast, arrived in Bangui at the end of 1890, just as the dry season was setting in. The post's French resident had recently been killed (and eaten, some said) by the people living nearby after having inadvertently been drawn into taking sides in a dispute between two villages (Kalck 1993: 55).[9] (Being a European offered certain advantages, perhaps, but clearly not unmixed with danger.) Still, Crampel and his party, organised into several European-headed contingents, struck out for points north in early 1891. By March, they were nearing Dar al-Kuti and al-Sanusi, who at the time had only just become a sultan rather than a trader.

Al-Sanusi was well aware by then of the Crampel adventurists' approach; his adviser, al-Hajj Tukur, had informed him of the interests and tactics of the interlopers. Al-Hajj Tukur was a Fulani from Sokoto, a well-established polity to the north and west (present-day north-west Nigeria), and a true adventurist himself: his career accomplishments included an escape from a Mahdist prison and a job as commercial agent for Sultan Yusuf of Wadai among the Azande (an imperial nation lying to the south, in the present-day borderlands between CAR, South Sudan,

[8] The most generous was the Baron Edmond de Rothschild, who was 'impressed by Paul Crampel's strong personality' (Kalck 1993: 49). A century later, one of Rothschild's successors made frequent trips to the Central African hunting zone in order to pursue big game. He enjoyed it so much that he even imported his own ultralight plane to use when visiting. When he stopped coming, Russian anti-poaching mercenaries repurposed the aircraft for their work, outfitting it with a mortar.

[9] Nearby residents had implored the official to protect them from some rapacious neighbours; when he did so, they came to hunt him down. With only a dozen unequipped, ill-fed Senegalese infantrymen on his side, the official was easy prey.

and the Democratic Republic of the Congo), where he interacted with the Europeans beginning to arrive there and learned French (Cordell 1985: 63). Messengers who had reconnoitred the Crampel mission returned to tell al-Sanusi of the substantial arsenal they carried: 'fifty rapid-fire rifles of diverse brands (Kropatchek [sic], Gras, Remington, Rubin), 175 flintlocks, 30,000 cartridges, more than 60,000 percussion caps, several hundred kilograms of powder, and a small cache of revolvers' (Cordell 1985: 61). Acquiring these goods would let al-Sanusi intensify raiding as well as advancing his position with his neighbours. Moreover, he had heard that Crampel's riflemen and porters were discontented. Four of the *tirailleurs* had deserted in February, and it appeared that Crampel was ill. The expedition sounded like easy pickings, and the value that could be taken from it overrode considerations of legitimacy or regard.

Probably the most pressing factor for al-Sanusi at the time of the Crampel expedition was his evolving relationship with Rabih b. Fadlallah, the great raiding innovator to his north. Rabih had visited Dar al-Kuti a few years previously, before al-Sanusi had made his large *zariba* at Ndele. At that time, Dar al-Kuti had no central leader, instead operating under the guidance of a revered Muslim scholar or *faqih*, al-Sanusi's uncle Kobur, who organised worship and mediated trade disputes. Kobur lived at a place called Kali-Sha, then Dar al-Kuti's largest town. Kobur disdained Rabih, who subordinated principle to the exigencies of hunting, maintaining that Muslims could not legitimately be enslaved by other Muslims. Rabih, for his part, enslaved anyone he deemed insufficiently tribute-providing, and local babies were taught from the cradle to fear him via an eerie lullaby: 'Rabih came, the bullets fell' (Cordell 1985: 56). But al-Sanusi, at the time a merchant who acquired wares by dispatching his 50 'guns'[10] to raid, made himself useful to Rabih by giving him ammunition at a time when Rabih's stocks were running dangerously low due to compromised supply routes. Rabih was powerful but surrounded by people who mistrusted him. French adventurists, who were making their first forays north from their camps along the rivers to the south, saw Rabih as rapacious (which was not an inherent problem) and uncontrollable (which was, because it meant that he would be difficult to turn towards French interests and projects). Sultan Yusuf of Wadai was a rival to the north. To the east, Anglo-Egyptian forces operating under the banner of abolitionism sought to capture slave raiders such as Rabih.

[10] That is, 50 *bazingirs*, each armed with a rifle. As with the practice of referring to elephants as 'ivory', hunters or other armed men would sometimes be referred to as 'guns' (Le Noël 1999).

As thanks for the ammunition, Rabih deposed Kobur and anointed al-Sanusi as his key interlocutor in the area. While Kobur's leadership, such as it was, had been accrued through his deployment of learned mediation, al-Sanusi owed his to his ability to acquire and provide. Al-Sanusi promised continued tribute as a marker of submission to Rabih. But, then as now, submission and tribute implied not renunciation of power but tacit agreement to a balance of that power, with al-Sanusi retaining considerable liberty to pursue his own ends. Public deference to Rabih indicated that al-Sanusi had removed himself from any rivalry. It did not mean that Rabih would police or otherwise control al-Sanusi, who, by facing Rabih with a non-threatening mien, in fact got greater leeway to raid because Rabih was less concerned that they were rivals.

Such was al-Sanusi's relationship with Rabih. But al-Sanusi also noticed that Rabih was increasingly isolated – due to, among other things, the blockade the Wadai sultan Yusuf had imposed because of his recalcitrance – and the isolation and weakness of his patron affected al-Sanusi as well. Al-Sanusi reckoned that if he did not claim the Crampel mission, Rabih would, and al-Sanusi would be made all the more dependent on his patron. Political power and organisation in the region were more spheres of influence than zones of control, their terms changing rapidly with the fortunes of their most powerful men.

Al-Sanusi sent a messenger to Crampel, now at the head of an underfed and demoralised party, in March 1891, warning him that he could not assure his safe conduct (Cordell 1985: 62). The letter could be read two ways: either as concern for Crampel's safety, or as a threat reminding him that this hunting zone was a place where people acquired through raids, not a place where such actions were policed and controlled.

A few days later Crampel was dead. *Bazingirs* sent by al-Sanusi had tracked and ambushed him with his advance party. Exactly how many people were killed has never been definitively established, but Crampel and two European deputies were among them (Cordell 1985: 62; Kalck 1993: 139–40). For al-Sanusi, the success of the raid was less about the number of people killed – though perhaps unavoidable, this was never the goal – but a matter of recouping their valuable possessions: Crampel's firearms and ammunition, as well as African prisoners or recruits (it is unclear whether they moved to Dar al-Kuti by force or choice) who could train them in the use of these new weapons and provide intelligence about places beyond their area of influence (Cordell 1985: 62; Dybowski 1893: 255; Kalck 1993: 139).

Al-Sanusi's capture of Crampel's guns left him better armed than Rabih, but having armaments was not an unalloyed advantage for al-Sanusi. It introduced a new concern about his status; now, Rabih might perceive al-Sanusi to be a threat. To avoid immediate antagonism, al-Sanusi made a show of deference to Rabih, but he dissembled. When Rabih demanded that al-Sanusi send him the captured weapons, al-Sanusi sent a few. But, he told Rabih, he swore on the Qur'an that there were 'no more weapons *on* the earth' (Cordell 1985: 65, emphasis in the original). This was certainly true: he had buried the others, at one go disguising his increased power and hunting ability, and in a way that was hard for Rabih to call him out on. While not a falsehood, it was an act of camouflaging, a careful positioning of information conveyed rather than a comprehensive explanation.

What was al-Sanusi's status in relation to people such as Crampel, and vice versa? Who could raid or acquire from whom? The answers to these questions depended more on opportunity than on principle. What was al-Sanusi's status in relation to the Wadaians to the north, and those allied with them? This question, too, was not settled, but al-Sanusi's location was always vulnerable: Kali-Sha was in the middle of a hard-to-defend dry floodplain. In 1894, several years after the Crampel incident, Sharif al-Din, the Wadaian governor of the Salamat, attacked al-Sanusi's *zariba* settlement. The onslaught lasted months. The Wadaians captured thousands to sell or enslave themselves, seized what ivory they could find, and made off with the ripening millet (Cordell 1985: 65–6). This was war by raiding rather than conquest, a war with the primary objective of acquiring goods, including humans. Al-Sanusi and his closest advisers managed to evade the attackers by hiding out in the caves and caverns on the rocky outcroppings that mark the area.

Al-Sanusi's successful raiding had not settled his status. Instead, it had made his *zariba* an attractive target for others. To the Wadaians, al-Sanusi seemed neither friend nor enemy but a rival and an opportunity. Relations among people in the region were certainly not a Hobbesian war of all against all, but it was a period marked by innovation in raiding and acquisition, and so the terms of relationships and claims to property were unstable and could be challenged or overturned. One component of that innovation had to do with journeying further from home in order to acquire value (labour, liberty, tribute) from people whose status was ambiguous but could be construed as 'not us'.

Once the Wadaians departed, al-Sanusi began to rebuild on the more defensible plateau that became Ndele. Under al-Sanusi's leadership, but with help from French adventurists, Ndele flourished. In 1897, his old adviser/mentor al-Hajj Tukur negotiated the first treaty between al-Sanusi and France, dealing with Émile Gentil, an officer adventurist on a mission to vanquish Rabih. The purpose of the treaty was 'commerce and alliance' (Senoussi–Gentil 1897: 1),[11] a claim to let exchange be their primary point of contact and otherwise mostly leave each other alone. Gentil promised that France would provide al-Sanusi with 100 Gras carbines, 5,000 cartridges, and 200 flintlocks within nine months, and then five Gras carbines, 50 flintlocks, and 2,000 cartridges per year after that (Senoussi–Gentil 1897: 1). Al-Sanusi promised to accord the French a monopoly on imported goods. Gentil and his men had little ability to monitor what went on inside al-Sanusi's walls, and both parties knew that the monopoly would be impossible to enforce (Cordell 1985: 70), but it symbolically accorded rights of acquisition and exchange to the French adventurists.

In 1900, Gentil and his troops eventually succeeded in killing Rabih, who they saw as dangerously intractable. Although Rabih's son tried to continue the fight, he never became the kind of successful raiding innovator his father had been (for instance, his father's actions expanded ideas about who could be raided). Better armed and with rivals such as Rabih vanquished, al-Sanusi was freer than ever to send his *bazingirs* out on raids, and thus began the most intense period of manhunting and *zariba* work under his authorisation (Cordell 1985: 105–6).

Around the turn of the twentieth century, a French *résident* and some *tirailleurs* set up near Ndele, and they needed livestock and other food and the saleable goods produced in the area, particularly ivory and rubber, as well as porters. In a treaty amendment signed in 1903, al-Sanusi promised to provide them. In exchange, he would receive an 'annual gift' of guns, ammunition, some currency (the immortal Maria Theresa thalers and French francs), and other French goods (Senoussi–Fourneau 1903: 2–3). The French also hoped to limit al-Sanusi's raiding, which they saw as potentially in competition with the acquisitive projects they wanted to launch, but they had few effective means to do so. The treaty also stipulated that al-Sanusi and his polity were now 'under the protection of the French Republic', but it continued to recognise al-Sanusi as the 'sovereign of Dar al-Kuti' (Senoussi–Fourneau 1903: 1), language recalling that political relationships in the pre-nation state era allowed for some flexibility or inconsistency about the assumption that a sovereign is a unitary wielder of power in a territory.

Manhunting by *bazingirs* continued. Most of this work could occur undetected by the French *résident* and his men. Paths into Ndele were narrow and surveilled by *bazingir* guards, making it difficult for those in French employ to sneak in and observe. Captured humans could be

[11] 'C'est un traité de commerce et d'alliance.'

brought in and out via the paths furthest from the French dwellings. But the French residents present during these years were not clueless. They knew that the *razzias* continued, even if they did not always admit the extent. They knew that al-Sanusi had not fulfilled the demands the treaty made of him, such as the provision of goods and tribute (Cordell 1985: 72). They knew, too, that al-Sanusi was becoming more dependent on them for the provision of goods as his other relationships (Rabih, Wadai) had been cut. Therefore, in 1908, they pushed for yet another treaty amendment. Al-Sanusi remained the 'sovereign', but now the text stipulated that 'the slave trade is formally prohibited' and al-Sanusi promised to 'end all *razzias* and military expeditions not approved by the French authorities' (Senoussi–Mongin 1908: 1).[12]

What must al-Sanusi have thought? The new treaty prohibited slavery, but it also required him to provide the French with porters, who were obviously themselves enslaved. Granted, slavery is a trickier concept than it might first appear. To be a slave means that another person holds rights to you and your (re)productive capacities, but the extent, duration, and scope of those rights can vary, as can the range of opportunities for slaves to exit that status (Kopytoff and Miers 1977). The people pressed into servitude as porters were not always long-term conscripts. They were rounded up, given a load to carry, and, once they had delivered it – if they survived – released. Everyone knew that the sultan's porters were coerced, their labour acquired without remuneration. Sometimes the practice was described as semi-voluntary, out of deference to a feared and respected leader, and sometimes simply as slavery. As the perceptive Captain Modat noted shortly after his arrival in 1909, al-Sanusi's 'mentality' was to see slavery as 'a means of governing', and *razzias* were his 'only commercial operations that are actually productive' (Modat 1909: 2).[13] When the new treaty came into effect, Modat began intercepting *bazingirs* and demanding that al-Sanusi release captives, but while both al-Sanusi and Modat had their justifications at the ready, neither respected the treaty's terms in their fullest spirit, nor had they likely ever expected to do so. Logistical concerns alone made it incredibly difficult to get the goods promised to al-Sanusi to him, and the French requirements of al-Sanusi were generally contrary to the realities of *zariba* politics, as al-Sanusi himself implied in his letters to the authorities in Bangui.[14]

[12] '[L]a traite en esclaves est formellement prohibée' and al-Sanusi promised to 'mettre fin à toutes razzias et expéditions militaires non-approuvées par les autorités françaises'.

[13] '[L]a mentalité de SENOUSSI pour qui l'esclavage est un procédé de gouvernement et les razzias les seules opérations commerciales vraiment productives.'

[14] Letters 1–4 (n.d.), ANOM, AEF/GGAEF, Carton D/4(4)/8.

By January 1911, the overgrown *zariba* town of Ndele was under increasing strain. Perhaps, that morning of 12 January, al-Sanusi was considering his situation. Following the 1908 treaty, the French military presence had grown, and by the end of 1909 it included several 'Europeans' (a catch-all covering all non-Africans): a captain (Modat) together with one lieutenant or sub-lieutenant, nine *sous-officiers* (non-commissioned officers), and one corporal. They were joined by a number of '*indigènes*' (none of whom were locally indigenous), comprising two *sous-officiers* and 58 *tirailleurs*. This made a grand total of 72 people (Government of Congo Française 1909). Ndele, according to a French estimate of the time, counted 15,000 to 20,000 people and 6,000 guns (Government of Oubangui-Chari 1911). Numbers on the ground therefore heavily favoured al-Sanusi. But he knew that the French officers among him were connected to a better-resourced polity elsewhere, namely France.

Al-Sanusi was also dealing with a running dispute with Djellab, a younger kinsman of sorts within the raiding fraternity. Djellab resided at Ouanda Djallé,[15] eight days' trek[16] to the north-east of Ndele, along the not yet demarcated border with Anglo-Egyptian Sudan (Modat 1910a). As Modat put it, al-Sanusi had accorded Djellab a '*droit de razzia*' (a right to raid; Modat 1910a). This *droit de razzia* was one version of a regional practice already at work for centuries, as we have seen: the grant to a hunter of freedom to raid in return for a proportion of the take, without any expectation that one would police or otherwise control the other.

An early account of such delegated powers of acquisition appears in the travel journals of Muhammad ibn Umar ibn Sulayman al-Tunisi, who visited Wadai and Darfur in the first quarter of the nineteenth century. In Wadai, hunting was restricted to a class of people, essentially the sultan's military officers. In Darfur, anyone who could present the sultan with the requisite gifts (a horse in full tack, for example, with a slave as groom) could request dispensation to hunt men and ivory. If the sultan accepted, the man would undergo an initiation during which he would be presented with a *salatieh*, a long staff that was the badge of office of the *ghazwah* or *razzia* leader (Al Tunisi 1845: 289). The sultan blessed the hunter's power, along the lines of the following:

> All those who accompany [the *salatieh*-bearer] shall be free from blame on our part – in testimony of which the present *firman* [edict] has emanated from our sublime generosity and our noble bounties. Far, far may all opposition be, all acts of malevolence, against this mandate. We have recommended to the bearer of this

15 Ouanda Djallé lies close to the Tata site of the anti-poaching ambush that opened the book.

16 This is based on travel of 25–30 kilometres per day (Modat 1910b).

permission to act with justice towards those who may follow this expedition, and to conduct himself with the equity and the moderation which the fear of God inspires. (Al Tunisi 1845: 290)

In other words, no earthly sovereign supervised the raiding operations – the 'fear of God' should result in a certain code of conduct, but people feel the potential for godly punishment to varying degrees. The sultan, therefore, could decide who to anoint as entitled to hunt, but it was not his writ to police the conduct of the raiding acquisition itself, in one of the numerous regional arrangements of 'dispensation to raid' as a mode of governing relationships. By the time al-Sanusi was on his hill at Ndele, these had come to include the French government's project of concessions, which officials justified on entirely different grounds but worked in much the same way (Coquery-Vidrovitch 1972).

But while this kind of forceful acquisition was not exactly subject to policing, it could still be done in such a way as to provoke, or to assuage, other adventurists. Djellab, 'thirsty for independence' (Modat 1910b), had begun to goad al-Sanusi, who said Djellab was not providing him with his due. Djellab countered that he was sending tribute, but al-Sanusi was not accepting it. Each accused the other of illegitimate killing and taking.[17] By 1910 they were feuding overtly. Al-Sanusi had more men and weapons, but Djellab occupied a superior position on his own well-defended plateau and his men repeatedly routed al-Sanusi's *bazingirs* and even took their cannon (Modat 1910a). At one point Djellab's men captured six porters working for Modat, who, furious, sent his *tirailleurs* against Djellab (Modat 1910b). Modat was beginning to understand that whatever had triggered al-Sanusi's ire against Djellab, al-Sanusi now also wanted Djellab's spot, which was profitably located, both by virtue of being a trading crossroads and by being so difficult to attack. In late 1910, al-Sanusi sent his military adviser, Allah Jabu, and several hundred *bazingirs* to definitively dislodge Djellab. If al-Sanusi resituated his key *zariba* at Ouanda Djallé, it would cause big problems for the French, because they would lose what leverage and cooperation they had managed to obtain from him.

Therefore, that 12 January, Captain Modat and Lieutenant Henry Grünfelder laid a trap. They told al-Sanusi to come out to greet a military contingent that was passing through on its way to Bria, to the east of Ndele. At 8 a.m., with the sun already strong, al-Sanusi emerged with his son Adam, as agreed. Modat had a document in his hand, which he

[17] Al-Sanusi told Modat that he had granted Djellab the right to 'exploit' the trader caravans travelling through the area, but that Djellab's men had killed several Muslim merchants in the process of doing so. Al-Sanusi sent *bazingirs* to send a message to Djellab that such actions were unacceptable (Modat 1910a).

pretended to be reading. Shielding his movements with the paper, he reached for his gun and shot al-Sanusi, who died immediately. Adam managed to shoot the lieutenant before he too was killed. This is how the sultanate's remaining local historians, Doungous Koro and Abdirahman Ade, explained the events to me a century later; they mostly accord with Cordell's account, but change which European fatefully pulled the trigger: 'After talking briefly with the sultan, the French officer [Grünfelder] quickly drew a pistol and shot them both' (Cordell 1985: 74). (Cordell was able to interview eyewitnesses.)

The accounts that made it into the colonial and military archives (which Cordell also drew on) camouflage the episode in several ways. They summarise the events and relationships up to that January morning in such a way that eliminating al-Sanusi seems to have been unavoidable; and they consistently refer to the act of killing as an 'arrest' rather than what it was – murder (Governor of Oubangui-Chari 1911). Calling the killing an arrest was not exactly false. It was, however, partial in both senses. It lent the appearance of state-like capacities when in fact what predominated were assertions of status through forceful acquisition – in this case of al-Sanusi's life and position. It attempted to place a factitious legal framework on a scenario that involved competing assertions of privilege.

Calling the killing an arrest also had the effect of discursively asserting French authority for the benefit of audiences elsewhere. The captain and his men represented law and order; al-Sanusi was a fractious subject to be arrested. In his report to the Governor of French Equatorial Africa, the Lieutenant Governor of Oubangui-Chari wrote: 'This is how Captain Modat, equipped with the powers that had been conferred on him, decided to arrest the Sultan Sanusi on 12 January at 8 in the morning. I do not yet have details on the manner [in which] the affair was undertaken and that cost the life of Sanusi and several of his loyalists' (Lieutenant Governor of Oubangui-Chari 1911). But on the ground in Ndele, the move was not seen by anyone as an arrest – it was a gamble (Cordell 1985: 74). Modat and those with him did not know how Ndele residents would react to al-Sanusi's death. If they fought back, Modat's group would be seriously outnumbered; the French were already hindered by a comparatively weak knowledge of the terrain.

Some of al-Sanusi's followers did fight back. Intermittent battles went on for several weeks, and some of his close associates retreated to oppositional positions on other *kagas*. But most fled, including beyond the putatively French territories to Anglo-Egyptian Darfur. The city of more than 20,000 (Lieutenant Governor of Oubangui-Chari 1911) that had grown around al-Sanusi's hunting and trading shrank to just a few thousand nearly overnight, and people fled from the surrounding area as well.[18] Ndele has never again had much more than half as many inhabitants as during al-Sanusi's tenure.

Trans-Saharan human and ivory hunting continued after al-Sanusi's death, and trade to the north and north-east remained important, but the scale of those activities decreased markedly without al-Sanusi to help organise them. Yet, in other ways, raiding and acquisition – less explicitly, but no less certainly – have remained central to the region's dynamics of profit and governance.

The adventurist is dead; long live adventurism

Hindsight can make it seem possible to look at this area as if it were never anything but an opportunity for colonialism. *Of course* the French won out over al-Sanusi, one might think. Ndele's intellectuals who speak of it today are more likely to attribute the shifting balance of power to the favour of the French to the vagaries of interpersonal intrigue. In my 2009–10 interviews there, the elderly raconteurs summoned up liminal figures – the young woman who slept with both al-Sanusi and Modat, the translators with their own agendas – as having instigated Dar al-Kuti's misfortune via their chicanery and betrayals.[19] They insisted that this supposedly inevitable episode turned instead on incidents of deception and luck. European accounts admit to their own use of deception and intrigue,[20] and Central African accounts include an appreciation of forces and power beyond that of any individual. Getting an idea of what really happened requires a willingness to readjust the telescope, to zoom in and out, and to pay close attention to the details that come into focus.

A longer view – telescoped out, one might say – indicates that, over the course of the nineteenth century and during the beginning of the twentieth, North-central Africa[21] was the location of a particular version of forcible acquisition and raiding. In part this was because it was an 'Islamic frontier' (Cordell 1985) where towns inhabited by Muslim merchants and scholars were emerging and facilitating long-distance

[18] Among the *transfuges* (deserters) was Djellab, who led his followers across the border into Sudan, where they remained. French attempts to lure them back for purposes of taxation failed.

[19] The woman had allegedly told Modat exactly which moment al-Sanusi would be vulnerable – immediately after prayers – as otherwise it would not have been possible to kill such a supernaturally protected person.

[20] For instance, Émile Gentil, describing his treatment of al-Sanusi: 'In order to avoid complications, I had to create a ruse' (Gentil 1902: 100).

[21] I borrow this geographical descriptor from Cordell (1983) to refer to eastern CAR, south-eastern Chad, and adjoining parts of Sudan/South Sudan.

connection and trade, but where most people had not yet converted and could be robbed or captured themselves.[22] As the nineteenth century drew to a close, Europeans began making steady inroads and launching their own projects of acquisition. The meeting of the Islamic frontier and the European colonial one, each with its own flexible ideas of 'us' and 'not us', established an unusually dynamic intersection for raiding and contact among people sometimes foreign and sometimes friendly to each other.

Mobility, security, and the freedom to raid without being raided in return were key to personal advancement. Any interest in control (of people and their ways of life, of territory) and management was subsidiary. The crucial variable remained 'exploitation', not 'conquest' (Santandrea 1964: 18), in contrast to the expectations that inhere in subconsciously normative state-centred political theorising.

Of course, the extent to which conquest – the establishment of a political system of control – is a goal of imperialism is an open question that depends on individual contexts. That conquest is a proxy for acquisition is an idea as old as empires. The argument that the profit motive was more important than other political or humanitarian aims is key to many understandings of imperial structure, as the works of Hannah Arendt (1973), Rosa Luxemburg (2003 [1951]), and Walter Rodney (1972) suggest. Particularly in Arendt's argument, imperial exploitation by creating new frontiers was a *necessary* outcome of the politico-capitalist needs of European nation states. The benefit of the term 'frontier' is that it makes the relation between the hinterland and the metropole always explicit. But too great a focus on the interplay tends to a determinism that understands what happens on frontiers as a function of metropolitan need, with the frontier seen as either a mechanism for accumulation or a tension release valve for the more established polity. The hunting zone defies these models. European metropolitan interests there were often amorphous, in a process of revealing themselves through the actions undertaken by agents on the ground. European adventurists were among a number of freelancers involved in raiding acquisition, which was only sometimes profitable in the sense of enabling accumulation. The raiding bases that proliferated in the region were connected to commercial and political processes beyond the spaces in which they were sited, but they did not have a simple function in relation to them. The hunting zone was

[22] Muslims had begun arriving in the area over the course of the eighteenth century, but only in the second half of the nineteenth did hunting/raiding for the trans-Saharan trades become a primary activity in the area.

neither a frontier nor a set of territorialised polities, then, but a '*zariba* system' (Cordell 1979).[23]

The imperfect French translation of *zariba* is garrison-entrepôt (*garnison-entrepôt*), a term Roitman (1998) found in the colonial archives on northern Cameroon and revived. She used the term to describe the enduring ways in which *corps habillés* (literally, clothed bodies – a regional term referring to uniformed state employees[Debos 2016]) participate in commercial-military activities, including seizure. This is a useful point, but it risks making *zaribas* seem like state projects, when in fact a *zariba* and its overseers – then and now – could have any of a range of relationships to the variety of existing political authorities (Santandrea 1964). They may have been *corps habillés* (a status that carries with it privileges and exceptions, but also vulnerability, as we will see in exploring the careers of anti-poaching guards), but this was not necessarily the case; they were adventurists, acquirers by definition, and they could also be seized from. Therefore, rather than focusing on polities – on *zaribas* as an idiosyncratic mode of state making – I have instead focused on adventurists and their varied needs for forceful acquisition, as well as their varied interests, which included profit and fame but also an attraction to more proximate contact with 'dangerous' people and places. Rather than the goals of control and discipline, which are frequently seen as the core of the ethical striving of both persons and their political institutions, they were involved in a game in which cunning and the exploitation of status uncertainty counted for a lot. This does not mean that adventurists had no obligations, norms, or other varieties of law, but that flexible self-styling and playing with qualifications in order to blend in across potential collaborative or extractive landscapes were more important than building an essential and coherent identity or adhering to principle.

With al-Sanusi dead, the official form of the area's political institutions shifted. Although he had sought to hide his slave taking from the French

[23] It is tempting to refer to the raiding bases as a 'network' to temper Santandrea's choice of the label 'system', but that would also be incorrect, for the *zariba* operators were often in direct competition. Each *zariba* operator was concerned primarily with ensuring (through threats of violence) that surrounding villages would supply only him with ivory, and that others would not interfere with his ability to bring that ivory to market. Therefore, there was a proliferation of roads, as German adventurist Georg Schweinfurth explained in the 1870s: '[N]o less than fifteen different roads, corresponding to the same number of different merchant houses in Khartoom, branched out towards the south and west from the localities of the Seribas into the remotest lands of the Niam-niam [Azande]. Wherever two of these roadways intersect, a serious collision between the parties concerned is almost certain to ensue' (Schweinfurth 1873: 418).

résidents and their troops, he otherwise made no secret of the importance of raiding acquisition as a source of his power. That ended with his death. Instead, people fled, and, at least on paper, the area came under French legal and bureaucratic colonial government control. Yet the French authorities never had the money or other resources necessary to consolidate their administrative capacity, and bureaucracy remained more an abstraction than a force to be reckoned with in the hunting zone.

Given the continuities in forceful acquisition, it is tempting to see it as a functional outcome of a geographical position or culture. But that is incorrect. In addition to the raiding al-Sanusi oversaw or otherwise profited from, his tenure at the head of Dar al-Kuti had seen movement towards political institutions and established relations of social status. He married young women from throughout the region, thus establishing familial ties and creating alliances. In Ndele, slaves could rise to become enfranchised – even entitled – members of the polity. In addition, al-Sanusi oversaw a system of dispute resolution. Although he was never as interested in conducting a census as the French, he had procedures to assess taxable status and collect tribute, which are the rudiments of the 'stationary banditry' said to be the basis of state modes of rule (Olson 1993: 567). Moreover, he distributed spoils among the people in his orbit, and this largesse drew people to him. If the French had not killed al-Sanusi, there is a good chance that quite a different political economy would have emerged, one not based primarily on raiding acquisition. With hindsight, this appears a great irony: the colonial attempt to impose a state-bureaucratic form with far from sufficient resources guaranteed that raiding acquisition would persist. There is thus nothing *necessary* about the persistence of raiding acquisition. The area, its features, and its people do not determine the mode of politics to the exclusion of other possible ways of organising things. Raiding is not some kind of uniquely 'culturally appropriate' way of being in the world (Roitman 1998: 301) for people from the region. Even minor changes could have taken things in a dramatically different direction.

Instead, through a number of historical contingencies potentiated by larger politico-economic processes – the intensification of long-distance trade, imperialist projects, capitalism – north-eastern CAR became a peculiar kind of space. It was not a frontier: that is, not a place shortly to be engulfed by larger polities or economies (Tsing 2003) or the starting point for a process of expansion (Kopytoff 1987). Nor was it a place entirely 'outside' these processes. People in what became French Equatorial Africa already had long experience with complex, changeable systems of exchange involving many currencies, from cloth to iron to salt, and long-standing connections to the rest of the world (Guyer 1993);

New World crops such as maize, manioc, and tobacco were widely cultivated when the first European adventurists arrived (Prioul 1981: 166). Rather, the area became an arena in which participation in broader political-economic processes has tended to draw on forceful acquisition, and to play out through particular improvised 'formalities of action' (Bayart 2000: 254).

There are striking continuities throughout this period's otherwise immense transformations. One is the mutability of status and power, worked out through sometimes delicate performances of assertion and acquiescence. Adventurists, both indigenous and European/incoming, acted on their own counsel without recourse to abstract ideas of governance – they seized opportunities as they arose in their quests for wealth, renown, and, sometimes, vengeance. At the same time, they dissembled about their intentions, frequently portraying themselves as merely vassals of more powerful bosses. Al-Sanusi, when asked to account for Crampel's death, said that Rabih had made him do it; on a later occasion, Modat told al-Sanusi to take his complaints about French incursions not to him but to the far-off governor. Maintaining their privileged status depended on being daring, resolute in action, and prudent, and on being fortunate enough to live to tell the tale.

Being able to tell the tale became increasingly important as under French colonial rule letters and reports served more and more as modes of accounting for affairs in the hinterlands. These communications could ignite faraway audiences with a wide range of interests and opinions, many sharply critical, such as people with humanitarian or anti-colonial sympathies in Europe. While raiding acquisition persisted during the colonial period, it was never celebrated or particularly well understood in France, and its perpetrators only occasionally sought to justify it along 'desperate times, desperate measures' lines. More often, they tried to manage to whom such practices became visible. Raiding and acquisition retained their prominence less because they were the expression of group or individual values and more because they were the improvised reaction to *conflicts* of values between people of uncertain relative status who came into contact and struggled to come to terms with each other.

3 Manhunts persist in an unfortunate colony

> This arrest was a deliverance for the populations of Kuti, ruined and devastated country, where long years of *razzias*, of massacres and of slave trafficking had only barely left a population necessary to maintain the 4,000 *bazingirs*, the hungry stock of the sultan, always ready for all kinds of brigandage.
>
> In ridding these populations of a slave trafficker whose authority rested on nothing but force and who was a sultan in name only, we have not breached any historical tradition; nothing natural or hereditary or consecrated by time linked the former little banner carrier of Rabih to the populations of the region who escaped his massacres and who he had settled by force around the centre of Ndele exclusively to feed his warriors.
>
> With him has disappeared one of the biggest slave merchants of Central Africa, and, one more time, it falls to the *paix française* to repair the ruins that 23 years of tyranny have accumulated in the region. (Government of Oubangui-Chari 1911)[1]

Thus wrote the Governor of Oubangui-Chari in a letter to his superiors at the Ministry of Colonies in Paris on the consequences of 'arresting' al-Sanusi. Calling the murder an arrest made it seem a manifestation of French law and order, rather than the culmination of years of manoeuvring during which al-Sanusi and French officer adventurists sought to draw advantage from their relationships while mistrusting each other's dangerousness.

[1] 'Cette arrestation a été une délivrance pour les populations du Kouti, pays ruiné, dévasté, où de longues années de razzias, de massacres et de trafic d'esclaves avaient à peine laissé la population nécessaire à l'entretien des 4000 bazinguers, réserve affamé du Sultan, toujours prête à toutes entreprises de brigandage.

'En débarrassant ces populations d'un marchand d'esclaves dont l'autorité ne s'appuiait que sur la force et qui n'avait de Sultan que le nom, nous n'avons porté atteinte à aucune tradition historique; aucun lien naturel, héréditaire, ou consacré par les temps ne rattachait l'ancien petit chef de bannière de RABAH aux populations de la région échappées à ses massacres et qu'il avait concentrées par force autour du centre de Ndele, exclusivement pour nourrir des guerriers.

'Avec lui a disparu l'un des derniers gros marchands d'esclaves du Centre Africain et, une fois de plus, il incombe à la paix française, de réparer les ruines que 23 ans de tyrannie avaient accumulées dans la région.'

The governor, in the timeless manner of the functionary, continued his report by appealing for more funding for his staff. Money was the overriding concern of officials in Oubangui-Chari: whatever aspirational goals they might have, their most pressing concern was their own poverty (Marchal 2009). In addition, key staff positions often went unfilled since French Equatorial Africa – and Oubangui-Chari in particular – had the reputation of being a career-ending backwater (Brégeon 1998).[2] Money from the ministry was never enough to establish a functioning administration, yet superiors demanded that certain infrastructural tasks, such as building roads, be accomplished. The only option, it often seemed to the local French, was to acquire what was needed directly from Central Africans. Goods that could be sold elsewhere – rubber, ivory – were valuable, but what they mostly needed was labour. And that had to be taken.

So manhunting, the *chasse à l'homme*, became the major project of colonial officials during the colony's early decades. Colonial officials might try to cloak the prevalence of manhunts in aspirational justifications. Among other things, they said that manhunts were a necessary first step to be able to eventually teach people the discipline of paying the taxes that were crucial for the benefits of civil life. But the violence and cruelty of labour manhunts were hard even for their perpetrators to explain away.

Many Europeans involved with manhunting during this period were well aware of the dissonance between the future-oriented goals used to justify their presence and the actual practices they allowed, or engaged in, or didn't punish. Relations with their distant overseers, at ministries as far away as Paris, remained stable, the immortal mill of French bureaucracy grinding predictably through dossiers of promotion or reassignment. On the ground in Africa, though, the remote colonial official was hardly assured of prevailing; his actual power over the Africans he was meant to be governing was vulnerable to rapid changes of circumstance. Space and distance were not the only great disconnectors; the colonial administrator was subject to the tyranny of time. A governor many days' walk away or a minister in Paris might be looking at the long term. For colonial agents, the present ruled: immediate needs crowded out other considerations. Presentism made itself felt in the most mundane yet inescapable ways: colonial agents, for example, knew only too well that five out of six died on the job in Equatorial Africa (Kalck 1971: 54) and wanted simply to survive their postings. Since there was never enough money for any but the most immediate needs, any aspirational

[2] It was where people with the lowest grades at the colonial training school would be sent, and a place of privation and isolation, particularly outside the capital.

inclination came into direct conflict with relational and temporal exigencies. And rapid acquisition, achieved by violence or the threat of it, was the most efficient arrangement. Violence as a means to the end of acquisition was the shortcut, the workaround.

The perpetrators of the *chasse à l'homme* were not insensible to its violence and its conflict with the values they claimed to hold. Looking directly at colonialist brutality, then, offers not a revelation of some new enormity, but an opportunity to consider its prevalence in spite of its uneasy coexistence with contemporaneous mores, and the improvised skills that people developed to navigate situations in which needs and values conflicted. How were violent events in the Central African interior perceived by imperial institutions and audiences? What were their long-term effects on relationships in the interior, shaped and affected by manhunting as a mode of acquisition? On neither level was law – colonial or otherwise – much of a guide for interaction. Instead, ambitious colonial officials learned the skill of camouflage: managing the faces shown to different audiences. Practices that would likely have been frowned upon, if not actively punished, by distant superiors were public secrets among local colonial officials. This way of thinking about violence and the officials' instrumental view of human beings – simultaneously acquisitive and dismissive of the value and status of other people – corroded the colonialists' undertakings.

Une véritable chasse à l'homme

Throughout all France's colonies, the *code de l'indigénat*, established in 1887 as 'the regime of administrative sanctions applied to colonial subjects', was the 'obscure core' of government (Mann 2009: 331). The empire was supposedly one of law, but in reality the *indigénat* divided citizens of France, who were judged and related to through law and bureaucracy, from the subjects of the French empire, who were at the mercy of colonial *commandants*' rule by unanswerable decree and arbitrary, spectacular punishment.[3] Achille Mbembe has termed *commandement* the core of colonial ways of thinking, consisting in the 'right to dispose' of the native, of his labour, and of its fruits (Mbembe 2001: 25). But 'right' is an awkward descriptor. The colonisers' powers were supposed to be limited. In theory, they could not apply *just any* sanction to the natives, yet many did do things that were prohibited and generally faced no penalty (Coquery-Vidrovitch 1972; Mann 2009). Their 'right',

[3] This is the overriding distinction; the *indigénat* also created other distinctions among colonised subjects (Mann 2009).

then, is better understood as arrogation. They took, stole, acquired, and seized – especially people's capacity for labour. That was how, particularly in the early decades of French involvement in Central Africa, colonial projects – those of the government and of the private companies granted territory to exploit – came to depend primarily on one thing: manhunts.[4]

The day-to-day concerns of colonial incomers to Equatorial Africa were above all logistical. How do you move people and supplies across long distances? In 1879, Henry Morton Stanley 'managed to have a steamer carried piece by piece overland to the Pool' on the Congo River (Harms 1981: 220). Some 15 years later, French colonial planners did the same in Oubangui-Chari, with the *Léon Blot*. But *how* did they do it? Infrastructure – roads, depots, etc. – is built to make things move. Much recent anthropological work has suggested that infrastructures can be understood as simultaneously material, constructed, and improvised (Anand 2017; Degani 2017), or that they can be immaterial and social (Simone 2004b). But the hunting zone presented the dilemma of logistics without infrastructure, either material or social. Instead, there were manhunts to make people into porters, and, later, roadbuilders.

Early European adventurists in Equatorial Africa needed huge amounts of goods and equipment. They needed great stores of rice for lean days or weeks; gifts – beads, cloth – for the 'chiefs'[5] they encountered; medicine – quinine and champagne, the great French cure-all – for tropical illnesses. They needed guns and ammunition; tents; giant cauldrons for water and cooking. They needed scientific instruments for specimen collection, geological samples, and photography. Some even carried food for the Africans working for them, although most left them to fend for themselves. As the nineteenth century drew to a close and the French-led war to the north in Chad intensified with the fight against Rabih and Wadai, the soldiers there increasingly needed cumbersome

[4] Getting people to work was a major preoccupation of colonial governments elsewhere as well. In French West Africa, more than half of all recorded punishments under the *indigénat* in the mid-1930s were meted out for the purposes of 'taxation and labour requisition' (Mann 2009: 342). But that was in West Africa, where some modicum of administrative structure had been created. The interior of French Equatorial Africa had very little in the way of governing institutions, but the labour needs of would-be administrators and exploiters were even more pressing.

[5] Europeans generally misunderstood the nature of authority in Equatorial Africa. When a European-led column arrived in a village, one man would usually come forward to serve as the interlocutor between the people there and those passing through. The Europeans assumed that this person was a chief with powers of command and that therefore he could tell others what to do. This was generally not the case. The individuals who came forward owed their positions to their careful representation and balancing of their constituents' interests. Failure to do this could cost them their position.

military equipment as well, including several steamboats. Engineers argued that the least bad way to transport them was to dismantle them and carry them north through Oubangui-Chari and into Chad. The concessionary company agents also had vast porterage needs, particularly to carry goods such as rubber and ivory to the rivers and beyond. There were even some European tourists – nobles who came with enormous retinues to collect as many big-game trophies as they could – and these parties required porters too (Mollion 1992: 179). Except on the navigable rivers, all travel was on foot, and all 'roads' better described as paths. Tsetse flies vanquished horses and other pack animals. Therefore, the Europeans' main preoccupation was securing African manpower to carry things.

The first French adventurists, such as Paul Crampel, hired porters near the coast, at Loango, to carry their goods. Through the decades of European presence, a labour market developed, with standardised payments (Dybowski 1893: 15), and myths emerged among Europeans to justify this system. 'A Loango is a porter; he is nothing else,' summed up Colonel Baratier (1917: 26), an adventurist in the final years of the nineteenth century. But as logistical needs became greater, the few people who could be signed up on the coast were no longer enough, especially considering that porters travelling long distances, far from their families and farms, had to be provisioned as well – which required even more porters. The Europeans concluded that it made more sense to find people along the way, who would be made to work for a few days at a stretch. Since they were close to their homes, the argument went, there was no need to provide them with food, shelter, or any other care.

Providing for porterage consumed all of the few adventurist-administrator-concessionaires' time (Mollion 1992: 71). Some Africans were curious about the Europeans in their midst and saw them as potentially useful as well as dangerous. Some even volunteered to help the Europeans with their loads. But most were indifferent to the payments Europeans offered in exchange for the drudgery of carrying heavy loads for days on end. Along the road that was emerging between Bangui and Chad, especially south of Fort Crampel (now Kaga-Bandoro), demand for porters was especially acute. But the people who lived in the area – who were wealthy and well fed – were especially uninterested in portering. When Émile Gentil lumbered through the area on his way north to combat Rabih, he was so desperate for porters that he resorted to remunerating people with the one currency they wanted: guns (Mollion 1992). The outcome was predictable: the next adventurists to arrive and demand porters were fired upon.

What options remained? Only the *chasse à l'homme*. The Europeans travelled with *tirailleurs* and *gardes régionnales* (regional guards) from West Africa or coastal Equatorial Africa for protection and to help hunt animals for food. These guards increasingly spent their time rounding up porters and ensuring that they laboured as energetically as was demanded of them. The needs of the moment determined how people of the interior would be engaged, which turned out to be seizing all the value they could offer, through their labour, and then discarding them.[6] Chamayou's description of the ruler-as-hunter's interest being to 'tax and consume, if necessary to the point of exhausting and even killing his subjects' (2012: 17), is apt. There was little effort to domesticate[7] Africans, but much effort to capture them, force them to provide their labour for projects that eventually ended, and then discard them.

Tales of the agonies of portering spread quickly among Africans in the areas where demand was highest. No longer did anyone volunteer to help. In an average expedition, a man was given at least 25–30 kilograms (50–65 pounds) to carry on his head. During the pressured drive to transport the steamboat *Léon Blot* to Lake Chad in the 1890s, each porter carried 60–65 kilograms (130–145 pounds) – nearly his own body weight. Jean-Baptiste Marchand, the leader of that expedition, would see people struggling and alight from his *tipoye* (a litter itself borne by men), grab the load to show them how easily he could carry it and how silly they were to complain, and then – quickly – hand it back.

> I literally drag my convoy. The poor people do just a few hundred metres and stop. At each moment I must lift them up again. To prove to them that their loads are not heavy I take one myself; I gaily carry it a little way and then hasten to give it back because these loads are seriously crushing. (Marchand cited in Baratier 1914: 75)

The obvious ironies pass unremarked.

Predominant European attitudes towards Africans at the time were at best patronising. But this is insufficient to explain the clear brutality maintaining a European presence required. For instance, some Europeans argued that Africans did not have the same food requirements, not being the same kind of person. One of Marchand's aides reasoned that 'half of what isn't enough for us would be too rich for them' (Baratier

[6] Some colonial officers (but more often missionaries) did not want to discard the Africans forced to labour for them. They advocated building schools and other biopolitical infrastructure (Modat 1909). However, there was rarely sufficient money or other momentum necessary to make those kinds of projects happen.

[7] I use 'domesticate' in the capacious way Scott (2017) describes the mutual habituations between people and state.

1914: 95).[8] However, the proximity that expeditions and manhunts entailed tended to offer visible evidence to the contrary. As another European in the same expedition said: 'In vain Captain Monnoye tries to dispel our fears and affirms to us that for a porter to walk he must not eat. We remain incredulous and full of pity. Lack of familiarity, no doubt' (Mollion 1984: 48).[9]

Similarly, some Europeans argued that Africans did not need shelter, since they were used to 'primitive' conditions. Drenched in sweat from the day's exertions, the conscripts would shiver as they lay on the ground, and many died of pneumonia or other illnesses during the cold dry-season nights, when temperatures can be close to freezing.

When it came to food, European officers generally served themselves first, and there was often not enough for the non-local regional guards, who instead fed themselves by taking from people living in the areas through which they passed or were stationed (Coquery-Vidrovitch 1972). If African interior residents fled in the wake of the regional guards' arrival, the guards would track down the women, rope them together at the neck, and hold them hostage, sometimes raping or otherwise torturing them, until the men returned (Mollion 1992: 102). This tactic was widespread among private companies' militias as well (Coquery-Vidrovitch 1972).

Manhunting quickly had profound effects on the areas where it became such an overriding practice. The area where European need for porters was greatest was home to the Manza, around what is today Kaga-Bandoro. Gentil, who signed the first treaty with al-Sanusi, wrote how impressive he found the Manza lands when he traversed them in 1896. 'We lose lots of time in discussions at every village that we meet (and they are many). Immense millet and manioc plantations surround them. Everywhere there is abundance and prosperity' (Gentil 1902: 43).[10] Just four years later, another adventurist, Fernand Foureau, was met by a markedly different situation:

> At each stream passed we saw the remains of once-flourishing villages where papayas, manioc, sugar cane, bananas, and cotton are rotting in the bush. The inhabitants, fearing recruitment for porterage, fearing at the same time the common theft of the Senegalese [*tirailleurs*], have fled away from the road and

8 '[L]a moitié de ce qui nous suffirait pas est trop gras pour eux.'

9 'En vaine le Capitaine Monnoye essaye-t-il de dissiper nos craintes et nous affirme-t-il que la condition nécessaire pour qu'un porteur marche est qu'il ne mange pas; nous restons incrédules et nous avons pitié, manque d'habitude sans doute.'

10 'Nous perdons beaucoup de temps à discourir à chaque village que nous rencontrons (et ils sont nombreux). D'immenses plantations de mil, de manioc, les entourent. C'est partout l'abondance et la prosperité.'

have raised houses a few kilometres in every direction, such that even though the region is quite populated, a traveller cannot tell. (Foureau 1902: 780–1)[11]

The hunts for porters destroyed social life among the Manza as well as causing famine that took many lives. As one colonial officer lamented: '[W]e track them in the bush where they prefer to seek refuge and die of hunger rather than carry our loads' (cited in Kalck 1974: 124). The captives were held in concentration camps called, in a chilling adumbration of George Orwell's Newspeak, 'freedom villages' (*villages de liberté*), which were in operation from 1900 to 1905 (Mollion 1992: 176). The hunt for human porters transformed the human, and the literal, landscape as thoroughly as the *bazingirs*' raids.[12]

While the seizure of labour and goods brought Europeans and Central Africans into closer proximity, these contacts did not transform into a civil relationship whereby Africans became subjects or citizens in any meaningful way. There was next to no administration of state authority, and quite a lot of interactions marked by entrainment that could give rise to tense collaboration or punishment and seizure.

The interpersonal mechanics of manhunting

Sociologist Randall Collins developed the term 'entrainment' to refer to the ways in which, when people meet, their interactions will never be merely the sum of freestanding individuals, each marked by their own culture, but instead they become attentive to the same thing or process, and emotionally involved with each other, so that whatever happens is born of this not wholly predictable contact. Entrainment is a helpful concept for thinking through the mechanics of manhunting and other

[11] 'A chaque marigot traversé on trouve les restes de villages autrefois florrissants où pourrissent encore dans la brousse les papayes, du manioc, de la canne à sucre, du coton, des bananiers. C'est le portage humain qui est la cause de la disparition de la population. Les habitants, redoutant le recrutement pour le portage, redoutant de meme le chapardage si familier aux Sénégalais, ont fui en dehors du chemin et ont élève leurs cases à quelques kilometres à droite et à gauche, si bien que, quoique la region soit très peuplée, le voyageur ne s'en aperçoit pas.'

[12] Thousands died in the porterage system; Georges Toqué argued that it was tens of thousands. Some were killed directly while many more died during the labour ordeal; pneumonia, starvation, smallpox, and sleeping sickness were all widespread. And many died in flight, which carried its own ordeals, or from the consequences of massively disrupted agricultural production. Death rates for porters on the '*route du Tchad*' were somewhere between 50 and 150 per thousand, about 10 per cent of the male population along the Chad route (Cordell 1994: 142). The impact was not felt equally, however, and so was probably much greater for certain communities and less for others, with the Manza hardest hit of all.

forms of colonial acquisition because they occurred through emotionally-intense confrontations. While it is tempting to portray the social scene in Central Africa at this time as being composed of separate and hierarchical groups (indeed, whites did enjoy privileges refused to others), there were important cleavages and rivalries even among those who would seem to have similar interests, and the stratified ways in which privilege was assigned could be overturned, whether during confrontation or ruse and avoidance.

These vagaries of power were especially apparent in the case of the people who actually did the work of manhunting: the *tirailleurs* and regional guards. Initially, most of these auxiliary forces were recruited in West Africa, but few Senegalese volunteered for missions to remote Central Africa (many coastal Africans, like many Europeans, referred to the people of the interior as 'savages' [Toqué 1996 [1907]]), and *la contrainte* (coercion to make any payments demanded) was harder to achieve in a place such as West Africa where people could be French subjects in a more meaningful sense. So the *tirailleurs*' ranks were filled with Equatorial Africans from those riverine and western regions where the colonial presence was a bit more pronounced. A handful of Europeans would be dispatched to a given post, with a contingent of these guards to press-gang for them. But the guards might have their own objectives or interests.

Joseph Eudes d'Eudeville, a colonial officer sent near the end of his career to the south-eastern post of Djemah in the 1920s, described the leader of the guards with whom he shared the post: 'He gets himself carried by *tipoye*, demands five or six chickens for his daily food, and beats the natives when they do anything that does not fully please or satisfy him' (cited in Brégeon 1998: 84).[13] The other guards and their wives spent most of their time raiding manioc from d'Eudeville's gardens, which they fermented into alcohol. As d'Eudeville understood his choice, it was either to keep the guards close, where they would constantly provoke him, or send them out to the surrounding area, where they would hunt and terrorise people in ways he saw as counterproductive in the long term even if they might serve certain immediate colonial needs (Brégeon 1998: 84).[14] He found the guards' actions deplorable, but he also needed them, and probably feared them, or at least felt his position of official superiority always potentially tenuous.

[13] 'Il se fait porter en tipoye, exige pour sa nourriture quotidienne cinq à six poules et frappe les indigènes quand on ne lui donne pas satisfaction pleine et entière.'

[14] D'Eudeville was also in the unenviable position of being the ranking administrator present in the wake of the death of 18 people given defective sleeping sickness vaccines by a medical team that passed through the area (Brégeon 1998: 81). Colonial cruelties were both planned and mundane, even accidental.

Although the upheaval of porterage manhunting was immense, it would also be incorrect to portray those who pressed people into service as invincible, or their dominance inevitable.[15] They were often dramatically undersupplied: in the 'capital of porterage', Ungourras, in the early 1900s, officials lacked chains for captives and had to fashion other restraints (Mollion 1992: 167). Colonial officials and their guards could be extremely brutal, but their position was also precarious. For one thing, the hunted people could flee. Many Africans who evaded the guards banded together, even forming a new polity of sorts in the bush, referred to by one colonial administrator in 1924 as a Hobbesian 'species of indigenous republic' (*'espèce de république indigène'*; cited in Mollion 1992: 164). Centred on a place called Koukourou (now a conservation area), this island of independence from European labour coercion held out for years. Colonial officials attempted to prohibit people from going to Koukourou, but they had little means to do any policing; the main effect of prohibiting travel there was not that people did not go but that it gave officials an excuse for the use of extra force against those few they caught. And the people hunted for their labour could also fight back, as many did (Nzabakomada-Yakoma 1986). As Sergeant Camus wrote in 1897: 'Bullets rained down with such density that I had to open fire just to not be totally ashamed to flee in the face of the savages and also to mark to these people that their gunfire is insufficient to prevent the French from passing, as they say' (cited in Mollion 1984: 56).[16] Equatorial Africa was known as a particularly rebellious region (Brégeon 1998; Lombard 2016d).

While interior Africans had no need for the Europeans or their guards, their would-be governors needed the Africans. Therefore, they needed to lure people towards them, while effectively doing nothing for them but relieving them of what they could be made to offer. The colonial adventurists did not see themselves as facing an enemy, but as capturing targets. What, then, was the right balance of violence and consideration? The framework of a ruler in relation to his citizens or subjects did not apply. Rather, the balance of violence and regard had to be continually recalculated in the context of an ongoing process of emotional identification and differentiation, violence, and the dominance of the material

[15] My word choice here is a hat tip to Dennis D. Cordell's critique of common arguments about slave raiding (Cordell 1994).

[16] 'Les balles pleuvaient avec plus de densité et j'ai dû ouvrir le feu pour ne pas avoir la honte de fuir devant des sauvages et aussi pour marquer à ces gens que leurs coups de fusil sont insuffisants pour empêcher, comme ils disent, les Français de passer.'

needs of the present over the needs of ethical consistency, or the needs of times other than the immediate present.

Manhunting beyond colonial officials

Porterage was only one of the needs underpinning manhunts, and colonial officials and their guards only some of the adventurists instigating manhunts in the remote reaches of Oubangui-Chari. Inspired by the profitability of Belgian King Leopold's privatised Congo, in 1899 the French government leased 700,000 of the 900,000 square kilometres of the French Congo (which became Afrique Équatoriale Française in 1910) to 40 companies, each of which would then hold concessionary rights to 'wild goods' in a given territory.[17]

The theory behind the concessionisation of the colonial endeavour was that the quest for profit would lead companies to invest in infrastructure and administrative capacity that the colonial government could then take over, along the lines of tax farming. The money paid for the concessions was also an infusion of capital (Levi 1988), which could in theory be used for colonial administration. Corruption marked the process, however, and much of the expected revenue never made it into state coffers (Coquery-Vidrovitch 1972).

Max Weber (1978 [1922]), working through these topics when the Equatorial concessionary system was at its height, analysed historically similar attempts at delegation. The central problem was clear to him: while governments have a long-term interest in collecting revenue, temporary beneficiaries of this sort of 'farming' arrangement do not necessarily share that concern, and that colours how they relate to people – namely, as entities to be extracted from and discarded, not as a flock to be shepherded – and the concessionary project as a whole. In French Equatorial Africa, little encouraged concessionaires to think of theirs as anything but a short-term, extractive enterprise. For one thing, the concession leases, initially for 30 years, were later granted only for ten. Also, the infrastructural inputs necessary to pursue anything other than a quick profit were immense, as colonial agents, government and business alike, well knew. Even leaning on brutal manhunting techniques, they continually fell short of the numbers needed for even their minimal

[17] Only two parts of Oubangui-Chari escaped concessionary company intervention: the areas around Kemo and Gribingui, which were reserved for hunting porters for transport to Chad; and Dar al-Kuti (although the latter was drawn into concessionary commerce through al-Sanusi's dealings with the Kotto concession, just to the south) (Kalck 1971: 51).

endeavours. The concession system nurtured some of the dynamics that characterised colonial government engagement, particularly those related to time and scale: the short-sighted focus on the needs of the present, the interplay between relationships in a locally unstable arrangement, and the staid unchangingness of a faraway bureaucracy that imagined that profit and humanitarian principles were an easy pair.

By adding more variables to the mix, concessionisation made any attempts at bureaucratic regulation of all 'hunting' even more fraught. Regulations passed in capitals far from the hunting zone often effectively became new opportunities for camouflage as much as dictates for action. At the Berlin Conference of 1884–5, delegates had decided that no monopolies would be allowed in the Congo Basin. The concessionary regime inserted ambiguity into this otherwise straightforward rule. Since the companies (temporarily) owned the land, they owned everything in it, and so they had unique rights to extraction, reasoned the lawyers involved (Coquery-Vidrovitch 1972). The concession system was a way of having monopolies without the monopolies calling attention to themselves – or, put otherwise, a way of camouflaging the monopolistic aspects of concessionisation.

By working with the agents of a 'secondary empire' (Bohannan and Curtin 1971), including the sultans of the Haut-Oubangui, concession-agent rule bears similarities to the 'decentralised despotism' that Mamdani (1996) diagnosed as the particular pathology of European colonial rule in Africa. Mamdani argued that Europeans needed coercive and despotic power for their mode of rule, and so when they engaged with 'traditional chiefs' they exaggerated or invented coercive powers, in the process fundamentally distorting what had been more reciprocal precolonial political systems. However, where Mamdani's decentralised despots were helping to shape people into long-standing colonial subjects in South Africa and elsewhere with a more extensive colonial footprint, in Equatorial Africa concessionary agents were interested in extraction in the present, not administration over a length of time. Concessionaires imposed head taxes, calling on 'chiefs' to help ensure their extraction, but these taxes were in kind, a system of forced gathering with no administrative aim. The law prohibited them from assigning such taxes, but there was no capacity to enforce it (Cordell 1994: 138).

Legal distinctions between government officials and concessionaires did not mean much in this remote area. For instance, only government officials could order labour manhunts, but in practice concessionaires used forced recruitment as well. Administrators, military officers, and concessionary agents all had judicial authority (Zoctizoum 1983: 77). The list of native crimes was at once precise and broad. There were

22 major offences, including such crimes as 'refusal to obey' (Zoctizoum 1983: 78), and colonial and concessionary agents could also play the rebellion card, claiming that their violence was simply a means of quashing nascent uprisings or otherwise enacted in self-defence (Coquery-Vidrovitch 1972). Among the most common punishments imposed were longer terms of labour.

The forced gathering of labour for concessionary projects therefore came to entail manhunts similar to those for forced porterage. The effect of removing the able-bodied from farming settlements could be devastating. Father Joseph Daigre, a missionary in Banda country (around Mbrès and Bamingui, just north and east of the area hardest hit by porterage demands), described the situation in 1920:

> Auxiliaries [militiamen] behave like police and hunt out all the gatherers who try to escape the ordeal. It is common to meet long lines of prisoners, naked and in a pitiful state, being dragged along by a rope round their necks. Countless poor wretches are taken along the remoter tracks, completely stupefied by the harsh treatment. They are famished, sick, and fall down like flies. The really ill and the little children are left in the villages to die of starvation. Several times I found regions where the people least affected killed the ones who were dying, for food. (Cited in Kalck 1971: 59)

All of this was going on in a climate increasingly marked by fear and mutual feelings of vulnerability, both of which were correlated with particularly brutal forms of violence (Appadurai 2006; Collins 2009). As Africans in the interior suffered miserably, many responded by developing effective ways of hunting the people who hunted them. Individuals or small groups killed concessionary agents in the middle of the night and raided their storehouses. Others organised into larger hunting parties. They attacked convoys, 'closed' the rivers that were the concessionaires' only means of exit, and otherwise frustrated concessionaires' colonial projects (Coquery-Vidrovitch 1972). In one case on the Ogooué River, they managed this feat for a full six months; the *Commissaire général* (commissioner general) had pulled out all the guards stationed there due to budgetary issues, a reminder that this colonial presence was more intermittent than omniscient. Although the Europeans and their guards were better armed and could mobilise institutional outrage more effectively than Africans, the incomers' dominance or security were hardly assured.

Nor did national origin or other registers through which identity could be expressed or perceived structure coherent groups of people at the interpersonal level. Parisian bureaucrats had thought that concessionary agents would be allies in their goals of profit, governance, and 'civilisation', but in fact in many cases the concessionaires proved truculent. Often, concessionaires were effectively more powerful than the very few colonial officials they operated among. One colonial officer lucidly summed up this competition of interests in 1910:

The difficulties the administrators encounter in the exercise of their functions come, on the one hand, from the existence of powerful concessionary companies that have long exploited the country without control and who relinquish to the administration those privileges that they have managed to obtain from the sultans and indigenous chiefs only under duress. On the other hand, there are also free colonists who have established themselves in the region who complicate the situation, because, natural enemies of the concessionary companies, they also oppose the rules of the administration, which, they believe, constrain them in their commerce. Innumerable problems stem from the fact that these colonists are not always very scrupulous in their choice of means of hindering the activities of the administrators. (Mordrelle 1910)

Big-game hunters were also seeking out Oubangui-Chari during this period. One of the most famous, 'Karamojo' Bell, reported that a colonial official in the deep interior of the hunting zone warned him that the other whites there were 'scum' (Bell 1960 [1923]: 135). Oubangui-Chari did indeed attract certain Europeans who sought greater leeway than rigid adherence to an ethical doctrine would permit. As the future general Charles Mangin noted when on a tour of Bangui to inspect the colony's troops in the early 1900s, 'As a sample of our race, the choice of [concessionary] agents could hardly have been worse. Unless the regime is radically changed, all kinds of abuse and vengeance will irremediably stain the history of this unfortunate colony' (cited in Kalck 1971: 52). Not all the concessionaires engaged in or encouraged brutality; much depended on the personalities of the people involved. Only a few succeeded in stripping Central Africa of its non-human resources and even fewer turned a profit (Coquery-Vidrovitch 1972), but it was not the law that checked excesses or organised obligations.

Those who undertook colonial-era manhunts were not all equal in their ability or interest in hunting others. Europeans were peculiarly keen to extract labour, and it was their impetus that led to the regional guards hunting people to be made labourers and seizing goods from people more stably resident in the hunting zone. In turn, the residents of the area hunted back, sometimes to claim the others' goods but more often to show that they were dangerous and to prevent the others from trying to coerce them. These proximate interactions and relationships were unstable and charged with emotion, and immediate needs were a driving consideration. But the features and dynamics of manhunting were also shaped by the relationships between the people in this zone and the bureaucratic and humanitarian landscapes elsewhere.

Tenuous institutional connections across distance

The century that has passed since the height of manhunting (1890–1930) has overturned the sensibilities that could explain the *chasse à l'homme* as dictated by circumstance. All that is left is the cruelty, and the correct response to that cruelty is opprobrium. But understanding manhunting requires more careful analysis. Relying on the moral superiority afforded by hindsight is unenlightening. Even at the time, *la chasse à l'homme* was not celebrated; more often it was abhorred or lamented even by its perpetrators. So why did it continue?

The key is the way in which people responded to the discord between the 'common sense' of colonialism and the perceived need to acquire from others against their will. One might consider, for example, that cruelty today would lead to nothing but more evil; demolition today would generate only a heap of toxic rubble tomorrow. It was hard for people for whom this was the predominant response to make a career in the colonies. Another reaction was to persuade oneself that it was a temporary measure: the bush fire today would generate far greener grass tomorrow. Some, as is always the case, focused primarily on themselves and their careers. Those who decided, whatever their reasoning, that they would not look too closely at the violence did so by developing camouflage.

The colonial commonplaces that today seem so unjustified, and that came into inherent conflict through their meeting with African common sense, all centred on money and labour. Europeans in favour of colonialism were guided by a sometimes contradictory collection of economic principles. These held that slavery was abhorrent, but people should work for money and anything else was immoral laziness. Yet only certain currencies were appropriate for use in Africa (Guyer 1995: 9), and colonies should not cost anything (an idea often credited to the prominent economist Pierre Paul Leroy-Beaulieu [Coquery-Vidrovitch 1972: 33]). And, ultimately, colonisation was necessary for the good of the nation, in particular because of what could be acquired there (see, e.g., Dybowski 1893: 1).

By the end of the nineteenth century, Europeans generally saw slavery – that is, working without pay in a long-standing relationship of ownership – as illegitimate and anachronistic. Indeed, even when other aspects of their presence seemed less salutary, Europeans could cite their efforts to eliminate slavery to legitimate their own imperial aims, in the process discounting those of trans-Saharan imperial networks into tropical Africa (although adventurists on the ground were more likely to recognise the perverse effects of even such do-goodism [Fabian 2000]). If Europeans had resorted to outright slavery, the chalice of moral superiority that French officials saw themselves holding would be revealed as a sieve. Europeans wanted Africans to work for them, ideally willingly, in exchange for payment. But Europeans only saw certain currencies as appropriate for Africans, particularly those that could not be converted into circulable wealth (Guyer 1995: 8–9). And interior Africans were generally uninterested in working in the ways Europeans demanded for the payment Europeans offered – largely cheap beads or other trade goods. Confronted with African refusal, Europeans justified forcing the Africans to work on pedagogical grounds: they were teaching the Africans to be less lazy. Alternatively, colonial officials might claim that the labour they demanded of Africans was legitimate because it was a tax, and respecting taxes was seen as a necessary marker of modernity, as was wage labour. This went some way to assuaging those concerned about the violence of the colonial endeavour. Forced labour was 'analogous to slavery' (Cooper 2000), but it was not slavery, and that was something to hold on to. But just how much force could be exerted on pedagogical grounds? The degree of force people in the hunting zone could justify to themselves ('It was the work of the guards, and they're out of my control'; 'I had no other option') was not the same as the level Africans could accept as reasonable, nor was it the same as the level colonial overseers – concerned citizens at home as well as government officials – could accept, nor was it something anyone could see as ideal. At best, it was a stage to endure to get to a better future.

How people in the hunting zone, particularly Europeans,[18] attempted to deal with the stress their immediate needs placed on their values could be tragicomic. The adventurist Jean Dybowski, on a mission to 'get vengeance for' Crampel's killing, needed to buy firewood for his ship's boiler as he made his way north towards Dar al-Kuti in 1892. The chief of the Bondjo (a subgroup of the Banda) he met when his wood reserves were critically low agreed to a sale. However, the women who had laboured to collect and prepare the wood refused, since the chief would keep the payment and they would lose the value of their labour, as Dybowski himself acknowledged. 'Demands rose from every side and it would have been wise perhaps not to insist, but we did not have the

[18] Unfortunately, the voices of West Africans working in Equatorial Africa – for instance, those of the early *tirailleurs* – often get lost, and a full excavation of West African/ Equatorial African francophone colonial relationships remains to be done.

choice, because the last pieces of wood that we had on board were already in the ovens' (Dybowski 1893: 156).[19] A sorcerer (Dybowski's term) performed rites on the wood to dissuade Dybowski from taking it, but Dybowski did not care. He paid the chief twice what the wood was worth in his opinion and began having it loaded onto the boat. 'The women stirred up the population against us, and the men were at the top of the embankment, ten metres above the surface of the water, and threatened us with their spears. But the wood is loaded, the machine whistles, and we depart, leaving the *indigènes* to their unjust anger' (Dybowski 1893: 156–7).[20] Dybowski knew that the chief was seizing – unfairly – the value of the women's labour, but he nevertheless characterised their anger as 'unjust'. Either he was not troubled by the perversion of the system of payment he saw as just, or he was attempting irony. Whatever the case, his own immediate needs trumped any interest in consistent values.

In the context of these inconsistencies around values and the frequent triumph of self-centredness, violence – in both the nature and the execution of the manhunt – became part of a repertoire of meaningful behaviour and skills. Rarely did anyone laud violence as an ideal practice, but it frequently became a tactic in order to acquire labour and other goods from people who saw little reason to give them freely. Unstable proximate relationships were also connected to the projects of faraway funders and colonial officials, who often preferred to avoid confronting inconsistencies around values and the instability of relationships in the African interior. European-initiated violence took forms that were meant to awe those in the immediate vicinity, but its perpetrators knew to keep it from the attention of overseers and humanitarians elsewhere, who would not understand the constraints faced by would-be governors in the area.

The violence of Africans in the interior strove for a different balance: for the most part, Africans did not want to attract too much attention from people elsewhere either, as this could lead to reinforcements being sent. With some notable exceptions, including the Kongo-Wara War (Burnham and Christensen 1983), for Africans, maintaining an irregular insurgency (playing along, hiding, undermining) afforded them greater

[19] 'Des réclamations s'élèvent de toutes parts et il serait sage peut-être de ne pas insister, mais nous n'avons pas le choix de la solution, car les dernières bûches de bois que nous avons à bord sont déjà dans les fours.'

[20] 'Les femmes ont ameuté la population contre nous, et les hommes sont au sommet du talus qui surplombe d'une dizaine de mètres au-dessus de la surface de l'eau et nous menacent de leurs sagaies. Mais le bois est embarqué, la machine siffle et nous repartons, laissant les indigènes à leur injuste colère.'

autonomy against a small, but potentially merciless and augmentable, colonial presence.

Those colonial agents with aspirations to more sought-after posts or higher echelons of the administration learned quickly that success required careful management of the views one revealed to one's far-off superiors, particularly in relation to violence. Colonial officials who described in detail the widespread hunting practices, which were considered brutal by much of the French public, or who otherwise reported honestly about the problems they faced were frequently demoted or reprimanded. In contrast, those colonial officials who wrote blithe missives about the ease with which they achieved their objectives were promoted and praised. For instance, a man named Coupé was deemed 'the ideal administrator' by his superiors, but he manipulated figures in his reports to make himself look better and refrained from mentioning the violence he oversaw (Mollion 1992: 73, 77). He hid in plain sight: he followed procedure but edited reports to blend in with the desires and expectations of the people in charge of his promotion. He developed the skill of camouflage.

Acts of violence were staged according to their audiences. Locally, the ideal was to shock and awe, and in so doing to cow others. Thus, in theory, less violence would be needed in the future, yet the spectacle might be prevented from coming to the attention of faraway administrators and humanitarians. Georges Toqué, who was based at Fort Crampel (now Kaga-Bandoro) from 1902 to 1904, came to symbolise the dilemmas inherent in the practice.

Toqué was something of a 'non-conformist' (Mollion 1992: 171). He believed that Africans could claim a civilisation equal to those elsewhere and took offence when they were called 'savages' Mollion 1992: 171), even though on occasion he did so himself. Like many of his compatriots, he advocated aggression when necessary; at the same time, the people he attempted to rule over actively hunted him. During a trip to reconnoitre the terrain in the areas west of Fort Crampel, more than 5,000 arrows (he counted them) rained down on his party (cited in Mollion 1984: 50).

Among the captives under Toqué's watch was a man named Pikamandji, who had deserted from the national guard and was made to work as a porter for his 60-day imprisonment. Pikamandji deserted again and abandoned his load in the process, the worst possible offences in an arrangement dependent on forced-labour logistics. Toqué's deputy, Fernand Gaud, decided to make an example of Pikamandji. He gathered the people of Fort Crampel, tied a stick of dynamite to Pikamandji's behind, and lit it (Smith 2015a: 22).

Tactics like this were not anomalous among the adventurists and the people working with them (Mollion 1992: 171). Nor should they surprise anyone who has read Foucault's (1977) descriptions of examples of gruesome bodily punishment (such as the dismemberment of Robert-François Damiens) in France prior to the nineteenth century. Spectacular punishment has frequently been an important means of coercing others. The difference here was that spectacular punishment was used and seen as scandalous simultaneously. Toqué wrote a letter to his superior describing what had happened. At the time, Brazza had been tasked with carrying out an investigation into the abuses of the concessionary regime in Equatorial Africa (Coquery-Vidrovitch 2014). Spectacular violence might have been a useful tool for the colonial officials, but it was not something to publicise. When it was recorded in such a form as to make it inescapably known to those who were obliged to be scandalised by it, some kind of action had to be taken. So Toqué's letter meant that he and Gaud were brought to trial. He claimed that officials had promised that he would be acquitted if he refrained from describing the atrocities in the porterage concentration camps that had been created in Oubangui-Chari. He refused. During the trial he argued that he had been following the example of his superiors, one of whom he had accused (in another letter that predated the trial) of being responsible for the deaths of 20,000 Africans made to serve as porters. Toqué was nevertheless found guilty (Mollion 1992: 170–2).[21] (His superior was never investigated.) Among other factors considered at trial, an analysis of his handwriting was entered into evidence – writing things down was doubly dangerous when, according to the science of the time, handwriting revealed a person's character.[22]

When Toqué's trial had made it impossible for him to pursue a career as a good, silent officer, he made a name for himself by eschewing all camouflage in favour of exposé, in the form of a tell-all memoir published after his release from prison (Toqué 1996 [1907]). He sought to make it more difficult for those not directly involved in the nitty-gritty of colonial projects to retain the selective vision they relied on, pointing out the metaphorical cracks that threatened to topple the pedestals on which they placed their reasoned principles. This was uncomfortable at best for the

[21] Toqué was executed after the First World War for writing articles for the pro-German newspaper *Gazette des Ardennes* (Toqué 1996 [1907]: 193–4).

[22] Toqué's handwriting was described as 'seductive' in style; among other conclusions to follow from that observation was the following: 'It is possible … that in sexual matters there are deviations.' His handwriting was also taken as evidence of a 'dual' character: 'brilliant spirit when it comes to taking action but of a questionable morality' (cited in Toqué 1996 [1907]: 196).

colonial and France-based authorities who advocated for and oversaw budgets and promotions, as well as for other supporters of empire. They had an interest in not poking around or verifying too much. Besides, that kind of investigating required human and material resources, always in drastically short supply.[23] By casting the problems as the fault of a deranged individual, as the verdict judged Toqué, administrators could keep the telescope focused only on his blemishes, and leave the rest of the scene beautifully hazy.[24]

[23] In 1920, Oubangui-Chari had 90 functionaries, 31 of whom were in the capital. Of the ten *circonscriptions* (districts), four were staffed by military officers because of a lack of personnel. There was no magistrate in the colony. Functionaries held multiple positions: one person was Head of Office for Finances, President of the Tribunal, and Head of Office for Automobile Transport. There was at most one accountant in the service of the administrator (Coquery-Vidrovitch 1972: 87).

[24] In his memoir, Toqué recounted that his bosses in the colonial ranks schooled him in just such tactics of camouflage (which Toqué – self-servingly but not necessarily falsely – presented himself as resisting). After a particularly brutal administrator, who Toqué refers to as 'H.', was killed by Central Africans he had tormented, Toqué wrote to his superior, M. de Roll, to explain the circumstances and the dire state of affairs in the area. Toqué advocated making the hostage-taking more humane, such as by giving hostages houses to sleep in, rather than 'keeping them outside like livestock' (Toqué 1996 [1907]: 64). In his response, de Roll first urged Toqué to shut up. Then he agreed with Toqué's plan to make the hostage system less brutal. He continued: 'React against this senseless habit of useless fusillades. In contrast, there should be immediate and pitiless repression of well-established cases of rebellion, major attacks, or assassination of recruiters – but against the culpable village alone and never against their innocent neighbours' (Toqué 1996 [1907]: 65). Toqué described this guidance as confusing: if the most brutal modes of hunting were bad, why was silence necessary? Not long afterwards, he had a conversation with de Roll in which the boss further explained his thinking. According to Toqué, de Roll was becoming exasperated with Toqué's failure to adapt to the requirements of the job, particularly in terms of managing information about hunting practices. Toqué had suggested they should write a report about H.'s death and the vengeance killings that followed. He said that his superior responded:

> Make a report! … Ah! But no! Enough already! … Everyone would abandon us, even Gentil, even the colonel, even though they know what's what. … It's us who would be wrong. No one would want to admit that the best way to have prevented H. from going crazy would have been to not leave him alone and without means in the middle of exasperated indigenes. For me, I have only a few months to live; I don't want to ruin them. As for you, with the future that you could hope for, your interest is to muzzle yourself. The worst grade you could have at the ministry is that of a pain in the arse. Remember this: it is not prohibited to kill negroes, but to talk about it, to be taken, or to leave evidence; and it is better to kill 20 negroes than to scratch one. The dead can't speak, while the scratched man would become a martyr in France. You would have a good time trying to explain but would never manage to convince that it's not you who's in the wrong. (Toqué 1996[1907]: 67–8)

In de Roll's comments and advice, as related by Toqué, it is less important to hold oneself to particular principles of how one should relate to other people (those concerns are present, but subsidiary) than it is to retain the leeway to represent oneself to people elsewhere, a leeway that can often best be assured simply by being quiet. While this is patently self-serving – and Toqué's account certainly should be read as self-serving in

Institutionalised forceful acquisition: taxation

When the violence of colonial projects in Equatorial Africa became known to people with humanitarian sympathies, it was a scandal, as was the case with the 'scapegoat' Toqué (Mollion 1992: 171). A trial or a fact-finding mission would follow and reforms would be passed, but there would never be sufficient means to implement them (Coquery-Vidrovitch 1972, 2014). As in the case of Foucault's prisons, reform was not a response to colonialism but a major component of it, and reform never managed to fundamentally alter the governing incentives people faced in this remote place.[25]

Still, things changed. Sleeping stations were eventually established for porters, and, by 1918, food was available for them at various stopping

addition to whatever truths it presents – it is also evidence of the conflicts of values that people in positions such as Toqué's faced in their work, particularly the dissonance they experienced between their sense that they were doing something for Africans' greater good, the need for violence to accomplish the tasks their superiors demanded of them, and those superiors' skittishness when it came to hearing about that violence.

[25] People did raise alarms – again and again. The first decades of colonial rule were marked by intense brutality, neglect, and intermittent scandals and public mobilisation against these depravities when they were brought to the attention of audiences with humanitarian interests, particularly in Europe. Today, people recalling the violence of that era and the mobilisation against it usually cite André Gide's book *Voyage au Congo*, published in 1927, in which he recounts a number of grisly incidents (including one in which 32 men, women, and children were killed by colonial guards). But although the most-cited today, Gide's account was only one in a series of exposés of violence in Equatorial Africa. Already in 1905, Brazza had overseen an investigation and subsequent report that catalogued abuses and advocated for reform (Coquery-Vidrovitch 2014). (Interestingly, this push for reform came from colonial officers – who were also accused of abuses – because they were angry about the concessionaires' arrogation of power.) Another reform effort was launched in 1907, yet another in 1910, and then another in 1927 after Gide's book came out. Another writer, Albert Londres, wrote a devastating critique of rule in Equatorial Africa in 1928. In his reportage, *Terre d'Ebène* 2012 [1928], both Europeans and Africans come across as being within hours of death – emaciated and ill to the point of being unable to handle any kind of moral compass. Each of these accounts is haunting and chilling on its own. Even those elements on the periphery of the stories that are the main focus stay with the reader, like that of women so depleted by slavery and porterage labour that their breast milk had dried up, their babies trying in vain to eke out some sustenance (Gentil 1902: 186). Sven Lindqvist opens and closes his own more recent account of colonial violence in Africa, *Exterminate all the Brutes*, with the same point, which is meant to emphasise the fact that his goal is not to provide knowledge of hitherto unknown horrors: 'You already know enough. So do I. It is not knowledge we lack. What is missing is the courage to understand what we know and to draw conclusions' (2014 [1996]: 13, 179). So here is my conclusion, which echoes Lindqvist's. Each time violence was 'uncovered', people with humanitarian sympathies saw it as morally abhorrent. This is understandable, and even correct. However, presenting it in this way shifts attention away from the fact that this kind of forceful acquisition violence does not occur because it is a deliberate programme as such. It emerges out of conflicts of values and conflicts in priorities. And simply declaring the violence abhorrent does not in and of itself resolve those conflicts.

points. (Of course, the food had to be acquired, including forcefully, and bringing the food to these spots required the recruitment of still more porters [Mollion 1992: 132].) By the 1920s, Central Africans' labour had been acquired for the building of roads, and automobiles became the new logistical beasts of burden. The concessionary experiment was most intensely pursued between 1899 and 1930, although it officially lasted until 1946, just like the *indigénat* (Coquery-Vidrovitch 1972), and in an altered form it continues today (see Hardin 2000, 2011; Smith 2015b on these contemporary forms). The written traces left by the Europeans also demonstrate an increasing regard for Central Africans (Mollion 1984). However, the Europeans' need for labour remained, and so manhunting continued as well, although not in as feverish a manner.[26]

Oubangui-Chari was stuck in a vicious politico-economic vortex. It was by far the poorest of all the French colonies. In addition, the cost of colonial projects was exceptionally high, given the expense and difficulty of importing materials, and the production of goods to help pay for them exceptionally low, in part because the concessionary companies had control over natural resources. Throughout the colonies, the French levied a head tax on all adult men; this was a tax for the right to exist. Since Oubangui-Chari was so poor and the human population so small, the head tax was the highest of any colony's. The tax was assigned as an annual number of francs due to the colonial authorities. Some concessionary officials made people pay head taxes to them as well, which was illegal but never prevented. In French West Africa, the tax rate peaked at five francs per year; in Oubangui-Chari it ranged from five to seven, or ten in Bangui. But even that difference does not capture the additional burden on the Central Africans. Only very few had any access to cash, and so they had to pay their head taxes in labour – and their labour was valued far more cheaply than that of West Africans. The backbreaking labour increased morbidity and mortality dramatically (Cordell 1994), and people fled to less-demanding colonies such as the Belgian Congo or British Sudan to avoid such a fate.[27] The tax became both cause and symptom of a vicious cycle of depopulation that began with the trans-Saharan manhunts and the arrival of new diseases (Cordell 1994).

[26] At the end of the 1920s, Europe and North America were descending into economic depression. Anyone who had hoped that the retreat of the concessionaires would be accompanied by an expansion in colonial infrastructure and welfare projects was disappointed. Funding and personnel remained extremely tight. In much of Oubangui-Chari – especially in the north-eastern hunting zones – the polity's administrative and surveillance capabilities continued to exist largely in name only.

[27] Colonial officials in the hunting zone fretted about '*transfuges*' – deserters. Some officials tried to figure out why people were leaving. Along the borders with the Belgian Congo

Taxation would seem to be the quintessential state-making enterprise. In a rational bureaucratic state, taxation is envisioned as an exchange of money for services, such as welfare and security. Moreover, it has an ongoing pedagogical purpose: it is a reminder of the ways in which one is subjugated to authority. These state-oriented objectives were among the justifications colonial officials used in explaining why the head tax was necessary. But in Oubangui-Chari, taxation was a mode of coerced extraction and little else – and the extraction was particularly intense. Government or private officials 'taxed and consumed, if necessary to the point of exhausting and even killing' (Chamayou 2012: 17). With the entrenchment of this peculiarly brutal and neglectful colonial rule, the chase component of manhunting became less important, but forceful acquisition did not stop.

An elderly blacksmith in Ndele recalled to me in 2010, for instance, that from the 1930s to the 1950s al-Sanusi's son Abdel Kader ('re-hatted' as sultan in the mid-1920s in an approximation of indirect rule) had a militia that rounded people up to provide labour – everything from clearing roads to watering mango trees to carrying *tipoyes*. They were joined by the regional guards, who would tie as many as a hundred people together to keep them from absconding. (Roping people together was illegal but not punished [Brégeon 1998: 164].) In the 1930s, one of the main governmental undertakings in French Cameroon and Oubangui-Chari was road clearing. Automobiles reduced the need for porters but increased the need for wide and flat roads, which people had to build and then maintain. All African men in the two colonies were therefore required to toil for 15 days per year to build roads. However, in Oubangui-Chari, the population was so small and the need so great that the legal limit of 15 days would never have been enough. Colonial officials faced conflicting demands: build the road, but do not abuse people. To do the former they would have to ignore the latter; to do the latter they would have to ignore the former. However, ultimately the people most important to the furtherance of these officials' careers were very far away, and many of them resolved the tension by circumventing regulations and keeping quiet about it. They managed the narratives about themselves and their work that circulated outside the hunting zone. Indeed, it was an open secret among the colonial set that one could

and Anglo-Egyptian Sudan, for instance, they reported that some people left in order to be part of plantation agriculture in Sudan that would give them the money to get married; others left because they found the British or Belgian colonial presence less onerous in its demands; and still others left because, after the First World War, French officials had issued a policy to cease the distribution of medication for sleeping sickness, whereas across the borders it continued to be dispersed (Natalini 1918).

force people to work for as long as was necessary to carry out the required tasks, provided one did not draw attention to the fact (Brégeon 1998: 163).[28] This was not a source of pleasure for most officials; in general they regretted it, but they saw few workable alternatives. This, then, is one of the defining features of being 'stateless' in a world of states, of playing hunting and raiding games at a time when caretaking, administrative politics are normative. It is not that people who are hunted and extracted from in these ways have been cast out, whether as enemies or as meaningless, but that their inclusion is caught up in an unrelenting dynamic of spoliation and camouflage.

The end of the *indigénat* without structural change

The *indigénat* system that placed native Africans in an inferior position to whites finally ended in 1946. Forced labour in Oubangui-Chari continued, however, and was officially ended only in 1954 by Louis Sanmarco, then administrator-in-chief of the colony. Unofficially, forced labour continued in some places, whether because plantation owners in rural areas did not know that the laws had changed or because they found it convenient to ignore them (Brégeon 1998: 172). Wages for labourers, to the extent they were given, were extremely low. In 1949, a person would have to work a hundred days in order to be able to buy a shoddy cotton *pagne* (Brégeon 1998: 179). Few would do this work by choice.

People who were 'hunted' in Oubangui-Chari had not been cast out of humanity. Nor were they hunted because they were 'enemies' against whom a war had been declared. It wasn't because they had been exposed, rendered 'bare life' by a decision to strand them neither inside nor outside the polity and thereby produce sovereign power itself (Agamben

[28] For instance, in 1937, Inspector Ruffel wrote a report in which he described some of the abuses of the forced labour system. Workers, and their supervisors, were assigned tasks rather than days' work. This was illegal. People who fled rather than complete the labour would be captured and forced to begin anew, regardless of how many days they had already completed. This was also illegal. In one case he cited, the escaped workers were brought back roped together, and led by a guard. This had also been made illegal. After reading the report, the lieutenant governor, Masson de Saint-Félix (after whom one of the national parks that were also being created around this time was named), agreed that tying people together with a rope was bad practice. But when Ruffel argued for ending the forced labour system, Masson de Saint-Félix responded with colonial pragmatism: where would he find the millions of francs that would be necessary to keep the roads in drivable condition (Brégeon 1998: 163–4)? The question was rhetorical. Both knew that the money was nowhere to be found. The occasional uncomfortable spotlight on abusive practices might engender new protective laws but the light would soon fade, while the labour needs and lack of non-coercive resources would persist.

1998, 2005). Nor yet was it because government officials decided that they should be exterminated or 'rendered as pests' (Mavhunga 2011: 152). Their bodies, their force, were vessels from which others could acquire labour.

By the late 1950s, the imperial system was coming under great tension. Read today, a 'top secret' military analysis from those years seems to suggest that colonial authorities had already given up on establishing any kind of effective state here:

> Oubangui, land of forested savannah, with its population clearly concentrated along the roads and its vast empty spaces, would be an ideal terrain for a guerrilla: it is easy to ambush along the main roads; costly to destroy bridges, culverts, and ferries that must be used for all itineraries; easy to disappear in the bush and there be invulnerable due to the difficulties of penetration and the near impossibility for aviation to locate isolated or small detachments; easy to organise in the same bush, away from inhabited places but in the old settlement and collection bases; opportunities to receive in these bases provisions from across both the eastern and western borders. In these conditions, the task of the forces charged with maintaining or re-establishing order appear particularly arduous. While neither the relief nor the climate make it impossible to undertake military operations, vegetation and the river systems constitute major obstacles to any rapid intervention ... Large spaces escape all control, and any operations could only be undertaken on foot, with the slowness and fatigue that this mode of transport entails. They will require large numbers because the Oubanguian bush, with its lack of horizon and the absence of any 'obligatory' route, is an 'eater of men'. (Government of Oubangui-Chari n.d.: 9)[29]

In 1960, six years after Oubangui-Chari's first class graduated from its first high school, the colony gained independence as the Central African

[29] 'L'Oubangui, pays de savane boisée, avec sa population clairsemée concentrée le long des routes et ses vastes espaces vides semble une terre d'élection pour la guérilla: embuscades faciles à monter sur les axes de pénétration, destructions payantes des ponts, ponceaux ou bacs que doivent franchir tous les itinéraires, possibilité de disparaître dans la brousse le coup fait et d'y être peu vulnérable par suite des difficultés de pénétration et de la quasi-impossibilité pour l'aviation d'y repérer des isolés ou de petits détachements; possibilité d'organiser dans cette même brousse, à l'écart des lieux habités mais dans les anciennes zones de peuplement des bases de recueil; possibilité enfin de recevoir dans ces bases un ravitaillement extérieur par la frontière de l'Est ou de l'Ouest. Dans ces conditions, la tâche des forces chargées du maintien ou du rétablissement de l'ordre apparaît comme particulièrement ardue. Si, ni le relief, ni le climat, ne s'opposent à priori à des opérations militaires, la végétation et le réseau hydrographique constituent par contre des obstacles sérieux à des interventions rapides ... de larges espaces échappent à tout contrôle; et des opérations ne pourront y être entreprises qu'à pied, avec toute la lenteur et la fatigue que ce mode de déplacement comporte. Elles exigeront des effectifs importants car la brousse Oubanguienne avec son manque d'horizon et l'absence de tout itinéraire "obligé" est une "mangeuese d'hommes".'

Republic (Kalck 1971). The 'unfortunate colony' became the 'unfortunate country'. Of all the former French colonies, CAR was the worst off, both financially and in terms of administrative capacity. The country carried its colonial burdens of penury and lack of personnel into independence. Even clerks had to be imported from France due to the lack of trained Central African personnel (Kalck 1971).

Accounts from these early post-independence years described two contrasting attitudes. Some emphasised the hope and excitement that surrounded the official end of French rule. Others decried the new leaders as *munju voko* – black-skinned whites – that is, they argued that independence was only a replacement of one privileged caste by another (Zoctizoum 1983). Both were true; although much collective energy was devoted to education and other state-building projects (Hardin and Zana 2014), from its founding the country faced immense structural challenges (Kalck 1971). Among other things, a system in which authority has been more about entitlement than about governing may be difficult to change (Lombard 2016c). But it was the decay and violence from the 1980s onwards that obscured the early hopefulness in the shade of challenges and problems.

Conclusion

Today, many postcolonial countries – and CAR in particular – appear weak, failed, or fragile: that is, like their once healthy forms have been emaciated by poor management. The poverty of that analysis becomes evident when one appreciates that it is the state form itself – its objectives, its modes of oversight – that has been so central to producing precisely the political forms that we now find in this part of the world. That is, over the twentieth century, the state form – first in its colonial configuration and then in its independent one – has provided a normative legal-ethical framework for protection, production, and violence. In CAR, the normative skeleton took on a grotesque version of Malinowski's 'flesh and blood',[30] a version that was very different from the embodiment adopted by states that had developed more reciprocally because of its inextricability from the dynamics and exigencies of the hunting zone. Instead of organising management, discipline, and production, and creating enduring institutions, agents of the state had always been mostly concerned

[30] At the risk of using an awkward metaphor, I am revisiting here Bronisław Malinowski's (1922) famous invocation of socio-cultural skeletons, flesh and blood spirits, and the 'imponderabilia' of daily life as the proper ethnographic objects, this time to suggest that these elements might not always coalesce as a coherent body, as Malinowski assumed.

with extraction and acquisition – sometimes for institutional ends, and sometimes for their own.

It was not preordained that forceful acquisition would prove so tenacious, its importance even enhanced, in north-eastern CAR. True, the vastness of the geography and the limits of the available finances were obvious from the beginning of the French colonial presence. But in contrast to those frontiers that permitted their exploiters to accumulate, north-eastern CAR was less clearly a site for profit and accumulation. It was a colonial appendix[31] rather than a heart. For most of the colonial period, it was classed as an 'autonomous district' rather than a *circonscription*.

But one can learn a lot even from an appendix, even if its function remains unclear. The particular problems of a space like this were a source of embarrassment to officials elsewhere. Spaces such as the hunting zone are not supposed to exist, and high-level officials would prefer to pretend that they do not, through tacit encouragement of dissemblance, for example, whether in reports to the ministry or in other communications. The overwhelming impression one has in submerging oneself in accounts of the colonial era is not that colonial agents and concessionaires experienced blithe assurance about the righteousness of what they were doing. Rather, it is that the values they espoused frequently came into conflict, and people's proper relations to each other were uncertain. (How *should* an African be treated? How *could* he be treated? How should an African treat a colonial official?) Colonial officials had incentives to deal with those value conflicts and uncertainties in ways that furthered their own careers and interests, rather than holding firmly to one set of principles.

Many intellectual traditions venerate consistency as key to ethical practice. The consequence, as James Laidlaw has pointed out, is that people who are inconsistent appear to be 'mere heap' from an ethical perspective (2013: 173). In fact, however, there are always trade-offs between controlling one's desires and values so that they overlap perfectly with those of one's group. Alternative conceptions (Laidlaw cites Nietzsche as the most influential progenitor of this tradition) instead name the freedom to be inconsistent as the better avenue to achieving personhood (2013: 174). In raiding, as a mode of acquisition, retaining the ability to be inconsistent allows greater individual success. And people who live in this manner are not 'mere heaps'. But it would be

31 Mads Brügger describes CAR as an 'appendix' in his documentary *The Ambassador* (2011), which includes a number of factual inaccuracies but also some evocative, if overly expansive, analytical gestures.

going too far to say that they have experienced their position as one of freedom – in some ways yes, but overall no.

So it is neither as linchpins of a global project of expansion nor as loci of utopian resistance to the standardising dictates of life in a centralised polity that hunting zone politico-economic tendencies are important. Raiding's importance in CAR lies in its having been, for more than a century, an improvisation in response to problems of scale, time, and values in a remote part of an imperial world, problems that inherently compromised deontological projects. This chapter has paid most attention to the workarounds colonial agents and concessionaires developed as they pursued their projects. But Africans were dealing with similar conflicts of values. Many Africans of the interior were intrigued by aspects of the new lifestyles Europeans brought with them but also saw Europeans' coercive, extractive drive as cruel and abhorrent. It was generally not possible for them to pick and choose – to take what was attractive and reject the rest. Studies of those African leaders who teamed up with the Europeans to implement indirect rule or to organise manhunts have tended to portray the Africans as greedy or immoral (e.g. Metefia 1982). But it seems likely that they, too, experienced conflicting values, a position Max Gluckman (1956) characterised as 'equivocal'.

With the human population of the area devastated by decades of manhunts and the arrival of new diseases, the presence of other animals – elephants, lions, giraffes, rhinoceroses, buffalo, Lord Derby elands, and many others – was even more striking, and even more attractive as a source of both livelihood or subsistence and profit. These animals became a major focus of the government and other incomers, including itinerant big-game hunters from around the world. Thus the official development plan for north-eastern Oubangui-Chari, and later CAR, was not to develop it but to devote it to conservation and hunting. In the 1930s, nearly all of the region was designated hunting or fauna reserves (later, some were made into national parks) or protected as a 'zone of hunting interest' (*zone d'intérêt cynégétique*). Safari hunting concessions were created around this time as well. They expanded further after the Second World War, when safaris became 'democratised', catering not just to aristocrats but to businesspeople and other wealthy hunters (Roulet 2004). Big-game hunting and conservation thus became a new node around which most forceful acquisition centred, and served to entrench many of the ways in which raiding organised politico-economic encounters while adding new issues to the mix. Humans and other animals participate in dynamics of confrontation, in the full range of ways they might play out, from connection to killing and acquisition.

4 Big-game hunting and regulatory sociality

A visit to Manovo

Boris-Harding's house lay at one end of the two neat rows of concrete and tin-roofed houses flanking the road through the conservation base known as Manovo, on the edge of Manovo-Gounda St Floris National Park, about two hours' drive (depending on how heedlessly one drives, and the state of one's vehicle) from Ndele, the nearest town. Boris-Harding is a *surveillant-pisteur*, a tracker-guard, whose job is to patrol the immense stretches of north-eastern CAR where the hunting of large animals is prohibited for all but the wealthiest of hunting tourists. He was among the *pisteurs* at Tata, in the encounter that opened this book. When Boris-Harding and his fellow tracker-guards are in protected areas and encounter people less dangerous than they are, they seize their material goods (largely tools – bicycles, shovels, rifles) and evict them, sending them back to their village or town. They hunt – sometimes to the death – those who gather the land's vital resources for themselves or their livestock, and do not submit so easily.

Boris-Harding had already been doing this work for nearly two years when I met him towards the end of 2009. His father and older brother had been *pisteurs* before him, and his own rather unusual name combined the names of two of the expatriates his father had worked with on anti-poaching ventures. His father left the job after he was shot in the shoulder by some hunters. His brother had come upon some herders/hunters while on his own. They broke his arm and he died of an internal haemorrhage. Boris-Harding explained that he had taken the job to get vengeance for the wrongs done to them. He also appreciated the respectability and connections he gained from having this paid job.[1]

The Manovo conservation base is an edifice of non-native construction in the midst of an area notable for its very limited circulation of imported

[1] Salaried jobs for men without a university degree are few in the region, and those unrelated to conservation and game hunting almost non-existent.

material goods. Even in its now dilapidated state, it is difficult to overstate the impressiveness of the conservation base in an area of very few concrete buildings. On the road from Ndele, one arrives first at the village, a settlement that sprang up around the base to cater to employees and benefit from the services and goods available. The village is illegal (technically, no human settlement is permitted inside the park), but the government in Bangui once recognised it as an official village. From Manovo village the road straightens and passes the church, the school, the shop, and the clinic, and two rows of tracker-guard houses, all built of concrete and roofed with metal. They once had proper metal doors with locks, also a rarity in the region, but those were all taken during a gap in conservation project funding. From there the road winds on, this time past a memorial to tracker-guards killed at work in the 1990s. Many have been killed since, but there is no money to update the plaque. Next is a giant garage hangar with a heavy equipment graveyard at the front. The backhoes and other massive vehicles were all brought in during the early, profligate years of conservation projects (the late 1980s and early 1990s) and used both for the construction of this base and for the clearing of hundreds of kilometres of new roads, to enable the increased surveillance of humans as well as other animals. A radio control centre, a building for training and offices, and a physical fitness area follow. Then the buildings stop, and the road continues for another kilometre, ending at a clearing with four three-bedroom villas. Initially designed for expatriates working on conservation, they are now occupied by the conservator and his *adjoint* (deputy), both Central African functionaries, and the mercenaries brought in to train the tracker-guards. When these houses were built they had electricity, hot running water, and air conditioning. The equipment for these luxuries is now vestigial. Down a path just wide enough for a Land Cruiser, one reaches, a kilometre later, the two-kilometre airstrip and its hangar.

The Manovo base is a testament to the fact that, although undertakings with the goal of governance in north-eastern CAR have been few, big-game hunting and conservation have been the key impetus for those that have occurred. Almost all of the region – an area larger than Portugal – has been consecrated national park or hunting reserve, or is otherwise off limits to humans.[2] CAR has the highest proportion of territory earmarked for safari hunting of any African country (Binot, Castel, and Caron 2006). Yet acquisition (of animals, foodstuffs, materials, and

[2] The conservation projects that became established in the 1980s covered 85,000 square kilometres – a larger area than Austria.

other wild goods) from uninhabited spaces remains the economic motor of the region and a source of innovation, cooperation, and connection to regional capitals (Piermay 1977; Roulet 2009). Grappling with acquisition – not managing people or production – has therefore been the primary interest of projects that have attempted to control others. But in order to do so, the would-be regulators of acquisition adopt the tactics of the people they would apprehend, and become illicit acquirers in their own right.

The coming pages present the twentieth-century history of acquisition of goods that have an ambiguous status in relation to property and law owing to their wild provenance and the plural norms engendered by developing long-distance politico-economic processes. I argue that these dynamics can be appreciated only through consideration of people and situations: that is, through the identification and entrainment central to the process of tracking and acquiring, whether one is a government official or a self-described poacher. There are social and mimetic elements at play that ensure that raiding and acquisition remain central to life in the area, even as some claim that their interest is in stopping them. This is particularly the case because the space is officially attached to a polity that is, formally, ruled by law, but which remains largely beyond its area of direct interest or concern. Deontological ethics are a casualty of this kind of legal-spatial configuration.

But I am getting ahead of myself. These features of recurring raiding acquisition are discernible throughout the intertwined history of the commercialisation of wildlife and its conservation. We will return to the comfortable chairs in the shade beside the flower garden in Boris-Harding's yard to hear more about his work. But understanding how Manovo came to exist and what it tells us about transformations in acquisition requires delving into the history on which it is built, and the ways that attempted regulation occurs through social situations – or regulatory sociality – rather than rules.

Colonial game-hunting laws: origins and limits

French colonial officials hoped that big-game hunting would be a way to salvage pride and make money in their territories. They had not become rich, unlike their imperial neighbours, King Leopold. The king's profits in the Belgian Congo had been the inspiration for the concessionary project in French Equatorial Africa (Afrique Équatoriale Française or AEF). But although concessions failed to produce much profit for the French, colonial officials could still boast that, while Congo had been emptied of animals, French territory retained a healthy population (Lavauden 1931: 8). To the extent that the colonial government was concerned with the north-eastern autonomous districts, its concern mostly turned on hunting, especially big-game hunting.

In Oubangui-Chari, passing hunting regulations and dispatching people to enforce them in straitened circumstances required would-be enforcers to become raiders themselves, tracking and taking from people whose status was vulnerable to officialdom but who could also prove dangerous. Hunting regulations written in faraway capitals were neither irrelevant nor a blueprint for ethical behaviour. They were instead a kind of scaffolding added to the landscape, an awkward structure that could be climbed and otherwise manipulated in order to create new opportunities for camouflage and new opportunities for taking, although the scaffolding also allowed opportunity – for fame or infamy – to be seen from afar. Government regulation of big-game hunting was part of the broader processes of acquisition amid status uncertainty that are the focus of this book. Even the most stalwart enforcers of hunting rules had to adopt tactics of tracking and trickery to catch the most resourceful 'poachers', and even the most incorrigible self-described poachers would sometimes admit the applicability or good sense of the law.

Understanding how hunting regulation solidified acquisitive politics rather than eliminating or controlling them requires attention to the logic that inspired it. In the government's view, big game was the area's main source of wealth, and therefore a potential source of revenue for its own coffers in the form of taxes and fees on hunters. Around this time, it was becoming more fashionable to believe that wild animals, rather than being pests to be eliminated or a perpetually regenerating reserve, needed long-term human stewardship and protection from unfettered commodification (Jepson and Whittaker 2002). The need for revenue from hunters and the need to stop people from hunting indiscriminately were often at cross-purposes. One way of dealing with the tension has been to make legal big-game hunting increasingly racialised and exclusive, as happened first through regulations and then, from the 1940s onwards, through safari hunting. Along the way, the features of the imagined ideal hunter have evolved, with those for whom hunting can be described as nothing but a profit-making endeavour particularly vilified.

Europeans were concerned about the profit hunting of those they termed foreign others ('Arabs') even during the period when it was clear that Europeans were the main instigators of the most extensive profit hunts. Just three years after al-Sanusi's killing, in 1914, a colonial officer who had 'made the rounds' (or been *en tournée* – the classic colonial activity in rural areas) in north-eastern Oubangui-Chari wrote that:

Elephants are found in large numbers both in the depressions and inundated plains and in the mountainous regions. Also many natives foreign to the *circonscription* come to devote themselves to hunting. Over the course of the month of January, a large number of these natives (Hemat Arabs from Salamat, Ouled Saî Arabs from Dar-Sila, Tayschė Arabs from Darfur, Yulus from Kafiakindji) were met and they perpetrate true massacres. A group of Hemat Arabs whose camp was on the Mamoun possessed 73 elephant tusks that had been procured over the course of one month. (Schmoll 1914: 10)[3]

Twenty years later, in 1934, an official posted to Birao wrote that the area 'knew a great prosperity just a few years ago, thanks to hunting ... The *circonscription* was then invaded by many Arabs, who had no occupation besides the pursuit of elephants and giraffes' (Boucher 1934: 51). The racist and nationalist tenor of both these reports is familiar to any student of colonial operations, as is the tendency to overlook the entanglement between the 'Arab' hunters and the often-European buyers. Nevertheless, it is interesting that the commodification of wild African animals that was so intense during this period was a source of mixed feelings for the colonial officials. They generally excused themselves from criticism, but they weren't wholly oblivious to the conflicts their presence inspired.

According to government logic, imperialism was a force here for the greater good. But it was only because of the expansion of mercantile capitalism, together with new gun technologies, that hunting could occur on such an intense scale that extinction became a worrisome possibility (Jepson and Whittaker 2002). While those involved in mercantile colonial projects generally saw profit and commodification as part of civilisational progress, in certain domains, including big-game hunting, focusing on profit above all came to be seen as a perversion. Big-game hunting was not kept out of the realm of commodification – far from it. But tensions emerged between its commodification and modern sensibilities about the value and status of both human and large-animal lives.

One way of managing the need for revenue from profit hunters (by this point there were no other saleable resources in this area, and very few humans) and the desire to limit profit hunting was to racialise hunting permits, giving licences only to 'Europeans' (a category that was more properly 'non-African', since it included at least one Baluchi [Rushby

[3] 'L'ÉLÉPHANT se rencontre en grand nombre aussi bien dans les dépressions et plaines d'inondation que dans la région montagneuse. Aussi de nombreux indigènes étrangers à la Circonscription viennent-ils se livrer à la chasse. Au cours du mois de Janvier, il a été rencontré une grande quantité de ces indigènes (Arabes Hemat du Salamat, Arabes Ouled Saî du Dar-Sila, Arabes Tayschés du Dar-Four, Youlous de Kafiakandji), ces gens font de véritables massacres. Un des groupes d'Arabes Hemat dont le campement était sur le Mamoun détenait 73 défenses d'éléphants qu'il s'était procuré en moins d'un mois.'

1965]) and then taxing the goods acquired through hunting. But even the high-level officials helping design this system recognised its many inherent weaknesses as a means to control or police hunting. For instance, in 1909, the Russian Prince Demidov travelled to the Haut-Oubangui region to hunt. He was fined 8,000 francs for leaving without paying the ivory tax for the 385 kilograms he carried home. In addition, he had subjected his porters to especially brutal conditions. Thirteen died. For their deaths, he was fined 6,500 francs. (The difference in amount gives a sense of French priorities.) The sanctions were mostly symbolic, however, as the prince had left the continent and the government had no way of making him pay (Mollion 1992: 179).

Until the rules were changed in the late 1920s, AEF was the last remaining place where, after buying a licence, a big-game hunter could shoot as many elephants as he liked, in a model reminiscent of the old *salatieh* system. As George Rushby, a British big-game hunter and later game warden, put it in his memoir:

> There was a vague but persistent rumour that the French in their territories still issued licences which permitted a hunter to shoot an unlimited number of elephants. That kind of elephant licence had once been common to most African territories but such licences had long since been abolished in British-administered countries and in the Congo. I decided to go to French Equatorial Africa to see for myself. (Rushby 1965: 82)

Elsewhere in the region, conservation was gaining symbolic approval, and commercial hunting losing it. As early as the turn of the twentieth century, British officials had established conservation laws and national parks in their colonies. In their Eastern and Southern African colonies, a corps of game wardens patrolled the parks and otherwise sought to prevent hunting, and when they encountered hunters, they locked them up rather than killing them. Game hunting still went on (and safari taxes brought in substantial government revenue), but it was considered more a pursuit for science or sport (trophies) than one of profit (Jepson and Whittaker 2002).

In AEF, and in Oubangui-Chari in particular, by contrast, hunting for profit and conservation were always thoroughly intertwined projects, however unlikely a pair they may seem.[4] Rather than national parks, the AEF government created hunting reserves, the first in Oubangui-Chari

[4] It was just around this point that more stringent hunting regulations were being developed. The credulously optimistic forester-zoologist Louis Lavauden thought that this tardiness in the project of conservation could serve the French well: they could adapt the best practices and learn from the mistakes of the British and Belgians. 'It seems that a few years ago [the period just after the First World War, 1920–4] the Belgian Congo was a remarkable country for big-game hunting. Today there is hardly any large game in the national parks' (Lavauden 1931: 8). ['Il semble qu'il y a quelques années le Congo Belge

in 1916.[5] In hunting reserves, big-game hunting was restricted so that the animals could reproduce, with the idea of preserving populations for future hunting. In the 1920s and 1930s, the government created several more hunting reserves, and eventually added fauna reserves and national parks. Almost all the north-eastern lands, except for the few towns and villages now relocated along roads by government diktat, were incorporated into reserves. There was colonial pragmatism at work in this land-use prioritisation: there was much that Oubangui-Chari did not have, but it did have big game, and the hunting was so rich that the government could charge much more for a hunting permit there than in other colonies. For instance, whereas in Gabon, Middle Congo (Republic of Congo today), or Chad a commercial hunting permit could be had for 1,000 or 4,000 francs, in Oubangui-Chari the same permit cost 10,000, because the expectation was that much more game could be acquired (Government of Oubangui-Chari 1929).

Fees from the hunting permits and the taxes on exported tusks were crucial to government revenues. Hence the 'rumour' that Rushby followed into Oubangui-Chari: that it was a place for unfettered hunting, as opposed to places where hunting had been figuratively 'fenced in' (his term). Nostalgia for a freer past is a frequent big-game hunter trope. But what emerges both in memoirs of European big-game hunters and in archival reports is not so much that freedom was curtailed as that government regulation added a new dimension to the serious game of acquisition amid status uncertainties. Animals participated in the game, too, when they moved on to better-protected parks and reserves.

The uncertainty injected by restrictive laws without sufficient resources to implement them could itself be a source of adventure. As Rushby put it: 'My men enjoyed the extra excitement of poaching trips as much as I did' (1965: 148). He described at length his most successful poaching stints, including one in the Mweru Marsh game reserve in Northern Rhodesia, along the border with the Belgian Congo. He was extremely successful because he was hunting in a game reserve where the

ait été un pays remarquable pour la grande chasse. Aujourd'hui, il n'a plus guère de grand gibier que dans les parcs nationaux.'] Considering that jealousy of the Belgians' Congo revenues was a prime motivation for the French colonial project in the first place, the decline in game must have brought some satisfaction to the still poor French. The human populations in their territories had plummeted, but they still had big game.

[5] It covered the area delineated as follows: a straight line between the sources of the Bamingui and Bangoran Rivers, the Bamingui until it meets the Chari River, and the Chari until it meets the Bangoran, and the Bangoran (Journal Officiel de l'Afrique Equatoriale Française 1917: 31). The advantage of delineation based on rivers was that it would be easy for people to know when they were in the reserve; the disadvantage is that rivers' locations can change seasonally and annually.

elephants had not yet learned to associate a rifle's report with grave danger. Traders purchased Rushby's poached ivory at a 25 per cent discount off the going rate, a loss Rushby considered reasonable, especially since it included a 'small consideration' so that the administrative officer would turn a half-closed eye towards the areas where Rushby was hunting, becoming complicit in his camouflage.

Rushby's enthusiastic poaching was not because he thought the government regulations were illegitimate. Indeed, in Tanganyika he was careful to abide by all such rules. The difference was that he thought he might like to live long term in Tanganyika, and being on the right side of the law was prudent. Elsewhere his interests were immediate. His actions were directed by the nature and duration of his relationship with a place and the people and other animals there, and his interest in working exceptions for himself. Similarly, although one could describe 'considerations' paid to officials as corruption, the characterisation misses the way in which doing this let them maintain hunting regulation as an entrée to acquisition, and the recognition shared by most people in the area – Africans and others – that the laws were discordant with local needs and priorities.[6]

Moreover, colonial officers were themselves heavily implicated in playing with the rules for their own ends, and particularly in order to take. This is not news; it was acknowledged by pretty much everyone not using camouflage to pursue acquisition without attracting attention. One official, writing in 1924, noted that, although four to seven tons of ivory were sold at government auctions in Ndele, perhaps ten times as much ivory was changing hands in the bush, where 'Arab traders' purchased it to trade to Europeans for gunpowder. Keeping this trade out of the centre of town was a nod to propriety, not a genuine attempt at secrecy. The local administrator claimed to be scandalised, but he was one of the biggest ivory profiteers (Brégeon 1998: 253), and he made the regional guards in his employ into his own troop of elephant hunters (Gaoukane 1986: 172).

Even the French zoologist Louis Lavauden, whose reports are chiefly noteworthy for their credulous optimism about the government's ability to apply strict conservation policies, admitted that the authorities sometimes applied regulations 'according to their pleasure, on the specious pretext that the regulation appears to them inapplicable. It's a very serious tendency among French colonial functionaries and one that

[6] There is thus a deeper history to the tendencies people have identified in the more recent push towards privatisation (Hibou 2004; Roitman 2005).

should be spoken about more frankly since it is quite general' (1931: 31).[7] They did not oppose or resist the regulations; they quietly ignored them, deeming them ill adapted to the exigencies of their situation. Given these various attitudes towards the law, mutable relationships, details of particular situations, and emotional entrainment played larger roles in determining what should be done than the law itself.

While the British created a system of game wardens to carry out their conservation goals, the French in AEF created a corps of hunting inspectors.[8] The fees they were meant to collect and other details varied among the colonies but the overall regulatory architecture was shared. It was clear from the start that, though the system was supposed to be a project of control, something quite different would happen in the hunting zone. Raphaël Antonetti, governor of AEF, and Auguste Lamblin, lieutenant governor of Oubangui-Chari, had refreshingly frank epistolary conversations about proposed hunting regulations. The frankness was due perhaps to Lamblin's exceptional length of stay in Oubangui-Chari: alone among lieutenant governors, he made it a home, staying from 1917 to 1929. (In contrast, the average length of a lieutenant governor's stint was six months, which seriously impeded the establishment of institutional coherence or vision [Brégeon 1998: 87].) Most officials saw Oubangui-Chari as an unpleasant way station and simply tried not to antagonise their superiors so that they could quickly move on. But Lamblin, rather than camouflaging for the sake of a career elsewhere, was committed to the territory.

The proposed hunting decree that Antonetti and Lamblin discussed stipulated that Africans who hunted elephants must relinquish the tusks to the authorities, in exchange for which they would receive a sum of about a quarter of the tusks' value. Meanwhile, there were plenty of European and Arab traders who were eager to buy the ivory at a more favourable price. How would that work? Lamblin noted that the main elephant-hunting areas in Oubangui-Chari were the eastern and northeastern zones, the areas at once most sparsely populated by humans and

7 '[S]elon leur bon plaisir, sous le prétexte spécieux que ce règlement leur semble inapplicable. C'est une tendance très grave des fonctionnaires coloniaux français, que nous devons signaler d'autant plus franchement qu'elle est plus générale.'

8 These hunting inspectors sometimes had greater resources at their disposal than other official armed forces (regional guards and other militia and police). The miserable colonial official in Ndele in the mid-1930s, Lignier, had to 'borrow' the hunting inspector's militiaman (Lignier 1936b). But they, too, were constrained by their budgets and by the widespread resistance to their application of the hunting laws. For instance, the annual report for Ndele in 1948 stated that the only case heard by the *Justice Française* that year concerned a 'rebellion' led by nine people against the hunting inspectors and the laws they attempted to enforce (Placet 1949).

least surveilled, where 'it is easy to realise that no effective control is really possible',[9] given that there were no roads or border posts along the entire length of the 600-kilometre border with Anglo-Egyptian Sudan. 'The hunters find themselves at home and rarely risk being disturbed'; 'we should expect that nearly all of what this region produces will escape us' (Lamblin cited in Antonetti n.d. [1929]).[10] Antonetti added to Lamblin's caution his own reminder: 'I don't think it is useless to signal here that since the state has been stripped of its dominant rights to the advantage of the *concessionnaires* the hunting legislation does not apply to them [concessionary agents]' (Antonetti n.d. [1929]).[11]

Despite such awareness of the inherent problems in the proposed hunting regulations, the text decreed in 1929 included all the provisions that seemed so unworkable. The practical disconnect between the policies determined in the metropole and their implementation fostered competing values, which many game hunters and hunting officials alike dealt with by camouflaging the ways in which they all acquired – often forcefully – in the context of uncertain status. Perhaps it was exasperation that led Antonetti to describe these travails explicitly. He had just learned that what he thought were proposed hunting regulations had in fact been decreed fully two months earlier.

> On the other hand, recognising the judicious motives and reasons of general or speculative interest which provoked the additions or modifications made to the initial text and from which the colony should benefit, I find myself, for this question of hunting, as for many others, in the presence of factual circumstances, of daily realities, which I find it difficult to ignore without exposing myself to working in vain, more façade than a profound revision, and all the more dangerous because the belief that the text's provisions have foreseen every circumstance and are fully applied will be even more in contradiction with the facts. (Antonetti n.d. [1929])[12]

9 'Il est aisé de se rendre compte qu'aucun contrôle vraiment efficace n'est possible.'

10 'Les chasseurs s'y trouvent donc chez eux et ne risquent guère d'y être dérangés'; 'on peut compter que la presque totale de ce qui proviendra de cette région nous échappera.'

11 'Je ne crois pas inutile de signaler ici que l'État s'étant dépouillé au profit des grands concessionnaires de ses droits dominaux la législation sur la chasse ne leur est pas applicable.'

12 'D'autre part, tout en reconnaissant les motifs judicieux et les raisons d'intérêt général ou spéculatif qui ont provoqué les additions ou modifications apportées au texte primitif et dont la colonie doit bénéficier, je me trouve, pour cette question de la chasse, comme pour beaucoup d'autres, en présence de circonstances de fait, de réalités journalières, dont il m'est difficile de faire abstraction sans m'exposer à faire une oeuvre vaine, plus de façade que de révision profonde, et d'autant plus dangereuse que la croyance que les dispositions d'un texte complet sont mineutieusement appliquées, alors qu'il paraît avoir tout prévu, se trouvera davantage en contradiction avec les faits.'

Antonetti here recognised the limits of central planners' ability to build a structured system of control for hunting in a hinterland space. The law seemed to provide for every eventuality, but it was so out of tune with the situation on the ground that hunters could clamber all over it.

From a different set of commitments, Rushby made a similar argument. After having begun his career as a commercial hunter of ivory in eastern Oubangui-Chari and elsewhere, he spent his last decades as a game ranger in British East Africa doing 'elephant control' – hunting elephants that had become too populous following strict conservation policies. Rushby argued that the only good game regulation was one made by those on the ground. Game reserves and parks were vast territories, and infrequent and unreliable communication and the fact that rangers spent at least nine months a year 'on safari' meant that they received visits from their superiors only every few years. 'Important decisions had to be made and carried out by the Game Ranger on the spot … Any attempt by a Game Warden to impose tight headquarters control over Game Rangers could not have worked' (1965: 176). According to Rushby, to be successful a ranger had to have almost total autonomy, even though he had a position within the government apparatus. Antonetti might not have been so candid or categorical about the limits of bureaucracy in managing hunting, but both understood that flexibility, discretion, and proximity would produce fewer moral tensions than rigid application of prescriptive principles elaborated at a distance.

So the prescriptive principles were there, in some spectral way, but both the acquirers and the enforcers had to be flexible in their interactions. The resulting entrainment often generated the sort of fleeting connection that makes the parties recognise a similarity they share, and push in the direction of mutual respect. Connection and feelings of similarity can feel dangerous, too, however, and can make vengeance – an act that seeks to demonstrate dominance in relation to someone who has challenged one's status – and forceful demands for autonomy seem necessary. A puzzle of the hunting zone is that, in the face of particularly extensive restrictions on acquisition, such restrictions remain largely powerless, and the level of violence particularly high.

Entrainment and identification

Real social life occurs through actual interaction, not through the abstract concepts we develop in order to (imperfectly) describe it. Law is also an abstraction, one that makes use of coercive, material, and symbolic backing, but it, too, becomes real in actual situations and practices. In everyday situations, people carry out continual micro-rituals – they comport themselves, or speak – that are the basis for why we do not appear crazy to each other (Goffman 1990 [1959]). There are other situations that, by dint of the competing interests, affiliations, or normative aspirations of the parties involved, are recognisably 'everyday events of crisis' (Kapferer and Gold 2018: 7). In these situations, 'heterogeneities of value in practice and the conflicts and tensions in interpretation and judgment' (Kapferer and Gold 2018) are more apparent than 'cultures' or 'systems' imagined as coherent wholes. In everyday events of crisis, people feel touched by 'heightened intersubjectivity', an intensified 'degree of mutual focus of attention' (Collins 2004: 35). However, the intersubjective encounter cannot play out through routine, and 'shared emotions and intersubjective focus' that 'sweep individuals along by flooding their consciousness' (Collins 2004: 32) can be all the more transformative. The plural, personalised, and situational ways in which people have thought about which forms of acquisition are 'natural' and which are 'unnatural' in the hunting zone and the categorical nature of government law have meant that encounters over big-game hunting have often been exactly this kind of 'everyday event of crisis'.

Competing claims to acquisition in the context of big-game hunting have tended to play out with violence, or the threat of violence. The forceful aspect lends them a particular frisson:

> Violent interactions are difficult because they go against the grain of normal interaction rituals. The tendency to become entrained in each other's rhythms and emotions means that when the interaction is at cross purposes – an antagonistic interaction – people experience a pervasive feeling of tension. This is what I call confrontational tension; at higher levels of intensity, it shades over into fear. For this reason, violence is difficult to carry out, not easy. Those individuals who are good at violence are those who have found a way to circumvent confrontational tension/fear, by turning the emotional situation to their own advantage and to the disadvantage of their opponent. (Collins 2009: 20)

Hunting guards and other agents of the law are not immune to fear and confrontational tension. Rushby described coming under frequent fire from the people he was supposed to be pursuing: 'Game Scouts operating singly and accompanied by only one porter had to move warily through bush where they knew poachers were operating. Frequently a Game Scout had to accept that discretion was the better part of valour' (1965: 154). Only once he had rallied all the other game scouts in the area would they attempt to intervene. The theoretical superiority afforded agents of the law could be erased by the features of the terrain, in terms of both the geography and the resources available – human, material, and symbolic (for example, popular perceptions of the legitimacy of projects of control). Laws could not be 'applied', as described in less pluralistic contexts, where status is demarcated more stably. Patchy resolutions were negotiated through confrontationally tense interactions.

Attempts to curtail game hunting in remote areas sapped government administrative capacity and made even stalwart would-be 'appliers' of the law into people who transgressed expectations about the legal and/or property status of valuables in order to acquire their quarry – in this case, 'poachers'. A particularly dramatic example is that of the Lado Enclave, the most infamous big-game hunting territory of the era because of its massive animal populations and disputed colonial ownership. Just smaller than Switzerland and nestled between Oubangui-Chari, Anglo-Egyptian Sudan, Uganda, and the Belgian Congo, it was initially claimed by King Leopold but was turned over to the British on his death in 1909 (Leopold 2009).[13] Lado was known for having the densest populations of elephants in Africa. One commercial hunter, William 'Karamojo' Bell, worked there and reported that the only factor impeding unlimited acquisition was its tall grass. He quickly had so much ivory that his party could no longer carry it, so they buried it. The tusks displaced so much dirt that there was inevitably a large hump above the stocks. In an unconsciously ironic instance of camouflage – hiding in plain sight, rather than masking or removing from view – Bell erected simple crosses to make the mounds look like burial plots – which, of course, they were, bringing elephants into the fold of human symbolic practice.

The switch from Belgian to British control created a period of flux during which Lado was overrun with hunting profiteers.[14] Area residents

[13] King Leopold hoped to use Lado as a foothold in order to also claim the Bahr el-Ghazal region to the north. That did not happen, despite his making a map with fabricated ethnic groups so that he could argue that they should not be split administratively. (Colonial officials obviously did pay attention to where ethnic groups lay when determining borders, despite arguments to the contrary they just always put their own interests first.) When the British blocked Belgian access to the Nile, Belgian hopes that the area would prove profitable because it would ease the export of rubber and ivory from Lado also failed, because it was so costly to get the goods all the way to the west coast. Eventually they reached an agreement that Lado would be King Leopold's personal property until his death, at which point it would revert to the British. The king sent African askaris (known locally as 'Tukutuku' after the sound of their guns) to secure the enclave's one administrative base, *zariba*-style, and they terrorised the area's residents (Leopold 2009: 466–7), but they did so primarily in the service of their own interests.

[14] Demand for ivory on the part of the American and European middle classes was near its peak, and demand for the coarser-grained female ivory was even higher (Collins 1960). The lack of control in the process of big-game hunting made Lado an attractive place to make animals into saleable goods. But to sell those goods, big-game hunters had to travel through places with at least marginally more stringent regulatory climates. They therefore developed an endless number of ruses to allow them to avoid onerous fines and taxes (Collins 1960). Regulation of big-game hunting, rather than a mechanism of

remember them as being as rapacious as their slave-raider predecessors; they raided people to be conscripted into porterage with similar gusto.[15] The few government officials present in or near Lado used much of their time on long, risky, difficult expeditions to hunt down those hunters they deemed poachers. Frequently they did not succeed. This meant that they were not doing any other 'important administrative business'. They saw stopping poaching as a necessary foundation for administration, 'in order to preserve the elephant herds and to establish a sound and secure administration amidst hostile tribes' (Collins 1960: 220–1). However, they never had enough people, money, or infrastructure to be effective. They could only sporadically hunt the poachers, and even that took most of their time away from other tasks, just as the *chasses à l'homme* had done with the French. Pretending to be able to control hunting (or, more charitably, aspiring to do so) created a cycle of non-administration, the effects of which were felt beyond the domain of game hunting and wild acquisition.

A single case demonstrates some of the vicissitudes of the scene. The British colonial official (later war hero and Henley champion) Charles Vincent Fox, and the American gold miner and commercial hunter James Wood Rogers memorably clashed in the Lado territory. Rogers was the most notoriously law-flouting of the commercial hunters, and in 1911 Fox set out to make an example of him. Even after a full month in pursuit, Fox still had no idea where Rogers and his band of 90 porters were. 'Deceived' by locals and 'hampered by torrential rains accompanied by cyclonic winds' (Collins 1960: 222), Fox dispatched a police officer to kidnap someone who could be forced to provide intelligence. This failed. Instead, Fox wrote, people in the surrounding area stood 'on the surrounding hills silhouetted against the skyline, barking like baboons, and laughing and jeering at our baffled pursuit' (quoted in Collins 1960: 223). So Fox took an even more irregular course of action.

> Making his way unnoticed to a nearby river, he quietly slipped into the water and floated downstream for about a half mile until he came upon a native filling a gourd with water. Floating noiselessly up to the unsuspecting tribesman, Fox pulled him into the water and held his head under until the man's struggles had ceased. By this time Fox's police arrived, dragged the unfortunate native from the water and revived him. In a few moments the terrified captive had put Fox and his men on the poachers' trail once more. (Collins 1960: 223)

control or something one could avoid in exceptional spaces, was an active part of the game of hunting itself.

15 Teddy Roosevelt raised a toast to the 'hunters of Lado' during a trip to East Africa around the same time, but this embarrassed his companions, and he recanted (Collins 1960).

Fox subsequently lost and regained the trail of Rogers and his party several times. The hills were so steep that supplies for the journey had to be hoisted by pulley, and the grass so tall and dense with dew and rain that everyone was perpetually soaked. The pursuit took more than a month of wetness, fear, frustration, tension, and determination. Eventually, Fox's group came to a rain-engorged river. A few made it across a bridge of creepers and vines before it fell into the river and disappeared. Fox was stuck behind, but those who had made it across found themselves beside the camp of Rogers and his band. They sneaked close, lined up their shots, and fired. Those in Rogers' party with guns fired back. Rogers was hit, apparently by one of his own men (Collins 1960).[16] Fox arrived as Rogers lay dying. Rogers' associate, 'Doctor' Pearce, told Fox that he was outside his jurisdiction. After crossing the river, they were in the Congo Free State, and Fox and his men were lawbreaking vigilantes.

Rogers died that night. His final words, spoken to his compatriot Doctor Pearce and reported by Fox in his account of the mission, reflected on the legacy of a life in which autonomy was more important than fidelity to principle.

> Well I have had my good times and my bad times. You remember what I have told you Doctor, I can't stand the religious people. If you are religious you have got to play up to your religion. I never had none so I could do what I liked. Well, Doctor, I'll soon know how I stand with all of your religious fellows. (Quoted in Collins 1960: 225)

While Rogers seems to have seen himself as a rule-hater, the point of being an outlaw is not to oppose regulation but to find or make exceptions to it. That was why it was so exciting. While Fox justified his pursuit of Rogers on the grounds that it would deter other 'poachers', Rogers' associate Pearce thought he made an ignorant assumption. Pearce told Fox that his pursuit of Rogers 'will probably give it [poaching] an additional fillip. The band of brothers [the poachers] will say we thought poaching had got rather slow but there is still excitement left in the old game now that there is a chance of being shot by the English as well as the Belgians' (cited in Collins 1960: 226).

[16] Confusion saturates violent interactions, which are felt in the moment and to which sense is attributed mostly after the fact. 'Contrary to our popular images of violence as something easy for people to do, violent threats most of the time abort – they do not get past the barrier; and when they do pass the barrier, violence is mostly incompetent, not hitting its target, or often hitting the wrong target, innocent bystanders or even members of one's own side, so-called friendly fire. In short: violence is emotionally difficult to carry out, and having a motivation is not enough' (Collins 2013: 135).

Indeed, elephant hunting (which colonial officials categorised as poaching) increased in the following years. By the 1920s, forceful acquisition had become less prominent in Lado. But the diminution owed at least as much to game hunting becoming less attractive in the face of the Great War and a dramatic drop in ivory prices (Roulet 2004) as to more effective enforcement of government-issued hunting rules.

Fox pursued Rogers because Rogers was forcefully acquiring in illicit ways, but in the pursuit Fox, too, forcefully acquired illicitly. He transgressed expectations about how people and property should be treated in ways that, in a moment of quiet reflection, he would likely have seen as morally compromised. Yet he did it because the dynamics of encounter seemed to require such methods. In a sense, he became a poacher, taking his quarry in territory outside his writ. In tracking Rogers, Fox and his party mimicked him, and those personal practices helped create entrainment even before they encountered one another. Fear and uncertainty are part of such processes: one seeks to forcefully acquire – whether as guard or hunter – knowing that one's target is likely to challenge the attempt.

Entrainment and its afterlives mark attempts at forceful acquisition. Entrainment can approach a feeling of identifying with another, creating the experience born of feeling that something has been shared. Hunters have long described such an experience – the conflicting feelings it gives rise to, and the ways in which they deal with them. That killing an animal entails both 'violence and affection' is something hunters sometimes experience as 'the ultimate paradox' (Boglioli 2009: xi). Of course, the charge is not the same if one is attempting to take humans (their life, their labour power, their liberty) rather than another kind of animal. But in both cases the possibility, the attempt, of forceful acquisition contributes to a further destabilisation of the status of the parties to the encounter. Interactions between humans and other animals demonstrate that intersubjectivity can cross species lines, even in the presence of force and violence, and that there are resonances between modes of manhunting and encounters between game hunters and large game. In particular, interactions between hunter and big game clarify how vengeance can become socially important: namely, as a means of (re)differentiating status.

Entrainment across species

Although written history of the hunting zone is limited, there is one prolific genre: memoirs by European game hunters who undertook their acquisitive work there. The racist, colonial, and patriarchal tone of such books is grating to the contemporary ear (Haraway 1984; Hardin 2000; Wonders 2005),[17] but however easy they are to pigeonhole as retrograde, it is harder to explain away their blend of recognising intersubjectivity while nevertheless engaging in violence. This goes against the popular supposition that violence is necessarily born of hatred or other modes of denial of sentience. Rushby wrote: ‘In view of the large number of elephants I have killed it may sound paradoxical, or even hypocritical, if I say I always had a feeling of regret, even sadness, each time I examined the body of an elephant I had killed. It may have been due to the respect and admiration I have for this magnificent animal’ (1965: 14). Cynical and self-serving? Perhaps Rushby was both, but his stories are emotionally complex even if that were the case.

Consider the following example: in eastern Oubangui-Chari, Rushby happened upon an elephant cow and her calf. The cow charged him at close range and, fearing for his life, he shot her dead. The calf was upset and charged repeatedly at Rushby and his staff of trackers. Finally they left, hoping that the rest of the herd would return to care for the nursing calf. When the humans came back the next morning, however, they found the calf lying dead beside his mother. Rushby concludes the story: ‘It is difficult to say what caused its death but one can well imagine what my feelings were’ (1965: 36). It is only difficult to identify the most immediate cause of death. The calf died because Rushby killed its mother. Rushby disavowed culpability for the calf's death. He saw himself as operating legitimately, in self-defence. One could plausibly argue that the elephant charged him because game hunters like him had changed the terms of human–elephant encounters. But that does not erase his capacity to be moved by intersubjectivity that crossed species lines – not enough to change his line of work, but in a way that marked him nonetheless.

Hunter memoirs must, of course, be read with care.[18] The point of a hunting tale is not to faithfully capture everything that happened; it is to

[17] Racism and sexism are undeniably elements of the way in which many big-game hunters have perceived the world and their place in it. But the world never conformed neatly to that vision. If these hunters represented nature as ‘a worthy brother of man, a worthy foil for his manhood’ (Haraway 1984: 45), it was not only because doing so served their interests. It was also because the creatures they came across imposed themselves in the hunting encounters as they played out. In other words, if the animals were ‘worthy’, it was not only because they were presented as such by the humans hunting them. It was also because, during the hunting process, they could make a claim to meriting regard that could be understood by a human, even though that regard could be Janus-faced.

[18] Because of the need to consider hunter memoirs in relation to their genre conventions, this chapter focuses on white hunters. The Africans who appear in these stories are generally referred to through a combination of racist, patronising, and ‘noble savage’ stereotypes. These descriptions say far more about the people writing them than about the people they purport to describe and to know so well. It would be too easy, and far too

tell a good story (Roulet 2004). A good story is not necessarily false. It is just that objectivity and comprehensiveness (the narrative equivalents of striving for ethical self-consistency and openness) are subordinated to the careful positioning of elements of self, so that certain features stand out while others are blended in or downplayed. Expressing the fullness of identity is subordinated to other processes of recognition and camouflage that determine renown and career success in relation to audiences elsewhere.[19] Thus, the challenge of reading hunter memoirs as a source of historical insight is to recognise the ways in which they are meaningful but also interested and partial accounts – without reducing meaning only to a matter of bias. Indeed, hunter memoirs, rather than an 'appendix' to the process of hunting, are a necessary and essential part of it (Dalla Bernardina 1996 cited in Roulet 2004), because while the encounter itself draws hunter and hunted into an interaction in which the human's distinctive representational capacity – language – provides little advantage and unsettles their status in relation to each other, the memoir allows the human to re-inscribe the status difference that the hunting encounter suspended and to explain it.[20] In addition, non-human

boring, simply to assess how these hunter authors measure up according to 'superior' contemporary values. Situational collaboration in hunting can temporarily remove racist cultural norms, to varying extents, in part because all stand before danger together. The lack of acknowledgement of African leadership in game hunting in this literature is nevertheless a limitation of the arguments in this chapter and one I hope will be redressed in future research.

19 Although it is most visible in the hunting zone, understanding camouflage as a way of orienting oneself in the world has far broader application. For instance, Western professional contexts demand extensive positioning or camouflage, particularly the removal of one's gendered or personal traits – such as care responsibilities – from the workplace (Moreno 1995). Camouflage helpfully shifts the discussion away from the limiting frames of truth and falsehood and towards a more accurate understanding of how people position themselves in landscapes.

20 Dalla Bernardina argues that, while philosophers have long occupied themselves with the question of whether non-human animals have rights (that is, are persons) or are more properly subjects, 'primitive' and rural societies (people for whom killing animals is part of daily life) struggle with a different question. In such contexts, it is generally taken for granted that non-human animals have personhood, in the sense of having rights. The question then becomes how to justify killing those non-human persons: how can they be deprived of the rights of personhood they had previously enjoyed (Dalla Bernardina 1991: 33)? Humans and non-humans alike engage in representation and action, but humans have an extra capacity to represent through language and thereby tell a story of how and why they did something in a moment of violence. Telling a story is an after-the-fact capacity that requires human symbolic modes, which are muted during the hunting encounter. When brought to bear later, they help bolster the human's assertion of difference from the being that was hunted. The hunting story is a way of 'nuancing the act [of killing] and potentially justifying it' (Roulet 2004: 322). The moment of giving life or death is short; the human urge to understand and explain what happened, and to gain social recognition from it, is of a much longer duration.

animals' representational capacities can be 'entextualised' (Rentería-Valencia 2015) in the stories hunters tell.

A generative move in the recent swell of interspecies ethnographies has been the turn to semiotics. Eduardo Kohn's (2013) adaptation of Charles Sanders Peirce's approach to communication in order to think through the life of the many species of the Ecuadorean Amazon has gained particular traction. Peirce argued that there are three main modes of representation: symbolic, iconic, and indexical. Symbolic representation is specific to humans and involves generating meaning from arbitrary signs, signs that acquire meaning only as part of a system of signs. Iconic representation consists of signs that are similar to what they represent, just as onomatopoeic words sound like what they describe. Indexical representation consists of signs that are affected by or otherwise correlated with what they represent. Non-humans represent both iconically and indexically. Attention to these modes of representation permits an appreciation of the active role non-humans play in life without having to mediate their participation solely through human symbolic representation, a highly imperfect translating device.

Building on Kohn's work, Rentería-Valencia describes the semiotic dynamism in which he participated through his observation of bighorn sheep hunting on Mexico's Tiburón Island:

> the 'thrill of the hunt' has nothing to do with the successful establishment of control over nature, but rather about the ephemeral articulation of sense (in terms of the decisions taken both by the hunter and by the prey) in a landscape full of open possibilities. And it is precisely in this open landscape, where those of us, observing in silence the dramatic scene unfolding before our eyes, were capable of relating to both ram and hunter, to life and death, to signs and symbols, and to the trail of meaning left behind. (Rentería-Valencia 2015: 102)

Bighorn sheep could not symbolically represent themselves, but their iconic and indexical modes of representation 'hitchhiked' in the big-game hunters' narratives (visual, oral, and written). Their appearance in a tale is mediated by the human teller. But that does not mean that their role can be reduced to simply that of foils, or that their participation is a figment of human creation.

The semiotic argument for non-human representation has produced important insights and agendas. But human–non-human hunting encounters could also be approached as a kind of social situation, as an interaction ritual marked by confrontational tension. Meaning is born of the encounter itself, and its 'senses' are mostly elaborated only after the moment has passed. The interaction ritualists (Randall Collins, as well as Erving Goffman and Émile Durkheim before him) focus almost exclusively on encounters among humans. Their 'social' is a human world. And, indeed, if we posit that a hunting encounter is intersubjective (as Collins defines entrainment), the risk in including non-humans in the analysis is that they cannot let humans in on their understanding of subjectivity (if they have one). However, it is clear that the hunted non-humans are not lifeless objects – they respond, contribute, and help make the encounters what they are. Since all parties to the encounter are reacting to each other, they are intersubjectively related, even though not all are involved in symbolically representing that intersubjectivity and they have different capacities for understanding it. In companionate (Haraway 2008) or domesticated interspecies relationships, intersubjectivity is obvious. It works differently in big-game hunting – the interaction rituals include violent ones marked above all by confrontational tension – but it is still present.

Mimicry is one way in which big-game hunters become entrained with other species. This can include mastering the calls of the animal one seeks to hunt. Long-time hunting zone game hunter Christian Le Noël learned to imitate a male lion's voice. To be loud enough to be a credible lion, he magnified his yowls with a megaphone. Lions occupy distinct territories, and hearing another male on his land would cause a lion to emerge to challenge his apparent competitor. In imitating a lion, did Le Noël become no longer fully human, but rather part human, part lion? This has been argued of Siberian elk hunters: that in the process of the hunt, they become a creature that is part human, part elk (Willerslev 2007). Big-game hunting in Central Africa does not support that 'strong ontological' (Keane 2013) claim, but mimicry and other techniques of the hunt help produce entrainment between humans and the animals they make their targets.

While a hunt can contain longueurs of little action, it also includes particularly charged moments of encounter, moments when principles or guidelines recede as the impetus to action, and emotions and split-second calculations come to the fore. Assessing what happened after the fact, people might be uncomfortable with it or unable to explain it. The Dutch photographer Ed van der Elsken, after his first and only hunting safari in 1957, wrote:

> I find I have been indulging in a great deal of moralising. I remember now that when I was in Africa, filled with the emotions of hunting, I knew nothing of all the noble sentiments and intentions expressed in my text. I often hunted enthusiastically and by no means always sportingly. Primitive instincts and passions arose in me, inciting me to capture, conquer and kill. I, too, was guilty of many dirty and cowardly tricks. I must admit this because it would be unfair if

I were to stand too much aloof from my comrades, who often stood by me in critical moments. (van der Elsken 1961: 24)

His participation made him complicit, but in retrospect it was difficult for him to identify any moment when he had been able to reflect and choose what to do, any moment when self-control could have been summoned. The morals he could espouse far from the scene of the hunt were different from those available to him during the hunting encounter itself.[21]

In his day-to-day work in the Netherlands, van der Elsken tried to capture the movement and improvisation of jazz musicians in still photographs,[22] and he experienced safari hunting as analogous: fast-paced, in-the-moment, un-choreographed. And in the case of hunting, also dangerous. Safari hunting drew him into life-and-death cooperation with people he saw as different; the other safari participants were not people he would have been friends with otherwise. Hunting encounters, as a mode of forceful acquisition, are not ethical free-for-alls, but they are nevertheless more subject to in-the-moment dynamics than other situations in which one may take time before deciding or acting. Arguably, the main reason for that situational intensity is the parties' shared capacity for force, in which we gain insight into vengeance (marking difference through force) as an impetus in social life, at least from the human perspective.

In big-game hunting (unlike, say, hunts for rabbits or small deer), humans and their intended game have the ability to kill each other. Humans kill more often and with an intensity that can appear

[21] In 1956, the year before van der Elsken made his trip, Romain Gary published his novel *Les Racines du ciel*, an early and impassioned case for the inhumanity of hunting elephants, set in the northern reaches of the hunting zone (present-day southern Chad), and its memorable characters and arguments were in van der Elsken's mind. Van der Elsken summarises Gary's intentions as follows:

> Gary says there is more to it than an animal's suffering. It has something to do with the grinning ruthlessness with which progressive civilisation and technique push aside or render inanimate everything that 'lags behind'. And so there are those who lag behind, black or white, with two legs or four. They are archaic and out-of-date. At the same time they are successful and well made. Purposeful creatures, with greatness, dignity and genuineness of their own and with their own right to live in the pattern of Nature'. (van der Elsken 1961: 24)

A film version starring Errol Flynn came out in 1958 (*The Roots of Heaven*, directed by John Huston). Gary's work was the driving force behind a wave of European and American moral outrage over elephant hunting, and van der Elsken implicitly endorsed Gary's call to protect the elephants.

[22] To use the terminology of this chapter, he captured *situations* in still photographs (Siegal 2017).

psychopathic, but they, too, can be vulnerable.[23] In his account of a lifetime hunting big game in CAR, Christian Le Noël told the stories of three fellow hunters killed by elephants. Other books include similar memorials. Of course, the humans hunted and killed elephants with vastly greater fervour than the elephants showed against them, but the results of the enterprise were not preordained and there was risk involved for the human hunter. One of the best-known big-game hunters in CAR, C. J. Pretorius, was deaf. An elephant approached him from behind, catching him unawares. The elephant swiped her trunk against him, and Pretorius died from the injury. Many big-game hunters desire precisely the particular kind of flooded consciousness one experiences in encounters marked by mutual dangerousness and the subsequent thrill of differentiating oneself from the other, whether by killing or by other means. To describe this killing as reciprocity, as subsistence hunters sometimes describe their kills (e.g. Nadasdy 2007; Willerslev 2007), would be wrong.[24] But so would describing it as no more than the exertion of white, masculine dominance over nature. In the midst of mutual human–animal dangerousness, status is at least temporarily less certain, and there is the possibility of an identification that can itself elicit concern, but also a desire for vengeance or punishment.[25]

In the wake of human killings by elephants, human hunters may announce a need for vengeance against the offending elephant. Pretorius's son Marcel, also a safari-hunting guide in CAR, tried to 'get vengeance' on behalf of his father, but failed. Others have spoken of the

[23] Many big-game hunters claim that tactics that remove the danger and work, such as hunting from a vehicle, are both morally vacuous or dubious and boring. They remove the entrainment, the social part of the interaction ritual (Le Noël 1999; Roulet 2004).

[24] In studies of 'traditional' hunting, it is common to hear of hunters striving for balance with their game. The hunters recognise the fearsomeness of taking life, but at the same time they see it as a necessary part of the world and their place in it. Some hunters even see the killing that goes into their work as a reciprocal exchange – literally, not just symbolically (Nadasdy 2007). Big-game hunting, being caught up in profit and imperialism, is instinctively imagined by liberal Westerners as entirely different: brutal, excessive, and unbalanced. And industries have indeed developed that remove the mutuality and chance that could go into hunting large animals, such as the 'canned hunts' on offer for wealthy tourists in Southern Africa (Schroeder 2018). Big-game hunters certainly do not share some vaunted ontological principle such as balance. Some big game hunters strive to maximise kills by any means, caring little for place or inhabitants over the long term. Others place greater value on the pursuit and on being sporting, and on personal discipline.

[25] 'Like the first love affair in one's life, the first dangerous animal one meets leaves indelible memories,' wrote hunting guide Le Noël (1999: 8). While it is left ambiguous in this instance, big-game hunters frequently portray their game as masculine until the point of conquest, at which point it becomes feminised, regardless of its actual sex. When it comes to big game, legally only males are to be hunted, but this regulation is a guideline only sometimes observed.

need to 'punish' elephants that maul or otherwise wrong humans (Grasselli 2007[26]).[27] 'It is a tradition among the French professional hunters that when an animal kills one of their numbers, others will pursue the animal and kill it. After all, that animal, once having killed a human, can become a rogue, a murderer that will kill any human it encounters' (Le Noël 1999: 22). Of course, the same could be said of the human big-game hunters: they pursued elephants with such a single-minded intensity as to strain the sense of how humans behave properly. These humans, too, were rogues.

Vengeance is a topic at once classic in anthropology yet also under-theorised, perhaps because it has mostly been studied in relation to people living in 'traditional' ways and has therefore been described as part of functional cultural systems. Big-game hunters' invocations of vengeance recall that it is a desire born of uncertainty over status, a desire to restore a feeling of dominance. After all, one seeks vengeance only

[26] Often one person will occupy different roles in relation to hunting and its regulation over the course of their career. Giorgio Grasselli is a good example. He began his career obtaining licences to shoot 'problem elephants' in Cameroon, a system with some similarities to the *salatieh* system of old. In the 1970s Grasselli decamped for what was then Rhodesia and became involved in another kind of hunting as well: that of 'terrorists' – the people fighting against the white-run government. Grasselli received paramilitary training and entered a special police unit of big-game hunters. In addition to operating tours for big-game hunters, Grasselli also hosted visitors – mostly Americans and South Africans – who wanted to 'do something for the cause' (2007: 177). These included an American bounty hunter named Dave, and a Chicago police karate instructor and owner of a demolition company named John, who came with his friend, the editor of *Soldier of Fortune* magazine. 'I took them hunting and we also tried to hunt out – though to no avail – very different kinds of prey, which was the object of their safari!' (Grasselli 2007: 177–8). These tourists, especially the Americans, who could 'buy any kind of weapon in the United States', were helpful in bringing in more guns and ammunition for the besieged white community, more and more of whom felt like they were being hunted, in their own houses, by the people Grasselli refers to only as terrorists. Later he hunted 'poachers' in CAR.

[27] Through conservation and animal control policies, vengeance against non-human animals became a prerogative of government in many African countries, rather than a matter for individuals, in the 1950s and 1960s. 'Problem elephants' (those that were going after crops and sometimes charging the people who tried to scare them away) became 'wanted' creatures. Problem elephants were those that transgressed the bush–village boundary and did not know their place in the human-decided spatial order of species. Hunting them was a way of re-differentiating them. And yet, as we have seen repeatedly, the intersubjective and entrained terms of the hunting encounter often undermined the differentiation that the instigator of the hunt intended to achieve. In some places, dedicated staff dealt with outlaw elephants. George Rushby, for one, had this job for the last decades of his career. He claimed to have killed hundreds of elephants in the name of reducing an unsustainable overpopulation. In other places, such as Cameroon, one could obtain a commission to kill the offending elephant, with payment coming in the form of the ivory the human hunter cut from the corpse.

against those one fears are similar to oneself, in relation to whom one feels a need to 'make a point', and the act of vengeance is a feat meant to say something about oneself. (Killing the mosquito that bites you is hardly an act of vengeance.) Vengeance is rarely neat, because it generally brings someone new into the relationship; the dead cannot seek vengeance, but their relations very well may. Although vengeance might be imagined as a means of restoring balance, it rarely does so. In fact, it is more likely to perpetuate itself. It is a means of bringing about collaboration (even if posthumous) among people, such as big-game hunters, who might like to think of themselves as solo operators or otherwise not prone to working together. Vengeance thus elicits how violence and status are claimed in relation to each other, and through interactions marked by confrontational tension and the possibility of 'going rogue' in relation to norms of judiciousness or care in less entrained moments.

Elephants cannot talk about how they experience rogue humans, but they have certainly changed their ways of life in relation to them. When Karamojo Bell came to Oubangui-Chari at the turn of the twentieth century, he described a place where elephants had not yet learned to be as afraid of humans as they were in places with longer histories of for-profit gun hunting: 'after the shot I was astonished to see elephant emerge from the busy parts, strolling aimlessly about, apparently quite unscared by the sound of a rifle. I went through crowds and crowds of them, getting a bull here and there. It was many years since I had seen elephant so unacquainted with firearms' (1960 [1923]: 160–1). This did not last. Many thousands of elephants were killed. Dragged into hunting encounters with 'rogue humans', elephants changed the ways they lived. They spent more time in areas with dense vegetation that prevented the rogues the line of sight required for effective use of a gun. (At close range, being stronger is a greater advantage than a firearm, since the guns of the time took time to load and aim.) Of course, the fact that certain species adjust their behaviour in relation to others is not evidence that the non-humans have experienced entrainment, but the moves they might make in the moment of danger – charging, running, alerting, huddling – show that they are not indifferent to circumstance.

As important as vengeance has been to big-game hunters' stories about themselves, they recognise that its value, too, can be disrupted by the particulars of confrontational tension in a given instance. In a story recounted by Le Noël, a hunting guide had been killed by an elephant, and Jean-Claude, a safari-hunting guide, undertook vengeance. He would know the elephant in question by the gunshot wound it had sustained during the previous altercation. Jean-Claude and his party tracked the elephant for a week. When they finally found the elephant, they were fully face to face, so close that:

> Jean-Claude knew he would be helpless if the elephant charged ... [T]he big elephant did not seem to be suffering from its wound. Then, as Jean-Claude lowered his rifle, the elephant turned around, dropped its trunk to the ground and retreated back into the forest gallery. The retreat was as sudden and as silent as its approach. The tusks were long and straight and while the trophy was not exceptional, it was good. Yet, something told the professional hunter not to shoot again at this elephant. It is hard to explain to one who has never flirted with death that there are times when you don't fire the rifle even though the adversary is close and coming. Strange things can happen. By the same twist of fate that made Jean-Claude decide not to fire at the elephant, it in turn elected not to charge Jean-Claude. This was a truly dramatic confrontation. Although he wanted to avenge his colleague's death, something told Jean-Claude that he should not shoot. There is indeed a thin line between the moment when you give life by taking your finger off the trigger, or give death by unchaining the thunder of your weapon. (Le Noël 1999: 220)

He could have added: or give death by swiping with a trunk and trampling. While we cannot know what guided the elephant's moves (or why the elephant did not do otherwise), the elephant and Jean-Claude faced each other, they could not ignore each other, and the threat they constituted to each other was central to the terms of that entrainment, even as, with distance, it contributed to Jean-Claude's changed consideration of his status in relation to this elephant as an individual, which likely informed his future actions towards elephants in general (although he continued to hunt them).

Big-game hunting is one story of how violence can be part of a meaningful repertoire of social relations, yet without necessarily arising from hatred or denial of the target's sentience. How is it that violence and growing intersubjectivity can go together, without ultimately calling the perceived plan to kill into question? When the creature killed is essential to subsistence, the hunter's justifications seem more reasonable than when the being is killed for some other, more obviously acquisitive, reason. In the case of manhunts, the justifications marshalled after the fact seem even more morally compromised. And yet we know that violence is not always enacted as a function of a cause (Collins 2009), such as hatred, nor is it always the culminating act of an enduring process of dehumanising othering. It is also crucial to consider the interplay between entrainment, a shared intensity of experience, and vengeance or other demands for acknowledgment of one's worthiness, an assertion frequently supported by showing oneself to be dangerous.

Conclusion: violence and the limits of controlling hunting

Violence, particularly in the form of forcible acquisition amid status uncertainty, has been an important part of repertoires of meaningful action in the hunting zone, but clear assignments of its morality are most easily made at a remove – spatially or temporally – from the encounters themselves. Those who are intimately involved in the encounters see them as bringing values into tension,[28] and, through the entrainment they entail, limiting the importance of deontological principle to the conduct of action. Within and between species, entrainment in interactions marked by mutual dangerousness creates its own kind of knowledge, accessed through encounters charged by emotion and physical danger, in which indexical and iconic modes of representation are more important than the symbolic language available only to humans. Those who attempt to control hunting are not immune to these tendencies. They are making their own claims to status through forceful acquisition.

One outcome of all of this is that regulation and avoidance of regulation, rather than being based on rules and principles, are based on more proximate, interactional moves. This means that regulation does not always tend towards consistency, or the pursuit of an ethical self, as ethics are frequently understood (Laidlaw 2013). But nor are acquisition or raiding ethics necessarily a matter of pure spontaneity. Rather, regulation amid raiding occurs through encounters in which parties can become entrained, and through that identification identify with another, and that identification can inspire protection and/or violence. These processes are far more illuminating of hunting or raiding and attempts to regulate it than the usual explanations, which frequently assume turpitude or corruption on the part of the people involved. Moreover,

[28] Big-game hunting and the enforcement of hunting policy include paradoxes and conflicts in values, both among humans and between humans and other species. Here are three realms in which this is the case:

1) Big-game hunting only became possible through the imperialist-capitalist world system and technologies (guns) developed for it. And yet relatively quickly governments decided that it was a realm that was to be protected from a drive for profit, and indeed profit hunters have consistently been vilified by other big-game hunters.
2) Even if we do not go so far as to describe tracking as a process of seduction (Kohn 2013), it requires mimicry and closeness, and in the process engenders an awareness of one's target's sentience; and yet the overall goal remains to kill. For game hunters and hunting guards, too, there is dissonance in this process.
3) Roles are changeable: the humans sent to stop 'poachers' were often themselves illicit hunters at one point in time. They understand the thrill of poaching at the same time as they know their job is to enforce the law.

these processes cut across and disrupt social categories, including those of species.

Other studies of places where regulatory authority is pluralised have usefully differentiated between (il)licit and (il)legal (e.g. Roitman 2005, 2006). What is illegal might not also be considered illicit by those involved, just as what is legal might not be considered licit. Hunting games tend to destabilise such categories. It is not that what is illegal is seen as licit, or that what is legally mandated is seen as illicit, but rather that people's understanding of the categories is in tension, resulting in ethical assessments that depend greatly on the details of situations as they play out. Who is involved? What do they know about each other? In what ways do their assessments of a counterpart's status shape their relationships? What actions are taken? How long do they intend to maintain the relationship with other humans, with other animals, or with the space? Big-game hunting and controlling it draw parties who are potentially dangerous to each other – game hunter and elephant; game hunter and hunting inspector – into contact. The contact can experientially entrain them in complex ways, making the regulation – legal or otherwise – more a matter of social situation than is the case in places where law and routine provide deep grooves that channel one's interactions.

But however they are understood, hunting encounters – between large animals and those who would hunt them, as well as between game hunters and those who would arrest them – have an emotional complexity that some deny and others maintain, without this diminishing their commitment to their acquisitive work. The importance of regulatory sociality and liberty amid competing claims to forcibly acquire became more pronounced as anti-hunting conservation policies became more confrontational in the final decades of the twentieth century.

5 The limits of law in coercive conservation

Seeing the hunting zone like a ...

James C. Scott (1998) described what it means to 'see like a state', and how state vision tries to override other ways of seeing. In the hunting zone, there remain many ways of seeing.

A geographer would see north-eastern CAR as wet, with a varied landscape of rocky plateaus, grassy plains, and forested savannah. A geographer would see a terrain once inhabited by many humans, now almost entirely empty of them. A geographer would see a puzzle. CAR is the 'most natural and easiest' means of moving from the Mediterranean and the Sahara south to Southern Africa, yet that has never happened; instead, it is a 'unique case on earth' for the near total loss of place names that has accompanied its loss of humans due to *razzia*, disease, and colonial manhunts (Boulvert 1996: 310).

A cattle herder would see in north-eastern CAR a land of grasses so rich[1] that heifers fed on it give birth to not one calf but twins. A herder would see a promised land of water even during the dry season, particularly compared with the increasingly parched lands to the north where herders spend the rest of the year (Tomety 2009: 11). A herder would notice very few humans making claims to territory, and if humans were around, the herder would find that he might negotiate use access to uninhabited land – or just take it – although the people with fields can also be unpredictable and may cause difficulties.[2]

Seeing like someone born and raised in this area, one would see it as home, with the comfort, pride, tastes, and habits that concept carries with it.

[1] The grasses in question are especially *echinochloa stagina* and *e. pyramidalis*, two varieties of wild millet (interview, 3 October 2009).

[2] The category 'cattle herder' is very diverse and includes young men pasturing herds many hundred strong as employees of big men (often military officers) in Chad and Sudan as well as family groups moving with their own herds. Central Africans describe the young men as unconcerned about making accommodations with others, and the families as more likely to develop long-term interests and relationships with people living in north-eastern CAR (Tomety 2009).

And yet it is also 'bizarre' (the term chosen by a friend from Tiringoulou, one of the area's few towns) because in a world supposedly divided into states, with their practices of creating and caring for citizens, people here are instead 'abandoned' by a state that does not care for them at all.

One of the very few government officials assigned to north-eastern CAR who actually travels to the zone would see an area without acceptable schools, and where managing money is risky and a hassle, because salaries are paid into bank accounts accessible only in the capital, Bangui. Such an official would see an area where everything relating to the use of uninhabited areas is illegal, although enforcement of every law must be negotiated.[3]

A conservationist would see an area of both crisis and opportunity. Crisis because animal populations have plummeted since the 1970s – published results for the last major wildlife survey for north-eastern CAR, conducted in 2010, bore the title 'Game Over! Wildlife Collapse in Northern Central African Republic'. But seeing like a conservationist, there is always hope: the authors also suggested that if the area were leased to private concessionaires to manage, the animal populations might rebound (Bouché et al. 2012).[4] Seeing like a conservationist, one would see this as an area where humans – those born and living in the area and those whose homes are more properly in Chad or Sudan – are hunting animals and/or herding their cows with no thought for the long-term sustainability of their actions. With the eyes of a conservationist, one sees north-eastern CAR as being different from other places because the government has assigned an unusually high percentage of land to conservation,[5] although officials in the capital have few proprietary interests in managing it.

[3] During my time in Ndele, I spent several mornings with the local tax collector, who was briefly resident in town. He explained every tax he was supposed to collect (market taxes, etc.) and described people in town as stubborn and unwilling to pay. Theoretically he could call on the local *gendarmerie* to support his collection efforts, but he had no direct relationship with them. In theory they were part of the same entity – 'the state' – but, in practice, they did not collaborate. And while he had a safe in which he was supposed to store the tax money he collected, a previous occupant of his post had lost the key, so instead he had to try to hide the money at his home, which inserted variables such as theft into his bookkeeping practices.

[4] Large mammal populations in northern CAR declined by about 94 per cent between 1978 and 2010, although the declines were not uniform across species. Elephants have been almost completely eliminated. Although the aerial survey method does not account for whether some have moved outside the area, it does account for the many elephant cadavers sighted (Bouché et al. 2012: 7004).

[5] Overall, some 16 per cent of CAR's territory is allocated to conservation (for example, it is a national park or hunting/fauna reserve), and 31.5 per cent is reserved for big-game hunting (the highest percentage in Africa [Binot, Castel, and Caron 2006]) – or, to be more specific given the recent (post-2007) collapse of the safari-hunting industry, it is

Seeing like an international humanitarian, one notices an area with profoundly difficult logistics that cause costs per 'beneficiary' to be higher than anywhere else in the world.[6] The humanitarian sees people who are impoverished and suffer from high levels of violence. And the humanitarian does not clearly see the details of that violence, which often remain blurred: 'armed men' attack a village, but their identity remains obscure and the following week this attack is superseded by another.[7]

Seen by an anthropologist – or, more properly, seen by me – the lands the maps denote as north-eastern CAR are special because all these different ways of seeing it, and many more besides, coexist, not always peacefully. No high modernist state has tried to 'see' this area through the hegemonic remaking that defines such states (Scott 1998). Instead, people negotiate licit practice while norms remain plural, and recourse to force or the threat of it is frequent. State laws and the international frameworks they latch onto (for example, conservation pacts) are important because they can facilitate connections to people and resources elsewhere, and because everyone in north-eastern CAR – 'local' or incomer – is familiar with the idea that the world is supposed to be divided into states and only states make laws. Most, though, do not think that CAR or its laws provide a usable framework to orient one's striving for an ethical life.

From my field of vision, north-eastern CAR is a striking case of conservation's struggle to survive violent competition. Throughout Africa, colonial-era conservation policies that stipulated vast parklands uninhabited by humans have largely continued post-independence. Conservation and the management of depopulated lands are particularly striking examples of how 'minimal' was the reform that characterised the shift to nation states on the continent (Mamdani 1996) – even the individuals involved often remained the same. Colonial officials created international conservation organisations to ensure that they could retain a key role in wildlife and wild-space management (Schauer 2018). In the last few decades, armed conflict – war, rebellion, robber gangs, and

reserved for *potential* big-game hunting concessions. These protected areas are not spread equally across the country but primarily cover the north-east (Roulet 2004).

6 Interview with international humanitarian administrator whose organisation works in every conflict hot spot, March 2018.

7 In Ndele in 2009–10 I would attend meetings at the United Nations office that would gather a few government representatives, employees of the area's few newly arrived international humanitarian organisations, and other local leaders to discuss 'security incidents', the details of which were generally obscure since they occurred in villages that few attendees had visited themselves. Newly arrived mobile phone towers created islands of communication, not networks; they 'hopped', to borrow the term James Ferguson (2006) has used to describe capital mobility in Africa.

armed exploitation of resources – has come to mark the region, and access to the parklands and the goods they contain has become all the more contested. This is the case in Cameroon (Kelly 2015), in Chad (Fay 2007), in the Democratic Republic of the Congo (Marijnen 2017), in South Sudan,[8] and in CAR – that is, in every country in this region, and beyond. North-eastern CAR provides one example of armed conservation among a number of comparable cases.

Many studies of armed conservation have tracked how it augments the power of the state or state-like actors, as well as the historical continuities of its modes of oppression in postcolonial locales (e.g. Büscher 2013; Devine 2014; Duffy 2010, 2014; Kelly 2011; Lunstrum 2014; Marijnen and Verweijen 2018; Neumann 1998, 2004b). In many ways, armed conservation in north-eastern CAR could be fitted into these narratives and arguments too. It has been particularly violent, though hardly one-sided. But where much of the focus in armed conservation literature is on struggles for political authority (or 'public authority' [Marijnen 2018]), much can be seen by looking at practices of forceful acquisition amid uncertainties about status. In pursuing those practices, authority (in the sense of control) is not necessarily an advantage. Although all these relationships are shot through with power dynamics, an examination of the roles of law and ethics draws out tendencies that a focus on politics and authority can miss.

A thicket of state laws continues to prohibit much of everyday life in the hunting zone, particularly regarding hunting itself, and significantly affecting wild acquisition and privilege. The laws are spectacularly out of tune with the realities of people's lives and the capacities of public authority in such a remote and infrastructure-poor space. State law does not reliably guide the actions of conservationists, the area's few state officials, others living in the area, or anyone else, although people give different explanations for why the laws do not, should not, or cannot guide their actions and interactions. And yet people living in the area recognise that state law is supposed to be special – more dominant or legitimate – and cite this as a reason why they cannot make their own law. Ultimately, then, all dispute- or access-regulating practices are perpetually negotiated and improvised.

The total illegalisation of life in a context in which state-like control is so enfeebled (whether enacted by official government employees or by others) means that the law tends simultaneously to be weak in determining what people should do and to be invoked in particularly overbearing

[8] Interviews with international conservationists in Juba, December 2011.

fashion when circumstances make it possible. Like colonialism, conservation is a geographically and socially discontinuous and multi-scalar project (Vandergeest and Peluso 2015; Verweijen and Marijnen 2018). Rather than an entity that manages 'its' population in a proprietary or shepherd-like way, conservation entails the interplay of audiences and enablers far from the space in question yet concerned by it (funders, conservation supporters, exposers of neocolonial abuse) with people on the ground, who participate in conservation without wishing to relinquish autonomy in managing their careers, relations, and needs for acquisition.

Given such dynamics, the concept of law (Hart 1961) is limited in its ability to guide inquiry into social life in the area. Even legal pluralism and its variants do not help much, since they describe overlapping and intertwined systems of reciprocal obligation that can be drawn on in relation to people or problems. Instead, armed conservation in north-eastern CAR draws out practices of making visible or hiding across social, geographic-physical, and legal-bureaucratic landscapes, to facilitate projects in the area and connections to areas beyond. It is a realm marked more by ethics than by law. Differentiating law from ethics is somewhat naïve (they are, of course, not mutually exclusive), but doing so accounts for the fraught obligations of reciprocity in this context, and it allows consideration of the interaction rituals between *particular* people engaging with each other in *particular* situations, rather than placing the explanatory emphasis on categories of people in their relation to abstract principles. So, while north-eastern CAR certainly has much to contribute as a study of armed conservation among other cases of armed conservation, it is more broadly relevant as a means to explore the interpersonal repertoires developed in the midst of situations in which law is not much of a guide to action.

A methodological note: although I strive to avoid prior normative assumptions, my access to different perspectives about the use of north-eastern CAR's spaces and resources was not equally easy with all people. In particular, the 'foreign' herders and hunters were generally inaccessible to me, and their perspectives are sketched through their 'entextualisation' and 'semiotic hitchhiking' (Rentería-Valencia 2015) in others' accounts. Without claiming to represent their points of view, then, my methods nevertheless allow an appreciation of the blindnesses and assumptions of those whose voices, documents, and practices I could observe and with whom I could engage directly. Others, too, had varied levels of interest in talking and spending time with me. Respecting people's preferences in that respect is key to ethnographic ethics and one reason why I try to be careful not to over-hastily assign causality to a category of actor and to appreciate situational and interpersonal circumstances and vagaries.

Illegality all the way down

Today, if a Central African in, say, Ndele, the metropolis of the northeast and the furthest town from the capital with an appreciable government presence, wanted to hunt legally, he would need to obtain a number of permits. First, if he wanted to hunt with a gun, he would have to obtain a firearm purchase authorisation, which costs 30,000–50,000 CFA (approximately US$60–US$100, or £40–£75) depending on the type of gun. With that permit in hand, the new gun-owner would still need to buy a gun and then pay an annual tax of 5,000 CFA (approximately US$10, or £8) to keep his *carnet d'arme légal* up to date. All such fees are levied on foreign-produced guns. Locally made guns, referred to as *ganapoint* (Berman with Lombard 2008), are illegal. They are, however, what most people use for their hunting.[9]

But suppose a Central African did obtain a foreign weapon and the necessary permits. (This never occurred while I was in Ndele, nor was

[9] In many ways, the current system is the perpetuation of the racialised colonial legal system. Where before, through the *indigénat*, race was the dividing line, now ability to pay is: for large game, for instance, the trophy fees are so high that no area resident could ever afford them. Central African historian E. Kouroussou Gaoukane summarises what colonial hunting laws did:

> White people, benefiting from impunity, were the first to violate hunting and firearms regulations … Central Africans could not understand why the administration would deny them what they consider their patrimony, the right of usufruct in common lands, which people had always used to feed themselves without any authority opposing them. (Gaoukane 1986: 172–3)
>
> [Les blancs, jouissant de l'impunité, étaient les premiers à violer les règlements sur la chasse et le régime d'armes … Le centrafricain n'arrive pas à s'expliquer que l'Administration le prive de ce qu'il considère comme un patrimoine, le droit d'usufruit sur les terroirs communautaires, et où l'on est habitué depuis toujours à tirer sa nourriture, sans qu'une autorité quelconque ne s'y oppose.]

In Oubangui-Chari, African hunting was rendered illegal in two main ways. First, African access to firearms was to be severely limited (Gaoukane 1986: 171–2); and second, African hunting practices – involving trapping, snares, nets, poison, and fire – were deemed less ethical than European ones and were therefore outlawed (MacKenzie 1988; Roulet 2004). Guns were seen as better because they could minimise the time it took for the animal to die. Interest in minimising the length of time it takes for an animal to die is relatively recent, and even today sometimes other considerations take precedence, such as not scaring away other potential game by firing another shot (van der Elsken 1961), or being able to claim that you killed with only one shot, even if it takes a long time for death to arrive (Loveridge 2018). Whereas women frequently participated in net hunting and other more collaborative methods, with the shift towards using guns their roles were eliminated.

there any record of its having occurred in the previous two years of record keeping.) He would now need to obtain hunting permits. These cost between 30,000 and 50,000 CFA depending on the type of game sought and must be renewed annually. In 2008–9 and 2009–10, the Ministry of Water and Forests office in Ndele issued exactly one hunting permit, and it was to a foreign safari-hunting tourist. Then there are all the restrictions on where one may hunt. Ndele is surrounded by protected areas – the country's largest national parks abut it (Figure 5.1) – and animal hunting is allowed in only a narrow buffer zone around the town. But the game has all gone from that area, so if one wants to actually catch an animal, one must go into the areas where hunting is prohibited.

It would be hard to overstate how disconnected from people's lives the hunting regulations are. Few people in Ndele have cash-based livelihoods, and the sums required to hunt legally are enormous in relation to people's day-to-day liquidity. (People can marshal surprising sums from relations when truly needed, no one sees abiding by hunting regulations as a serious need.) Moreover, game meat is much prized. It is not eaten because there is nothing else, but because it is far preferred to other sources of calories: it is tastier and more filling, and in smoked form lasts longer (Roulet 2004).[10] Game meat is a hugely important part of the region's gift economies (Lombard 2013a). I saw it, usually smoked, for sale in the Ndele market nearly every day.

So, to all intents and purposes, it is impossible to hunt legally, but people hunt quite a lot. Safari hunters, because they transit through Bangui, where licence checks are more frequent, and because they have more access to cash and familiarity with institutionalised regulation, are more likely to obtain gun and hunting permits (Roulet 2004). But that does not mean that legal hunting rules necessarily determine their practices more than they do for others. Accounts of safari hunters breaching hunting and conservation rules are legion (e.g. those recounted in Le Noël 1999; PDRN 1995). In sub-Saharan Africa, 'the transgression of the rules of the hunt, whether legislative or deontological, is an everyday reality' (Roulet 2004: 285).[11]

It is not entirely accurate to present hunting regulations as transparent, though out of touch with people's realities. Even the people tasked with implementing the law have little in the way of legal texts at their disposal, and only occasionally do they receive word when regulations change. At the Ministry of Water and Forests in Ndele, the effective head

[10] My own interviews.
[11] '[L]a transgression de la règle cynégétique, qu'elle soit législative ou déontologique, est chose commune.'

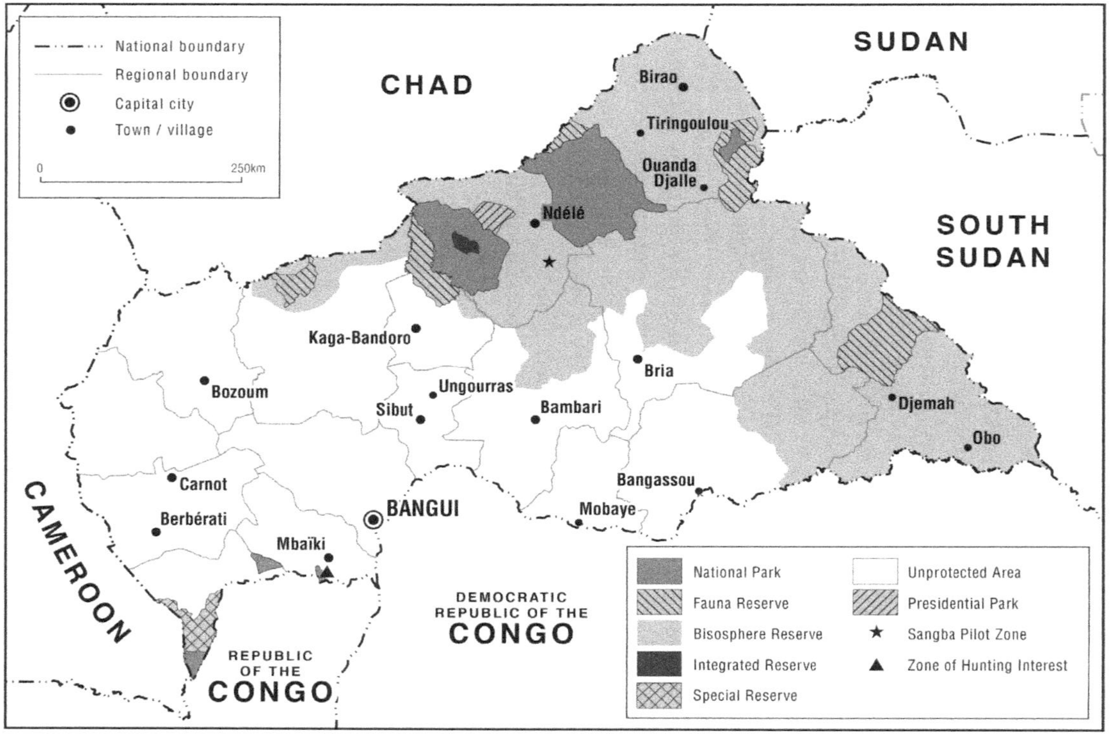

Figure 5.1 Map of protected areas in the Central African Republic

of office,[12] Marcel, had only a copy of the 1958 register for Afrique Équatoriale Française, a tome the thickness of several telephone books that recorded all the colonial government's decisions that year. At home for safekeeping (government offices have a tendency to be looted), he had a copy of the wildlife law of 1984. He brought it to show me one day, and I carefully read its articles 81 through 93, which regulate the ivory trade. Hunting elephants was legal then but was banned later that year (as Marcel well knew), but he did not have access to printed versions of any subsequent texts. Were he to seek to enforce hunting regulations (not something he frequently did), it would be difficult for his targets to know whether he was faithfully applying a government rule or issuing his own command.

Yet Marcel was fully cognisant of the bind that legal hunting regulations imposed on people in the area, even though he saw those people – Muslim, hot-tempered – as essentially different from him – Christian, a successful farmer of marketable crops (tomatoes and spinach). Marcel argued that the key '*compétence technique*' (technical competency) that was required for someone in his position was that of flexibility. In theory, his job required him to seize any and all meat that had been procured in parklands and protected areas. This is where most meat in Ndele comes from, due to both the depopulation of animals in the buffer zone and a lack of consensus as to exactly how large that zone is. As Marcel explained to me during one of our many hours-long conversations spanning the mornings when he was in the office:

> The law in the parks is very harsh. It is truly categorical. All humans are prohibited from entering the park. You can't even pluck a leaf, or kill a single animal. All is prohibited.[13] But Ndele is right inside the park. If we didn't allow people to go into the parks a bit, no one could live here. There would be no city of Ndele.

For these reasons, Marcel said, the laws placed a heavy moral and practical burden on him. 'It weighs on you,' he said on multiple occasions, often accompanying the statement with a slow shake of his head.

[12] I write 'effective' because, according to the organisation chart, he was only the third in command, but his two superiors either were not in Ndele or did not come to the office. This is yet another example of a case of no one wanting to be known to be in charge, since then claims could be made on them. Claiming that the person pulling the strings is in fact someone who is not present is also a useful way of defusing tension when conflicts arise.

[13] According to the letter of the law, the rules are not as harsh as Marcel described. People *are* allowed to enter national parks. They can pluck leaves, too. They are simply not supposed to hunt or use unsustainably the valuable things found there.

'Sometimes, in one's capacity as an African,[14] one is obliged to close one's eyes.' He further explained:

> The peasant will say, 'That meat is my life, my livelihood,' pleading for you not to take it. He will say, 'I will give you this' – either money or a part of the meat – in exchange for you not seizing everything. And then people complain that we are corrupt! So you see, it is a very technical work that we do.

In Marcel's conception, 'technical' work was defined by balancing interests, negotiating, and allowing people (including but not limited to him) to make a living through acquisition.[15] And, indeed, whatever the laws say, acquisition in all its forms, particularly from wild spaces, has been key to livelihood and profit, and a major realm of innovation – both in terms of wild goods and in terms of the kinds of seizure or tribute claimed by people such as Marcel.[16]

When it comes to forceful acquisition in the hunting zone, there is 'illegality all the way down',[17] and these practices are not well captured by invoking 'law'. This is an unusual argument for an anthropologist to

[14] 'In one's capacity as an African' is a poignant statement of the continuing colonial hierarchies of positioning in the world; see also Ferguson (2006) on speaking 'as an African'.

[15] There was another reason for the delicate nature of Marcel's work, namely that the hierarchy that was supposed to secure his control of the guards subordinate to him was unstable. As I recounted in an earlier article (Lombard 2016a), Marcel was occasionally terrorised by the guards whose jobs owed much to their having proven themselves dangerous. This was a variant on 'keep your friends close but keep your enemies closer': more precisely, 'ignore the negligible but placate the potential threats'.

[16] 'L'agriculture nourrit; la cueillette rapporte' – 'Agriculture feeds; gathering brings returns,' say Central Africans (cited in Piermay 1977: 348). That is, farming is a way to feed oneself, but making money entails being skilled at obtaining goods located in areas not generally inhabited by humans. To the extent that figures exist, they bear out Central Africans' assessment. Agriculture is an important source of nourishment, but so is gathering, and gathered products can be sold more easily and at higher prices than anything cultivated (Piermay 1977). Cities have been growing, and new urban residents desire the goods and tastes of their rural roots as well as of the 'exotic' north. The most-needed product is wood, in branch or charcoal form, for cooking fires, as well as wild grasses used for roofs, and bamboo. Fish and game meat (smoked and fresh) is also in high demand, as is honey. Ironically, some of the other products in demand are those people developed a taste for through the colonial forced labour regimes. The rubber they had been made to collect was only one part of the plant (*Manihot glaziovii*), and the leaves make for a tasty boiled sauce. Other wild products go to export markets; these include the bark of the *Rauvolfia vomitoria* root, which has pharmaceutical uses, Ethiopian pepper (*Capsicum frutescens*), and wax (Piermay 1977: 347). These trades – pretty much all illegal or at least illicit – have arguably been the source of greatest innovation in the rural economy and constitute important connections between urban and rural areas. By the early 2000s, thousands of tons of 'bush meat' were being sold at the main markets in Bangui each year (Roulet 2004).

[17] Here I am riffing on the expression 'turtles all the way down' – a colloquial way of referring to the problem of infinite regress. In the expression, the Earth rests on the back of a turtle; that turtle is standing on another; and so on for as far as anyone can travel, and beyond.

make, as one of the driving goals of legal anthropology has been to broaden the scope of what counts as 'law' since Bronisław Malinowski (1926) did just that in the first fieldwork-based legal ethnography. It was more common at the time to argue that 'primitive' people had custom but not law. Malinowski agreed that the Trobriand Islanders he studied had customs, but he added that they also had law in the form of a system of obligations. During the early decades of legal ethnography it remained necessary to explain the content of the category of law (if not define it) in order to bolster the claim that non-Westerners had it (e.g. Llewellyn and Hoebel 1941). With the capacity for law established as universal (at least among scholars), a new focus arose: namely, to argue for a porous conception of law that encompasses everything from government statutes to neighbourhood arrangements (Sousa Santos 1987). The benefit of this argument is that it captures the way in which legal questions are socially embedded in realms beyond those of formal law.

But there is also a drawback in broadening 'law' or leaving it vaguely defined. In classic legal anthropological definitions, law was understood as obligatory,[18] entailing a reciprocal understanding of what should happen following the breach of a value or right (Pospíšil 1972). In north-eastern CAR, state law takes up space, yet without providing anything like a guide to action or facilitating reciprocal obligations. People in north-eastern CAR recognise the privileged status of state law to the extent that they feel they cannot make their own laws,[19] but state law organises neither obligations nor duties in the zone.

Instead, there is a mix of ideas, practices, and justifications related to proper access to the space's wild sources of wealth. Some herders (many of whom also hunt) pay taxes to heads of villages for the right to acquire from open spaces, principally grass for their cows and wild animals to eat or smoke and transport for sale elsewhere. Others pay similar fees to the personal agents of the few mayors in the area. Some people welcome conservation projects and their rules for managing wild spaces and what they contain; others decry them. Many support conservation but denounce its strictures when they apply to them. In short, there is no coherent system of reciprocal obligations or duties organising access to the open spaces' saleable and livelihood resources, and people adapt principles to the particularities of 'ethical moments' (Zigon 2007: 138) when routine does not channel their actions. Some people describe

[18] Obligation is different from coercion or morality (Hart 1961), and it is what makes law law, as opposed to something else.

[19] This lack of law-making authority comes up frequently when conflicts over conservation strictures arise.

actions that are illegal according to the letter of the law as morally licit. This is similar to how Roitman (2006) described cross-border traders in northern Cameroon. But their justification often rests on a claim that an exception made for 'us' is valid, but it should not be made for 'them', where membership in either category depends on the configuration of the situation (people, circumstances, etc.). The son of a local notable caught hunting or mining in the park, for instance, will generally have more powerful defenders than a peasant who insists that he was hired by a conservation tracker-guard to mine in the park but then has everything seized by a rival tracker-guard.[20]

Perhaps, then, north-eastern CAR is yet another case where illegalisation is a driver of increasing disorder, as Jean and John Comaroff have argued (2006). But disorder is only one of the possible consequences when law is displaced by ethical considerations of what should be done in tricky or novel situations and by the use (or threat) of force in the face of status uncertainties. Living in some key senses 'without law', people have developed skills for profitably pursuing their careers and livelihoods. Subsequent chapters use histories of armed conservation to examine what those skills have looked like in terms of ethics and coercion. But first it is important to further set the scene of what armed conservation has looked like.

Not just us and them

Conservation initiatives in north-eastern CAR are the continuation of a decidedly colonial legacy. Time and again, outsiders present African practices of acquiring goods from uninhabited spaces as destructive and unsustainable, to use the recent jargon. In many cases, these claims of African destructiveness have simply been wrong. Think of the colonial officials who saw 'Arab' hunters as singularly destructive, even though it was European commercial hunters who instigated the killing of the largest numbers of elephants and bought from those 'Arabs'. More recently, take the case of desertification, diagnosed in many places in Africa. Scholars and aid or policy people all argued that overgrazing by cattle was causing landscapes to become deserts. More careful, less polemical study has led to the repudiation of the idea of desertification in general (more common are cycles of drought and rain, which may be longer or shorter) and in particular of the idea that pastoralists are uniquely destructive (Behnke and Mortimore 2016; Benjaminsen 2017; Brockington 2002).

[20] Incidents with these basic features occurred during my fieldwork in Ndele.

However, the fact that many ideas about how best to manage Central African lands and wild animals have relied on colonial and racist arguments does not mean that other ways of thinking about acquisition and its future are inherently more enlightened or moral. People in the hunting zone are not content with their place in the world. They lament the changes they notice in the wild landscapes around them, which seem drier and devoid of the animals – giraffes, buffalo – that older people vividly remember encountering on their long childhood walks to school. They have been innovators, including in technological realms, as Clapperton Mavhunga (2014) describes in the case of hunting and wild-space work in Zimbabwe. But whereas Mavhunga relies on the framework of a repressive, racist colonial 'them' and a dynamic, active, and moral African 'us', north-eastern CAR does not fall into such a neat dichotomy. This is first because 'African' is a highly differentiated and stratified category, and second because, regardless of whether balanced and coherent modes of 'natural acquisition' existed at some point in the past, Africans have long been involved in forceful acquisition for profit or coercion too, and it is hard to separate these things. Indeed, interlocutors in north-eastern CAR recognise two, seemingly contradictory, things: that the taking of wild goods for long-distance commerce is probably not going to be possible forever; and that gathering in some form has been a major source of well-being and profit making in the hunting zone.

Both Central Africans and proponents of conservation agendas from outside the area share a language for speaking about their fears that trends in wild acquisition have made it an example of self-devouring growth. 'Foreigners', they agree, are the authors of the most destructive forceful acquisition. By the early 1980s, large groups of men, mostly from Sudan or Chad, appeared in north-eastern CAR's conservation zones. Arriving with automatic weapons (AK-47, FAL, and G3 rifles), porters, and pack animals, they departed laden with meat, honey, and ivory. Central Africans and conservationists described the hunters as 'Sudanese' or 'Chadian' or else used the term of the moment for men-at-arms of the Chad/Darfur borderlands: in the 1980s, it was *Murahaliin*; in the 2000s, *Janjaweed*.[21] This carries the same implications as colonial descriptors: Arabic-derived words name the rapacious 'Arabs' destroying CAR's patrimony. However, the characterisation was not incorrect so much as that it allowed Central Africans – officials and others – to deflect attention from

[21] Central Africans use the term *Janjaweed* to refer to people they identify as being among eastern Chadian or Sudanese itinerant men-at-arms; people trying to raise funds for conservation use it because the fearsome reputation attached to this category is well known.

their own involvement (direct or indirect) in acquisition, including by force, in the zone.[22] Such practices have been the main mechanism for this region's inclusion in wider economies for some 150 years, and Europeans instigated many of them. The packs of hunters and porters who descended on eastern CAR from the 1970s and 1980s onwards were not so much a new phenomenon as the resuscitation and reinvention of the practices used during the last ivory booms, some 70 years earlier, and led by al-Sanusi and also by hunters such as Bell and Rushby.[23] Central Africans have been eager hunters too. President-turned-emperor Jean-Bédel Bokassa drew much of his revenue from his (camouflaged) control of ivory hunts, and famously enjoyed hunting big game.[24]

Herders could also be described as destructive foreigners.[25] Cattle have become an investment strategy for the region's wealthy and

[22] This is an example of what I have called 'cunning victimhood': presenting oneself as the victim of more-powerful players, and in so doing drawing greater profit from it. It is neither a contradiction in terms, nor is one of the terms truer than the other (Lombard 2016d).

[23] Ivory hunting has declined since 2009; the elephants are pretty much all gone from north-eastern CAR (Bouché et al. 2012). There have, however, been some incidents of hunting the smaller forest elephants of south-western CAR, which had largely been well protected, both by wildlife guards and by their location far from the Sudanese and Chadian locales many ivory hunters call home. New armed conservation efforts have been deployed to south-western CAR to stop the ivory hunters.

[24] Jean-Bédel Bokassa developed all manner of camouflage to profit from elephant hunting. In the early 1970s, his first wife's sister, together with her partner, founded a firm called La Couronne, which operated just like the concessionary companies of old. They were the official buyers of all ivory. People bringing ivory to La Couronne would say that they had collected the ivory from elephants they had found already dead; as it was difficult to verify this, the claim provided effective cover with regard to the hunting and gun regulations. Ivory became an even more important source of currency as Bokassa's other sources of wealth dwindled due to his idiosyncratic policies. La Couronne's control over the ivory trade was noteworthy, although the extent to which the governing elite and their associates benefited from the sale of ivory was not. This situation continued: for instance, in 1980, a French businesswoman was reported to have requested the purchase of 20 tons of ivory, and the '*autorisation exceptionnel*' was signed by Bokassa's successor, David Dacko (Onana 1998: 196, 199–200). When I attended the World Food Day celebrations in Obo, in far south-eastern CAR, in December 2009, several vendors had stocks of ivory (as well as a baby chimpanzee) to sell to the visiting high-level ministers. When I asked, they said that the ministers were their best customers. When it comes to rare wild products, regulation is subordinate to other values around meaning privilege, and exception, and the degree of people's authority is reflected in their ability to draw advantage from those values.

[25] The number of cattle pasturing in north-eastern CAR has indeed increased, although there is little aerial surveillance to make a reliable count. The armament herders carry has increased as well, whether as protection from cattle rustlers or robbers (the region's sedentary residents have given the herders the nickname *banquiers ambulants* – 'mobile bankers' – because of the wealth each cow represents), to engage offensively against those who would stop their movement (Tomety 2009), or in order to hunt. Some herders

powerful, including high-ranking military officers in Chad and Sudan. They are good business, particularly for sale to the growing number of meat-hungry city folk in Nigeria and elsewhere, and herds are maintained at far larger sizes than those of 'traditional' pastoralists. Many herders give their cows veterinary drugs that contaminate the water for wild animals; such drugs are both for sale and distributed free of charge by humanitarian organisations in Darfur such as the Red Cross or Veterinarians Without Borders (Woods 2016).

Categorisation in terms of 'foreigners' and 'nationals' and their allies uses public-facing, alliance-building language. However, it doesn't do justice to the connections that exist amidst stratification. Everyone can agree to dislike foreigners in the abstract. In terms of actual practice and situations, one is more likely to find shifting patterns of 'insiders' and 'outsiders' (Kelly 2015) who sometimes collaborate and sometimes come into conflict. For instance, many herders, including the young men accompanying, say, a Chadian general's herds, pay people living near the lands where they graze a kind of *droit de pâturage* (entitlement to graze). Some farmers grow crops they know will appeal to the herders, such as millet, expecting the possibility of commerce. And among Central Africans involved in wild acquisition, there are tiers of privilege and connection to powerful people not resident in the zone as well.

Safari-hunting concessionaires in north-eastern CAR have also long been major claimants not just to wild goods, but to wild space. Prioritising safari hunting has been the official legal strategy for 'rationally' managing wild animals, because safari hunters are supposed to pay enormous fees for any trophies they wish to take home. The selling point for Central African hunting safaris was that here you could have a real hunting experience – long treks on foot to track truly wild animals – as opposed to the more 'domesticated' tamer hunts of East and Southern Africa. Today, there are no safari-hunting concessions left in north-eastern CAR, although there are a couple elsewhere in the country.[26]

travel in family groups, in ways people recognise as similar to the practices of generations past. Other herding groups consist entirely of young men in the employ of urban bankrollers from Chad or Darfur, and they do a lot of hunting – for ivory and meat – as well. People tend to describe this as a new development, and in some ways it is, but it is quite a similar organisational style to that of *salatieh*-bearing in centuries past.

[26] When safari hunting was more of a going concern, safari guides and their clients were a diverse bunch. (Roulet 2004). While some foreign hunters were attracted to CAR by the appeal of treks testing their inner toughness and providing rejuvenating solitude (as Valéry Giscard d'Estaing described his love of safari hunting in CAR [Faes and Smith 2000]), others took advantage of the possibilities for shortcuts and massacre in a place that was effectively lawless (Le Noël 1999: 162).

The emergence of well over a dozen rebel groups since 2006 has made it a nearly impossible business.[27]

The various claimants to north-eastern CAR's wild goods tend to agree that there are more conflicts over these matters than would be ideal. There is less consensus, however, about exactly how things should be resolved. Armed conservation aid projects have only intensified the negotiation and denunciation through which people have long struggled to adjudicate acquisition in the face of conflict among people without shared dispute-resolution practices and the illegalisation of everything by state law.

'Project Conservation'

Conservation became an overriding concern of governance in north-eastern CAR in the 1980s in large part because of the impetus from a few charismatic and determined individuals. Elsewhere, it has largely been a state prerogative, but in CAR a wide range of people have been involved.[28] And while in theory all of these people share the same goals, they have often come into conflict, collaborating only when circumstances compel them to do so. This is a second striking aspect of CAR's armed conservation efforts: they have entailed much force and rivalry, but at the same time they allowed for the kind of blurred vision that can allow competing projects to coexist.

There is a long list of people who have mobilised for the armed enforcement of conservation strictures in CAR since the 1980s. It includes French soldiers, EU-funded conservation project employees, safari-hunting guides, and others. These discrete categories blend when one looks at the particular people involved, however. The same French officer who once led missions 'securing the border' came back to work as a mercenary training the EU militia; a number of safari game-lodge trackers went on to work for other conservation militias (and dozens

[27] In late 2006, I shared a dinner with a rueful safari-hunting guide who had been driving a new Land Cruiser stocked with all the alcohol and other treats his clients would expect through Ndele a few weeks earlier, en route to his camp. A rebel group, the UFDR (see Chapter 8), took the town, and while doing so they stole the Land Cruiser. When the French military flew in to push back the rebels, they also destroyed the safari hunter's vehicle (either that or the rebels sold the vehicle to Sudanese transporters – I heard competing versions). Another of our dinner companions was an insurance-claim investigator, and they discussed the optimal strategy for presenting this claim to the insurance company: an 'act of God'? The truth seemed unlikely to work.

[28] This is changing through the promulgation of 'public–private partnerships' – many of which look very much like these early armed conservation initiatives in north-eastern CAR.

eventually joined rebel groups). Similarly, the lines between these people and their opponents blur when looking at particular individuals. Many of the *pisteurs* working for the anti-poaching militia today were themselves formerly 'poachers' like those they now target. They and their bosses claim that this gives them a kind of embodied knowledge that makes them more effective. But the changeability of roles does not ensure reduced conflict among the people involved. Personalities and interests both change and clash.

The first people to argue for an increased conservation presence in the protected areas were the safari-hunting guides. They used to employ Central Africans as trackers to help their clients hunt game; now the same employees would also hunt poachers. One long-time safari-hunting guide, Matthieu Laboureur, described in a swaggering, cowboyish memoir how he came to conclude that extreme measures were necessary. His father had been a professional hunter in francophone Equatorial Africa since just after the Second World War. Beginning in the late 1960s (with a gap when he fell out of favour with Bokassa), he had operated a safari concession officially the size of Swaziland. Unofficially, the *concessionnaires* roamed more widely, including into the surrounding national park – Manovo-Gounda St Floris. After seeing the remains of some elephants, Matthieu Laboureur wrote, he felt a keen solidarity with the animals, and worried that he too could become the hunters' target. He lamented the hunters' apparent freedom from oversight while claiming such freedom for himself: he and his men would ambush those they identified as marauding hunters (Laboureur 1988: 12).

Safari guides such as the Laboureurs did their anti-hunting hunts on their own, figuring out their own modes of negotiation, contest, and coercion in relation to the people living in the area and other would-be users of their concessionary spaces.[29] In the mid-1980s, a development occurred that was apparently a massive shift: the EU organised, authorised, and funded an enormous conservation initiative for north-eastern CAR. This project, initially known as the *Programme pour le développement de la région nord* (PDRN, or Programme for the Development of the Northern Region)[30] would bureaucratise and 'rationalise' (the project's term) conservation in the region. However, although the project

[29] Matthieu's memoir includes a photograph of roped-together prisoners (illegal, but a useful practice in a place with little in the way of constraints such as handcuffs), whom his father was holding at the makeshift gaol he operated in the grounds of his safari lodge. This was a kind of holding cell to be used until the relevant authorities could be roused.

[30] Later it became known as ECOFAC (Ecosystèmes Forestiers d'Afrique Centrale/Forest Ecosystems in Central Africa) and then ECOFAUNE (Ecosystèmes Faunistiques/ Faunal Ecosystems).

conservationists and the Laboureurs liked to think of themselves as operating very differently from each other – Laboureur in a rough and ready way, the projects in the mode of rational-bureaucratic development – the contrast was not always so great. Some of those working for the conservation projects – the most successful – shared Laboureur's orientation towards stopping hunters through manhunting and other forms of forceful acquisition and operated in ways rather similar to his. But because of their bureaucratic connections, they had far greater resources at their disposal.

That armed conservation, as a development-aid project, came to be deployed in north-eastern CAR owes much to a few people who worked carefully to make it happen in the face of donor discomfort with funding armed endeavours. One of these people was Jean-Marc Froment. Originally from Belgium, Froment studied biology with a focus on conservation and wildlife management. He has devoted his career to working in remote African protected areas with small human populations, many of them also marked by ongoing histories of violence. He arrived in north-eastern CAR in the early 1980s under the auspices of a 'technical cooperation' project funded by the EU and the Food and Agriculture Organization of the United Nations (FAO). His job was to train the area's hunting guards. What began as a primarily scientific and technical undertaking – teaching the guards to identify flora and fauna, and so forth – transformed into something else as he became increasingly concerned about the hunting and raiding ramping up all around them.

Froment became convinced of the need to do much more concerted policing of the parklands to stop ivory hunters and herders and to arrest the southward creep of the desert's edge, while also bringing economic benefits to the area's residents – in the familiar 'have one's cake and eat it too' utopianism of projects that claim to merge conservation with development. He teamed up with Enrico Pironio, another former FAO fieldworker who worked for the EU on environmental aid to Central Africa. Together they led a drive to launch a conservation project, which became the PDRN, for north-eastern CAR.

The term 'project' had a more specific meaning than it does now.[31] A project was a donor-funded and -led initiative that created an organisation with its own coherence (and, most importantly in this respect, its

[31] In the rest of this chapter, I capitalise 'Project Conservation' when describing this type of intervention. Much donor funding in the 1980s was disbursed using this kind of structure. Subsequently, in the midst of concern about the 'corruption' and poor governance of African states, it became more popular to channel funds through international NGOs, which would reproduce their modular way of operating by opening a national office in the country in question.

own budget) but was formally attached to a ministry. It could be said to be bolstering state capacity, which donors saw as self-evidently a good thing. This was despite the fact that none of the people involved – whether working for the *ministère de tutelle* or the project – saw the project as being of the state.

In the case of the PDRN, the *ministère de tutelle*, the relevant ministry, was the Ministry of Water, Forests, Hunting, Fishing, and Tourism. At the time of the PDRN's formation in the mid-1980s, the Water and Forests ministry had 368 employees and an annual budget of 10 million CFA (about €31,000). In contrast, over the first 15 years of EU funding, the projects received a total of about €50 million for a staff of about a hundred, not including short-term workers such as those hired to clear trails at the beginning of the dry season (Lloveras 2002). As an infrastructure undertaking, the PDRN was bigger than anything the region had ever seen. It entailed the clearing of hundreds of kilometres of roads and landing strips, the creation of anti-poaching bases whose permanent buildings are more extensive than those of any of the region's major towns, and the importation of heavy machinery and other expensive equipment. All this was marshalled for the following goals, as described by the PDRN's founders:

> To maintain the protected zones of the northern region in their natural state and to thereby conserve the advantages that the country and regional collectivities could draw from it: (i) in an indirect manner by the conservation of natural ecosystems and their role as an ecological barrier against desertification, notably the national parks Bamingui-Bangoran and Manovo-Gounda St Floris; (ii) in a direct manner by the improvement, management, and use of natural fauna resources of the northern region. (d'Espiney, Tello, and Delvingt 1993; cited in Roulet 2004: 42)[32]

In order to preserve the northern region in its 'natural state' (in fact, the way it had become after many decades of raiding), the PDRN built massive bases at Manovo, Bamingui, Gordil, and Sangba (Figure 5.2). They also organised and financed the construction of hundreds of kilometres of '*pistes*', narrow tracks just wide enough for a vehicle to pass through the bush.[33] The *pistes* were necessary so that the '*service de*

[32] '[M]aintenir les zones protégées de la région Nord dans leur état naturel et de conserver ainsi les avantages que pourraient en retirer le pays et les collectivités régionales: (i) de manière indirecte par la conservation des écosystèmes naturels et de leur rôle en tant que barrière écologique contre la désertification – notamment les parcs nationaux Bamingui-Bangoran et Manovo-Gounda St Floris, (ii) de manière directe par l'aménagement, la gestion, et l'utilisation des ressources fauniques naturelles de la région Nord.'

[33] Clearing paths just wide enough for a Land Cruiser proved harder than expected. They planned to construct 360 kilometres of *pistes* but managed only 150 in the first two years (PDRN 1990: 73).

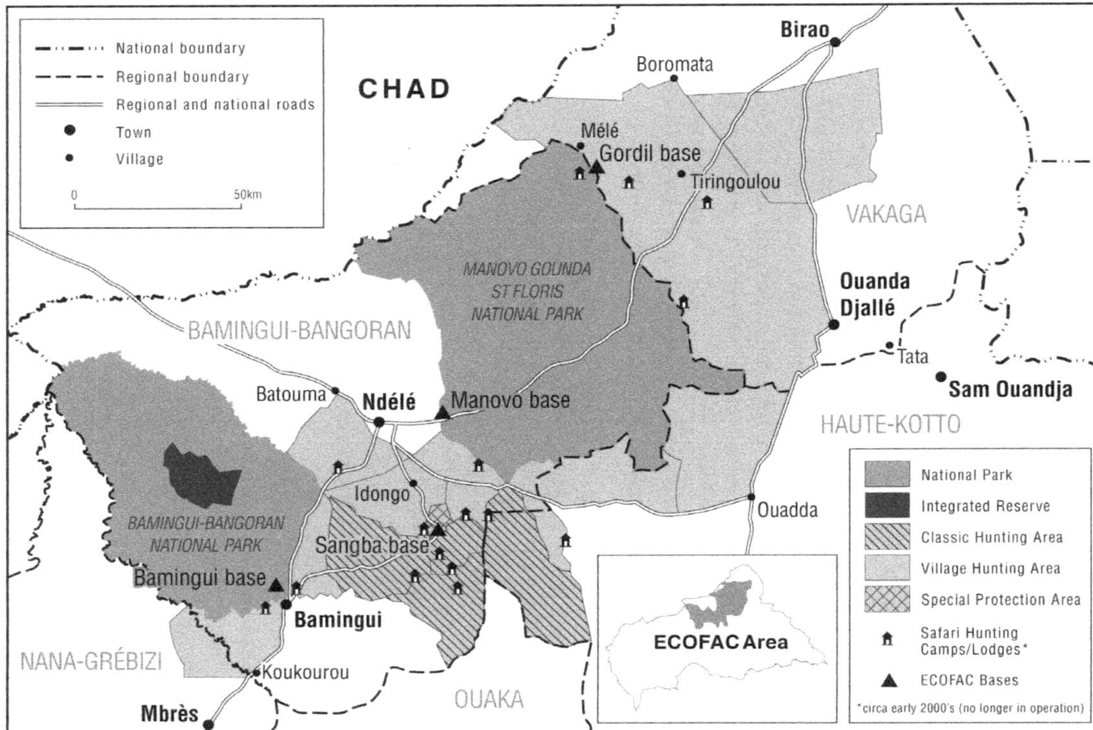

Figure 5.2 Map of ECOFAC's area of operations

surveillance et de protection' (surveillance and protection corps) created by the PDRN, consisting of *pisteurs* (tracker-guards), would be able to carry out their role of overseeing the parklands. In the first decade or so, the *pisteurs* were involved in monitoring the region's ecology in addition to working to keep these areas free of other humans and livestock. Later, funding diminished and the competing claimants to the area's wild goods became more forceful, and manhunting became a more prevalent part of the *pisteurs*' work.

The technical term for their manhunting was *lutte anti-braconnage* (LAB, or the fight against poaching). With LAB, the *pisteurs* were to enforce the hunting and conservation laws and conduct people who did not abide by them towards legal sanctions. However, the skeletal legal edifice in north-eastern CAR – basically, a tribunal in Ndele – only intermittently heard cases. The tribunal was often closed due to a lack of personnel; the sultan-mayor of Ndele (al-Sanusi's grandson) would claim the prerogative as his own to free detainees, and tribunal employees were known for themselves breaching the law.

Armed enforcement of conservation and hunting areas has a centuries-long history (Thompson 1975). Critical scholarly accounts of these practices and projects often contrast two groups of people involved in them: agents of the state or other state-like actors (Trouillot 2001), who seek to dominate, territorialise, and discipline, often using violence (Brockington 2002; Büscher 2013; Duffy 2010, 2014; Marijnen 2018; Neumann 2004a [1996]; Peluso 1993); and local populations dispossessed of land and resources and forced into new kinds of poverty, despite rhetoric and practices meant to inculcate 'local participation' (Alexander and McGregor 2000; Devine 2014; Hardin, Remis, and Robinson 2014; Kelly 2011; Neumann 2001; Robinson and Remis 2014). These accounts usefully correct advocacy narratives that prioritise the lives of charismatic megafauna and marginalise the humans living alongside them (Baaz et al. 2015). The deleterious effects the critical accounts identify are indeed present. But focusing on control (whether for the sake of economic gain, biological conservation, capitalist transformation, or anything else) miss the more personal stakes at play for people during particular confrontations.

Rather than quests for hegemony or control of other people, north-eastern CAR has seen claims to privilege and entitlement – to status – in a context in which status is mutable. Conservation has been neither a state project nor the project of a 'state within a state' – a project of actors seeking to establish public authority (Marijnen 2018). Instead, almost all successful people are flexible with rules and relationships in the service of acquisition, whether of wild goods, status, or dignity

(Lombard and Tubiana n.d.) or precedence over others. People who are in certain respects allies – safari-hunting guides and conservation project staff, for example – can sometimes find themselves at odds with each other. The ability to control other people over the long term (cited as a conservation project priority) is ancillary to the negotiation and denunciation that happen on the ground. While the tools for perpetrating armed violence are not shared equally among all parties, all of them are able to threaten and hide in powerful ways. As they do so, any hegemonic interests are frustrated, and serious games of forceful acquisition and status claiming proliferate.

Negotiation and denunciation amid social fractiousness

Armed conservation in north-eastern CAR has entailed a lot of coercion (*pisteurs* are forceful acquirers, including of the lives of those they deem illegal outsiders and of whatever goods they can seize from others in the parklands) and a lot of forced ententes and other kinds of collaboration. Armed conservation led to manhunts marked by both seizure and killing. Yet at the same time people forcibly maintained their ability to pursue inconsistent projects unmolested, a kind of brokered autonomy. Some used camouflage in order to achieve autonomy, playing with types of forceful acquisition across scale – for example in relation to the inhabitants of the region's large towns; in relation to the occasionally rousable government in Bangui; and in relation to the international conservation and aid donors of various kinds. These dynamics are less noted in the conservation literature, which tends to emphasise the forcible aspect of phenomena such as dispossession or failures of enforcement, due to corruption, for example, while also making a firm distinction between 'locals' (whose claims are generally seen as more valid) and 'outsiders' (who – fellow nationals or not – work in neocolonial ways and therefore are presented as inherently morally compromised).[34] Some analyses make an assumption that 'the state' is the fount of legitimacy: this is the underlying conceit of all development aid. Others, critical of state coerciveness, assume that the 'local' perspective is legitimate. But who counts as a local? Neither 'the state' nor 'the locals' can muster a stable

[34] For a helpful corrective to the tendency to divide between local (native) and outsider (European/American), see Hardin (2008), who in its place suggests an 'ethic of intimacy'.

and inclusive system of principles of obligation and duty: that is, of law. Instead, everyone makes moves during 'ethical moments' because they have to deal with conflicting, if sincerely held, values, and they live in a context in which policing is difficult, obligations and reciprocity are compromised, and the bonds of association and cooperation can change.

The usual categories brought to bear to understand hunting ('locals', 'foreigners', 'poachers') are more unruly than they might seem at first. Central Africans resident in the north-east as well as conservation project documents differentiate between 'local' and 'foreign' poachers. The first refers to those whose families farm in the area, the latter to those who live more itinerantly and move between CAR and Sudan or Chad. These 'foreigners' are the ones who are vilified as operating on an 'industrial scale', showing up in the protected zones with dozens of men and pack animals, the better to massacre elephants and any other large game that they can sell in South Darfur and beyond. 'Locals', on the other hand, are frequently portrayed as hunting primarily to feed their families. This is only partly true. Locals hunt meat to sell, and they also sometimes hunt elephants and other protected species, and they often do so in the *salatieh*-like employ of a government official or other wealthy person from the capital. These days, however, the *salatieh* staff takes the form of the dispatcher's gun and bullets.

The fractiousness, and complicity, of the 'locals' was not unknown. Many specific incidents were noted in reports. One technical consultant hired to write a report for the conservation project (not someone with a long-term interest in employment in north-eastern CAR, in other words) was particularly sharp in his phrasing: 'How could one think it right to punish villagers for crimes when the [local] functionaries do not behave in solidarity with the state programme[35] that [Project Conservation] represents?' (Lundgren 2009: 3).[36] But the category 'local' could usefully camouflage the unruliness of how the conservation project actually plays out.

[35] That the author presents it as a 'state project' reflects aspirational diplomatic niceties; it is not a statement of analytical fact.

[36] In full: 'Le comportement de certains agents de l'État dans la région n'aide pas à diluer la pagaie sur le plan sécuritaire (collecteur des impôts accompagnés par des agents armés dans les camps de chasse, devant les clients; braconniers saisis avec les armes des fonctionnaires; braconniers remis pour procédures juridiques, rapidement libérés; préfet donnant autorisation aux pêcheurs de pénétrer les zones de chasse sans concertation préalable avec les gestionnaires; l'agression physique d'un locataire de chasse par des pêcheurs restée sans suite, etc.). Comment vouloir sanctionner les villageois pour délits quand les fonctionnaires ne se comportent pas de manière solidaire avec le programme de l'État que représente l'ECOFAC-ZCV?'

The category 'local' became even more fractious because only some locals had the chance to benefit from Project Conservation's 'participatory' components. Many villages and all the major towns (Ndele, Kaga-Bandoro, Bamingui) in the area were left out: sometimes because they did not fulfil technical qualification criteria, sometimes because of running disputes between those overseeing the organisation of participatory projects and notables in the area, and sometimes due to a combination of factors (PDRN 1998). Initially, participation involved a variety of development initiatives (beekeeping workshops, game farming, etc.) for some residents of the area. That transformed into a system whereby people living in the area around safari-hunting zones or conservation areas were to be enlisted in a trade-off. They were to refrain from hunting animals or otherwise making use of wild spaces and their resources, and in exchange would receive large portions of safari-hunting revenues, to be managed by village and local committees.

Versions of safari-tax revenue sharing with people living around parklands have been tried in a number of African countries after the apparent success of Zimbabwe's CAMPFIRE programme. (Subsequent analysis showed CAMPFIRE to burn less brightly than had once been suggested [Alexander and McGregor 2000].) In CAR, it was called the *zones cynégétiques villageoises* (ZCVs, or community hunting zones).

A couple of things are particularly noteworthy about the ZCV in comparison to other such programmes. One is that the amounts intended to devolve to the village-level management committees were set substantially higher than elsewhere in Africa.[37] Another is that, although the ZCV rules were supposed to be the legal arrangement governing safari hunting, taxes, and the people living nearby, government officials in Bangui never took the steps necessary to provide that *reconnaissance légale* (legal recognition) (European Commission n.d.a) over the course of decade when the ZCVs were functioning reasonably well, from about 1998 to 2009 (Granier 2010). Villages associated with a ZCV could get a decent amount of revenue through their involvement; in 2008–9, to give one example, the ZCV steering board bought two tractors and spent 4.5 million CAF (in the United States) on photo-printed T-shirts and caps to distribute for World Tree Day (Roulet 2009: 13), in addition to the money that was managed on a village basis. But, ultimately, it all rested on ethics and negotiation.

The ethical questions grappled with by different actors were, of course, different. For instance, safari operators were likely to raise the following

[37] Interview, September 2010.

issues:[38] What is the right thing to do, the thing that I see as associated with the kind of person I strive to be? What do I need to do in order to keep my business operational, and keep employing all the people I support here? What can I get away with, and, relatedly, do I want a long-term relationship to this place and the people here? It is difficult to align the answers to such questions, but an underlying issue cuts across all of them: To whom/for whom am I responsible? *Pisteurs*, villagers, and others faced competing demands too: family and other relations' expectations of distribution and largesse, personal aspirations to dignity and renown, a feeling that opportunities for advancement are rare and must be taken – to name just a few.

Tiringoulou is a town in north-eastern CAR that was once a successful participant in the ZCV, drawing substantial revenues from safari-hunting concessions in the surrounding area. When I spent time there in 2009 and 2010, the head of the ZCV committee, local doctor Mezzan Ramadan (brother of Tiringoulou's most famous denizen, Yaya Ramadan [see Chapter 7]), described for me the benefits of Project Conservation when it 'worked well' (*a bien marché*). Tiringoulou would take in receipts of 20–30 million CFA per year (approximately US$40,000–US$60,000) and used the cash to pay the salaries of 12 nurses and 18 teachers in the various villages of the *commune* (county). Each received 25,000 CFA per month, without fail. Leftover cash went to such things as paying villagers to repair the roads in the wake of inevitable rainy season damage, or stocking up on medicine and food for times of need. Mezzan was amazed that so much could come from just a few safari guests.

The most recent safari season, 2008–9, had been disastrous, however. A Frenchman named Gérard Bernard had rented two concessions – Tiringoulou 1 and Ouandja 1 – with the stated intention of operating safaris from them. However, he was strikingly unsuccessful as a guide, bringing in only one client. They did not provision properly for the hunting journey and did not have enough food. The tourist left after only a week, halfway through the usual duration of a safari. And Bernard 'poached' (Mezzan's term) in another guide's concession, the space demarcated as Tiringoulou 2. At the annual meeting between ZCV staff and safari operators when the safari season closed in June, Mezzan presented a list of taxes Bernard owed. These included 9,635,000 CFA for his use of a concession other than his own; 6,805,000 CFA and 4,793,000 CFA for the concessions that he had signed on for but did not end up using (Mezzan called this the *protocol de base* – even if you do not use the concession, you must still pay for it, just as you would if you

[38] These questions came up in my interviews and conversations with safari operators and in their statements in Project Conservation reports.

rented a house but did not inhabit it); 1,000,000 CFA in trophy fees for a lion he had killed; plus various other taxes.

When these sums were presented at the meeting, Bernard became upset. The meeting lasted all day and into the night and broke up with the intention of resuming the following day. But Bernard – 'the bandit' (*le bandit*), as Mezzan termed him – left on a night flight to Douala, and by the next day he was in France. Mezzan emailed Bernard a few months later. He replied that he had just had part of a lung removed and was suffering from renal colic and needed to recuperate. He had left behind a vehicle in Bangui, which Mezzan hoped could be confiscated to pay the overdue taxes, but it was parked at the offices of a diplomatic organisation with tight security, and for the time being it was inaccessible.

This, at least, was Mezzan's account. I emailed Bernard but never received a reply. One can imagine a few justifications he might have offered: he did not have the money to pay; the sums demanded were unreasonable for someone like him who was just prospecting (he never set up a lodge or fixed camp). Mezzan's own calculations of the amount due varied. The first time we discussed it, in October 2009, Mezzan estimated the final bill to be 20–30 million CFA; the second time, in March 2010, his calculations came out at 50 million. Imagining oneself in Bernard's place, one could understand why he might see the sums as negotiable, or unfairly inflated.

A report intended to bring expertise to bear on the improvement of the ZCV, published as the Tiringoulou–Bernard controversy was heating up, notes that concessionaires who do not pay what they are supposed to pay never face any sanction. Their licences are always renewed. However, the author also notes the concessionaires' concerns:

> Discouraged by the non-evolution of the situation in the northern region [i.e., the continuing rebellions], the private operators are quite fatalistic. They do not believe the situation will get better and seem to count only on their own resources to be able to draw a minimum profit from their hunting activities. Even though they pay for their services, they do not consider the management committees real business partners. They expect nothing from the state either, and they hope that the performance of the management committees will improve to the level they expect but they offer only very little in order to facilitate this improvement. Since neither the state nor the ZCV want the concessionaires to leave, the concessionaires feel like they are in a position of strength and manage their businesses the way they want, regardless of what the protocol says. In a context like this, it would be particularly delicate [difficult] to convince these companies to accept a new protocol that would impose penalties if terms are not respected. (d'Huart 2009: 23)[39]

[39] 'Découragés par la non-évolution des choses dans la région Nord, les opérateurs privés sont très fatalistes. Ils ne croient pas à une amélioration de la situation et ne semblent

Also, people aiming to collect ZCV revenue did not always respect the protocols' terms either. They expected concessionaires to pay for the full area they rented, even when people from the nearby villages were farming, inhabiting, hunting, fishing, or otherwise using these spaces for their own purposes. Some villages are completely surrounded by concessions and, if they did not encroach on the concessions, residents would struggle to feed themselves (Lundgren 2009). To summarise: whether one was a resident of a ZCV village, or of a village excluded from the ZCVs, or was a safari-hunting concessionaire, the rules were so out of tune with the exigencies of life they offered little in the way of ethical guidance, and nothing in the way of law. This does not mean that people did not treat each other with respect. Even during a three-year gap in Project Conservation funding (2004–7), which deprived the ZCV of some of its institutional and financial support, most safari-hunting concessionaires continued to pay, and most community managers continued to carry out their responsibilities (Roulet 2009). It just means that law and rules were less the source of behaviour than ethics, situations, and personal relationships, and in navigating them people have different priorities and values.

The *pisteurs* employed by Project Conservation were similarly socially fractious. They came from villages and towns around north-eastern CAR, and they have included people from a number of groups that today are described as 'ethnic'.[40] Historically, Gula have been the most numerous, but many left to join a rebellion in 2006. Others include Banda and Yulu, as well as a few Runga, although they too left to join a rebellion in 2008. For reasons of both personality and history (in some cases, their great-grandparents were on opposing sides of the *zariba* dynamic), many are suspicious of each other. They live on anti-poaching bases such as Manovo with their families. All are from villages or small towns

compter que sur leus propres ressources pour retirer un bénéfice minimum de leurs activités cynégétiques. Bien qu'ils paient pour leurs services, ils ne considèreent pas encore les C.GEST comme de réels partenaires de business. N'attendant rien de l'Etat non plus, ils espèrent que la qualité des prestations des C.GEST évoluera vers le niveau qu'ils attendent, mais n'offrent que très peu d'ouvertures pour faciliter cette évolution. Comme ni l'Etat, ni les ZCV ne souhaitent le départ de ces Locataires, ceux-ci se sentent en position de force et mènent leur entreprise – Protocole ou non – comme ils l'entendent. Dans un contexte comme celui-ci, il sera particulièrement délicat de convaincre ces sociétés d'accepter un nouveau Protocole imposant des pénalités en cas de non-respect de ses termes.'

40 It is true that the name of the 'ethnic group' is associated with a distinct language, but the properly 'ethnic' character of these groups is more of a recent differentiation, since French colonisers encountered a social tangle that they struggled to separate into groups (Kalck 1959). In fact, the people living in north-eastern CAR were all buffeted by and reorganised through the *zariba* period and are thus reflective of recent re-mixings and movement (Sikainga 1991).

and are used to life where everyone knows each other. The bases are artificial villages: they are not cities, where you can get by allowing strangers to remain strangers, but not villages either, where residents generally expect to live until they die – which gives them an incentive not to make too much trouble for themselves or others. On the bases, personalities clash; people accuse each other of witchcraft or other anti-social behaviour; wives are 'stolen'; and *pisteurs* are frequently reassigned to other bases, sometimes to resolve these tiffs and personality clashes. Western employees and other overseers move frequently too. Base life does not lend itself to developing consistent or formalised ways for people to relate or to regulate disputes.

The *pisteurs*' leader is described in Project Conservation-speak as a 'technical assistant' (usually abbreviated to AT from the French). Although there is no rule stipulating this, the AT has always been a white, Western man. Despite his modest title, he is the one who can compel the *pisteurs* to get up for dawn calisthenics and who organises and leads their anti-poaching raids. Being visibly in control can be a liability, and the titular camouflage serves everyone's interests. The expatriate can claim not to be operating in colonialist mode (he is just a technical assistant, after all) while the *pisteurs* and other project staff can claim that the title is meaningless since clearly the foreigner dictates everything, and thus they justify their own inconsistencies of practice.

The technical assistants develop close bonds with some of the *pisteurs*. Their housing is segregated. Generally, *pisteurs* live on one part of the base and expatriate and high-level staff on another. But in other respects they are deeply involved in each other's lives, including in dangerous situations in which they depend on each other for safety. At the same time, everyone knows that an AT's tenure is likely to be short. Whenever someone leaves for a vacation, he might not return, for whatever reason.[41]

Legally, the *pisteurs*' work should follow the same procedures that were developed for the occasional patrols carried out by colonial armed forces in the 1950s, since they have not changed since then.[42] At that time, the government had begun to worry about the increasing number of 'Arab'

[41] This happened during my field research, for instance. The AT went home to spend Christmas with his son in France and was fired; he was eventually allowed to return to pick up his things and called me to say goodbye but said that we should not meet because if others saw us it would cast suspicion on me. He felt that he had been fired because he was pushing back too strongly against 'local' poachers who had connections in the capital and were providing a good revenue to well-connected people. He was re-hired, however, a couple of years later.

[42] Only in the 1950s was a colonial army organised for Oubangui-Chari. Previously, the regional guards – known more for capriciousness than professionalism – had been the backbone of the security forces.

(Muslim or foreign) herders and hunters in north-eastern CAR. The government termed these patrols '*actions de présence*' – making the rounds, including in the protected areas; they literally 'showed the flag' by conducting flag-raising ceremonies in villages. It is a telling term because it provides a reminder that the rest of the time they were *not* present. Despite reports of an 'invasion' of Arabs hunting and herding, the soldiers on those rounds only sometimes encountered any such outlaws. When they did come across hunters or herders, they were to follow the following procedures:

> The individuals in an irregular situation will be made to give a statement and will be handed over to the district chief. In the event that, despite the measures taken, certain individuals manage to escape, their goods will be seized and their camps destroyed. A statement will similarly be taken. It remains understood that there will be open fire in the case of rebellion or legitimate self-defence. (Bordier 1959)[43]

The protocol also stipulated that cows found in protected areas or that had not passed through immigration controls should be shot, along with any pack animals, especially if their keepers refused to heed the guards' directives. In one incident, the Birao administrator shot 167 cows, a move his superior judged correct ('*il a eu raison*') (Cedile 1956).[44] The same policies remain in place, but people disagree over how they should be implemented. Some ATs worry that shooting cows will antagonise in ways that undermine their overall goals; others boast about the 'millions of CFA' (as opposed to the number of cows) they destroy by killing them.

In the 1950s, as today, it was difficult to follow the principle that someone caught in a protected area or in an otherwise 'irregular' situation should be transferred to administrators for judicial proceedings. In 1958, the military leader of a three-month 'Action for presence and control of the Sudanese' (*Action de présence et contrôle des soudanais*) mission in the Birao area noted that no administrator had accompanied his group, which would have made it easier to follow legal protocol. He concluded: 'It is evident that, without the aid and the assistance of the

43 'Les individus en situation irrégulière feront l'objet d'un P.V. [procès-verbal] et seront remis entre les mains du Chef de district. Dans le cas où, malgré le dispositif adopté, certains individus auraient pu s'échapper, leur biens seront saisis et leurs campements détruits. Un P.V. sera également établi. Il reste entendu que le feu sera ouvert en cas de rébellion ou de légitime défense caractérisée.'

44 In 1956, government officials proposed that entry to Oubangui-Chari be denied to all Mbororo herders, who had (and still have) the reputation of being exceedingly truculent. In the wake of the killing of two guards in Birao in 1959, President David Dacko repeated this suggestion, but his French advisers reminded him that it would be impossible to enforce, as well as discriminatory (Bordier 1959), apparently forgetting that they had proposed the same thing three years earlier.

administration, the dispatch of these units or the renewal of the Birao campaign will be useless' (Commandant Militaire de l'Oubangui-Chari 1958).[45]

The parts of a governmental bureaucratic machine are supposed both to be connected to each other and to move. In the hunting zone the government did neither. But while the actions undertaken did not achieve the ends the more optimistic might have hoped for, they were not useless: they helped inaugurate the modes of anti-hunting raiding that later became prevalent.[46] In particular, those early actions established a practice of acquisition through seizing material goods and of manhunting, now undertaken as a mode of policing. This was not a rupture with the past but the renewal and reinvention of practices and tendencies with long histories in the region.

Conclusion

To say that seizure is a long-established mode of regulation in the region (Roitman 2005) is true, but it misses the nuance in how people perceive and justify taking. In English, seizure tends to have a polemical connotation. Seizure goes against an ideal of private property and private bodies. That ideal goes a long way towards defining the proper status of things and persons, even though it is often breached in practice. Status is not so clear in north-eastern CAR, however. Property may be taken if it is being used in the wrong place or context, but which context is 'wrong'

[45] 'Il est évident que, sans l'aide et l'appui de l'Administration, le détachement de ces unités ou le renouvellement de la campagne de BIRAO ne serviront à rien.'

[46] The isolation and frequent neglect of bureaucratic legal bodies have continued. During my fieldwork in the hunting zone, the tribunal at Ndele, which should have tried anyone detained by the area's law enforcement agencies, was inactive. Only the clerk and a secretary showed up to open the dark building when I visited. The president and prosecutor had both been dismissed following a dispute over, among other things, the trafficking of game meat. (After a few months in Bangui, however, they were reassigned and promoted.) Their intended replacements never showed up. A few people were deposited at the town jail by *pisteurs*, but those who could rustle up the money from relations in town would pay the guard to free them. Those who could not do this were eventually freed by the clerk, who reasoned that they had already been there longer than their sentences would have been if they had been tried and found guilty. The previous year (2008), before the president's and prosecutor's dismissal, the tribunal was occasionally open and a handful of people were tried after being caught in protected areas. One said that he had heard that someone had come to town looking for a hunter, and he proposed himself for the job. He killed two guinea fowl and a lion 'in legitimate self-defence'. The man who had hired him took the lion skin and fled, as did the five other people in the hunting party. The unlucky defendant was given a 30,000 CFA fine (which should have been paid to the *agent spécial*, but there was none in office) and sentenced to a year in prison. However, he neither served the sentence nor paid the fine; he did not live in Ndele and could slip away.

(parkland and its buffers) and which is 'right' (villages and their immediate environs) is a distinction that is neither clear nor widely agreed upon.

Lives may also be taken. Sometimes taking a life elicits a major outcry; sometimes it does not. To note that the status of people and things is less certain in north-eastern CAR than in places where law and government are more institutionalised is not to say that seizure is more accepted – it is only to acknowledge that acquisition, including forceful acquisition, is a way of both profiting and making claims to status.

In recounting this history of armed conservation, I am not pulling back the veil of the Project's ideology to reveal the ugly face it has been hiding (Maurer 2005). My investigation has not revealed previously unknown happenings and this is not an exposé, even though the details might be new to readers. Much of what I have presented here has been written about, discussed, and even lamented in Project Conservation's own reports. This suggests two avenues of inquiry. One would investigate by what means people deal with the conflicts of values that arise in the context of conservation. The second would examine when and why certain issues became problems necessitating action, and when it remained possible to ignore them. Pursuing these lines of inquiry requires careful consideration of the various potential audiences and constituencies for conservation, from those living in the hunting zone to Project Conservation funders and scandalised humanitarians elsewhere. For both, camouflage and denunciation are two main repertoires of action, and they are the focus of the next two chapters.

6 Camouflage skills*

Those who feel disenfranchised or otherwise disconnected from the law must defend their claims 'by force or stealth', argued E. P. Thompson in his masterful study of the transition from social means of organising the acquisition of wild goods to a system of law in eighteenth-century England (Thompson 1975: 240). People in north-eastern CAR are certainly disenfranchised and disconnected from their state's laws, and they defend their claims by force and stealth, just as Thompson noted. But how does such stealth work? A common-sense understanding might consider it a matter of efficient hiding, but that is not how it works in north-eastern CAR. People involved in acquisition and conservation have not hidden or otherwise removed themselves from view. Instead, they have cultivated camouflage, blending in across different social and bureaucratic landscapes because doing so helps them further their own acquisitive or status projects. Camouflage, a hunter's skill, works best when those directly interested and others who could refocus their telescopes both end up scanning the landscape only through blurry sights, whether because that is easier, because they feel powerless, because they have been co-opted, because they are tacitly cooperating, or because they agree with the act. After all, camouflage does not make one invisible. It simply makes it possible to keep doing a variety of things without obviously flouting the practices that those invested in normative or consistent principles would expect. Camouflage is most powerful among people with certain privileges as regards their manner of seeing and being seen, and those people have developed implicit ways of working together. The collaborative aspects of camouflage, and their entanglement with shifting social positions of privilege, were on full display in Ndele in early 2010 following a dispute over who could acquire diamonds in the area, and where.

* Some of the material in this chapter has been published previously in Lombard (2016a, 2016b).

Competing claims to acquisition

In January 2010, the Ndele jail went from being nearly empty to overcrowded in a single night. Eighteen people – among them two village chiefs – had been locked up after *pisteurs* caught them mining in a protected area. The captors, who received a bounty for equipment they seized, took the villagers' pumps, shovels, bicycles, and everything else they found. A few days later, the village chiefs and a few others paid their way out of prison with 6,000 CFA each (about US$12/£9) handed directly to the prison guard. The court clerk freed the others as well in the hope that doing so would be a protest, a 'shock' to cause the central government to staff the tribunal, which had not heard a case in nearly a year. It did not work. His superiors continued to enjoy their salaries from a leisurely distance, remaining in the capital while he and a secretary continued to open the doors of the non-functional court every day. No one seemed to notice. The tribunal remained unstaffed.

Although the alleged miners were no longer in prison, in town a sense of grievance spread as people told and retold the story and added their own commentary. I discussed it with my friend Aziza, president of the Ndele branch of the Central African Women's Association and a brilliant and driven person who went on to become Ndele's first woman mayor. Aziza was livid at how the *pisteurs*, some local and others from elsewhere in the region, had acted. The few solidly constructed houses in Ndele – made with imported cement and paint – were the 'fruits of diamonds', as she put it; diamond mining was the only activity that brought material wealth to the town. I began to hear rumours that the dispossessed miners were working to rally people to attack the *pisteurs*.

A few days later, a government minister happened to pass through on an early campaign visit. On such rare occasions, government officials make a show of listening to their constituents, who have no means of holding them to account for the promises made but accept the gifts offered; this is what I have elsewhere called 'promissory politics' (Lombard 2015, 2016d). In the midst of the airy promises, though, other things can happen. In this case, one of the arrested village chiefs disrupted the platitudes to angrily recount the injustices he and his fellows had suffered, how the *pisteurs* had beaten them and seized all of their possessions. The minister might have turned to the prefecture's top functionaries, the *préfet* and the *sous-préfet*, for further explanation, but neither were in residence.

The *sous-préfet* was embarrassed to have missed his chance to demonstrate his usefulness in negotiating. Ndele residents saw him as nearly as foreign as the town's Chadian and Sudanese merchants. Although he was a Muslim like most of the locals, he was from CAR's south-western rainforest region. But he cultivated and was proud of his negotiation skills, and defusing tension after the diamond-mining seizure would have been an opportunity for him to shine. Therefore, he took the quickest transport he could find back from the capital, reappeared in town a couple of days later, and summoned all the interested parties – local notables and miners, as well as the anti-poaching project staff – to a meeting.

On the day before the meeting, the *pisteurs* blasted into town in late afternoon,[1] filling the backs of two Land Cruiser pickups.[2] They wore their regulation green and brown camouflage and carried their guns and canteens. Many wore black sunglasses, an unusual sartorial choice in the region but essential to looking the part as a militiaman. Here in town, their camouflage uniforms did not make them blend in, but stick out. They looked fearsome, and that was the point.

The morning of the meeting was as relentlessly sunny as every February morning in Ndele. The *sous-préfet* stood in the door of the meeting hall at the mayor's office, where he had asked everyone to assemble. He greeted people as they came in and helped them find seats. The highest-level people sat on chairs on a raised platform at the front. The rest sat on benches arrayed in two columns with an aisle down the middle. Like a wedding usher, the *sous-préfet* asked me, 'Which side are you on, anti-poachers or diamond miners?,' implying that the columns of benches were thus divided. (In fact, most people on the benches, on both sides, were broadly of the opinion that the *pisteurs* had overstepped their authority.) He quickly responded on my behalf: 'Neither! You're a gold prospector, on the side of gold prospectors!' This was an oblique reference to my being an American, and a joke. I sat at the side, near the front.

Soon the hall was packed, with not an inch of unclaimed bench and standing room only around the perimeter and at the back. The *pisteurs* and their bosses (the 'national conservator' and 'deputy national conservator' assigned to Manovo base) arrived last. Some of the guards stood at the back, next to the main doors, holding their weapons. Their superiors took seats on the raised platform at the front and awkwardly but carefully set their guns aside. To join Project Conservation, they had been pulled from the civilian ranks of the Water and Forests Ministry and they did not have the assurance

[1] They were a fairly common presence in town; before they went on missions, they would have to lay in provisions from the market, the only market in the area that could provide enough foodstuffs for LAB teams for several days in the bush. On those visits, they would chat with family, friends, and acquaintances. But, on this occasion, they kept their distance.

[2] One pink face stood out among the others. It was that of the AT (or, to use the term he professed to prefer, mercenary), who, although not officially in charge, effectively commanded the *pisteurs*. He did not attend the meeting, instead passing the hours at a bar in the centre of town.

and familiarity born of long handling of firearms. Notably absent were any representatives of international humanitarian organisations or international organisations, although, over the last couple of years, both had established offices in town (the UN's with the highest and most impenetrable wall). They considered these kinds of political matters interesting but not their concern, and, in any case, their employees were too busy with reports and grant applications to spend a morning sitting and listening.

The *sous-préfet* called the meeting to order just before nine. He explained that its objective was to identify a definitive solution to the tensions, namely an 'agreement among people' ('*entente entre azo*'). To start things off, he recounted the facts: the miners said they had had their things seized from them while they were outside the park, in the buffer zone. The *pisteurs* said they had found the miners in the park. The miners said they had been wrongfully beaten and dispossessed. The *pisteurs* said they had not. The miners said the *pisteurs* were now using the miners' equipment for their own in-park mining. The *pisteurs* said they were not. Meeting attendees agreed that the *sous-préfet* had correctly characterised the heart of the dispute – the park, he said, can bring riches when it is well managed, and therefore what was needed was a 'definitive compromise' ('*ti tene kpale ni a hunzi biani*').

One by one, people rose to share their knowledge, stories, questions, and concerns. Many gave eloquent speeches, mostly in Sango with some French thrown in. The best orators drew hearty applause. Some interlocutors styled themselves peacemakers, arguing that both sides had valid concerns. Others drew applause for pointing out the unjust imbalance between the well-equipped armed *pisteurs* and those they targeted: 'A man who farms and works hard and saves and buys a bicycle, and then he gets caught and his bicycle taken and suddenly he is a poor man!' But in general people were impressively aware of the trade-offs and competing claims at stake.

Many spoke of the problem of 'the texts' ('*les textes*'), meaning laws and other conservation rules. People made frequent and explicit reference to the texts being out of touch with people's realities. As one would-be peacemaker put it: 'Let's return to the reality that this population needs to be able to live, and I pose myself the question of whether all the modern Central African laws are applied in all their vigour.' In other words, why should this be the one domain in which law was taken as determinative, above other social considerations?

Several hours in, attempting to shift the meeting from the 'recounting grievances' to the 'providing solutions' phase, the *sous-préfet* noted that 'in light of all these declarations it comes out that there has been misconduct all around. There is no need to exaggerate. And the heart of the problem would be to attack the texts that determine the parks, but that is a very long procedure' – and one that would take place far from Ndele and its surroundings and require the intervention of international forums (*'les instances internationales'*).[3] The key task, then, was to find a '*mango tere*': an understanding allowing people to secure their livelihoods without making a total mockery of the conservation laws and inviting the scrutiny of donor bureaucrats. Or, as the *sous-préfet* summed it up, '*Mbi bâ, mais mbi bâ pépé*' (I look, but I don't see – in other words, I look the other way, you hide in plain sight). The deputy head of the anti-poaching programme implicitly agreed, saying: 'There are certain kinds of things that we can't speak about in a heterogeneous setting like this one. For example, if the leader of the miners wants to work in a particular place he should come and see me so we can talk just the two of us, and without telling other people I could give him an authorisation.'

When the *sous-préfet* adjourned the meeting, well after noon, no decisions had been taken – but that was not the point. The miners were asked to obtain copies of the park maps and the laws governing diamond mining.[4] They were also to make suggestions to the anti-poaching project about areas where they should be allowed to mine – laws or no laws. No formal recommendations had been made before I left Ndele a month later. A couple of weeks after my departure, Ndele was attacked by an armed rebel group that had been based on the road to the north of town, and people's concerns shifted.

The meeting itself was the important thing here, even without any concrete resolutions; it was both a mutual show of force and strength, and a forum for negotiation and the mutual reinforcement of camouflage strategies. The *pisteurs* showed strength and latent force through their military costume and comportment. But the miners and their supporters also showed that their interests could not be ignored. They had drawn their dispute with the anti-poachers from the bush into town, where there were witnesses who would preserve its history. In the space created by this mutual show of force, all parties could agree on two things: first, that flexibility regarding laws, alternately using them and ignoring them, was useful to accommodate the largest number of the actors involved. Second,

[3] The presentation of laws as imposed by foreigners is not entirely correct (when it comes to laws, there is a tutelary relationship between donors and government officials that officials accept), but putting it that way had both pragmatic and self-serving aspects – pragmatic in that they were absolutely right that changing the laws would be near impossible, and self-serving in that it made it possible to disclaim responsibility for making decisions, or accepting accountability for them after the fact. It is another face of what I have called 'cunning victimhood' (Lombard 2016d).

[4] None of these maps had been brought to the meeting; the representative from the *brigade minière* (the Ministry of Mines) had only recently arrived in Ndele and had no idea what the geographical rules were.

they agreed that people should work to manage the circulation of information about one another's activities and enterprises across scales.[5]

Unavoidable camouflage, cultivated camouflage

One of the defining traits of peasants is that they are 'in no way economically dependent' on the state or other actors 'trying to tell [them] what to do'. Peasants often meet attempts to exercise authority by ignoring them, or with some other 'combination of confrontation, negotiation, subversion, acquiescence' (Graeber 2007: 167). Only committed anarchists, however, assume that all authority is inherently unwanted. In northeastern CAR, people are used to and feel entitled to some autonomy, but they are also aware of the oddness of their own position – that is, that they live in such an administratively emaciated place – and although they may see current arrangements as necessary, they do not see them as optimal. This double edge extends to how people think about armed conservation, and understanding their relationship to it requires understanding 'ambivalent statements, contradictory attitudes, incompatible values, and emotional internal clashes as research objects' (Berliner et al. 2016: 5). In fact, consistency is not always a paramount ideal; freedom from self-consistency may even be a prized value, overriding other values such as a desire for order (Scheele 2015).

People caught up in armed conservation enforcement in the hunting zone do not see disorder as an ideal. Nor do they believe in conservation as a utopian ideology in the manner of its planners and backers. They are far more likely to describe themselves as having to make do in the fallout from the far-from-ideal world they inhabit. They claim and appreciate autonomy; indeed, they depend on it. But few are satisfied with this state of affairs. Naturally enough, Central Africans experience attempts at control as attempts at seizure, with the polemical edge (unjust, unfair) that term suggests, and they reject such attempts when they can. Yet people also see downsides to the fact that no one is implementing control in a rational-bureaucratic, impartial way. People see the state's absence

[5] In order to reach these two common stances, it was also helpful to create an external, clueless 'boss' (in this case *munju*, non-African, together with the state/international laws) who could serve as a repository for blame for the policies many people found objectionable and also as the figure who held responsibility for any effort to regularise the flexibility that life in the area requires. Or, to emphasise the less exotic aspects of these dynamics, the discussion at the meeting was a local version of a conundrum that often bedevils collective projects: do we try to change the structure, or do we find a way to work within it? In this case, it was agreed that changing the laws would be next to impossible, and therefore working stealthily within the system was a better option.

as a problem, even as it leaves them able to claim opportunities and to operate with more leeway than they would enjoy in more closely surveilled places (Lombard 2015). Even the long-term funders of armed conservation, who have themselves cultivated stealth in the form of camouflage in order to keep these projects funded, recognise that the projects' overall record is poor.

Camouflage is particularly useful in the context of discontinuous social, geographic, and bureaucratic landscapes, the locus of conservation projects today and colonial ones before them. That is, rather than a state or state-like entity that manages 'its' population in 'its' territory, conservation projects in Central Africa have entailed the interplay of interested funders, conservation supporters, and exposers of neocolonial abuse far from the space in question, with residents who participate in conservation without feeling that participation removes their need for autonomy in managing their careers and relations.

Camouflage as interpersonal skill and resource

Throughout the armed conservation years, access to parkland resources has been widely contested – sometimes overtly, sometimes surreptitiously. Access to parkland resources is highly contentious, not just because no one agrees on the limits of the parks.

Some *pisteurs* turn their position – geographic or administrative – to acquisitive advantage. Anti-poaching bases lie within or beside the parks, offering both staff and the villagers who serve the projects privileged access to game, fish, diamonds, and other wild goods.[6] To the extent that locally based project staffers note these practices in their reports, they describe them in moral and individualised terms. For instance, in September 1990 an anti-poaching guard arrested a hunter he found in the park. Both were slightly injured during their disputation, the hunter more gravely. The anti-poaching guard was then locked up – 'totally without justification', said the project staff – at the detention centre run by the Bamingui *gendarmerie*. The *gendarmerie*'s 'apparently inexplicable' reaction, indicated project staff, was due to the fact that its local head was an avid organiser of hunting parties and wanted to send a signal to potential enforcers that he would not accept their actions. Now that he had been outed and transferred, though, there developed a 'close collaboration' between the

[6] Without the programmes that are, in theory, meant to prevent and patrol these trades, the Manovo, Gounda, and Sangba base villages would not exist. According to the law, no one is allowed to live in the parks and the villages are illegal, but they were nevertheless officially recognised by the government.

gendarmerie and the *pisteurs* – the implication being that the head of the Bamingui *gendarmerie* was the sole corrupt actor (all quotes from PDRN 1990: 9). However, read together, two decades' worth of conservation project reports show that the involvement of *pisteurs* and government functionaries in the gathering of wild goods was persistent.

Interestingly, some anti-poaching guards and people living in conservation areas have expressed to me wholehearted support for the most draconian of conservation measures. The prevalence of wild acquisition by people who also averred the need to end it through adherence to hard-line conservation and anti-hunting policies seems inconsistent. How can they accept salaries for jobs intended to end the acquisition of wild goods at the same time as they support usages that contravene conservation action and principles? Were they simply lying, or otherwise self-interested? Justifying one's own exception to the rule may be the most human of traits.

But self-interest is only one part of the picture. In the hunting zone, no one has the material, human, or philosophical resources (and perhaps not even the desire) to thoroughly control everyone else. Some people – for example, or especially, project staff – are present only briefly and others live out their lives there. Many of the conflicts that arise can be hidden, either because they are well placed to escape oversight or because it is in the interest of the privileged to look but not see. Such circumstances hardly facilitate consistency according to abstract principles. Instead, freedom from self-consistency appreciates in value, along with negotiation skills and the ability to threaten or invoke force. People may quickly agree to collaborate, particularly with those passing through. And they do want to work together. But they also must look out for themselves, and the attempted control they have experienced hasn't seemed transparent and fair but arbitrary and unjust. Therefore a willingness to think flexibly rather than scrupulously follow rules means that they can balance their own interests in imperfect and unpredictable circumstances. Privilege is a key factor in these camouflage games. There is a public secret that certain people – especially but not only *corps habillés* and those who can call on them – enjoy special exceptions from rules. Sam, a guard at the Water and Forest Ministry office in Ndele, inadvertently showed how expectations of privilege allow for the belief in opposing systems of rules.

Sam was the leader in recounting a story many in town were discussing at the time when I approached and joined him and his fellow idle employees on the porch. Sam was a cosmopolitan. He dressed in clean new clothes, including brand-name tracksuits, rather than the cheap Chinese knockoffs intermittently available in the market in Ndele. He also had greater facility with metropolitan life than any of the others – he had a bank account and he spoke excellent French. Sam seemed intent on moving up in the world, and, unlike many other ambitious young men, the confidence that it was only a matter of time. Sam was telling the story, and the four others present added commentary and moral inflection.

The story concerned a man named Clovis. Like the group on the porch, Clovis worked for the Ministry of Water and Forests, but he was posted further north and east than Ndele. Clovis had received a leave, and he hitched a ride on the back of one of the Sudanese commercial trucks[7] that provide the only motorised transport in the area to visit his family in Bangui.[8] When one travels outside the capital, even just a few kilometres, one is obliged to return with food, preferably meat; if you don't, your family might turn you away. Partly this is because foodstuffs are much cheaper outside the capital and one can obtain much more for one's money. It is also because the kinds of food available outside the capital are hard to find elsewhere, and items such as smoked meat from the north-east's large animals, including buffalo, are prized. The intense flavour means that a little can make a lot of people feel well fed. Even conservation project staff (especially conservation project staff!) would be expected to bring smoked meat for family and acquaintances when they returned to the capital. The West African nuns who staffed the Catholic mission in Ndele quickly learned how disappointed their Central African sisters in Bangui would be if they arrived for a visit without meat and dutifully stockpiled buckets before a journey south. Smoked game from the north-east is almost all illegal, both because no one gets the required permits and because the areas around the roads are almost all protected no-hunting zones.

Wishing for a good welcome when he finally got home, Clovis carried a sack of smoked meat. The truck was stopped by project *pisteurs*. They demanded to search everyone's belongings. Clovis was dressed in regular clothes. If he had worn his camouflage work uniform, perhaps he would have given the impression of having status as 'one of us' and they would have skipped him. But they did not. He was searched like all the others, a humiliating process (Lombard 2013a). The guards took his meat, even though Clovis carried a *laissez-passer* (see below) from the Water and Forests Ministry office at Ndele. Such papers are a service some *kota azo* (big people) provide to smooth what can be an arduous journey through roadblocks to the capital. They are material proof of the person's

[7] On their journey south from Sudan towards the DRC the transporters sell manufactured goods including toothpaste and plastic kettles for handwashing. In southern CAR and DRC they purchase coffee, which they then take back to sell in Sudan.

[8] It can also be possible to hire a motorcycle and driver, but that is prohibitively expensive for most people.

relationship with someone due deference and exceptional status, a status that should be transferable (to a degree) across the relationship.

As Sam told the story (in Sango), the others present interjected, saying how angry they would have been to be treated in this way. Sam agreed with fervour: 'If it were me in Clovis's place, the whole town would know what happened. I would not let them get away with it.'[9] The threat in that statement was clear to all of us. Moreover, everyone agreed, the *pisteurs* were out of their jurisdiction. Their work was not on the road, only in the bush. The lone woman employee of the office, a secretary, said she frequently bought meat from the *pisteurs*, a statement she offered as proof of their hypocrisy. She added: 'And the paper Clovis got from the head of office here – doesn't that have any value for them? And if tomorrow they were the ones to show up here in front of our authorities [who would, she implied, treat them with the same lack of deference], how would they feel? It's not right.'[10]

The conversation then switched to other topics. Two men discussed their stomach problems (dysentery, they wondered?), and then a few stepped away to deal with a dispute that was in progress at the Water and Forests-operated roadblock some 50 feet away.

Later that morning, I chatted with Sam (in French now) about the conservation strictures for the area. They seemed impossibly harsh to me. How would people get enough to eat if they couldn't hunt? Sam disagreed. The laws served the greater good, he argued. He began an explanation that could have been used for one of the conservation project's funding requests, so clear and unequivocal was its defence of hunting regulations. He illustrated his points by noting how much more money people stood to gain by refraining from hunting – that is, from ceding such rights to tourists who would pay vast sums in taxes, most of which devolved to the ZCV – as opposed to the small and temporary gain of hunting for oneself. I said I was sceptical. He continued to disagree, arguing that what I described as draconian prohibitions are a good, rational system for Central Africans.

In the span of just a few hours, then, Sam went from energetically defending his privilege to hunt and transport meat ('If it were me in Clovis's place …') to carefully yet emphatically explaining why he and other Central Africans should cede such rights. One way of interpreting inconsistency of this kind would be to say that, in his conversation with

[9] In Sango: 'Tongana mbi yeke na place ti Clovis mbi yeke ziya ni na ala pepe. Azo kwe ayeke hinga tene ni.'

[10] In Sango: 'Na mbeti so autorité ti ge asala so ake na valeur ape? Mais tongana kekereke ala la akiri ge, ala yeke sala tongana nyen?'

me, he was simply telling me what he thought I – a white foreigner of presumed humanitarian/conservation sympathies – would want to hear. That was likely a factor, as is the tendency to agree with rules while making exceptions for oneself. But social scientists have often been too quick to attempt to grapple with an inconsistency by 'dissolving one side of the paradox' (Steinberg 2013) in exactly these ways.

In fact, coercive conservation in north-eastern CAR has been many things at once: eagerly supported, deeply contested, and actively resisted. Many people in the area describe how they used to encounter all kinds of wild animals when out and about and now are lucky if they cross paths with that resourceful scavenger the baboon, or crop-eating warthogs. While they do not mourn that their fields are less likely to be ravaged by elephants, they link the loss of animals to the other dispossessions they've known in recent decades, brought on by increasing armed conflict in the region. Whereas once the only thing slowing children on their way to school was an encounter with a lion or buffalo on the road (not, in fact, something that happened very often), more recently schools have frequently been shuttered and are always understaffed and ill-equipped. People worry that children allowed to roam might encounter violence or be kidnapped for ransom. The two trends – the decline in wild animals and the rise in armed conflict – are intertwined. Rather than resisting armed conservation, then, people have gone along with the proscriptions associated with it while making use of the state's absence, the vastness and sparse human population of the space, and the possibility to negotiate to do other things as well. Sam's statements are evidence not of insincerity or irony but of his skill with camouflage. Camouflage shifts away from the requirement of sincerity and towards the productive management of inconsistency, showing different facets in different settings.

Camouflage thus has some parallels with the linguistic concept of code switching: that is, using different languages for different interlocutors to express a range of ideas and orientations towards the world. It is about how people blend in or hide in plain sight in multiple 'epistemic communities' (Miller and Fox 2001) simultaneously. But 'code switching' and 'epistemic communities' both suggest that an actor makes choices in relation to his or her somewhat static conception of the surroundings. Camouflage further draws out the ways in which people help or hinder each other in these endeavours, making camouflage a fundamentally social and relational process.

Consider the *laissez-passers* like the one Clovis held, also referred to as *services*. These are documents – sometimes just a scrap of paper and at other times a typed sheet with official stamps – that a functionary prepares for someone wishing to avoid search and seizure at roadblocks. The functionary might provide the paper for a fee, or as a gift. (Interestingly, according to *les textes*, state officials caught in breach of conservation and hunting laws are supposed to receive double the penalties assessed others. This is yet another example of how law is divorced from the realities of camouflage and privilege as they play out.)

During my time in Ndele, people talked about the last prosecutor assigned to the tribunal in town. He was a prolific *service* issuer. He transported large quantities of smoked meat to Bangui, both for his family and for sale, and also sold or donated *services* to others so that they could do the same. The wording of the documents varied, but their effective meaning was that the bearers' goods should be treated as if they were the property of the issuer of the *service*, thus exempt from search. (*Kota azo*, important people, are generally exempt from search and seizure, but, of course, status as *kota zo* can change.) For the most part, the *service* lets its bearer and their goods hide in plain sight. It was helpful in a way for road-blockers and other searchers, too – they could avoid looking more thoroughly without making an open mockery of the whole search process. The *service* reiterated the relationship between the person blocking the road and the person issuing the *service*: neither exactly hierarchical nor cooperative, but acknowledging common privilege in relation to visibility and seizure. By abiding by the *service*'s terms, road-blockers lost some revenue, but they knew that, in the long run, doing so saved them greater hassle. An irritated prosecutor could have called them in for a protracted and expensive hearing on spurious charges, for instance. Thus, while camouflage requires individual skill, it is all the more effective in social contexts where everyone participates. When others acknowledge the benefit of the camouflage game, it is easier for people to pursue inconsistent projects simultaneously, without the dissonance becoming an issue. People who refrain from participating in the game often find themselves marginalised.

Camouflage is a skill, that is learned. It is one expression of the social aspects of an 'economy of appearances' (Tsing 2000); It is also a means of working together without joining a group or community. Fundamentally, it is a means of managing visibility in the context of relationships that entail neither explicit collaboration nor avoidance, and are partly structured by claims to privilege.

Camouflage is social; it requires others' participation, which one cannot control. A jealous or spiteful colleague might draw attention to another's camouflage, making that person impossible to un-see, and thereby pushing them out of the ranks of the privileged. Making camouflage lose its ability to hide is often a matter of naming aloud the multi-scalar entanglements of a stateless-state space. That is, it often entails making it impossible for the non-resident people who are supposed to be providing legal and bureaucratic oversight to turn their faces away from contradictions. Exposing camouflage in this manner is far from a surefire method for obtaining what one desires, but, combined with other methods – threats, for example – it can help force negotiation. In the case of the Ndele prosecutor, the conservation staff, goaded by an energetic AT, decided to pursue him for his hunting, for reasons both of principle and personal dislike. The prosecutor's trafficking was publicly aired and he was removed from his post. He was promoted a few months later, however. The AT was summarily fired a few months later – by his account, because he had too-zealously pursued those gaining from the 'local' bushmeat trade.

Bureaucratic camouflage across scales

It is a remarkable achievement that Project Conservation has continued for as long as it has. Aid projects of this type are supposed to 'build capacity' so that 'the state' can take over on its own; they are not meant to continue indefinitely. Funding is supposed to be contingent on measurable progress. And a development funder such as the EU is not supposed to fund a militarised undertaking (Marijnen 2017). But EU-funded armed conservation in north-eastern CAR ran from 1987 to 2004, again from 2007 to 2010, and restarted in 2012 – despite the fact that EU staff in Bangui declared categorically in 2003 that the endeavour had 'failed' (Pampaloni 2003). Dozens of guards were killed on anti-poaching patrols, and people continued to hunt and herd in off-limits spaces. The wildlife populations have been decimated. But despite armed conservation having stepped in for the state yet without acting state-like in exactly the way donors shied away from, and despite it not seeming to achieve its goals, organisers managed repeatedly to breathe new life into it. This was because they, too, became adept at using camouflage. They found and created possibilities for hiding in plain sight at the intersection of bureaucratic procedure and the characteristics of remote spaces.

Central Africans and foreigners interested in operating in CAR tend to share the assumption that 'the state' should be the entity that organises and controls people and territory and credibly claims a monopoly on violence.[11] They also agree that a state of that kind is not present in CAR.

[11] An exception is the people attracted to CAR because it seems like a place that runs on greasing palms; these include Mads Brügger's undercover character in his documentary *The Ambassador* (2011), set in CAR.

Their normative, teleological commitment lets them resolve this tension: if a state of that kind is not present, it is because the existing apparatus needs a bit more money and 'capacity', not because it operates according to other principles, or in response to other exigencies. When it comes to conservation, the state's absence is often presented as an opportunity for private concessions that can work more efficiently. Proposals of this type generally elide the possibility that 'the state' and other actors might not be in perfect symbiosis, as in this iteration:

> The plan includes the possibility to split the parks into blocks of more manageable size. The blocks could then be rented to private operators. This would enable the state to regain control and then manage areas that have been effectively abandoned. (Bouché et al. 2012: 7010)

The passage could have been written by the architects of the Afrique Équatoriale Française concession debacle (1890–1930). The idea is that concessions will develop state-like capacities that 'the state' can recuperate for its own, but that never happens. Concessionary politics (Hardin 2011; Smith 2015b) allow people to step in and act in the name of the absent state without submitting to the thorough oversight and reciprocity that are supposed to be its hallmarks. And while there may be a number of people who see themselves as acting in the name of the state, none of them are very state-like in their way of going about things. They are all more hunter-like in their orientation and practices. This is true not just of the Central Africans, but of the aid donors and other expatriates. Using camouflage in the midst of bureaucratic rules and procedures can be a powerful and exciting means of operating and a way of furthering projects when institutional structure and principle would seek to curtail them. Without 'camouflagers', north-eastern CAR might not get any aid at all.

Camouflage is a pragmatics of action in a hard-to-police and often ignored space. Most scholarly attention to camouflage assumes it to be a military technique, a technique of statecraft (Jusionyte 2015; Povinelli 2011). But hunters, raiders, and other forcible acquirers use it too, including to subvert statecraft. Camouflage can be used to navigate bureaucratic landscapes, taking advantage of their affordances[12] while not being bound to them.[13] It is not simply something that 'the state'

[12] Webb Keane defines an 'ethical affordance' as 'aspects of people's experiences of themselves, of other people, or of their surroundings, that they may draw on as they make ethical evaluations and decisions, whether consciously or not' (2014: 7).

[13] Some might counter that state actors often do things that go against the ideologies of stateness, and that such actions are central to statecraft (Jusionyte 2015; Roitman 2005). There are two disadvantages to that argument. One is that it risks making anything anyone associated with the state does into 'statecraft', and in so doing broadens the category of 'state' to the point that it no longer describes anything specific. Another is

(whoever or whatever one sees as comprising that state) uses for its own purposes, but a way people subvert or co-opt aspects of the state or institutional resources for their own ends.

A number of anthropologists have drawn attention to the leeway that remains within the apparent strictures of laws and bureaucratic procedures. Veena Das (2007) has argued that state laws and procedures are fundamentally illegible, both for people tasked with carrying them out and for those who come to 'the state' as supplicants or applicants for particular services. As a result, the state is imbued with magical, unpredictable capabilities alongside its rational-bureaucratic ones, and, in fact, the two modes are intertwined. Similarly, Ilana Feldman (2008) makes the point that it is possible not only to have government without a state, but that government is the product less of law than of the things that civil servants do. Both recognise that skilled civil servants arrayed in a bureaucracy can create unexpected outcomes. But where Das is primarily interested in the power of the state to make visible and recognise, and Feldman is primarily interested in the reproductive capacities of leaderless bureaucracies, bureaucratic camouflage draws out a different aspect: namely, bureaucratic actors' ability to strategically use forms to disguise the details of those actions that are contrary to organisational principle – without breaking the law or failing to follow procedure. In the case of EU-funded armed conservation, the people who 'read' reports in order to verify that protocol has been followed understand what they have read. But, in refraining from asking further questions, they enter into the weak social relations of complicity in allowing privileges beyond those originally envisioned.

For instance, a person involved in organising funding for armed conservation in CAR cultivated skills to use bureaucratic money in non-bureaucratic ways, to blend in with the letter of bureaucratic procedure while nevertheless doing what he wanted. He repeatedly deferred his own promotion because he knew it would bring him to a different level in the organisation, one where he would lose access to the institutional and personnel terrain that he had so assiduously studied, knowledge crucial to making his camouflage work and to the sense of power and efficacy he drew from it. While someone less creative with rules, and with a greater desire for advancement, might have concluded that supporting conservation in the midst of a war would cause more problems than it would solve, he was convinced that something must be done to try to save the animals, and committed himself to finding ways to do it, however imperfect the results.

that it makes it harder to account for the ways in which people talk about ideal state practices and distinguish those from the actual practices of state actors in their midst.

One challenge to pursuing LABs (coercive anti-poaching patrols) under EU auspices was that the EU sees itself as a development funder. Armed projects are therefore difficult to justify unless they are in direct support of state forces, for example through security-sector reform projects. Armed conservation is a grey zone because it creates an extra-state militia that, while technically attached to a ministry, was functionally separate. The militia's weapons and ammunition were to be supplied by the government, and the EU would fund the rest. However, the *État centrafricain* that signed the project protocols was perennially unreliable when it came time for project staff to ask for its contributions. Project employees lamented the *pisteurs*' insufficient weaponry in the face of foes who were well supplied as a result of the wars in Chad and Sudan. So they had to get creative. For instance, in the early years it was possible to sneak in ammunition under the general budget category of '*pièces détachées*' (spare parts). Hiding this expenditure in the 'spare parts' budget line did not require transforming the ammunition into something else, or covering it up with a mask – ammunition is, after all, a kind of 'spare part' – it simply required finding a way to describe it so that it would blend in under the budgetary radar, so to speak. Safari hunters also sometimes provided material, and from time to time the government distributed munitions. From 2007, a safari hunter-funded private organisation paid for some of the martial aspects of the project, such as hiring mercenaries.

Moreover, the attitude of many at the headquarters in Brussels resembled that of colonial officials – they preferred not to know the dirty details of protecting wildlife and biodiversity in Central Africa. It suited their own career interests to 'look, but not see', as the Central African idiom has it.

The structure of the EU bureaucracy itself helped. For instance, the EU has been working for some time to change the formerly dyadic relationship between Brussels headquarters and recipient capitals by bolstering regional offices – in this case, Libreville in Gabon – and by developing programmes that cover multiple countries so that officials can share experiences and plan transnationally coherent policies. In theory, regionalisation would make projects less top-down and more accountable. In practice, EU staff in Bangui told me, it meant that reports for projects they were funding were often sent to Libreville first, eventually making their way back to Bangui long after strategic decisions had been taken, making it even more difficult to keep track of what was going on.

By 2000, the EU's appetite to fund a stand-alone conservation project in CAR had dwindled, but regionalisation offered new opportunities for camouflage. Using hunting tactics, project supporters were able to fold the CAR-only PDRN into a regional endeavour, ECOFAC, which began in 1992. ECOFAC was created as a vehicle to pursue the biodiversity and rainforest conservation imperatives of the 1990s, and it covered the various Equatorial African rainforests.[14] (If you are struggling to keep up with the acronyms, note that their proliferation, too, can assist in bureaucratic camouflage, simply by causing eyes to glaze over.) North-eastern CAR is, of course, not a rainforest. But the zone was slipped in nonetheless – on a regional map, the distances seem short and it was close enough to the other projects to seem a plausible addition.[15]

CAR's forested savannah was an anomaly in another way, too. It was the only one of ECOFAC's sites to include funding for armed, coercive patrols, justified on the grounds that the 'participatory' safari-hunting revenue-sharing system would be untenable without an anti-poaching presence. But CAR's northern region effectively disappeared amid the hundreds of pages of reports about the other ECOFAC sites. In my perusal of the EU archives on armed conservation in Bangui, I noticed a shift as CAR-focused projects gave way to the regional ECOFAC. Now, in addition to various minor reports on CAR, there were massive tomes with long sections on each of the various participant countries' projects under the ECOFAC umbrella. In a short section at the back, I found the reports from north-eastern CAR. The new dispatches seemed hollow compared with the old, detailed reports on CAR. But for someone without that archival perspective, the new reports probably would not raise any alarm bells indicating that more study was necessary.

With the exception of the few people with a long-term interest in these projects (such as the promotion-avoider mentioned above), most EU officials working on conservation in CAR cycled out after just a few years, and institutional memory was very limited. One particularly perceptive official evaluating the funding request for ECOFAC IV (2007–10) wrote that 'the general impression given by the ECOFAC funding request is that this is the first project of its kind. No quantification of the gains of the previous phases is given' (EC: n.d.a).[16] However,

[14] At different times it has involved the Democratic Republic of the Congo, the Republic of the Congo, Cameroon, Equatorial Guinea, São Tomé and Príncipe, and the south-western tropical forests of CAR.

[15] Officially, the northern CAR component went by the acronym PDZCV – the second-generation name for the PDRN (ZCV stands for *zones cynégétiques villageoises*, a revenue-sharing scheme for people in safari-hunting areas). However, people generally referred to the project as ECOFAC.

[16] 'L'impression générale que donne la PF d'ECOFAC est qu'il s'agit d'un premier projet de ce type: aucune quantification des acquis des phases antérieurs n'est donnée. Le chapitre 3.2 "problèmes spécifiques" fait une description qui pourrait correspondre au démarrage d'un programme de conservation plutôt qu'à un projet de lutte contre la pauvreté en cours depuis plus de dix ans. On pourrait en déduire que les objectifs prévus les trois phases précédentes du programme, n'ont pas été atteints.'

most of the time such elisions slid past unnoticed. Despite these misgivings, ECOFAC IV received its funding.

Regionalisation also created new opportunities for budgetary camouflage.

> The monitoring of the budget allocated … has suffered from the distance between the coordination cell and Bangui; this monitoring hurt the project a lot because it cost between 250,000 and 300,000 CFA to bring the financial records to Libreville where they are verified and where the accounts are controlled and the reimbursements are made.[17] (European Commission n.d.b)[18]

In 2010, fully 85 per cent of the PDZCV's expenditure was 'unallowed'. By the time this was discovered, however, it was too late to recover the improperly spent cash. Although reports eventually made their way back to the European Commission's Bangui office, the environmental officers there found it difficult to keep up with the stacks of reports that accrued on their desks,[19] and they had limited incentive to read them closely, given that important decisions were generally taken elsewhere.

Bureaucratic procedure can, of course, be turned to ends of camouflage by those who believe that their interests and vision are better served by doing so, and doing so is possible even in capital cities (indeed, offices in Brussels were key sites in armed conservation camouflage). But it is particularly exploitable, or cultivable, when the geographical territory in question is far from the hub of bureaucratic activity – such as in stateless-state spaces like the hunting zone. This is yet another consequence of its inconsistent status – stateless, yet within a state – in the midst of the normative nation-state order. 'The state' has become an a priori repository for deontological legitimacy. But in places where 'the state' works in ways far from the roles imagined in its ideal type, people are left without a normative ethics that fits their lives. This is particularly evident in relation to the use of violence. States are normatively

[17] In 2010, fully 85 per cent of the PDZCV's expenditure was 'unallowed'. By the time this was discovered, however, it was too late to recover the improperly spent cash.

[18] 'Le suivi du budget alloué à la composante a souffert de l'éloignement de la cellule de coordination de Bangui; ce suivi a coûté assez cher au projet lorsque l'on doit payer entre 250 à 300.00 francs Cfa pour acheminer les pièces comptables à Libreville là où elles sont vérifiées et où les mémoires sont contrôlés ainsi que les remboursements sont effectués.'

[19] This was part of how I got access to the archives: after hearing of my interest in armed conservation, one official suggested that I read the archived and contemporary reports and summarise them for her, as she would never have time to read them all herself. Indeed, she had nearly a year's backlog of reports to read, and her job description did not include perusing the archives.

understood to claim a monopoly on violence; state and international law assess the legitimacy of violence in relation to that principle. But in places such as north-eastern CAR, the fiction of a state monopoly on violence is difficult to uphold in the face of constant evidence to the contrary, so people assert both the importance of the principle and the need to take things into their own hands.

This state-violence-legitimacy node is thus another way in which north-eastern CAR is a place of confusion and opportunity, and it is another aspect of the state – as a normative landscape – in which one must carefully position oneself. This is not because 'the state' as an agglomeration of actors proceeds in any corporate fashion or otherwise inquires into what is going on. It is because, in this UN nation-state order, certain kinds of violence appear problematic to international observers and others with humanitarian interests, none of whom seeks to claim full control of the area but many of which are intermittently concerned about its affairs. 'The state' is supposed to claim a monopoly on the use of force; it is supposed to be the entity conducting policing and the like. Therefore, coercive and potentially violent projects such as anti-poaching work that claim to act on behalf of the state and to be a force for strengthening state capacities may draw little attention (even if their actual effects are the opposite). In contrast, those that position themselves as private or otherwise non-state actors can attract much more scrutiny.

For instance, Bruce Hayse, an American doctor, adventurist, and philanthropist, attracted much attention – mostly negative or incredulous – when he decided to launch Africa Rainforest and Rivers Conservation (ARRC) Inc. in 2002. Under a private mandate from the CAR president, Ange-Félix Patassé (in office 1993–2003), ARRC would employ mercenaries and Central Africans to police poachers in the eastern third of the country (Clynes 2009; Lowy 2002). ARRC ended up never conducting a single patrol.[20] Still, the group has proven to be a useful thought experiment for people interested in describing the creation of enclaves outside state control. For instance, anthropologist James Ferguson adduced ARRC as a key demonstration of new forms of corporate/private governmentality on the continent (2006). A law review article charted the tangled web of international and domestic laws that might assess the legality of the militia's actions and concluded with only a qualified verdict: 'If the

[20] Hayse had hired a South African of ill repute to lead the militia, and swarms of rumours (diamond dealing, death threats, embezzlement) quickly clouded the organisation's reputation. Its equipment, vehicles, and bank balances disappeared.

shooting of poachers on sight were established as murder' – as opposed, for instance, to self-defence or necessary protection of biodiversity – 'no similarly persuasive rationale would excuse Hayse's protection strategy for the Chinko Basin' (Shanahan 2004: 253). (I heard about the article from a long-term conservationist in CAR, who found its fixation on capital-L Law inexplicable to the point of immorality given the circumstances the conservationists faced.)

Meanwhile, none of the coverage mentioned that, at the same time ARRC was attempting to establish operations, ECOFAC *pisteurs* – funded by EU money – were doing the same type of work elsewhere in the country, under a similar kind of concessionaire autonomy. The journalistic coverage of ARRC was also silent about how widespread violent anti-poaching policies are. A number of African governments have equipped their park guards with standing shoot-to-kill orders – among them Tanzania, Kenya, Zimbabwe, and Malawi (Neumann 2004b: 814). Instead of condemning militarised anti-poaching as such, the articles on ARRC seemed to find something inherently worrisome about the *private* character of the intervention; had it been clearly an action of the state, it would not have drawn the same attention. But stateless-state spaces such as the hunting zone defy category. In these spaces, the claim of relationship with the state, whether abstractly or in practical terms, can be a means of gaining greater leeway to pursue one's own interests. Just as al-Sanusi's 'submission' to Rabih and the French was a means not of submission but of recognising and suspending mutual threat, conservation projects developed institution-facing fronts that excused potential overseers or whistle-blowers from paying too close attention. Presenting a non-threatening mien could allow much more freedom of action, including towards the ends of acquisition and other projects.

Conclusion

In his study of the shift from social and relational to legal and private property-oriented ways of managing wild goods and spaces in England in the eighteenth century, British historian E. P. Thompson had the benefit of centuries of hindsight. The 'force and stealth' he identified as key to the intermediary period – when people still held on to social modes and had not accepted legal ones – were eventually supplanted by greater acceptance of (or acquiescence to) law, courts, and police as the proper arbiters of access to goods and space. In England, that shift occurred in conjunction with broader societal transformations that were under way at the same time – the end of feudalism, the rise of industrialisation. North-eastern CAR is on a very different historical trajectory.[21] That does not foreclose the possibility that stealth and force could transform in other ways, as indeed they have through the rise of rebellion and humanitarian-modulated arrangements such as displaced person settlements. But everyone in north-eastern CAR feels that degrees of 'stateness' (Nettle 1968) are decreasing, not becoming stronger, and many experience that as a problem.

How exactly camouflage-stealth will fare as a means of facilitating projects in tension with each other or with the institutional foundations of funding organisations remains an open question. Camouflage is a skill that people can develop in order to help each other use those institutional structures for their own gymnastic endeavours without drawing attention to the ways in which they might be causing the bars to creak or strain. People have to at least tacitly work together in order for it to be effective, and though the social ties created that way are weak, they nevertheless help define the mutable bounds of who gets to enjoy privilege when it comes to acquisition and access and related projects. And while this is particularly obvious in relation to happenings in remote places, there is little to prevent it occurring in capitals too.

[21] I try not to be deterministic even when historical continuities are profound, as in the issues of manhunting and disputable status that have marked north-eastern CAR. Empirically minded people like me tend to be sceptics. We tend to look at what has happened in the past, decry it, and use our rejection of it as part of a rationale for doing things differently in future. Much good has been accomplished by variations on this process. But armed conservation has been a utopian project, and its backers' refusal to let go of the hope that it will work is hard for the empirically minded to value perhaps to our detriment.

7 Denunciation and liberty*

In Chapter 4 I promised a return to the shade beside *pisteur* Boris-Harding's house, and a seat in the low wooden lounge chairs common in the region – a less throne-like version of the Adirondack chairs I grew up relaxing in outside the houses of my childhood in New England. Many of the guards and their families treated the base housing as exactly what it was: temporary lodging. But Boris-Harding and his wife and two young children tended their yard with precision. He had observed the cosmos and marigolds that beautified hunting lodges' grounds, and had once admired a yard full of sunflowers in Bangui. Both reminded him of scenes glimpsed in movies. He had asked proprietors for seeds and strove to recreate a bit of foreign refinement at his own place. While I chatted with Boris-Harding about his life and work, the older of his children intermittently came and leaned on his knees, intent and silent as she listened to a language – French – she would learn when she began school a couple of years later.

At that point, late 2009, Boris-Harding had been working as a *pisteur* for less than two years, but he had already been promoted from a rank-and-file tracker-guard to a team leader in charge of about eight guards. He was 27, less than two years my junior. Although he was relatively new to this work, he had grown up around it. His father had worked as a safari lodge *pisteur*, and Boris and Harding were the names of expatriate hunters and anti-poachers his father had worked for and admired. Boris-Harding had continued the tradition in choosing his children's names. They had received the names of the current AT, with whom Boris-Harding was especially close, and a conservation scientist from the more profligate era when his father was working and there was money for endeavours beyond the LAB and the ZCVs. His father worked for one of CAR's most famous safari-hunting guides, Matthieu Laboureur. According to Boris-Harding, one day his father and fellow *pisteurs* were

* Parts of this chapter have been published previously in Lombard (2018b).

seizing 500 elephant tusks when the people who had killed the elephants caught them. His father was shot in the shoulder. He was airlifted to Bangui for surgery and recovered. 'But because my father is illiterate he did not follow the dossier well [he did not know how to navigate the bureaucracy], and the money was diverted [*détourné*, the usual Central African word to refer to this type of corruption]. He never saw the money. That's what made him angry, and he decided to return to farming.'

Boris-Harding's older brother had become a *pisteur* and radio operator at a safari-hunting lodge to get vengeance for the way in which his father had been treated. He experienced the attack on their father as an assault on his personal integrity, on his status as a person worthy of respect. The sons wanted to show that the denigration had been wrong, and their subjecting the author of the injustice to similar treatment would be evidence of that wrongness: this is the proper state of affairs those advocating vengeance wish to bring about. One day Boris-Harding's brother saw a bush fire and was on his way to check it out so that he could alert his fellow *pisteurs*. Along the way he started following what he recognised as the tracks left by herders on horseback. He was alone; three of them found him. They beat him and broke his arm so badly that he could not walk. He haemorrhaged internally and died there in the bush.

Now it was Boris-Harding's turn to claim vengeance, this time on behalf of both his father and his brother. That was exactly how Boris-Harding spoke of it: he became a *pisteur* to get vengeance for what had happened to his family. (There were other important reasons, chief among them that *pisteur* was very nearly the only salaried occupation in the region, and that he was good at it, and took pride in being good at it.) Other *pisteurs* used the language of revenge, too: *vengeance* in French, or *futa kula*[1] in Sango. Vengeance is not just a quest to balance out a harm, in the functionalist way it has sometimes been represented. It is a demand for status and respect in a context in which that status has been compromised or assaulted.

Six months after Boris-Harding finished training, he was alone on a bicycle when he came upon a horse-mounted 'poacher' (his term). They were abruptly face to face, not unlike Jean-Claude and the elephant he tracked (see Chapter 4). 'I shot first and I sent the guy to heaven, and then

[1] *Kula* means both vengeance and debt; indeed, these are thought of in similar terms in Sango. (Sometimes Sango speakers using French will refer to a mission of vengeance as collecting on a debt.) *Futa kula* is the verb form.

I killed his horse and I cut off its tail as a form of evidence. People congratulated me, and I was promoted to team leader!' (cited in Tubiana 2018).[2]

The idea that access to the goods available in spaces not inhabited by humans *should* be regulated by law is a recent invention. Even in relatively densely populated and government-intensive places, the move to a law for the open spaces was slow, fitful, and contested, workable largely because people's sources of income and livelihoods shifted, and because they learned to be good Fooles, in the Hobbesian sense[3] (Hoekstra 1997), breaking covenants contrary to their interests as stealthily as possible. But if stealth proved to be a communicative undertaking, force is one as well. What does force in the context of armed conservation and acquisitive politics intend to communicate? What witnesses do its authors want to impress? People in the region who would shudder at it? People elsewhere who might be scandalised? What values underlie their moves? *Pisteurs* often use the idiom of vengeance to answer those questions or to explain why they pursue manhunts.

Vengeance has often been thought of as a mode of law, for instance in the form of *lex talionis*, 'an eye for an eye' (Miller 2005). In its legalistic formulation, vengeance is proposed as a mechanism that permits balancing. If you take my eye, it is just that I take yours, as the biblical cliché puts it. The prospect is supposed to deter people from ever doing such a thing, and to ensure that harm will be allocated equally if they do. This strikingly law-centred mode of vengeance is one that is already headed in the direction of contemporary judicial systems. State courts, rather than a rupture from vengeance-thinking, 'effectively limit [vengeance] to a single act of reprisal, enacted by a sovereign authority specialising in this particular function' (Girard 1977: 15).

The *pisteurs*, in contrast, are not operating in a context of judicially-managed vengeance. Theirs is a socially-organised vengeance, and vengeance of that kind can quickly become 'an interminable, infinitely repetitive process' (Girard 1977: 14). While even participants recognize that their actions in the name of vengeance will also be destructive, participating seems necessary. As René Girard noticed,

> In Greek tragedy, for instance, there is not – and cannot be – any consistent stand on the subject. To attempt to extract a coherent theory of vengeance from the

[2] 'J'ai tiré le premier et j'ai envoyé le gars au ciel, puis j'ai tué son cheval et lui ai coupé la queue, comme preuve. On m'a félicité et passé chef d'équipe!'

[3] The Foole plays an interesting role in Hobbes' text. The 'Foole' has noticed that there are times when self-interest and the keeping of covenants do not align. Hobbes allows that in such cases a person might break a covenant, not loudly or explicitly, but silently, weighing the risks of getting caught (Hoekstra 1997).

drama is to miss the essence of tragedy. For in tragedy each character passionately embraces or rejects vengeance depending on the position he occupies at any given moment in the scheme of the drama. (Girard 1977: 15)

And that is a key element: people's positions – as victors or as victims or something in between – shifts. That's why actions in the name of vengeance are inherently claims to status, claims to affix a position that nevertheless keeps getting overturned. Who will enjoy the privilege of not being messed with? Who can be subjected to depredation or other insult? Vengeance is particularly valuable to people without reliable access to institutional protections of persons or property. In order to keep that focus on mutable status and relation, and to keep some distance from the legalistic expressions of vengeance, I here develop an alternative analytical category: denunciation. Denunciation is a mode of claiming sovereignty – only not towards the traditionally ascribed sovereign values of unitarily controlling people and territory, but towards liberty: that is, towards asserting one's dignified status in the midst of forceful acquisition.

Manhunting and categorising violence

Anti-poaching manhunts such as Boris-Harding's encounter on the bicycle or the Tata ambush that opened this book are an outcome of circular reasoning about the mutual dangerousness of the parties involved. *Pisteurs* say they are hunting 'poachers' because the poachers are hunting them; the poachers say it's the other way round, and so on ad infinitum. The manhunts are violent, even lethal. The *pisteurs* kill people; some of those people kill *pisteurs*. This much is obvious. It is what the killings are evidence of, and what they do, that is contested and unclear.

Some people find them appalling. Others argue that the killing of humans is a lamentable, but justifiable, response to herders' and hunters' illegitimate acquisition. That framing, however, relies on the assumption that state ways of regulating acquisition have a prior legitimacy, a notion contradicted by ways of operating on the ground.[4] For this area is not part

[4] Prior assumptions are the foundation for any aspirational, utopian project, certainly including the building of a state. However, I am more interested in understanding what has been going on in north-eastern CAR, and the stories and observations I have collected offer little support for the assumption that a controlling, territorialised state is on its way (see also Lombard 2016d). *Pisteurs* would sometimes reference the law, and the fact that they were simply doing their utmost to uphold it. Any kind of exploitation or presence in the parks is 'strictly prohibited', they would say, and so any action they took against people violating that rule was morally justified. But this seems incomplete at best in view of the extent to which *pisteurs* were themselves involved in doing 'strictly prohibited' things in the parks (and, in fact, some of what they claimed was strictly prohibited was not, according to the letter of the law).

of a polity with material and symbolic coherence. That raises questions about the categories relevant to understanding the communicative aspects of violent force, and, in particular, the killing of one human by another. What does the violence do, in addition to taking the life of a person?

In more coherent (less disputed) polities, much thought has been devoted to precisely that question. Answers differ depending on whether the dead person is an insider or an outsider. There are two main ways to frame the killing of insiders. One sees the killing as a breach of the most fundamental of all rules, an aspect of *jus gentium* (Geertz 1973): thou shalt not kill, and if thou dost, thou shalt feel the force of the law. The other is to see the killing as a sacred act whereby the vitality of one person is appropriated to enrich and revive his fellows – a sacrifice, as in the case of a soldier. But since normative order is so inherently tenuous in north-eastern CAR, neither law nor sacrifice explains what manhunting does.

The killing of outsiders is usually considered an act of war. Then, the person killed is an enemy, an existential threat to the existence of the polity or group. *Pisteurs* sometimes use the language of war to describe their work. 'It's a terrible, terrible war,' sighed one older *pisteur* who lived a few houses away from Boris-Harding,[5] words his fellows sometimes echoed (see also Tubiana 2018). Framing the action in terms of war achieves several things for the *pisteurs* and other proponents of armed conservation. It asserts the gravity of the problem they confront, and it is a way of speaking that is effective in rallying people – an 'enemy' is an energising target.

Critics of armed conservation often use the language of war and militarisation as well, because from their perspective, a militarised approach is excessive and wrong and should be opposed. Indeed, 'militarised' indicates something of the way in which equipment and training have become part of the self-fashioning of the people involved in anti-hunting raids; certainly it indicates the life-and-death stakes this work has taken on. But while war is an emic discursive category (though with various implications) among *pisteurs* and their critics, it is not such a helpful category for a social analysis attempting to include the practices and perspectives of all the people involved.

One reason to avoid 'war' as a framing metaphor is that, although most of the *pisteurs*' training is in military and counterinsurgency operations, they are not in fact authorised to use force. The original project document for the PDRN laid this out especially clearly, but the essential doctrine has remained the same:

[5] 'C'est une guerre très, très terrible.'

> The lieutenants, for the protection of wildlife and their *pisteurs*, should never use any violence against delinquent people. They have, however, the right to legitimate defence of self and other. In case of an attack, beating, or shots, they have the absolute right to defend themselves, to respond to violence with violence and to gunshots with gunshots. There will be no infraction or crime such as homicide when the wounds were required for the necessary legitimate defence of self or other. (PDRN 1985: Annex 3)[6]

While framing documents go only part way towards explaining what actually happens in the hunting zone, the formulation is informative. The *pisteurs*, it says, do not have enemies. Instead, they encounter people who challenge their status with violence, and they are authorised to respond with the same. 'Legitimate self-defence' has always been an element of just war theory, but in the hunting zone the concept has a long history of serving another purpose: it is a means to justify, and to hide in plain sight, violence enacted in the course of forcible acquisition, as happened during the concession experiment. (Coquery-Vidrovitch 1972). People also use it to avoid sanction when caught hunting a protected large animal – a lion, for example. The details of encounters are often impossible to verify after the fact. Was Boris-Harding's killing of the mounted man an act of self-defence? *Pisteurs* would say yes, because they argue that if you do not shoot first, you will be shot. (The defunct 'poacher', of course, is never around to give his version of the story.) Self-defence is yet another way in which violence in the zone is removed from the realm of law – that is, from processes of fact finding, justice, and accountability[7] – and brought into a realm that is social, but in which coerciveness is used by many and towards varied ends, and certain people use it in order to make claims about their

[6] 'Les lieutenants de la protection de la faune et leurs pisteurs ne doivent se livrer à aucune violence sur les personnes délinquantes. Ils ont cependant le droit à la légitime défense d'eux-mêmes et d'autrui. En cas d'attaque, de coups, de coups de feux, ils ont le droit absolu de se défendre, de répondre à la violence par la violence et aux coups de feu par des coups de feu. Il n'y a ni crime ni délit lorsque l'homicide, les blessures étaient commandés par la nécessité de légitime défense de soi-même ou d'autrui.'

[7] In using the term accountability I am referencing Mary Douglas's description of how E. E. Evans-Pritchard went about his work. She noted that he started by looking for what people felt required accountability (some kind of sanction or reckoning): 'The effort to classify kinds of accountability in different social systems requires a careful sifting of information. The method carries its own internal-audit system. Theoretically, payments of debt and executions of justice, when they cover the whole of social life, should tally. If they do not, there is something more to research and explain' (Douglas 1980: 3). In the hunting zone, there is no social realm that is so well self-contained as to constitute a coherent 'internal' that neatly balances out. And even if there were, getting an omniscient view of what happens in the bush would require supernatural powers. But people still think about, and take action in relation to, what they feel is a wrong, although there is a built-in uncertainty about the details.

status, and that of others. At certain times it comes closer to familiar descriptions of war. *Pisteurs* may, for instance, base their judgements regarding the use of force on the physical appearance of the other: does he look 'local' or 'Arab'? But I propose an alternative framing, which better captures the competing demands for status and acquisition through shows of force.

Manhunts around conservation are part of a game of sovereignty. Sovereignty, that most ephemeral and yet foundational of concepts (Bartelson 1995; Roitman 2001), requires some exposition. Many European philosophical accounts describe sovereignty as unitary (one sovereign in control of people and a place), but that does not accurately describe politics in much, and arguably most, of the world (Benton 2009; Keene 2002; Maine 1915 [1888]). Many of the unitary accounts assume that sovereignty and state go together, even if they describe different aspects of power. Because so many accounts of sovereignty are based on studies of states or state-like actors and institutions, sovereignty tends to be a concept that has a particular relationship to law. The sovereign is the supreme adjudicator, the one who can make law that must be respected when everyday ways of resolving things fail. In cases of this kind of 'strong' sovereign, philosophers have argued that what differentiates the sovereign is an ability to decide when the law will be set aside in order ultimately to uphold the law (the 'sovereign exception') (Schmitt 2005 [1922]), or who shall be cast as 'bare life' (neither included nor excluded from the polity) (Agamben 1998). In the contests around coercive conservation in north-eastern CAR, that kind of sovereign is not present. Nevertheless, there are people who claim sovereign-like powers, successfully, at least for a time. That is, they 'get away with' (Graeber 2011: 658) violence or other behaviour that exceeds social or legal bounds, and such exceptional behaviour is part of a claim to the right to make decisions about how to live. These contests around coercive conservation are, therefore, useful as a means to consider other facets or expressions of sovereignty beyond those that occur jointly with state-like forms.

Thinking about sovereignty beyond the state is an old interest in anthropology, one most notably championed by those studying 'stateless' or 'primitive' societies. I draw inspiration from that tradition while rejecting the idea that there is a dichotomy of state and primitive. Consider Grégoire Chamayou's discussion of manhunts (in this case perpetrated against people accused of being 'wolf-men') in European history. Chamayou argues that the sovereign's signature capacity to declare someone a fugitive and therefore attackable by anyone was actually a mark of the powerlessness of his sovereignty:

> By permitting everyone to attack the fugitive, the sovereign also fell into a dangerous contradiction: authorizing someone to kill the condemned man was equivalent to delegating the sovereign's prerogatives to the mass of the people … The political secret that was betrayed by hunts for wolf-men is that, historically, sovereign power was relatively powerless. (Chamayou 2012: 27)

But Chamayou gets it wrong: it is not that sovereign power was powerless, but that it can take forms other than that of 'the' (unitary) sovereign, and it is therefore necessary to explore the features and consequences of other modes of sovereignty. Denunciation is one such mode, and coercive conservation lets us explore it.

Who can denounce?

In studying conservation manhunts, I puzzled over two acts of killing humans, the different ways they became stories, and their very different outcomes. The person at the centre of both cases was Matthieu Laboureur, born in France but raised on his father's safari-hunting concession in north-eastern CAR and employer of Boris-Harding's brother. The concession was officially the size of Swaziland, but Laboureur and his employees and guests roamed and took action in a far wider area. Laboureur wrote in a youthful memoir, 'Me, I am ready to go to the end … That is to say, to kill if it is necessary' (Laboureur 1988: 12). He said he had made a 'pact' with the elephants – to kill anyone trying to kill them – and he described doing just that. He and a couple of Central African wildlife guards ambushed a group of hunters, killing five people and their pack animals and seizing their stock of ivory. Laboureur's story turns to his caring for an orphaned baby elephant and his attempt to win the affections of a beautiful American tourist (spoiler alert: he succeeded). He describes no concern about the men he killed and no effort to ascertain who they were or otherwise account for their deaths. The safari-hunter memoir is a tall-tale genre, not an exhaustively-reliable account, of course. But I came across many accounts of similar killings described in other, less flamboyant sources (for example, reports of internationally funded conservation projects) that were also never followed up.

Then, in January 1990, Laboureur and his father, Jean, were doing their rounds when they came across a few men. People give different accounts of what happened next, but all acknowledge the outcome: Gilbert Bangandombi-Kotali was shot dead. Bangandombi-Kotali was working as a road clearer for the PDRN. Rumour had it that he was also one of the president's personal purveyors of game. The killing of one of their own roused the conservation project staff to action, and they demanded an official *procès-verbal* (statement), which Jean gave. He said that he and his son had been out for a drive with another guide and their respective wives when they came across some poachers who were not speaking Sango, CAR's national language. (It is the first language of few people in the region, but the one used by most when in heterogenous company.) Without further explaining what had occasioned the act, Jean said that he shot and killed Bangandombi-Kotali, with one shot from an M16 and another from a Revolver. One shot hit his hip and the other went through his chest and perforated his spine (Djouma 1990). Conservation project staffers found his account suspicious. They noted that the area was not known for a poacher presence and that Matthieu habitually carried the M16. (In popular understanding, 'everyone knows' that Matthieu pulled the trigger.[8]) Following this killing, Jean left the country to which he had devoted his entire adult life, never to return.[9] Note that he was not tried for the killing – it was not treated as a criminal matter. But he could not remain in the area. Neither could his wife; according to the conservation officer reporting on the incident, she had 'enemies' among the conservationists and did not feel safe.

When Bangandombi-Kotali was killed, Project Conservation and the Laboureurs had been attempting to coexist for about two years. The project staff argued that the Laboureurs had arrogated national park and other areas beyond their concession, and that those spaces were properly project preserves. Project staff described the Laboureurs, derisively, as would-be sovereigns and 'impossible' to work with.[10] And, indeed, the Laboureurs had killed people, in circumstances that are usually seen as the preserve of sovereign power. But Bangandombi-Kotali's killing stopped them. Why did it become a problem, when the deaths of the poachers Matthieu described, or those that project conservationists were responsible for, did not? Part of the answer lies in nationality: Bangandombi-Kotali was a resident of the area; Matthieu's poachers were more itinerant. However, in other cases, the killings of transnational actors most certainly have become controversial, so that cannot be a sufficient answer. A further part of the answer lies in the personality clashes between the Laboureurs and project staff, all looking

[8] For another story of a conservationist father taking a fall for his son, this time in Zambia, see Goldberg (2010).

[9] For most of the subsequent 25 years, Matthieu ran the family business, although the profusion of rebel groups over the last ten years and general insecurity have pretty much sunk the safari industry in the region.

[10] 'Generally speaking, the hunting companies continue not to accept the PDRN … A few conflicts have arisen and it is clear that real dialogue with these companies is impossible' (PDRN 1990: 35).

for ways to discredit each other. But their mutual dislike is not so much explanatory as is the impetus it provided for people to mobilise relationships after a death and enact a moral-performative project on behalf of the killed, and on behalf of the people participating. What is important is the particular form that call for attention takes.

The young Laboureur, almost inadvertently, illustrated the problem of calling attention to transgressions in the bush. Describing the people he killed in the first instance, he wrote:

> They are without scruples, and assured of impunity. Who could denounce them? If they surprised us they would not hesitate to take us down. Easy to exterminate five men [the size of Matthieu's party] when you're the stronger ones. Much easier than massacring a troop of elephants. Tomorrow, they would cross the border into their own country. Five cadavers in the bush are quickly swallowed; there would not remain even a trace after a few hours. (Laboureur 1988: 91)[11]

Laboureur's emphasis was misplaced. He overstated the role of geography. Although the area is vast and there are few people, those factors are not in themselves determinative. Remote spaces are indeed active sites for dehumanising violence in which victims are construed as killable animals (Bjork-James 2015; Gordon 1986), but the fact remains that only some bodies are 'swallowed', while others, including those of peasants such as Bangandombi-Kotali, are not. The status of people and things, then, is not quite as categorical as it is sometimes presented, and to understand why some deaths become problems in the space and beyond, and others do not, we must transform Laboureur's rhetorical question 'Who could denounce them?' into a literal one. Who *can* denounce? Laboureur's almost offhand question, once expanded upon, helps explain the repertoire of action through which contests occur over the legitimacy of extra-legal killing such as conservation-related manhunts and other forceful seizures.

Denouncers call out another as part of a bid to assert their own privileged status. Actions are underlaid by values, even if they are not made explicit, so looking to those instances where people use force in order to denounce also tells us something about the values they hold. People denounce to awe witnesses without necessarily including them as fellows.

[11] 'Ils sont aussi sans scrupules et assurés de l'impunité. Qui pourrait les dénoncer? S'ils nous surprenaient ils n'hésiteraient pas à nous descendre. Facile d'exterminer cinq hommes quand on est les plus forts. Beaucoup plus facile que de massacrer un troupeau d'éléphants. Demain, ils passeront la frontière de leur propre pays. Cinq cadavres, dans la brousse, c'est vite avalé, il n'en reste plus trace au bout de quelques heures.'

Most studies of denunciation have focused on Western cases in which denunciation plays out through a state or religious enforcer. People might denounce their neighbours to the secret police, which carries out punishment (Fitzpatrick and Gellately 1997). The identities of enactors and audiences are clearly differentiated in terms of the people who compose them and what their respective roles are. Some (e.g. Arendt 1973) have even considered denunciation to be a particular product of totalitarian regimes. Perhaps those living in sites of contested sovereignty have not been considered denouncers because lawbreaking is thought of as the only sort of thing one denounces. But people living in places without coercive law also have values that they might fight to maintain. Elsewhere in the region, for instance, anarchy, or autonomy, is valued more highly than order (Scheele 2015). In many places that are neither authoritarian nor anarchy-loving, people's statuses are frequently challenged and the bounds of collaboration are obscure. Denunciation can be a means of popularly asserting both status and those bounds, as happened during the French Revolution (Lucas 1997). These are dramas in which people's positions in relation to each other shift, in large part because of what they do in the midst of denunciation and its effects.

People participate in denunciation because some principle fundamental to their understanding of the world and their position in it has been contravened. But what that principle is – what value it expresses – can vary widely, from law and order in a totalitarian context to anarchy in a government-rejecting one. To say that a value underpins action is not to say that people see it as cosmologically ideal; rather, it means that when people rise up, they do so in defence of something they see as important given the situations they confront. In north-eastern CAR's colonial and conservation histories, denunciation seems to have been oriented towards liberty, in the sense of freedom from molestation – what Isaiah Berlin (1969) termed negative liberty.[12] Theirs is not a protest against violence exercised in the name of claiming sovereign prerogatives nor against the idea of rules. Nor is it a means of declaring autonomy. Rather, they denounce in order to participate in projects beyond their place of residence that directly or indirectly involve coercing others and to contest who is a legitimate target when those projects problematically overlap.

Whatever else it might be, the demand for freedom from molestation is a response to the exploitative and violent ways in which north-eastern CAR has become involved with long-distance trade and political

[12] For a fascinating discussion of the ambivalent value accorded this kind of liberty in another African locale (Guinea), see McGovern (2015).

processes, to which this book testifies. In many cases, these processes destroyed whatever 'order' existed (Dupré 1982) and created newly ambiguous relations of power (Balandier 1966) in which claiming liberty was part positive value and part survival skill.

In instances of denunciation in north-eastern CAR, there is a two-part claim: 'You cannot remove our liberty; we can circumscribe yours.' It is an assertion of status and privilege where both are often disputed or compromised. Bangandombi-Kotali's death was not denounced with physical violence against the person(s) who caused it, but the liberty claimed by the person who accepted responsibility was removed, in the form of his having to leave this space. Denunciation accompanies and even propels struggles to elaborate and enact privilege amid disagreement. It requires, and helps conjure,[13] parties who jointly defend their status. This defence takes the form of action they would denounce as illegitimate if they were the target and asserts their sovereignty over those they instead consider targets.

Denunciation, liberty, and exceptions

Early employees of armed conservation endeavours in the 1980s said that, at first, it was possible to talk to hunters and herders and explain limits. But, over time, tensions rose, conversation became rarer, and manhunts ending in death more common, particularly with regard to 'foreigners'. People with homes in the villages and towns around the parklands were also subjected to seizure. Theoretically, all such events were simply *pisteurs*' efforts to apply laws, but circumstance placed them far outside the world of consistent law or norms, and inspired ways of working – surveillance, seizure, killing – that were more flexible, opportunistic, and capricious than are supposed to occur in systems of law.

Manhunting is dangerous. Many *pisteurs* are killed, too. The shared dangerousness can get lost in media portrayals of armed conservation, stories all too often populated by caricatures – thuggish or heroic guards, impoverished locals, rapacious foreign poachers, Western conservationists who care more about wild animals than Africans do. But a guard can be both thuggish and generous, even in relation to the same people; a 'local' could side with the conservationists in one instance and against them in another. In the case of north-eastern CAR, it is misleading to speak of one group as being opposed to another, or even one nationality as being opposed to another. The illegalisation of everything while 'the

[13] I borrow this evocative term from Danilyn Rutherford (2012).

state' is absent means that all local order (legal or cosmological) is fundamentally multiple and contested, and people's affiliations can shift depending on circumstance.

In short, conservation in north-eastern CAR became a locus for sovereign-prerogative violence from multiple sources. *Pisteurs* hunted 'poachers' (their assessment) and herders. Parkland interlopers hunted the guards, dozens of whom have lost their lives during the 30 years of anti-poaching patrols. A few months before I arrived in north-eastern CAR five (out of about seventy total) had been shot and killed in an ambush, an event that continued to weigh on the remaining guards. The event caused them to rename former collaborators as hostile and untrustworthy. The people living closest to the attack site, in a ZCV called Krakoma, must have been complicit, they reasoned. *Krakomiste* became the new synonym for traitor.

There is no comprehensive account of how many people the guards have killed. But there are many fragmentary accounts and allusions. Some conservation project reports refer to people killed with euphemisms – 'foreign poachers neutralised', for instance. One report, under '*animaux abattus*' (animals slaughtered), listed two camels, eight donkeys, and three men (PDRN 1990). One person who had led *pisteurs* in the early days admitted – with the mix of wanting to shock, boast, and also acknowledge the outré nature of the work I came to associate with mercenary tales – that he had found a successful tactic: locate the elephant hunters' camp and then lie in wait west of them until dawn. At five, they would rise and pray towards Mecca, making it easy to ambush them. As a terror tactic, some Russian mercenaries working as anti-poaching patrollers in the mid-2000s were known to have severed the bodies of the people they killed (Tubiana 2018).

Anti-poaching guards were working under difficult circumstances. One could argue the guards' work was inherently morally corrupt, but they were sent to do a job, and the people they targeted were not simply victims and often vociferously protested against the ways in which those involved in conservation practice treated them. Armed conservation's grisly side shows how sovereign-prerogative violence and denunciation of it in the service of claiming exception from others' rule enforcement again became central to the region's politics during the final decades of the twentieth century, as they had been during the first few, when raiding in the air, believing that the project had indirectly for slaves and forced labourers dominated. Who was rightfully denouncing and who was behaving egregiously depends, of course, on one's position, which itself can change over the course of these actions – witness the former Project collaborators who became '*Krakomiste*'. Those denunciations aim to claim status in the form of freedom from molestation – in other words, an exception to be enjoyed by those doing the denouncing.

Not all acts of forceful acquisition – of lives, of things – are denounced. The ability of the person targeted or killed to mobilise relations, even from beyond the grave, is crucial in determining the extent and weight of the denunciation. What is mobilised is not a 'group' activated by the targeting of their own, but relations – people who feel implicated because of their closeness to the victim. And that mobilisation works along different lines depending on particular instances and aims. In this unstable mix, denunciation lets its practitioners reject the use of egregious coercion against them, and that refusal often takes the form of their use of egregious coercion against those they see as their tormenters. In this state of affairs, both violence and alliance inhere, stability much less so. Denunciation is an attempt to claim status as privileged by liberty for those who participate in it.

Denunciation in action

Idongo, a village lying not far from the Laboureurs' concession, became the conservation project's 'model village' in part because people there readily agreed to the conservation project's terms. Idongo abutted several profitable hunting concessions, which meant that people there benefited handsomely from the ZCV system whereby nearby villages stood to collect the taxes and fees paid by safari hunters. And, indeed, the project brought welcome resources to the village. As one French journalist describing the project in 2003 praised, modern forms of security and governance had arrived in Idongo: for example, 'the elderly have a right to a small pension' (AFP 2003). Later that year, anti-poaching guards caught several people from Idongo hunting in a protected area and seized their guns. The next night, the guards caught the son of the president of the village's conservation committee, with a few others, in the act of hunting and jailed him. However, the following morning many Idongo residents, joined by at least dozens of people from nearby villages, stormed the conservation project base. They destroyed the radio post. They attempted to confiscate the anti-poaching guards' weapons. Some were shooting their own guns, mostly into the air. Villagers ripped the clothes from at least one guard's back.

Others living in the area had been dispossessed or jailed before without any popular uprising. But in this particular case, people were roused or mobilised. The conservation committee president, a man with some influence, had seen his own son arrested, and he convinced others that the anti-poaching guards' actions had violated basic norms of civility and respect. Not just immediate family members of the detained but others too felt affronted to such an extent that they participated in denouncing it, to communicate that *we are not people who can be walked all over like that*. This was vengeance, but not of a law-like kind. When people from Idongo attacked the anti-poaching base, the possibility of punishing damage that had been done to them, or demanding compensation, was overshadowed by their interest in communicating their rejection of demeaning treatment, which seemed like a statement of *you are less than us*. In contrast, an assurance that they would not be molested – negative liberty – was a meaningful marker of respectful status.

A sense of common cause often brings people together to become a group that will respond to violence. This is an old idea in anthropology: when violence against an individual is experienced as an assault on 'us', and an attack by 'him' can be construed as one by 'them', new forms of mobilisation, including war, become possible (Kelly 2000). While the question of who is a friend and who is an enemy has been fundamental in understanding war and sovereignty in much Western theory, here that distinction is less important than the question of who will help protest against unjust or demeaning would-be sovereign behaviour – in a word, alliance. To ally to denounce a discrete episode does not foreclose future collaboration with those one is now denouncing; it is not about 'my group against yours' but about shifting who belongs to the category of privileged by liberty and who that of potentially being at others' mercy. The relevant boundaries of socio-political association are negotiated and reformed through such encounters. People might collaborate, teaming up to counter others, while in other instances the lines would be drawn differently, and they would find themselves in opposition.[14]

The Idongo brouhaha ended with the anti-poaching guards releasing the captured villagers in acknowledgement of an understanding that all involved would work harder to give each other space to pursue their undertakings – the familiar idea of 'I look, but I don't see'. And, indeed,

[14] In one case in 2009, a *chef de patrouille* sent a team of miners to an area rumoured to have been the site of vast colonial-era diamond extractions, deep in the park. The miners dug for several days until they had deep pits. Once they were ready to 'rinse' and pluck out the diamonds, another *chef de patrouille*, accompanied by several guards, burst in and expelled them from the park, taking over the rinsing – and the diamonds. Miners generally abide by the *droit d'oeil* – the right of sight – whereby anyone who spots a diamond claims a percentage of the profit, even if that person did nothing more to unearth it than spotting it on someone's shovel (ICG 2010). The first *chef de patrouille* insisted that he had nothing to do with the seizure and that he lost out on the deal as well, but, whether or not this was true, the contracted miners never got back the equipment that had been taken from them.

this is what they mostly did. Denouncing did not create new enemies. Rather, it changed the practices they would use in relation to each other.

In north-eastern CAR, people have tended to seek freedom from molestation in their projects rather than help to establish consistent and universal regulation or submission to hierarchical modes of organisation (Lombard 2015). But even if thoroughgoing control has not been a major objective of would-be governors, certain people have emerged as visionaries and have an impressive ability to rally people. One such person, Yaya Ramadan (brother of Mezzan Ramadan, the physician in Tiringoulou), died violently in 2002; the events that preceded and followed his death are another example of cascading processes of denunciation. The frameworks of neither criminality nor war fully capture the dynamics at work around Yaya's death, which came after the repeated meting out of sovereign-prerogative violence and preceded a years-long process of back-and-forth denunciation. The terminology of crime does not go far enough to describe a conflict about vengeance and status, with judgement visited on those the denouncers intended to intimidate and distinguish themselves from.

Renowned as a Muslim cleric and a visionary, Yaya Ramadan was able to rally his fellow Gula speakers and others in the area around his home town, Tiringoulou, like no one else. People called him Caliph, and they still tell stories of his more-than-human powers. The area has little in the way of organised associations; there are no farming cooperatives or similar initiatives. But when the Caliph asked people to do something, or suggested a policy, they listened. In the late 1990s, armed conservation staffers explained to the Caliph that combating hunters and herders would bring revenue because it would permit safari-hunting businesses to operate in the area. Caliph Yaya immediately saw the appeal of this scheme for his family, friends, and associates and asked to participate in the hunt for parkland interlopers (Roulet 2005).

Many Tiringoulou residents are armed, mostly with Kalashnikovs or hunting rifles. About 20 men joined the Caliph to scour the parks and other restricted-access areas. This was far more support than the conservation project staff had received elsewhere. It showed initiative and organisation to an extent that surpassed how others had greeted conservation. (Most, like people from Idongo, accepted the project's terms but rejected attempts to enforce them.) The anti-poaching project archives detail the Caliph's militia's success in taking. Here is what they took in one operation: 750 kilograms of smoked meat seized, five pack camels slaughtered, and two hunters 'eliminated' (PDRN 1998: 34). Note that word, 'eliminated': those killed were neither enemies vanquished, acquaintances killed criminally, or friends sacrificed for a greater good – these people were simply taken out. The victims were neither inside nor outside the bonds of any locally relevant political association; their lives were simply taken, in the process giving proof to the sovereign liberty claimed by those who killed them.

In early May 2002, Caliph Yaya and his men had another fruitful hunting patrol. They killed two poachers, according to a later report, as well as nine donkeys, and confiscated 1,500 kilograms of meat. In examining the bodies of those killed, they found a scrap of paper. It was a receipt delivered against payment for the right to graze and hunt in the area, issued by another local notable: that is, they had run up against an assertion of right to assign privilege and access to acquisition mirroring their own. The Caliph and his militia were less applying a law than attempting to transcend the messy realm of law by asserting their ability to seize from others, and they ran into conflict with someone who had pre-empted their authority to decide about privileges to take wild goods.

Just a few days later, on 8 May 2002, associates of the poachers ambushed the Caliph while he was driving through the bush. He was shot and died on the spot, as did three of those accompanying him. (Their associates also managed to kill a few of the attackers.) Being such a singular person, he elicited a tremendous denunciation of his murderers among all those who counted him as a relation. People rallied to attack those they understood to have authored the Caliph's death: Hemat and Ta'isha herders who move between north-eastern CAR and northern pastures in Chad and Sudan.[15] Two *pisteurs* close to Yaya also threatened the regional head of the conservation project, rushing him and shooting in the air, believing that the project had indirectly caused Yaya's death. Their show of force caused no permanent rift. The *pisteurs* remained with the project and faced no sanction because they were valued as tough fighters (Mbitikon 2002: 3).

By 10 May, more herders, many armed, and others in Chadian military uniforms had crossed from Chad to CAR. They set fire to five villages, killed several people, and took hostages. A little over a week later, the deceased Caliph's supporters killed about one hundred Sudanese herders near the village of Mossabio, north-west of Tiringoulou near the border with Chad. This kind of violence continued, with varying details, dimensions, and participants, for several years (Roulet 2005).

[15] While some of the ambush party had been killed, the culprits could never be definitively identified because the content of that category kept expanding as a result of the conduct of ensuing battles, which raised suspicions about.

Figure 7.1 The ‘rehabilitated’ mosque in Tiringoulou; the imam lamented its continuing disrepair

The Sheikh Tidjani, an Islamic authority revered by most in the region and living near Nyala in South Darfur, eventually became involved as a mediator. In late 2005, the Sudanese government promised material aid to Tiringoulou. They would rebuild its mosque and provide a gift of cash. With those promises, overt hostilities wound down. The eventual mosque refurbishment struck the villagers as a mockery, and the money never arrived. People in Tiringoulou found this deplorable, but they did not know to whom to complain (Figure 7.1). Mistrust across the region remained high, a feeling that was only exacerbated by the post-2005 turn to rebellion. (The area has seen the creation of more than a handful of rebel groups since then, including some who joined a successful assault on the capital in March 2013, who remain major actors [see Lombard 2016d].) Yet alliances, even between people with tense relationships, like the conservation boss and his threatening subordinates, continue to be frequent too.

The attacks and counterattacks after Yaya’s death look a bit like feuding or raiding, formerly a fertile genre of inquiry in the anthropology of violence (Beidelman 1961; Evans-Pritchard 1940; Peristiany 1965). Feuding and raiding are back-and-forth attacks between groups subject to fission, fusion, and changeable alliances, attacks motivated by a variety of material and moral aims and subject to varying degrees of institutionalised peace-making mechanisms (Evans-Pritchard 1940; Radcliffe-Brown 1940; Sahlins 1961). All those factors were indeed at play in the longer processes of violence of which Caliph Yaya’s killing is an example. The constitution of the parties in conflict changed dramatically over the course of the hostilities. Gula and Runga (categories described by both historians and people in the area as ethnic groups, although their boundaries and relations change) first worked in solidarity and then increasingly came to mistrust each other. Attacking and being attacked gave rise to suspicions. Are you really on 'our' side? Or did you aid or abet those attacking us? Both Gula and Runga generally found Kara and Kaba suspicious.

But overlooked in discussions of feuding or raiding, classically understood, is that liberty is a reason why people participate in these altercations. Compensation, honour, punishment – or some combination of these – may be important to those involved in denunciations in north-eastern CAR. However, their interests are not just in balancing out a wrong – by exacting payment for a wrongful death, say – demonstrating superior prowess in a valued skill, or defending their honour, but to assert a relationship between the parties involved: a relationship in which 'you' cannot usurp 'my' liberty, as proved by my disrupting yours. Denouncers protest against the violent subjection without inclusion that others have forced on them.

Of course, they do not always succeed, even in the short term. One can execute sovereign violence – killing, burning villages – and not get away with it. This uncertainty of outcome is lost in the idea of the sovereign decision. In that conception, the decision speaks for itself and can elicit no reply other than submission (Schmitt 2005 [1922]). The Caliph Yaya, a person who authored the kind of killing that has been called the hallmark of the sovereign, was himself killed by people who claimed sovereign prerogative. But that only becomes clear by continuing the analysis past the moment itself and considering it as an event in the longer process of using sovereign-claim violence to denounce others' enaction of it and obtain a measure of privileged status or liberty.

Here is one more example of denunciation in action. In early 2009, four members of an anti-poaching militia unit based at Gordil, the furthest north and east of the anti-poaching bases, together with the foreign 'technical assistant' leading them (the AT was an expatriate former military officer effectively in charge and was Boris-Harding's *binôme* or partner), were transporting an injured fellow *pisteur* to the Tiringoulou airstrip for evacuation. Their route passed through a national park. While crossing this stretch of land they encountered a large herd of cows. The guards wanted to shoot at the cows. 'They are right in the middle of the park!,' the *pisteurs* lamented. It felt like a provocation. However, the AT counselled inaction, for they were too few to defend themselves if they found that the cattle were accompanied by well-armed minders. Equally, even though the *pisteurs* might depart prior to reprisal, the herders might construe the villagers nearby as complicit with the guards and attack them, and the *pisteurs* wouldn't be there to defend against any such action.

The truck soon came to a village, Mélé. The village head (*chef de village*) waved down the vehicle. He implored the *pisteurs* to shoot the cattle. The AT explained why they could not do so. But the village head persisted. The cattle's presence was an affront he could not countenance. He promised that 20 men from Mélé would join the *pisteurs*. The technical assistant explained that they would not be able to stay to protect the village. But, afraid of losing face, he agreed that they could jointly go after the cattle, to send a message to their minders. He doled out ammunition to the new temporary members of his team. During the ensuing firefight, one herder was killed. The *pisteurs* continued to the airstrip and sent the wounded guard to hospital.

The next day, however, *Janjaweed* (in the Central African sense, see Chapter 5, p. 127) surrounded the village and held it hostage. Some observers said that there were 40 armed *Janjaweed* – including some mounted; others as many as 80. In any case, there were enough to demand, with credibility, blood payment of 10 million CFA (about US$20,000/£15,000). Contributions were cobbled together from Mélé residents as well as from others sympathisers. The armed attackers received a large enough portion of the cash they had requested to agree to pull back.

When the herder was killed, his relations demanded redress in a manner consistent with a legal mode of reasoning that many Muslims in the region understand *sharia* to dictate: payment should be levied against a wrongdoer to compensate for the harm caused to the family by losing this productive and cherished member. However, the matter did not end there. About a month after the Mélé incidents, a few *pisteurs* were in their homes on the Gordil anti-poaching base. Hundreds of armed herders or *Janjaweed* surrounded them. They did not fire any shots; they did not need to. Their superior force was obvious to all involved. The anti-poaching guards understood this show of force to be a denunciation expressing the sentiment: 'You cannot infringe on our liberty, because we could do much worse to you.' Shortly afterwards, the anti-poaching unit abandoned the Gordil base. The herders who confronted them were right: the guards could not usurp their liberty. The relations among those the guards sought to counter or kill were too strong and wide, and they mobilised to denounce in their turn.

Desires for punishment and honour may all have factored in to people's participation on that occasion. More fundamentally, their action demonstrated that they were the ones who could enact sovereign-prerogative violence, not the anti-poaching guards; that they could establish status and privilege in relation to how they would live, and how and what they could acquire. Enjoying such exceptional status is generally not a stable position,[16] the marker of one group or class as opposed to another. Circumstances shift interests, influence and who cooperates with whom. Though denunciation does not create durable sovereigns, what is being contested remain matters of sovereignty.

Conclusion

Violence in the context of armed conservation is part of contesting sovereignty. The question of sovereignty – rather than law, war, or resistance – in armed conservation violence in north-eastern CAR offers new insights into both violence and sovereignty. While most studies of sovereignty are based on cases where the state or state-like actors are important players, north-eastern CAR has a more varied landscape in terms of potential participants in sovereignty. Yet the problem that sovereignty, as a concept, is a response to – namely that some people subject others to 'outside of normal bounds' treatment as part of claims to be able to determine how to live – is also relevant in this context. Therefore, here are a few insights about sovereignty that come from this study of denunciation, which might be more broadly relevant. First, claims to sovereignty occur through repertoires of practices, and while the decisive 'sovereign exception' identified by German theorists of power working under Nazism like Carl Schmitt and Walter Benjamin is one, denunciation is another. Second, claims to sovereignty are processes, and those processes end up re-shuffling people's positions in relation to each other, power, and status. Third, when one's position is uncertain or feels precarious, it can feel all the more important to assert it forcefully. And finally, the values that claims to sovereignty seek to enforce are not necessarily culturally-derived but the product of social situations and circumstances beyond any individual's or group's preference. In the case of denunciation around armed conservation, few saw it as an ideal, but many participated in it.

René Girard argued that sacrificing a scapegoat helped people without judicially-organized retribution avoid interminable cycles of vengeance. The crucial factor in making a successful scapegoat was that this was someone who did not have the kinds of relations who would be so angered by the violent action that they would rise up to enact a reprisal. In the course of coercive conservation in northeastern CAR, some people were killed and their deaths did not elicit reprisal. But they were not effective scapegoats, in Girard's sense, because others were killed too,

[16] Indeed, in the following years, the Gordil area saw the emergence of several rebel groups of changing makeup and alliances.

and those others *did* have the kinds of relations who would rise up in protest – in denunciation. It therefore seems worth being cautious about saying that scapegoating/sacrifice is inherently functional, in the sense of a system that works toward a neat, preordained end. But while there is much to lament in a state of affairs marked by violence amid competing sovereign claims, it also puts on display a kind of active participation that more judicially-organized systems foreclose. Vengeance in the mode of denunciation, as a process of sovereign claim-making, is a vernacular in the genre of tragedy. But tragedy is not all disadvantage and damage. Part of the appeal of participating in denunciation is that doing so perpetually rekindles hope that the future, and one's social position in it, can be different, and better. Understanding denunciation therefore requires toggling between acknowledging its often-deleterious effects and appreciating that it pulls people in because they are un-resigned to this fate.

Postscript

The reader may be wondering whether conservation has accomplished any of its backers' goals. What about the wild animals? Some conservation project reports note gains in wildlife populations during periods when LAB was pursued intensely. The ententes between users of the space who could agree to help each other do not seem to have dramatically undermined this result. However, reports also acknowledge that, during any break in LAB,[17] wildlife hunting and other illicit uses of protected areas and their resources rise again, quickly erasing any gains. Overall, the situation today is bleak. This situation is certainly not due to LAB, nor can LAB be blamed for not being able to effectively curtail the claiming of wild goods in the long term (even though *pisteurs* have participated in wild acquisition too). In addition to challenges posed by various anti-control, pro-autonomy tendencies, the region has been pulled into war and conflict economies, and armed conservation has been embedded in this.

In 2012, ECOFAC was rolled into a new initiative, ECOFAUNE. Most of the old staff remained, though. The country director, Florent Zowoya, stayed on in his post. When we reconnected after a few years in 2014, Zowoya explained that they were shifting their approach. 'We have

[17] Breaks occurred due to gaps in funding approvals from Brussels, and also because of such things as employees holding out for higher salaries when contracts were up for renegotiation. (Salary disputes slowed down the roll-out of ECOFAUNE by about a year.)

been in a war with the herders and the poachers for a long time and it caused many, many deaths. We used armed force and there are no results to show for it. Therefore, we are now trying a more humanistic approach.' This was to begin with a remapping of the zone to work out how to share access to the space and its resources with fewer violent conflicts. For the first time, the project has even hired someone of an ethnicity associated with cattle herding, a Peulh (a broad and diverse ethnic category that includes many of the herders from Niger) who also speaks Hausa. They sent him north to talk to the herders and discuss with them, a kind of dialogue that has been difficult for conservation project staff for years.

There is more to the story behind this shift, however, as Zowoya also acknowledged. Since 2012, CAR has been at war. Of 92 conservation project anti-poaching guards in north-eastern CAR, all but 28 joined the rebellions, deserted, or died. All but 16 of their guns were seized by rebels or opportunists.

A few years after those setbacks, the project has been slowly rebuilding its forces. The 'humanistic' phase is fading now in favour of a return to manhunts (Tubiana 2018). The EU staffer in Brussels who helped conceive the projects and successfully camouflaged them over several decades has retired. The guards have just a few guns among them. A few men have gone from being *pisteurs* to rebels, and the claim-making repertoires and broader political processes of which those career shifts were part have changed dramatically.

Conservation in north-eastern CAR has been marked by an unstable mix of opportunism, frustration, feelings of abandonment, and demands for autonomy, all of which can run at cross-purposes. One way of working around the conflicts has been the pursuit of *mango tere*, an entente, so that people can pursue their own projects. Doing so provides income-generating opportunities of various kinds in a region whose residents lament its dearth of them. But no one really sees this system as optimal, especially since it is a precarious ground to hold if one is seized from. Although conservation does not have the elevated status among Central Africans that it does among some in the West, Central Africans are not happy that the wildlife is disappearing. Some do not think that it is disappearing as fast as the conservationists say; others think that foreign 'others' are the sole authors of its destruction; still others are indifferent to the animals. But they agree there are issues around access to wild goods that need to be resolved, without agreeing how to do that. Nor can we turn to some kind of magically sustainable 'tradition' as a way of moving forward, ethically, in the face of these problems. Acquisition of wild goods has always been an entrée to innovation and change, including participation in long-distance trading from remote corners of the world. Innovation has no inherent moral status. It is what one turns it towards that matters. One of the major innovations and disruptions of processes relating to status and force in north-eastern CAR in recent years has been rebellion. But even its authors, a few of whom we'll get to know better in the next chapter, see it less as a liberation project than as one of the few options left to them given their place in the world.

8 Force and status in rebellion*

Introduction

'It is because of the rebellion that the NGOs came here,'[1] General Damane Zakaria said during one of our conversations in Tiringoulou.[2] The sun was beginning to set on a late October day in 2009. Many people

* Some material in this chapter was previously published in Lombard (2018a).

[1] On this day, and on the various other occasions when I met him between 2008 and 2011, Damane spoke only Gula, although he understands a good deal of Arabic, Sango, and French (and, indeed, Gula contains a number of loan words from French and Arabic). He was slouched, as one does to minimise the pooling of sweat, in one of the Monobloc chairs one finds all over Africa, but when standing he looms over six feet tall with a stocky build accentuated by the loose, long robes he favours. Damane's translator, the head of the local *collège*, sat beside him. The translator, in a suit and tie and carrying a briefcase, was, weight-wise, perhaps less than half Damane's size. The contrast was striking: on the one hand, the massive, Islamic-styled general, with the relaxed posture of a person who takes for granted his right to take up space; on the other, the prim headmaster rebel, with his French-style dress, slight build, and deferential manner.

[2] Damane was correct, but not comprehensive, in making this claim – rebellion was one reason for the humanitarians' arrival. Rebellion left people displaced and otherwise in visible material need, and it took a form that facilitated humanitarian work. Rebels – who have organisation charts and (potentially) fulfillable requests – can be negotiated with, so that humanitarians can do their work unmolested, or not unduly so. Other kinds of armed actors – of whom the region has many, such as robbers – are not generally so amenable to collaboration and/or are considered criminal and hence illegitimate interlocutors (Lombard 2017). Another catalyst was timing and geography: Damane's UFDR emerged at a moment when international conflict watchers (international organisation employees, diplomats, etc.) were fixated on Darfur, which lies just to the north and east of Tiringoulou. They wondered whether the fighting in north-eastern CAR could be linked to Darfur (either empirically or discursively, through tactical slippages). And, if so, whether engaging in CAR, whose government and rebels welcomed international actors, would be a way to do something about Darfur without having to deal with the recalcitrant Sudanese government. A third was personalities: people such as Damane and the UN coordinator in CAR at the time, who wanted to show himself an effective fundraiser and administrator and so was far more engaged than almost anyone else in the role, before or since. The 'objective humanitarian need' was, of course, another factor, but it had been present before as well – the denunciations following Yaya's death (2002–5) caused hundreds of deaths and displacement on a broad scale, but no humanitarians arrived to deal with this 'intercommunal violence', as such attacks are glossed in the international organisation vernacular.

Figure 8.1 Formerly the home of Yaya Ramadan, this compound now houses a medical humanitarian organisation

had spent the day harvesting peanuts. Damane was speaking in his capacity as the leader of the Union des Forces Démocratiques pour le Rassemblement (UFDR, or Union of Democratic Forces for Unity), a rebel group that had emerged exactly three years earlier. Damane had signed a peace agreement with the government in mid-2008 and gained the title of 'presidential adviser'. His fellow UFDR members were still waiting for the kind of dignity that comes from a salaried job. They felt that the government had promised salaried jobs and other forms of material entitlement, but nothing had changed. Damane continued, 'Do you know how long MSF and UNICEF[3] have been working in CAR?' He answered his own question before I could: 'For a very long time – 30 years, or maybe more. But none of them set foot here [in the north-east].'[4]

The General and I were sitting in the shade of a *paillotte*, a thatch-roofed outdoor structure without walls, almost as good a sitting spot as a mango tree for catching the breeze while avoiding the sun, outside the concrete house that had once belonged to the Caliph Yaya Ramadan (Figure 8.1).[5] Inside the house, taxidermied antelope heads and other

[3] Médecins Sans Frontières, or Doctors Without Borders, and the UN International Children's Fund.

[4] A handful of humanitarian organisations – among them UNICEF and MSF – have indeed been operating in CAR for decades, but a major increase in their presence did not occur until 2007, with another, even larger, increase, in 2013–4.

[5] It was one of only a few concrete residences in town. Damane owned the only new one, built with money he received as a presidential adviser. He did not live there, though, as he preferred his familiar compound a few hundred metres away. His rebel-leader house was a showpiece. Painted bright turquoise (paint cannot be purchased in north-eastern CAR, so obtaining it means having access both to markets elsewhere and to the capacity to transport goods) and located at the crossroads at the centre of town, it displayed wealth and marked the status of people in Tiringoulou as people with connections and means.

wild trophies still looked down from their spots high on the walls, but they were dusty. The main room was now crammed with tables, chairs, desktop computers, wires, printers, reports and folders, the walls covered in maps. These material markers made the house's new use easily identifiable: it was a humanitarian organisation's office, in this case that of an American medical charity that had been operating in town for a couple of years. Mezzan Ramadan, Yaya's brother and the person who had brought the complaint against the French safari guide, owned the house now, renting it out on his late brother's behalf. The charity also employed him as a doctor at the town clinic they supported. Conservation had pretty much ended in Tiringoulou. This year, 2009, following the events at Mélé and their fallout, the nearest project base, Gordil, remained shuttered. Rebellion and humanitarian action were quite literally insinuating themselves into the material and social infrastructure conservation had left behind.

Rebelliousness and intervention by outsiders have long histories in this part of the world, but the particular forms they have taken in the last 15 years are new.[6] Major shifts include the growth of conscious self-styling as *rebels*, and the arrival en masse of the people I have elsewhere called the 'good intentions crowd' (international organisation officials, aid organisation employees, diplomats, and others who understand themselves as 'external' and altruistic yet have become central participants in post–Cold War African rebellion). Both rebellion and international intervention have dramatically affected the area's serious games concerning forceful acquisition and contested status. The adventurous lives of four men involved in these shifts for the last few decades illuminate the shifts and the continuities. These men are not heroes.

[6] Since 2006, well over a dozen rebel groups and less-organised armed mobilisations have emerged in CAR, many in the north-east. Since the late 1990s, there have been more than a dozen international peacekeeping missions in CAR (Olin 2015), and locals have developed particular stances of self-positioning in order to interact with them. Rebellions have frequently been inspired by egregious acts of acquisition or force and denunciatory reaction. The president hears that people in a particular region are restive and might challenge him, so he sends his personal guard to the hinterland to make a display of force: burning villages, attacking those who cannot flee (Bigo 1988; Lombard 2016d). Those attacked feel aggrieved at the arbitrariness and injustice, and if they have the means to mobilise denunciation, they do so. Their own shows of force tend to look similar to those of the government troops – they take a town or village, targeting only the generally ill-equipped government armouries and offices. They move from remoter areas to bigger towns in the direction of the capital. They hope that making their dangerousness evident will change their status. Previously ignorable and irrelevant, and even targets of raiding, they feel that being dangerous is the best way to demonstrate that they merit regard. The most tangible evidence of regard is being accorded a salary, but brotherly interaction (eating together, speaking man to man) can be meaningful as well.

They have not accomplished what they desired, but their sense of irony, their appreciation of new experiences and connections beyond the place where they live, and their roles as fathers and mentors have filled their lives in the periods of waiting that stretch between the moments of active encounter and the use of force.

The originating events for rebel groups such as the UFDR took the form of denunciation. The president in Bangui largely ignores what happens in the north-east, but in early 2006 then president François Bozizé had got word that there was a rebellion brewing there that might seek to topple him. His patron, Chadian president Idriss Déby, was also concerned that people in the north-east were facilitating the equipping of rebels hostile to him and even allowing them to use north-eastern CAR as a rear base, so he pushed Bozizé to take action. Bozizé dispatched his personal Presidential Guard to the area. They mounted a spectacular show of force against Tiringoulou and villages nearby, killing people and burning houses, to communicate to locals that they ought to stay in their place. He demonstrated his immunity from violence and dispossession by subjecting them to it. However, these actions made people in the area only more incensed at the abuse, and they mobilised to denounce the attack on them. Men of fighting age took to the bush, where they regrouped, trained, and planned their own spectacular shows of force. These they enacted, beginning with an ambush on CAR's north-easternmost town, Birao, in late October 2006, where they destroyed or seized any government assets they found, such as a small weapons stockpile. They made similar shows of force in several other north-eastern towns, on a trajectory towards the capital, over the following month. These rebellious shows of force, are a further new instance of the kinds of hunting encounters described elsewhere in this book. It is useful to see them as hunting encounters themselves, as it clarifies the way in which such an encounter is a moment of instability in mutual assessment: are we fellows? Are we antagonists? Can we ignore each other? And how do my rapid answers to these questions shape what I will do next? How do things tip in relation to the 'thin line' (Le Noël 1999: 220) between killing, letting be, or caring for? Demonstrating a mutual threat or the ability to kill can force deliberation as to whether one can be considered a fundamentally similar kind of being, rather than ignorable or otherwise irrelevant. But what comes of that consideration? A French aerial assault forced the UFDR to retreat,[7] and they eventually negotiated with the government.

[7] France has a long history of intervening in Central African conflicts, whether in support of or to depose a sitting president.

With those attacks, the members of the rebel group continued the tradition of denouncing what they saw as egregious seizure against them and those they considered fellows.[8] They sought to communicate that they could not be treated that way. However, they did not want simply negative liberty, to be left alone. They hoped that by showing force they would appear as people who merited regard, in the form of material largesse and status, and that the involvement of the good intentions crowd would help them leverage their demands. By calling themselves and self-consciously acting like 'rebels', they staked a symbolic claim in the international diplomacy/aid world, one they hoped would make them identifiable as political actors, not bandits. Their mobilisation thus took on new aims and meanings in the evolving post–Cold War context of aid and the concern about 'failed' or 'fragile' states such as CAR.

So far, the rebels have largely been disappointed in their aims. They, and the people they live among, do receive humanitarian aid, but they consider such aid insignificant and temporary, a handout at the discretion of the giver. They seek instead the kind of material largesse that they felt should be assigned to them as an acknowledgement that they are worthy of being included among those who receive, an entitled status they felt that they would never obtain unless the president knew they would be dangerous to him until they were appeased in this way. Of the humanitarians, Damane concluded, 'They are mocking us' ('*Ils se moquent de nous*').

I sat in on meetings between humanitarians and Damane's fellow Tiringoulou residents during which the humanitarians explained their offers. Hundreds of people from nearby villages had temporarily settled in Tiringoulou, judging the town safer than their hamlets. The humanitarians proposed to provide a household kit – a jerrycan, a tarpaulin, soap, some plates, etc. – for each displaced family, with 'family' defined precisely as at most one adult man, one adult woman, and their biological children. The humanitarians had noticed that some men had registered with multiple families. People in Tiringoulou saw this as the

[8] Violence always communicates something; it is never just 'brute' or 'barbarian' force (Richards 1996). Rebels in the hunting zone used attacks and threats to display their dangerousness in order to make a claim to mattering, a claim to being people who merit regard, as opposed to people who can be disregarded or forcibly acquired from. The UFDR was not the only one of CAR's more than a dozen rebellions born of denunciations around egregious seizure and who could commit it (Lombard 2016d, 2017). From the perspective of rebel group members and other participants in rebellion, their attacks have been a response to presidential troops' illegitimate forceful seizure from them. The president and his troops attempt to dismiss rebels' claims by calling them bandits or mercenaries. Both sides share the belief that displaying dangerousness is part of a socially meaningful and effective repertoire of action.

obvious work-around given that many men have several wives. To whatever extent the humanitarians understood local life, their agencies' rules would not accept alternative family structures and instead termed such moves corruption. Failure to stop this could compromise their future funding. From the perspective of people in Tiringoulou, such nitpicking was evidence of profound and insulting stinginess. Central Africans have come to desire distributive politics (Ferguson 2015; Lombard 2016c) all the more fervently over the last few decades in the context of state decay and international intervention. Humanitarian aid falls far short of the 'rightful share' they seek. People in the hunting zone are painfully aware that their government has always failed to live up to norms of bureaucratic welfare statehood, and those who participate in rebellion of various sorts hope to shock powerful distributors elsewhere into providing for them – not just occasionally, but over the course of their lives.

The status of people living in north-eastern CAR was compromised and uncertain even before the rebellions began to emerge. Central Africans in the capital area learned well – and still believe – the colonial government's argument that Muslims in the north-east are not nationals, but foreign imperialists bent on dispossession, even after several generations' residency on CAR territory. The status of north-easterners is all the more compromised and uncertain now. By attacking towns and seizing what they found, they focused attention on themselves, but ultimately this has only reinforced the idea, prevalent among people in the capital, that the rebels are rapacious foreigners. While the rebels have not achieved the kind of entitled status they hoped for, and in many ways their grievances have been fuelled rather than assuaged by the way in which humanitarians work with and around them, they recognise that they sought and achieved a measure of adventure in their lives, including in the form of encounters with new lifestyles and ideas.

The careers of a few men, most of them former or current *pisteurs* and rebel officers, offer evidence of this. Like those of status seekers and adventurists before them, their careers are shaped by the peculiarities of the hunting zone and its frustrations and opportunities. They are adept at finding ways to collaborate with people and projects beyond their place of residence. They have learned skills of self-positioning in relation to a variety of potential audiences. Even here, though, adventurous or confrontational moments are the exception. They spend most of their time waiting. While they wait, one of the things they do is to tell stories. It is something of that rhythm I hope to capture in retelling their biographies. Rather than the story of the 'scandal' that internationally funded *pisteurs* became rebels, or the story of 'tragic' and 'pathetic' aspects of extraversion (Bayart 2000), their own accounts are full of irony, of frustration and inertia, of trying to gain more than a partial view of the horizons they might aspire to reach, and which they feel others are actively obscuring. They tend to be ambivalent about the fact that violence has been so useful to them; they are not unaware of its costs. Ultimately, rebellion has not removed or replaced acquisitive politics or established status stability so much as it has changed the landscape and added new actors.

Soumaine Ndodeba

> 'Sometimes I ask myself why I was born here. The Central African Republic sure is a bizarre country.'

Thus said Soumaine Ndodeba (Figure 8.2), also known as Colonel (now General) Tarzan, in October 2009, early in my field research in north-eastern CAR. We sat in the shade of an old mango tree near his house in Tiringoulou, drinking sweet, hot, black tea from small glasses and shelling freshly picked peanuts. When he described his home as bizarre, I thought about offering some anthropological banality about how every place is weird in its own way. Then he laughed, and I joined him. In calling his home bizarre, Soumaine was making a moral claim: that this is

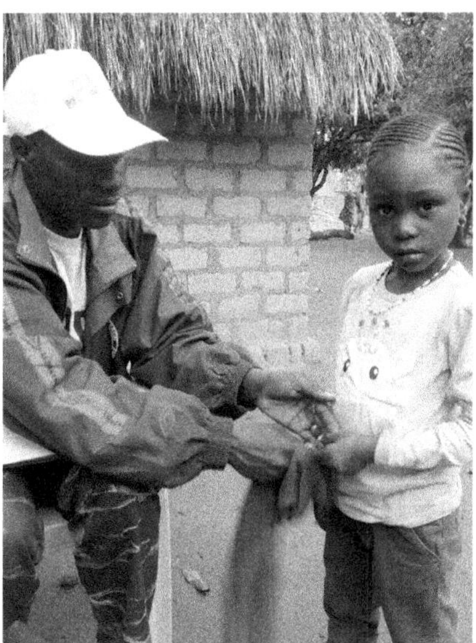

Figure 8.2 Soumaine Ndodeba helping one of his daughters put on a shawl outside his house in Tiringoulou

not how things should be. But he could also view his situation with a sense of humour, or at least irony.

Soumaine has been a leading participant, at an operational level, in forceful acquisition and status projects over the past two decades, a period of considerable transformation. He has worked as an anti-poaching guard, a rebel, and a children's and youth rights advocate and coach. He began his working career in 1997, joining the PDRN as a *pisteur*. He received military and tracking training from the expatriate technical assistants on the projects, referring to them by their first names or nationalities (French, Swiss, American, British). Project funding went into decline in 2004. From then until 2007, two Russians, ex-Foreign Legionnaires, camped out on the Sangba base during the dry months, the safari season, from December until about June. They led a select group of *pisteurs* drawn from the project militia's ranks on operations against hunters and herders, and Soumaine was among them. They were paid by the Association pour la Protection de la Faune Centrafricaine, a charity largely funded by safari hunters.[9] Soumaine remembered his Russian boss as 'very strong' and 'very hard' in his approach to the work they undertook. Soumaine appreciated the fact that the Russian had continued to call on the satellite phone for several years after he departed, promising to return and avenge those killed in his absence.

The Russians were the ones who gave Soumaine the nickname Tarzan. He refrained from saying why. They gave everyone in the militia nicknames, assigned when people did something foolish, clumsy, or otherwise worthy of a ribbing. They anointed a mild-mannered older gentleman Zidane after the headbutting footballer; another *pisteur* was dubbed Terminator. The Russians had multiple names, too, including those they were known by in CAR that they had adopted after they left the French Foreign Legion. The nicknames were practical: a way of speaking to one another without revealing their home identities – that is, *noms de guerre*. They are yet another reminder of how adventurists strive less to express their fullest sense of self and more to strategically self-position and retain the ability to move around and be flexible. Nicknames allow a person to obscure other social identities while among people who may be hostile.

While Soumaine was working for the Russians, in April 2006, he got word that Chadian rebels had used the airstrip at Tiringoulou, his home town, to ship in weapons, which they then carried off into the bush to the

[9] The Russians operated with a concession-type dispensation from the president, which took material form in a letter they brandished in the face of anyone who stopped or questioned them, such as at roadblocks or traffic stops during their visits to the capital.

north. Tiringoulou residents alerted the government in Bangui by radio. Shortly thereafter, Presidential Guard soldiers arrived. They made a dramatic show of force, attacking people and burning homes. They particularly harassed those who had camouflage uniforms or other signs of arms-carrying occupations, such as current or former safari camp guards and *pisteurs*. The actions were an accusation (*you have supported rebels*) and a threat (*you had better not do that again*; *you had better know that we can hunt you*). In the wake of the attacks, Soumaine returned to Tiringoulou to check on his family. But he quickly left again. He went back to the bush. He walked for two days, navigating by water points, and eventually found a group of his fellows from the area who were convening to figure out how to counter the attacks. The group included a few other *pisteurs*, some young men who had been working in diamond mines, and others – primarily young men already trying to make a career beyond agriculture, without much success. It was then that Soumaine became *Colonel* Tarzan, a rank bestowed on him for the military training he had received during his decade hunting people in the parklands. In the bush, he trained the others in his specialised skills of tracking, evasion, and attack.

At the end of October 2006, Colonel Tarzan and his group launched a surprise attack on Birao, the north-easternmost town in the country. Their attack, like those of the Presidential Guard that preceded it, bore some resemblance to the style of the *bazingirs* of old. They arrived in the pre-dawn twilight, shooting to cause terror and excitement and to send people fleeing. The group, the UFDR, was particularly interested in the symbolic as well as the material resources of the state that were at least minimally present in Birao. They captured what weapons they could from the minimal arms depots, and they ransacked offices, leaving chairs, desks, and papers overturned. Those few state officials present could not have effectively defended themselves by staying in place and fighting back; instead, they fled into the bush with everyone else. The UFDR took one town after another in this fashion, moving towards the capital. They made it as far as Ndele. At that point, French soldiers supported by Central African soldiers used aerial firepower to push them back towards the north-east. I visited Ndele a couple of weeks later, in December 2006. Many people were still living beside their fields, rather than in their houses. A couple of old government vehicles were now little more than burned-out hulks. But otherwise all traces of the rebels were gone.

Pushed back, UFDR members hung around in their home areas (Tiringoulou and Sam Ouandja) and oversaw artisanal mining operations (ICG 2008). Meanwhile, the Cotonou, Benin-based politico-military entrepreneurs who claimed to speak for and lead them, Abakar Sabone and Michel Djotodia, signed a peace agreement with the government in mid-2008, as did General Damane Zakaria, who led the UFDR on the ground. The effective outcome of the agreement was similar to that of the treaties between al-Sanusi and the French a century earlier: the parties would no longer overtly threaten each other, and the president would offer some largesse in exchange for this laying down of arms. Damane got his presidential adviser sinecure and control of the diamond mines; the president got the assurance that Damane would not go after him, and might possibly counter others who would.

For the operational leaders of the UFDR, including Soumaine, though, this was not what the agreement should have entailed. Soumaine wanted to be included, to be 'integrated', to use the Central African term of choice when referring to those who draw a government salary as a member of the civil service. He wanted to be a part of the state, not an auxiliary. In fact, one reason why he joined the UFDR was that, when a batch of project *pisteurs* was selected to join the Water and Forests Ministry, no one from his home prefecture, Vakaga in the far northeast, was chosen. Only those from areas closer to the capital made the cut. This was a provocative form of discrimination, from Soumaine's perspective, one that denied their status as people and saw them as beneath consideration. When I met Soumaine in Tiringoulou in 2009, he was waiting for the DDR programme (disarmament, demobilisation, and reintegration) he had been promised, part of the 'post-conflict toolkit' expected from donors these days.[10] Soumaine expected that the initiative would bring him some training and money, and also a government job, perhaps in the security sector since that would fit with his experience, ideally in an office somewhere.

Any such 'integration' was continually postponed, however. Once a peace agreement was signed, humanitarian organisations could come to the area without too much fear for their security. Tarzan turned to them as a source of skills and training, and to offer his connections. He was known in town for being good with children, from toddlers to grown youth, and also for his ability to mobilise them, and the American medical charity in town deputised him as its local children's rights advocate. They also taught him to coach football, in the hope that the area might one day host a friendly league.

But a larger DDR never came. In December 2012, Soumaine and many other former UFDR members joined a new alliance of men-at-arms, from the region and beyond, who were making a newly concerted attempt to claim the capital. Calling themselves Seleka ('alliance' in

[10] I discuss these programmes at length in *State of Rebellion* (Lombard 2016d).

Sango), they succeeded in taking the presidency in March 2013. Tarzan was shot as they were approaching the capital and airlifted to Gabon for medical treatment. When he returned to CAR he went straight home to Tiringoulou to recuperate. From there, he was sent to Bambari. By this point, his group, whose membership largely overlapped with that of the old UFDR, was calling itself the Rassemblement Patriotique pour le Renouveau de la Centrafrique (RPRC, or Union for the Patriotic Renewal of CAR). (In part, the new name engaged the debate over whether Seleka was composed, as its opponents claimed, entirely of foreigners; the RPRC was explicitly identifying itself as non-foreign.) Soumaine was given the rank of general and charged with ensuring group discipline. Many of the new recruits knew him only as General Tarzan. He does not mind the nickname; it is a marker of a certain kind of prominence to be known by one. But outside his arms-carrying work, he prefers his birth name.

As an officer with the capacity to discipline and organise others, fluent in the language of humanitarian actors and human rights, he again became a useful interlocutor for the aid and international organisations working in town. He helped them recruit child soldiers for a project demobilising them. He helped oversee a project that paid young men and women to do manual labour and listen to peace education lectures. He hoped that project would be brought to other towns, as he saw it as being truly transformative for participants, who worked side by side despite having traits – being Christian or Muslim, for example – that would otherwise have funnelled them into hostile factions.

I caught up with Soumaine in mid-2015, when he was back in Tiringoulou for Ramadan, which was about to begin. (There were rumours that an armed group was lurking and could possibly attack, so his return had probably not been purely social.) We met at his compound, a few modest but immaculately kept daub-and-thatch houses in a shady spot near the centre of town. His children were a constant presence. A 12-year-old son served tea and food with expert manners, turning a curious ear to our conversations. He remained always a few feet away, anticipating our every need – offering the water kettle for us to wash our hands, repositioning our chairs to avoid the harshest sun. A five-year-old daughter often stood between her father's knees; she also watched and listened (Figure 8.2). Visitors were a constant presence, too. Soumaine had just got home the day before, and a stream of people came to greet him, to ask after his health and for the latest political news. Soumaine would pop into the house, re-emerge, and slip many of these visitors something – often a bit of cash, but also other valuable goods, including, to one young man, a hunting rifle and ammunition. With me, he shared perhaps the most delicious roast chicken I have ever eaten. It was a reminder that, for all the acquisition he had done in his life, he had probably done just as much sharing and distributing, if not more.

In addition to catching up, the political situation was a focus of interest among all of Soumaine's visitors – those who had lived near Tiringoulou their whole lives and those just passing through, like me. With fellow residents, he spoke Gula and referred often to the elusiveness of '*hurriya*', an Arabic loan word meaning freedom. With me, he spoke French and used the term '*liberté*' (liberty). These two terms corresponded, in his usage, to Isaiah Berlin's (1969) notions of positive liberty and negative liberty. *Hurriya*, he said, was the freedom of being at ease: you have a job, your children go to school. 'Like the Dinka in South Sudan once they got their own country.' Liberty, meanwhile, he described through an example: Muslims in CAR are stopped at roadblocks, and even if they produce an identity card they are treated as foreigners and have to pay extra; they are subjected to undue and unfair molestation. How one is treated when one tries to move around the country is one of the most obvious of status markers. Muslims such as Soumaine from north-eastern CAR felt that their claims were always summarily dismissed.

Soumaine has been fairly successful in his adventurist career. He went from the PDRN and ECOFAC, where he worked as a guard, to an elite private anti-poaching militia, and then became an officer in a rebel group, an interlocutor with humanitarians, even a humanitarian worker himself. This is the trajectory through which ambitious people throughout the region become successful. Soumaine had the initiative and imagination to learn from, even to enjoy, his experiences along the way. But if he had, in the political vernacular, 'done well' (de Waal 2009), he saw the limits to his success. He knew he had not managed to claim a government salary-derived status, and he was becoming ever more articulate and insistent in his demands for both *hurriya* and liberty, although he knew that his hopes for them might prove a 'cruel optimism' (Berlant 2011).

Joseph Zoundeiko

General Joseph Zoundeiko was another *pisteur*-turned-rebel, also from Tiringoulou. He joined the *pisteurs* at around the same time as Soumaine and, like him, was chosen by the Russians during the project funding gap.[11] When I met him in Tiringoulou in 2009, he was in the same

[11] His nickname had less local salience than Tarzan's; perhaps that is why it wasn't taken up in the same way. Zoundeiko's renaming came one day when he was making tea using a small gas stove. The stove exploded, and Zoundeiko was dubbed Marconi for reasons that remained obscure to him.

position as Soumaine: a rebel officer awaiting disarmament. His rank as commander of the zone (*chef d'Etat-major*) placed him above Soumaine, which meant that he had access to arenas and responsibilities that Soumaine did not. For instance, Soumaine could find UFDR members and ask them if they were interested in talking with me; Zoundeiko would travel to Bangui to be part of seminars about disarmament largesse modalities. Zoundeiko also had more responsibility for keeping tabs on the increasingly restive '*éléments*', as he referred to UFDR members.

Zoundeiko had mastered multiple rhetorical styles. International Committee of the Red Cross (ICRC) representatives make the rounds of armed group leaders to sensitise them about international humanitarian law, for instance, and Zoundeiko quickly learned their terms and came to see such organisations as a potential source of leverage. He was also a great storyteller, particularly of tales of altercations. When I was in Tiringoulou, I stayed at Yaya's old house, the one now occupied by a humanitarian organisation. Zoundeiko would sometimes come to this spacious and fenced compound to visit the Central Africans working there. He did not have to speak loudly or with great flourishes to hold their rapt attention, even when speaking in Sango, a language not used in everyday life by Gula-speaking Tiringoulou residents. He told, for instance, of how a couple of times bullets had hit Soumaine only to bounce off him, implying that Soumaine had some powers and protection that were not of the visible world.

On a visit to Tiringoulou in early 2010, I caught up with *Chef d'Etat-Major* Zoundeiko. The day before, a stranger passing through town had been caught stealing the penises of several men in town. The phenomenon of genital theft has been reported throughout West and Central Africa since the turn of the millennium. It has mostly been studied as an African 'urban rumour' (Bonhomme 2009), a form of suspected witchcraft emerging from the fractured, uncertain, and mistrustful social worlds of rapidly growing cities swollen with newly arrived villagers.[12] But it had come to remote Tiringoulou too, in the person of a man (a Chadian or Nigerian, people surmised) who stopped briefly in town as part of a longer journey on the back of a Sudanese transport truck. In the market, the traveller purchased tea, and when he took it the tea seller noticed an electric tingling in his whole body, and had the distinct sensation that his member was gone. One or two others fell victim to this man. I visited one

[12] Anxieties over genital disappearance or change in the midst of societal upheaval have been widespread around the world. The fifteenth-century tome the *Malleus Maleficarum*, for instance, recorded instances of witchcraft in what is now Germany and its environs and is full of cases of penis snatching.

of the victims, who appeared genuinely ill, weak, and suffering. Mezzan Ramadan, in his capacity as the town doctor, said that while the penis was not wholly gone, it had lost all its force, and there was nothing he could do to help repair that kind of injury.

Almost as quickly as the incidents occurred, people in town mobilised, gathering their Kalashnikovs and other weapons and surrounding the sorcerer-thief. But Zoundeiko and other UFDR members intervened. Zoundeiko later explained to me that if he had not done so, the thief would have been handled vigilante-style, with angry women in the lead, which would have reflected poorly on both Tiringoulou and the UFDR. So instead they questioned the man. At first he claimed that he wasn't guilty, but then he accepted responsibility, saying that he had only denied his guilt because he thought that they would punish all travellers. They locked him up in a holding room at the rebel-occupied *gendarmerie* shed while they decided what to do. When they came back just at the gloaming hour of about six in the evening the door was locked, but the man inside had disappeared. No one could explain it. He must have used his occult powers. But at least he was no longer bothering Tiringoulou. (The penises eventually returned to their original strength, or nearly.)

Others told a different story: they said that UFDR leaders had executed the presumed thief. Either way, I was struck by Zoundeiko's care to tell a story that would not breach the international legal norms drilled into him by the humanitarians. 'International opinion' ('*l'opinion internationale*') was a motif in my conversations with Zoundeiko around this time.

For instance, Zoundeiko had heard that President Bozizé had recently given a speech in which he stated that he had handed over 340 million CFA (about US$0.5 million) to the steering committee in charge of DDR. But still nothing happened on the DDR front. It was true that the steering committee had sent a few representatives to Tiringoulou the year before to discuss the process with the UFDR there. One of them handed over 3 million CFA (about US$5,000) as a thank you. The Tiringoulou group accepted the money, but Zoundeiko found it troubling. To make it official there should have been a receipt, signed in Bangui and countersigned in Tiringoulou, attesting that all the money had reached its intended beneficiaries. But this money was just given informally, and they had no way of knowing whether they had received their due. During a subsequent visit to Bangui, Zoundeiko asked the vice president of the steering committee (himself a former government employee and rebel political leader) what had happened to the 340 million. The vice president replied, 'That's above my pay grade' ('*Cela dépasse mon niveau*'), and that was the end of the conversation. People living in north-eastern CAR or with interests in the region have turned the blurry vision of capital-based overseers to their advantage through camouflage, as happened during the colonial era and during armed conservation. But people in the north-east also have trouble getting a clear view of the capital's horizons, and they find this deeply frustrating.

Back in Tiringoulou, Zoundeiko said to me, repeatedly, that he told his men to 'stay calm. It is international opinion that will judge.' That is, if they waited patiently now, it would be clear that whatever action they took later was a legitimate response to the way in which they had been treated. He saw *l'opinion internationale* as a reservoir of moral norms that he could consciously position himself in relation to and thereby gain leverage through its organisations and ideas.

Zoundeiko and the others waited a further two and a half years. That was when their old political leader, Michel Djotodia, approached them about joining Séléka. UFDR members say that they joined right away; others following events have said that they joined only after Séléka's likely success became clear. Either way, they were not the most fearsome Séléka contingent, but they were a crucial sector of Central African participation. (The alliance included many veteran men-at-arms from the long wars in the Chad and Darfur borderlands.) Since the UFDR had signed a peace agreement with the government, the group members needed to rebrand themselves, hence the RPRC. Zoundeiko was named Séléka's military chief in May 2014. His name and picture made it into international news reports, but the alliance had already foundered.

On my visit to Tiringoulou in mid-2015 I spent time with Zoundeiko while he, like Soumaine, was home for a Ramadan rest after a year away in Bambari. He had some new scars since I had last seen him. And he was frustrated. He was also even more comfortable with rebel and humanitarian language, and with making bigger demands. In 2010 he had recognised that only some 'elements' would be brought into the security forces and the civil service; now he called for all the 'children' (youth) to be integrated. He spoke at length on the topic:

> At the Forum [Bangui Forum, a national political dialogue] we collaborated well but the government doesn't want to collaborate directly with us. We have intellectuals who have not been incorporated. If people want durable peace the youth should be integrated into the military. We're Central Africans too. The foreigners should be repatriated. What about us? We're sick of the foreigners too ... Michel [Djotodia] has been excluded. When things don't work out there will be people who will follow him [i.e. start another rebellion]. Look at us: we had signed peace accords and everything, but since [then] we were just endlessly waiting. Well, we couldn't wait forever. Even if they do a forced disarmament, that won't bring peace back here. One person might have ten or 15 weapons [note: there are few, if any, who have this many]. If they take one, he still has a lot.

> And even if they take them all, weapons are proliferating across the borders here so it would be easy to get more. Who can secure this area? The international community can't do it. And the army can't do it – the army is an ethnic army, the sons of ministers only. Whenever a problem happens, they just flee … I participated in the Bangui Forum. I spent 25 days in Bangui for it. We all want peace. We also need for our demands to be taken into account. There has to be some balance. We have made our recommendation; we have prepared documents. I'll find them for you so you can see. There was a peace agreement in 2008 too. If things aren't resolved we will always take up arms again. We will go and fight. We are well trained – much better than the army. Me, I've been trained by Americans, French, people like those Russians. Twenty of us could easily take 100 soldiers.

Then he used a metaphor: 'Better to treat this illness. You don't just give any old medicine and expect that the person is going to get better. No. You need the medicine that is adapted to the illness.' Rebellion was a symptom of the malady, the abandonment of and seizure from his home region; the cure was the kind of regard that integration into the public service would demonstrate.

In his past as a *pisteur*, Zoundeiko had been shot several times. In 2001, he was caught in a confrontation with poachers who shot him in the knee. The other *pisteurs* had to run, leaving him to hide for a full day. The scars remained: raised pink tissue showing both the bullet's entry near the knee and its exit on the back of his thigh. Another time he took a bullet in the stomach. Yet another time, a bullet grazed him just behind the ear. In February 2017, he was hit again. He and some of his cohort had joined the Front Populaire pour le Renaissance de Centrafrique (FPRC, or Popular Front for the Renaissance of CAR) to try to definitively cow the other main armed group, the Union des Patriotes Centrafricains (UPC). But before the battle, Zoundeiko was hit by a bullet fired from a UN peacekeeper helicopter. He died where he fell.

Zoundeiko's success – or at least his persistence – was furthered by his ability to anticipate how potential onlookers, whether inside or outside the zone, perceive violence across geographical, legal-bureaucratic, and social landscapes, and to position himself in response. Displays of force can galvanise collaborations across these landscapes, but they are risky. Zoundeiko's death saddened me, but I also knew that he, better than most, knew exactly what kind of game he was playing.

Hamad Hamadine

One morning in March 2010, I stopped by the UFDR-staffed gendarme shack in Tiringoulou to try to find someone to talk with me. As my eyes adjusted to the dim interior I quickly recognised Hamad Hamadine, who stood out both for his advanced age – born in 1950, he had beaten CAR's life expectancy by a couple decades already – and the crutch he leaned on in place of a leg, lost in the denunciatory battles after Yaya's death. Hamad's knowledge of French had earned him a role as a UFDR spokesperson. When I approached him and the few others present they fell quiet, and Hamad explained that they were discussing 'top secret' plans about what they would do if DDR and other entitlements they expected did not materialise. Their language of secrecy was no cover. It only added a frisson to the obvious message: that they could and might attack anew, that they were still dangerous, that they should not be overlooked.

Hamad and I had spoken several times by that point. He was the oldest armed-group member I got to know. His career reflects the vicissitudes as well as the adventures of hunting-zone life; it was a life full of *élan* and tragedy. Hamad now lived again in his natal town, Ouandja. But he was on an extended visit to Tiringoulou, having heard that Tiringoulou residents, grateful for his role in denouncing Yaya's murder, had expressed their thanks by collecting money that would let him buy a prosthesis in Bangui. However, the person who had been charged with taking care of the money had gone to Bangui, several days' journey away, for his brother's funeral. The fortieth day of mourning had recently passed, so perhaps he would be back soon and Hamad could ask about the cash. Hamad was simultaneously hopeful and sceptical as to whether he would ever get the money.

As a teenager, Hamad himself had gone to Bangui. Bokassa had recently taken power in a coup and had created the Jeunesse Pionnière Nationale (National Youth Pioneers), which Hamad joined. He later served three years in the army. This was the period when Bokassa had grand plans, such as the construction of the Jean-Bédel Bokassa 'model village' to be built 22 kilometres from the centre of Bangui. Hamad was given the job of overseeing its construction, following plans Bokassa obtained in China. They conscripted workers from the country's main prison, Ngaragba, as well as students from the technical high school who needed internships in order to graduate. Overseeing construction was a good job, but he ran into problems. 'You know, we Africans … especially in terms of matters of women …' he began, vaguely. Then he put it more plainly. He had taken up with the wife of another overseer. He was chased from the worksite and feared he might be imprisoned, but he managed to flee to Sudan.

He spent two years in Nyala, in South Darfur, where he taught French at a night school. Then he returned to CAR to work as a diamond prospector (as an *exploitant* or financer/organiser of digging) in Sam Ouandja and Bria, north-eastern CAR's two main diamond towns. He made a lot of money this way – millions of CFA in a year. 'But back then we didn't know how to manage money. We had a lot of fun with women and drinking. Look at me now: no longer working age and without money.' Yet he did not seem to regret his past. Rather, his seemed to be a version of the sentiment expressed by safari hunter Giorgio Grasselli (who worked in CAR in the 1990s), who wrote that 'an adventurous life hardly agrees with parsimony and a disposition to save money' (2007: 107).

While working as a diamond-dig financier in 2002, Hamad got word through 'Radio PDRN'[13] that Yaya had been killed, and he knew that he should return to Tiringoulou to help denounce the killing. So he did, and because he had worked as a local defence officer in Bria, he was made a *directeur d'attachement*, a leader among the 85 (by his count) who were joining for battle. It was in one of those engagements that he was shot in the foot. He was evacuated to Bangui in the conservation-project plane and was treated at the Hôpital de l'Amitié for a month, but the wound suppurated and in the end they amputated to the knee. He returned home.

When the UFDR emerged, he was not able to join as a fighter, but he lent his French-speaking skills to the cause, proudly showing me a collection of business cards from international journalists who had visited and consulted him. The BBC and RFI (Radio France Internationale) had both interviewed him, multiple times. And now here we were, sitting together and chatting in the shade under the eaves of the house he stayed at in Tiringoulou. He showed me copies of some of the UFDR's most important documents, such as their demands to the government, which he kept with him at all times, for their safety. Together we read the newspapers that friends had brought back from Bangui for him.

Hamad had lived a full life, chasing adventure and not just survival. However, he, like so many other armed-group members, understood that his position in the world – in a state and yet stateless – was an aberrant one. 'We have seen and heard how the whole of France mobilises if one soldier is lost. Our government here, do they do that, even when thousands of our own die?' The answer to this question was too obvious for either of us to waste time discussing it.

Hamad and many of his fellows felt intense privation – poverty, but especially the suspicion that they were disregarded by their countrymen (the 'bizarreness' of their position in the world, as Soumaine put it) – at the same time as their lives showed creativity, flexibility, and periods of

[13] 'Radio PDRN' was Hamad's (and others') term for the conservation projects' radio communication system; by that point the PDRN had become ECOFAC.

good fortune and bad. Hamad's life has been cosmopolitan in ways that counter most stereotypes about rural Africans. But he is also subject to the whims of others – the man who should have held onto his prosthesis money but probably will present excuses; the UFDR leaders who tell conflicting stories about their contacts with the government – in ways that are deeply unsatisfying. In rebellion, Hamad and his fellows strove to merit regard, to be recognised as worthy of entitlement by their government rather than abandoned. They wanted to force a moment of status reckoning with the president and others in power, to turn a fickle and capricious kind of dependence into a steady and strong one.

Boris-Harding

During a conversation with Boris-Harding beside his Manovo house in late 2009, he brought up the issue of the impending end of EU project funding. Projects are authorised for a certain number of years only (usually no more than two or three, though four or five was once common); this one would end in a few months. With it Boris-Harding would lose his source of income and again be cast out into the ranks of the un-statused and unsalaried. He hoped I would help plead his case by bringing his concerns to the far-off bureaucrats who would decide whether to relaunch the project. Boris-Harding implored:

> Seriously, the European Union must continue to finance this project. We *pisteurs* are really well trained. Me, personally, I am capable of training 20 or even 80 men. We could go and launch a *coup d'état*, or a rebellion, or become bandits if we don't have work. Think of it – there are 60 or 70 of us guards. We could really cause problems if we don't have work. We are here. And we are here to show the outside world that we are working.

Boris-Harding strove for respectability, to be recognised for his merit and accomplishments. His salaried job as a *pisteur* helped him achieve that. *Even Boris-Harding*, I thought ruefully as I listened to his threat. Even someone as scrupulous in his job as he is is willing to breach norms to make a living. Violence and rebellion are easy, and arms-carrying occupations interchangeable.

Only five years later, in December 2014, when I met up with Boris-Harding unexpectedly in Bangui, did I begin to question my interpretation of those remarks. War had arrived in the country in earnest in the form of Seleka and subsequent fall-out and mobilisation, and more than two-thirds of his fellow guards had indeed joined armed groups or been killed. But not Boris-Harding. He remained with the anti-poaching project, even during the periods of scarce funding.

Nine months earlier, during exercises for the anti-poaching militia, he had been carrying a backpack when the grenade inside exploded; it was four years old, with a loose pin. He could see his intestines hanging out and spent the night on the nearby conservation base in agony, unsure of what would become of him. The French expatriate training him, with whom he was close, organised a flight to the capital, surgery, and a month-long hospital stay. Boris-Harding then returned to the north-east. I found him in the capital because he had to visit intermittently to follow his disability claim through the various ministries that might one day approve it.

I reminded Boris-Harding of the threat he had made to join or start a rebellion. He looked down and said that though he did not recall the remark, 'I may have said that, yes …' His words trailed off.

I realised that, rather than making a statement of how easy it would be for him to turn to violence, Boris-Harding had been making a threat, a kind of speech act, as a way of asserting how far he would be willing to go if his needs were not met. He was making a display of dangerousness in the hope that it would bolster his claim to the worthiness of regard implied by a salaried job. Boris-Harding's life underscores the point that arms carrying is not just about perpetrating physical violence, accidental or intentional, even when it is undeniably pervasive, as are threats of violence. Boris-Harding was ready to make rhetorical statements to display his dangerousness, but when the time came he wasn't ready to follow through. (Other factors pushing him away from rebellion included the fact that his fellow *pisteurs* saw him as a goody two shoes, and that, although he had grown up in the area, his family roots, with the responsibilities family relations entail, were elsewhere. This also made others less sure they could trust him.) Boris-Harding had dreamed of joining the Foreign Legion, and before the grenade incident he was preparing for the journey to France. That dream now seemed impossible, both because of the lingering effects of his injury and because the French AT who was helping him, his *binôme*, had been killed in a motorcycle accident in France.[14] Boris-Harding

[14] The AT's story was part sordid, part tragic. He had worked as an anti-poaching AT in the late 2000s, then lost his job, but was brought back in 2013 after President Bozizé was ousted. Work was minimal in the midst of the war going on at the time. One evening in Bamingui, a town that is also an anti-poaching base, he got into an argument and beat a man nearly to death, departing rapidly in the project Land Cruiser to Bangui in the middle of the night. The man he had beaten had died by morning. Despite the potential for this to become a galvanising incident (attitudes towards the French were not favourable at the time, and a former French soldier beating a poor Central African to death would have been good ammunition), there was no outcry. One day the AT was leaving the national stadium after a weightlifting workout when his Land Cruiser was attacked by armed men who shot him multiple times. Armed attacks occurred frequently those days, so it was easy to blame it on criminality. But it seemed extremely suspicious

continues to work as a *pisteur*, and is now among the most senior – his grinning, confident face features prominently on the project website. He remains hopeful that someday the wild animals might return, breathing new life and meaning into the endeavour. In 2018, he, too, was in a bad motorcycle accident and spent weeks recuperating in the hospital in Bangui. Violence tends to have some meaning or purpose, but harm and danger are also banal parts of life for people in this part of the world.

Shows of force, violence, and status

Members of rebel groups use particular communicative forms of violence to claim entitled status. In so doing they are able to create proximity, even if it is temporary or illusory, to national and international sources of regard they previously lacked. They see the value of 'the state' as an entity capable of confirming status through the provision of a government job and its salary (Lombard 2016c). The value of other markers of 'stateness' – government-imposed rules that are enforced, for example – are more disputed. Rebel groups end up taking on state-like functions, with varying levels of enthusiasm. They have generally seen themselves as placeholders waiting for 'the state' to arrive, but have increasingly accepted that they could discharge these roles in the long term if properly funded and deputised by the government, as Zoundeiko suggested.

Post–Cold War peacekeeping projects of all kinds have sent contradictory messages about violence.[15] Humanitarian action is founded on the

that they targeted him in exactly that way, and many were sure that it was a crew from Bamingui come for vengeance, disguised as criminals. Despite being shot and bleeding, the AT managed to steer away from his attackers and crashed into the roundabout known as 'United Nations' after the monument to the organisation at its centre. The French military was alerted, and he was airlifted to France for treatment. He recovered and returned to CAR intent on vengeance. Before he could make it back to the north-east, however, he took a holiday in France. He was driving his girlfriend on his motorcycle along a twisty southern French road when a van coming in the opposite direction veered into his lane, instantly killing both of them. He used to speak frequently of his love for and pride in his son, a teenager when his father died, and he and his girlfriend had just had a baby daughter.

[15] For instance, in 2003, François Bozizé, former chief of staff of the armed forces, fired in 2001 because of concern about his loyalty, confirmed that suspicion by claiming the presidency in Bangui with a congeries of armed men. They were too disorganised to be a 'rebel group'; instead, they were an assortment of people, mostly Chadian with some Central Africans thrown in, who had been promised a payout to help claim the capital (Debos 2008). Bozizé's successful claim to power involved coordinated support from all the region's heads of states (including France), who were exasperated by then president Ange-Félix Patassé and decided he needed to go, with Bozizé as a tractable replacement (Smith 2015a). Although there was some international condemnation of the coup, Bozizé was not forced to step aside. Instead, he benefited from substantial international aid dedicated to 'rebuilding' the state.

principle most famously promulgated by Henri Dunant (later co-founder of the ICRC), which posits that violence is always bad, always a source of suffering and illegitimate gain, with no potential for moral righteousness. But to the extent that humanitarians and other interveners cast an occasional glance at the hunting zone, it is violence there that attracts scrutiny, not more peaceful forms of protest or mobilisation; it is violence that most readily leads to the disbursement of aid of various kinds. Violence is simultaneously bad and an invitation to engagement. If one assumes that the involvement of international actors decreases future or potential violence, this is not inconsistent. But at least in a few places – CAR, DRC, and South Sudan come to mind – that assumption has not been easy to sustain as violence has continued despite intervention. In these places, rebellion has begotten intervention in a cyclical pattern for decades.

Since September 2014, the UN Multidimensional Integrated Stabilization Mission in CAR, MINUSCA, the largest peacekeeping force (12,000 strong) in CAR's history, has been deployed there. Its presence keeps more than a dozen armed groups in a holding pattern for the most part, with violence now occasional but nevertheless persistent. Displays of force, at least, are harder to make since they would be taken as a direct provocation to MINUSCA. But, as Zoundeiko and others pointed out, these interventions have not removed the possibilities for rebellion in the future. North-eastern CAR is still a stateless-state space, and force, acquisition, and stealth remain key ways of positioning for people trying to make a career in the area. Central Africans and interveners alike are left struggling to work through the inconsistencies and conflicts of values that help sustain the use of violence in the region.

Achille Mbembe has argued that war has become central to the 'contemporary African subject's representation of life, of the political realm, and – in particular – of the relationship to death' (Mbembe 2006: 299). But war is about using violence to harden distinctions between friends and enemies, whereas these rebellions are a means of forceful seizure to gain status and regard.[16] The result, if the rebels are successful, is not friendship. It is regard: that they will not be violently molested, that they will receive some kind of just share of payment as a material marker of their status. In this respect, there is continuity between rebellion and long-standing hunting-raiding practices in the region, such as the dance between al-Sanusi and the French. What is new is the bigger role played

[16] I am not the first to note that contemporary African rebellions and violence do not seem to turn on distinctions between friend and enemy (Debos 2016; Hoffman 2011; Vigh 2006, 2009).

by the good intentions crowd,[17] who both participate in and disrupt these dynamics.

People in the hunting zone have no other means of forcing confirmation of their entitled status. 'Integration' into the civil service, with the salary to match, is a way of indicating value in a mutually stipulated system. The monetary aspect is important primarily because each payment, in a lifetime as a civil servant, reinforces one's status and one's ability to support others, both of which are key to social recognition and to inscribing oneself in people's memory – and these are more important to participants than remuneration *tout court*.[18] Their goal is not unlike the purpose of animal-hunting stories; it is not just about sustenance but about honour, validity, and making a name for the teller. Participants are after status in a place where status is a particularly fraught designation mediated by the capacity to use force.

Conclusion

Both camouflage and displays of force are part of the normal and meaningful repertoire of action in this part of the world, and rebellion is one form these displays can take. Rebellion makes effective use of the semiotic registers of those with material resources to distribute, particularly the good intentions crowd but also the government. It is a mode of extraversion – a way in which Africans have made creative, productive use of their dependent position in the world (Bayart 2000). It was not purely humanitarian need or suffering alone that led humanitarians to conclude that their ministrations were warranted in north-eastern CAR. The upheaval took a form to which they were attuned; they understood it and they had adapted tools to deal with it. Rebellion fit their intellectual landscapes in a way that other forms of violence do not. This is partly simply for practical reasons: humanitarians can negotiate access and security with rebel groups; doing so with bandits or other armed actors is far more difficult. Partly because the rebel groups make the factitiousness of the state's claim to control of its territory and population apparent, this is a problem from the perspective of international order in the UN-era world.

Displays of force have long been a means for members of rebel groups to enter new landscapes and move around in them; they have offered new arenas in which to contest their positions. But in order to remain there

[17] Humanitarian voices of concern are as old as European colonialism in Central Africa, but only recently have they developed such an extensive on-the-ground presence.

[18] See Lombard (2016c, 2016d) for more on these dynamics of citizenship through salaries.

they must continue to blend in with the stipulated semiotic terms. They have scope for action within this landscape, in other words, but little range to challenge its parameters or affect its shape or features. And what the armed group members have found is that this landscape is primarily interested in policing, in managing the 'given distribution of social places and roles, ways of being and saying such that some activities are visible and sayable (located in the order of the logos) while other activities appear to be nothing more than noise (are located in the realm of phonos)' (Povinelli 2011: 50, discussing Jacques Rancière's concept). Policing does not paralyse everything, nor is it inherently wrong. But the regard armed group members and others in the hunting zone have pulled together proves less tangible than they had hoped. They still feel that they are mostly ignored, rather than being treated as people with status.

While members of rebel groups would like their shows of force (which often take the form of forceful acquisition) to automatically demonstrate that they merit regard, these shows of force can be overturned by the next forceful encounter. Rebel group members know this all too well. Many have been involved in acquisition, especially forceful acquisition, under different auspices and different guises their whole adult lives, and while this involvement has brought skills, money, and even some renown, for many their sense of failed expectations and their relative privation have also grown. In the twenty-first century, the increasing role of international organisations in places such as CAR appears to be a new factor – one that, through its modes of programming priorities (dealing first with the dangerous and the victims), promised to bring entitlements for the benighted. But while positioning rebellion in this international landscape of concern can be a means of gaining leverage vis-à-vis a president and drawing new largesse to the country and the sites of rebellion in particular, it generates new constraints for all parties. Yet even in the midst of those constraints, people find opportunities they had not envisioned, as Soumaine, Zoundeiko, Hamad, and Boris-Harding all did in their different ways.

9 Sovereignty and distribution amid forceful acquisition

> 'Are you a hunter?'
> 'No, but I hunt.' Roulet (2004)

So begins Pierre-Armand Roulet's study of hunting tourism in Central Africa. The question was almost the tagline for his research. But although he was the one doing the fieldwork, he wasn't asking the question: his local interlocutors asked it of him. They wanted to know what he knew about hunting. Are you one of us? Do you understand what we do? Can you talk about us without bias?

Pastoral politics – governments of care, biopolitics, and managed production – have become a worldwide norm, even despite neoliberal and austerity policies designed to roll back government involvement in daily life. Industrialised production became a norm alongside it, even if less fully realised in some places than in others. In such a world, forceful acquisition, of which hunting is one iteration, is an aberration. It is not the way things are supposed to be. And so someone who is hunting, who is asked about his hunting, wants to know: do you get this, or are you here to judge?

I am not a hunter of animals; I do not hunt with a gun. But in the broader sense of searching for opportunity and insight amid potentially dangerous, potentially empathetic others in the recesses of interior Africa, my research, too, has been a process of acquisition – not, though, a forceful one. My inquiries have shown that hunting games – forceful acquisition amid uncertain statuses – rather than aberrant, are a logical, if not a necessary, accompaniment to the recesses of state making and long-distance trade. That makes them both hard to judge and difficult to celebrate. There is freedom and autonomy, of a kind, in the hunting zone, but care and ministration are elusive, and their absence complained of by inhabitants.

Soumaine Ndodeba and his fellows were quite aware of what they were missing. Hamad Hamadine, the UFDR spokesperson, pointed out that when French citizens were lost or kidnapped or otherwise in trouble anywhere in the world, the government would come to their rescue. And meanwhile the Central African government did not even care for those citizens who stayed within the country's borders. How could this be?

Ndodeba saw his life as positioning himself to take advantage of the few opportunities he found in the abandoned bush (his description) where he happened to have been born. Those opportunities had an important economic component, but they also involved 'open[ing] up multiple possibilities of becoming – particularly those possibilities that are capable of being "conversant" with a broader world' (Simone 2004a: 136).

This book shows the ways people like him operate, given their starting point in a sparsely populated, nearly roadless area never properly claimed by any forces of politico-economic centralisation. It is about the mode of integration of these spaces into broader networks of exchange and circulation. Through attention to the practices and positioning of adventurists such as Soumaine, as well as attention to what or who is being taken and how the process of acquisition engenders shifting assessments of status and thingness, regard and disregard, we can understand the creation and maintenance of an area neither fully inside nor fully outside any formal polity, and its important place in relation to the rest of the world.

Still, while this book's heart beats in a very remote place, the lessons it offers apply even in places that are seemingly far less remote.

Remote places used to be what one might call the province(s) of anthropology.[1] This has changed. For one thing, urbanisation – in the world more generally but especially in Africa – has been intense and impossible to ignore. For another, doing things differently from one's predecessors is a means to bolster one's claim to greater theoretical sophistication than they ever had. Remoteness would seem to have lost its cachet. The creative potential of cities is newly fascinating (Bonhomme 2009, 2012; Hecht and Simone 1994; Koolhaas 2007; Mbembe and Nuttall 2004; Simone 2001, 2004a, 2004b).[2] Scholars have described the importance of cities as jumping-off points to collaboration that overcomes the limits of location (Simone 2001, 2004a). Staying put

[1] This has never been as true as the stereotype would suggest: for instance, innovative work by anthropologists at the Rhodes-Livingstone Institute and elsewhere was already exploring city life in the 1930s onwards (Schumaker 2001).

[2] Of course, some scholarship and much popular reporting sees the opposite in African cities – disease, dirt, and chaos, all leading to death and misery for far too many.

is no longer enough (Ferguson 2006); working across scales is necessary to gain status and make a name for oneself.

Simone has argued that these processes work through the creation and maintenance of 'reference points': ideas or associations that act as platforms that can be shared by a wide range of people with divergent beliefs, aims, and backgrounds, so that they can get along. Different people have different assumptions about the meaning or expectations associated with those shared points of reference, but they can provide enough common ground to collaborate, provided fellow travellers do not inquire too directly about the divergences. Shared platforms offer some safety amid seas of strangers; they provide some confidence that one will be able to work with one's fellows. Simone concludes: 'African cities are especially available to these opportunities precisely because they appear to be outside effective control, and thus anything can happen' (2001: 23). He acknowledges that the ways of the bush are making inroads into the city. 'What had been the purview of the so-called bush now runs rampant through the city, and there is little recourse to effective mediation or clear boundaries.' But he doesn't appear to regard the bush as a site for the kinds of creativity he identifies except insofar as he describes bush cities in the form of the garrison-entrepôt, the remote trading hubs described by Janet Roitman (1998, 2005).

This book, in contrast, is about bush that is bush. Not frontier, exactly, but with no large towns and certainly no real cities or major commercial hubs. It chronicles a history of interscalar relationships and collaboration, about how people working in such a space participate politically and economically in a larger world. If scholars of new urbanism implicitly set up the non-urban as a locus of stolidity and non-creativity, the experiences compiled here bring that assessment into question. For example, Bonhomme (2009) argues that witchcraft rumours are a specifically urban phenomenon, since in the village, gossip is common, but rumours rare. Yet the witchcraft rumours he studies are vibrantly present in remote rural areas as well (Lombard 2013b). Whether dynamics identified in urban areas are unique to, or a function of, urbanity is a matter for study, not presupposition; the question of what is city-like about cities requires comparison.

Similarly, those who had thought of slotting this book into a 'weird Africa' category might consider parallels between its focus and other places in the world. Too often, when I present this research, I sense audience members pulling back, focusing on the violence, perhaps, and thinking, 'Whoa, that is *different*.' Perhaps it is. But we can only know through comparison. Ethnography doesn't facilitate comparison unless one works with a team, and research funding for group projects has become rare. So please help. As a scholar of a remote space, I have been intrigued and inspired by analysts' characterisations of city life, which resonate with what I have observed in my research locales. Might they find parallels in the material I present here? These questions lay out the necessary next step: to be able to figure out what really is a function of cityness and what of remoteness, and what transcends category.

Forceful acquisition and status uncertainty, after all, can occur in many places, and are certainly not culturally specific. The people in this book do not come from some unitary culture. Some were born in the area, some were born far away, but they all have work interests here in this place of little infrastructure and few institutions, a context that offers certain 'affordances' (Keane 2016) that nudge people towards developing skills to acquire, use force, and deploy stealth. An analytic of acquisition amid status uncertainty – raiding and its ramifications towards either hunting or war – identifies similarities of operation and of the dynamics of encounter between people, and even with other creatures in the mix. It is a serious game. The personal orientations, deeds, and encounters among the actors in it offer a clearer picture than a look at any group in the area, as if it were a coherent culture unto itself. It is true that these acquisitive tendencies show up most clearly in a 'stateless-state' space such as north-eastern CAR, but it is equally true that they are not the sole preserve of these kinds of spaces, and that forcefully acquisitive projects often depend on the participation of people far from the zones of direct action.

Adventurists need two skills in particular: one is camouflage; the other is the capacity to display force. Camouflage entails learning about one's surroundings and positioning oneself strategically, to blend in, to avoid unwanted notice, and to retain an important measure of autonomy. Camouflage is not simply a trick that those invested in the normative order of the world (state, nation, law) use to cover up the people who do not fit in well. That is, it is not simply a way of covering the 'dirt' that is found around the edges of the 'clean' categories (to use Mary Douglas's [1966] terms), immobilising it as if it had been swept under a rug. It might function that way for some, including the faraway colonial or donor officials who find it easier not to know too much about the messy details of life in Central Africa. But it is also an improvised skill that allows an entrée for those who do not quite fit otherwise, which they use to show some facets but not all, controlling others' perceptions of identity and intention and managing their positions in relation to the spaces they hope to inhabit, the goods they plan to access, and their position in bureaucratic and social landscapes that transcend their physical location.

There is a kind of freedom that comes from blending in. One can do other things at the same time, since one has established oneself as not meriting extra scrutiny. Such a way of working will never permit climbing the hierarchies of power in the world, and it is unlikely to bring great and lasting riches, but it can bring an adventurous career, and a living that includes windfalls if not the steady predictability of a salary and a pension.

Camouflage is a skill deployed through communication; it is one element in a dialogic process of perception. That is, it involves the perceiving agent and that which – or who – is being perceived. And one frequent element of that dialogue, another skill that people develop, is a capacity for dangerousness. The personal orientation of raiding covers times when one seeks to blend in and other times when one seeks to communicate that one is dangerous. That communication of dangerousness might have any one of a range of objectives: to get others to leave one alone; to threaten others until they extend some benefit; to get them to do as one demands. Note that this is a matter of capacity, not necessarily its implementation. At times, a person might judge it worthwhile to make a display of dangerousness; at other times that capacity might remain in the shadows. Even when a display does happen, it may entail violence, as in the spectacles of punishment by colonial administrators, but it may not. An elephant may begin a charge and then, its point made, turn and disappear.

Both camouflage and displays of force require in-the-moment assessments, but 'assessment' may imply more analysis than is involved. Really, these are questions of perception or sensation, or the entrainment of confrontational tension:[3] perceiving or sensing similarity and difference. Those perception sensations may be fleeting, quickly overturned by another impression, or they may endure, but in both cases they cast shadows over future relations between the individuals involved and those to whom they tell their stories.

Storytelling is a means of creating social and material relations – think of the many readers of big-game hunter memoirs who saw their hoped-for futures on the page. Or, for that matter, think of those gathered to listen to General Zoundeiko recount tales from his and his fellows' work as rebels. In both cases the stories were the product of the storyteller's

[3] In the West, people tend to differentiate between perception and sensation, with the former imagined cognitively and the latter embodied. Elsewhere, people understand the two as intertwined (Geurts 2002), which may in fact be a more accurate description of how people experience the world.

careful positioning of himself in relation to his intended audiences, but the connection was no less real for that. Similarly, faraway readers of conservation project reports might have the sense that they know what is occurring and continue to approve funding. But many stories, jealousies, and projects never made it onto the typed page. This, of course, is always the case, whether one is talking about a project in a remote place or one in a much more highly trafficked zone. But the camouflage aspects are more pronounced when one is talking about the remoter areas, because the exigencies of forceful acquisition must be made not to stand out as unacceptable anomalies next to the pastoral and productive norms that are more dominant in other places.

Raiding and violence

Another reason to think about this area through its practices of raiding is that it lets us appreciate the ways in which violence can be a normal part of governing relations without having to think of that violence as a process of war, or war in the making, or recovery from war. The dynamics involved are very different from those of war, with its friends and enemies and protracted battles. The hunting-zone dynamic involves tracking and learning about one's intended quarry, even coming to feel some similarities with it, before charged moments of encounter when one demonstrates one's dangerousness, or is vanquished, or enters into fellowship or collaboration. These processes are creative, the relations established by them less stable than the usual categories of political belonging, such as 'citizen' or 'subject'. There is freedom in such a state of affairs, a kind of autonomy of self-regulation. But it is a freedom nevertheless compromised by the difficulty its protagonists have in accumulating the wealth and benefits they understand to be part of more pastoral ways of being governed.

Early anthropologies of conflict saw it as important to their cataloguing of interests to delineate discrete categories. War was distinct from feuding, which was distinct from raiding, which was itself something entirely different from hunting. War was open conflict between two groups, with no accepted means of bringing the fighting to an end. In feuding, in contrast, there existed some institutionalised means (mediation or similar) of bringing the fighting to an end. Raiding has been seen in two main ways: as the material-acquisition aspect of war and political expansion; or as cyclical or otherwise back-and-forth acquisition (such as cattle raiding). Hunting is frequently seen as something different, with its violence downplayed in a variety of ways: for example, via the kinds of rituals people engage in to account for their taking of a life.

The neat categorical lines are far more blurred in practice, however. Soldiers fighting a war might raid to pursue their ends. The French army in Algeria in the 1840s is a particularly infamous example. Officers adapted what they argued was a local fighting technique, *razzia*, in their pursuit of colonisation. A *razzia* was a 'swift and brutal' raid against 'others' (if not enemies), with the objective of acquiring their valuables and displaying force more than killing. 'The gist of a *razzia* was to attack with overwhelming force against unprepared herdsmen or settlements. Because resistance against such massive incursions was futile, the victims could flee without disgrace and without losing face – and eventually reciprocate' (Rid 2009: 618–19). French military re-makings of the *razzia* meant that the army was able to seize needed supplies and, especially, food. These *razzias* also became a new form of war 'among the people' (in contrast to the rise of military professionalism in the conduct of war in Europe, which stipulated differentiating between soldiers and non-soldiers) and included brutal incidents such as the burning alive of more than 600 Algerians in a cave (Rid 2009: 629).[4]

French re-imaginings of the *razzia* served their own colonial ends and departed in certain respects from the raiding practices of those who preceded them in these lands, but the basic traits were the same: violent acquisition amidst contested claims to life, status, and property. And, indeed, that tendency to acquire in the midst of upheaval or otherwise uncertain relations characterised many different aspects of the intense involvement of interior Africa in long-distance trades in the eighteenth and nineteenth centuries, particularly the newly intensified *razzias* for humans to be made slaves and, during the later period, elephants for their ivory. The increase and spread of raiding are often explained through the 'predatory state thesis': that is, the idea that polities in the process of construction or centralisation were composed of predatory raiders who ravaged people living in more decentralised ways. The reality was far more varied. While raiding and capturing people to be made slaves were indeed crucial for these developing raiding polities, other people – those usually referred to as the passive 'reservoirs' for the centralising polities – strategically participated in and avoided the rush to acquire as well (Cordell 2003; Ewald 1990). As the demand for acquired goods (especially humans) rose, so too did the pressure on people to 'circumvent established codes of conduct pertaining to the capture and enslavement of others' (Hubbell 2001: 38). Young men

[4] French military *razzias* are a clear historical antecedent to contemporary counterinsurgency practices (Rid 2009).

who felt sidelined by existing hierarchies and opportunities had an incentive to innovate in raiding in ways that put the kinds of solidarity or alliance that had helped villages stick together in the past under new stress. People who were previously seen as safe, as 'us' (such as a neighbour's children), became targetable for seizure and sale (Hubbell 2001: 38–9). Their status, in other words, became uncertain and contested. They could be acquired – or sold – rather than being related fellows.

As the above suggests, innovation is not always directed towards finding ways to struggle for justice amid oppression or to preserve values and practices. It can also transform those values and practices. One classic example of this is innovation in the form of commoditisation and marketisation. Older anthropological accounts of cattle raiding in East Africa, for instance, conjure up a precolonial situation in which all raids were sanctioned by elders, the goal of raiding was to reproduce families and clans, and the cattle circulated and were exchanged endlessly among people in a given region (e.g. Evans-Pritchard 1940). That began to change once cattle could be sold for cash. Now, young men would raid cattle on their own and sell the captured cows to butchers for sale in the region or for export to the Middle East. They also stopped respecting the previous moral distinction between raiding (taking cows from people considered 'other' – a feat considered valorous) and theft (taking cows from people considered 'us' – considered cowardly), and the spoils of their raids were not shared but spent by the raider thieves themselves (Fleisher 2000, 2002).

Lately, much of the attention to innovation in hunting has focused on how it is re-emerging as a military practice. In northern Europe, military officers have long recruited hunters, who brought to war their specialised skills in reconnaissance, ambush, and skirmishing, and they often then became integrated into the military body. The Norwegian military still has a special forces unit called hunters (Danielsen 2018). As the animal hunters and sometime soldiers were replaced with soldiers who used hunting skills, their hunting or raiding origins have become less apparent. This is changing now that weaponised drones are becoming so widely used by the world's powerful armies.

The rise of drones has occasioned new interest in grappling with manhunting as an element of political practice. One of the things that has seemed most troubling with these drones is the extent to which they remove reciprocal danger from the process of pursuit and killing. Much of Western military innovation has been dedicated to enabling killing at a greater distance, and hence at less risk to the would-be killers (Lindqvist 2001), but drones still seem to mark a rupture in the extent to which they achieve this goal. The result is that, as French philosopher Grégoire Chamayou put it: 'The whole world, it is said, is a battleground. But it would probably be more accurate to call it a hunting ground ... While warfare is defined, in the last analysis, by combat, hunting is essentially defined by pursuit' (Chamayou 2015: 52). But the tricky thing about weaponised drones is that they both rupture and recombine elements of war and hunting, so that it becomes difficult to position them in existing analytical categories or genealogies of forceful practice. They 'remix' elements of soldiering, hunting, and other kinds of armed work, creating new dynamics without historical antecedent and with repercussions that are not fully known (Gusterson 2017).

In the midst of the uncertainties and remixings created by drones, the history of the hunting zone and forceful, acquisitive practice there raises a few helpful elements and questions. One is caution about how powerful drones actually are. In theory, they make surveillance omniscient and totalising. In practice, their capabilities are as shaped by the terrain as are those of most other technologies. The US and Ugandan militaries searched for Joseph Kony and the remnants of his much vilified Lord's Resistance Army in eastern CAR for eight years (2009–17), to no avail. The area is densely covered with thickly canopied trees and other tall vegetation, and aerial surveillance is mostly possible over roads and towns. The bush remains a space of refuge, with or without drones. The UN mission in CAR also uses drones (non-weaponised) and has found them to be far less powerful than they had hoped, since the images they collect still require interpretation by people familiar with the terrains in a more personal way, and since they can capture images only of well-inhabited spaces or roads. Drones have not transformed the hunting zone into the area where prey are assembled for targeting that Chamayou seemed to imagine in his idea of a 'hunting ground'.

In addition to caution about overstating the power of drones, the hunting zone also suggests that we consider more fully the hunting and acquisitive aspects of drones, and not just their effects on the conduct of war. Most studies have focused on the latter, on drones as forces that are transforming warfare. But one could also ask different questions of drones. For example, how are they transforming the ways in which taking (of lives, in this case) creates new kinds of political relationships? What, if anything, is accumulated in the process? It may be that the acquisitions from hunting by drone are just as susceptible to being overturned as the other kinds of forceful acquisition this book has explored. Drones depart from the kinds of raiding described in this book in the extent to which they alter the conceit of (potential) parity in the encounter: that the parties be worthy matches for each other. But, on the other hand, drones seem to broaden the scope of political relations in the world other than those of citizenship. In much Western political philosophy, the sovereign is supposed to protect and nurture a population, whose members constitute a reserve of wealth. At the same time, the sovereign can ask those members to expose themselves and die on behalf of that polity. Drones disrupt those relationships. No longer is the fact that the sovereign is asking people to expose themselves a basis for their claims to substantive citizenship, because the people asked to kill are not exposed in the same way as they were before. Once they are no longer citizens in the entitled or rights-bearing sense of that term, the pastoral, care-taking norms of politics might also shift. In that case, drones are heralding not so much a remixing or rupture as the spread of the kinds of exploitative and interested but also fitfully collaborative political relationships that have long existed through the raiding games in north-eastern CAR.

Raiding and sovereignty

When I conceived the research that became this book, I was particularly eager to include this place – north-eastern CAR – and the dynamics here in discussions of the ways in which sovereignty works in the world, and to see how understandings of sovereignty would change if forced to take places like this into account. But sovereignty, as a concept, is a shape-changer (Anghie 2007; Bartelson 1995), and thus the discussions around it become hard to pin down. Some argue that sovereignty designates a kind of unitary, totalising power (Agamben 1998; Schmitt 2005 [1922]); others that it has always been divisible, with different capacities held by different actors (Keene 2002; Maine 1915 [1888]; Sassen 2006). To a certain extent, the differences stem from whether one is studying sovereignty as a theory and/or an ideal espoused by political activists, or looking at sovereignty as it exists in the world. My research methods place me in the second camp, and when you place yourself among people, the inherent relationality of life – and, yes, sovereignty too – is impossible to ignore (Grant 2011; Rutherford 2012). I have proposed different ways of thinking about sovereignty as it is lived in north-eastern CAR (Lombard 2012, 2018). Approaching things in this way is a means to recognise the complications and contradictions in people's lives.

But this region's history, and the importance there of forceful acquisition and disputable status dynamics, also inspires reflections on sovereignty in the 'grand theory' sense. First, a definition. Sovereignty, I think, can be boiled down to the relationship between claiming or enacting a capacity for exceptional violence and being able to determine how a set of people will live (see Lombard 2018).[5] At certain times and in certain places, sovereign claims by one corporate group or another are only infrequently challenged. In other places and at other times, people heartily contest others' claims to sovereignty. In the former scenario, control over people and territory is fairly stable. In the latter, control over people and territory is much more uncertain. North-eastern CAR and its acquisitive politics are decidedly in the second category.

Thus, perhaps one could say that raiding and sovereignty have a fundamental relationship. For sovereignty to be consolidated, to be unchallenged, raiding must not be very prevalent. And when, in contrast, raiding predominates, sovereignty cannot be consolidated and will be challenged, for example in the manner of the denunciations described in this book. Raiding declines as sovereignty is less contested; as sovereignty is more contested, raiding increases.[6] This observation resonates with classic theories of state building, of course, but there are two main insights into it that my approach to CAR can add.

The first is that, while there is a teleological bent to much of the literature on state building and sovereignty (the idea being that politics moves in the direction of consolidation), the persistence of raiding – not as *necessary* to states in the manner ascribed to frontiers, but as a persistent accompaniment, and as a marginal but adventurous way of life – shows that trajectories in and out of raiding and sovereignty can change.[7] This point is particularly striking at this moment when both states and regional organisations seem to be consolidating and fracturing simultaneously. For instance, the EU is under major stress, but the African Union is taking on an ever greater role in security and peace-enforcement operations. The second is that my analytic provides a way of thinking about raiding that is at once fine-grained, looking at personal orientations and encounters, and broad, thinking about raiding that includes but is not limited to its capture of non-human animal forms. It unites insights from hunting (narrowly conceived) and contested politics, bringing clarity to both.

In the years after I conducted the bulk of the research for this book, Central Africans have been through a particularly rough period. Violence went from predominantly threat and show of force to a more war-like condition (Lombard 2016d). While most Central Africans wish and hope that the war is over, there are still currently about 14 armed groups in the

[5] This definition is inspired by Cattelino (2008) and Graeber (2011), among others.
[6] My thanks to Fred Appel for inspiring these comments.
[7] Here I am echoing Nolutshungu's (1996) classic observation about the state, based on research in Chad.

country. A massive UN presence helps keep the fighting sporadic, shifting from one place to another, rather than steadily engulfing more territory with enduring war, but it is unclear how the situation will develop in the months and years to come. Many Central Africans both participate in and decry the raiding dynamics described in this book, such as the pursuit of autonomy rather than conceding to being controlled and ruled. To be fair, attempts to control though the decades have relied on brutality and shows of force that arguably *should* be contested and contravened. It is thus neither with celebration nor with criticism that I close this book, but with an appreciation of those who opened their lives and archives to me, and with the hope that Central Africans will find ways to resolve what they see as the deleterious elements among the contradictions of their lives and their place in the world today.

In particular, one element that is lacking is distribution. Although it is a central element in studies of 'traditional' hunting – that is, of animals for the sustenance they can provide (Grinker 1994; Hellweg 2011; Marks 1991, 2016; Willerslev 2007) – this book says little about the division of what is gained through forceful acquisition such as raiding. One reason for this was the shared sense among everyone living and working in the zone that distribution of all kinds was not working as it should. People speaking about what they appreciated about al-Sanusi and the sultans who superceded him always began by naming the same virtue: they distributed food. When they were present, no one could go hungry, people said. During my research, the sultan was absent. A few humanitarian NGOs provided minimal goods and agricultural training, but people experienced these rather like Damane did: they felt that they were being belittled. (However, this sentiment did not preclude their participation.) Seizure has a long history as a mode of wealth creation in the region, but it has always been vehemently contested. When it has not, it is because the terms of distribution afterwards appealed to those who might otherwise challenge it. Those questions of distribution and how they relate to or mark status are currently quite unsettled, and they have been for some time. Understanding the mechanisms and terms of distribution – who can do it, to whom, and what can be distributed – might begin to remove the thorns from the brambles of raiding acquisition and status uncertainty. Doing so is a task for research and also for those in the hunting zone who wish to improve the terms of cooperation in their stateless-state space.

References

AFP. 2003. *A Idongo, les anciens ont même droit à une petite pension*. Bangui: Agence France-Presse (AFP).

Agamben, Giorgio. 1998. *Homo Sacer: sovereign power and bare life*. Palo Alto CA: Stanford University Press.

2005. *State of Exception*. Chicago IL: University of Chicago Press.

Al Tunisi, Muhamed Ibn. 1845. *Voyage au Darfour*. Paris: Chez Benjamin Duport.

Alexander, Jocelyn and JoAnn McGregor. 2000. 'Wildlife and politics: CAMPFIRE in Zimbabwe', *Development and Change* 31 (3): 605–27.

Anand, Nikhil. 2017. *Hydraulic City: water and the infrastructures of citizenship in Mumbai*. Durham NC: Duke University Press.

Anderson, Benedict. 2006. *Imagined Communities: reflections on the origin and spread of nationalism*. New York NY: Verso Books.

Anghie, Antony. 2007. *Imperialism, Sovereignty and the Making of International Law*. Cambridge: Cambridge University Press.

Appadurai, Arjun. 1990. 'Disjuncture and difference in the global cultural economy', *Theory, Culture and Society* 7 (2): 295–310.

2006. *Fear of Small Numbers: an essay on the geography of anger*. Durham NC: Duke University Press.

Appel, Hannah C. 2012. 'Walls and white elephants: oil extraction, responsibility, and infrastructural violence in Equatorial Guinea', *Ethnography* 13 (4): 439–65.

Aravamudan, Srinivas. 2009. 'Hobbes and America' in Daniel Carey and Lynn Festa (eds), *The Postcolonial Enlightenment*. New York NY: Oxford University Press.

Arendt, Hannah. 1973. *The Origins of Totalitarianism*. New York NY: Houghton Mifflin Harcourt.

Autesserre, Séverine. 2014. *Peaceland: conflict resolution and the everyday politics of international intervention*. Cambridge: Cambridge University Press.

Baaz, Maria Eriksson, Didier Gondola, Esther Marijnen, Judith Verweijen, Paul Katembo Vikanza, Koen Vlassenroot, Tatiana Carayannis, Kevin Dunn, James Fairhead, Stephan Hochleithner, Chrispin Mvano, Eric Mwamba, and Blaise Muhire. 2015. 'Virunga's white savior complex: how the film distorts the politics and people of Congo', *Foreign Affairs*, 5 March, <https://www.foreignaffairs.com/articles/africa/2015-03-05/virungas-white-savior-

complex?cid=rss-africavirungas_white_savior_complex-000000> (accessed 24 April 2015).

Balandier, Georges. 1966. *Ambiguous Africa: cultures in collision*. New York NY: Pantheon.

Baratier, Albert. 1914. *Vers le Nil: souvenirs de la Mission Marchand, de Brazzaville à Fort Desaix*. Paris: Fayard.

1917. *Au Congo: souvenirs de la Mission Marchand, de Loango à Brazzaville*. Paris: Fayard.

Bartelson, Jens. 1995. *A Genealogy of Sovereignty*. Cambridge: Cambridge University Press.

Bayart, Jean-François. 2000. 'Africa in the world: a history of extraversion', *African Affairs* 99 (395): 217–67.

Bayart, Jean-François, Stephen Ellis, and Béatrice Hibou. 1999. *The Criminalization of the State in Africa*. London: International African Institute and James Currey.

Behnke, Roy and Michael Mortimore (eds). 2016. *The End of Desertification?: Disputing environmental change in the drylands*. New York NY: Springer.

Beidelman, Thomas O. 1961. 'Beer drinking and cattle theft in Ukaguru: intertribal relations in a Tanganyika chiefdom', *American Anthropologist* 63 (3): 534–49.

Bell, Walter Dalrymple Maitland. 1949. *Karamojo Safari*. New York NY: Harcourt, Brace.

1960 [1923]. *Wanderings of an Elephant Hunter*. Newton MA: C. T. Branford.

Benjaminsen, Tor A. 2017. 'Let the desertification zombie rest in peace', Climate and Conflict blog, 4 December, <https://blogs.prio.org/ClimateAndConflict/2017/12/let-the-desertification-zombie-rest-in-peace/> (accessed 9 September 2019).

Bennafla, Karine. 2002. *Le Commerce Frontalier en Afrique Centrale: acteurs, espaces, pratiques*. Paris: Karthala.

Benton, Lauren. 2009. *A Search for Sovereignty: law and geography in European empires, 1400–1900*. New York NY: Cambridge University Press.

Berlant, Lauren Gail. 2011. *Cruel Optimism*. Durham NC: Duke University Press.

Berlin, Isaiah. 1969. *Four Essays on Liberty*. Oxford: Oxford University Press.

Berliner, David, Michael Lambek, Richard Shweder, Richard Irvine, and Albert Piette. 2016. 'Anthropology and the study of contradictions', *Hau: Journal of Ethnographic Theory* 6 (1): 1–27.

Berman, Eric G. with Louisa N. Lombard. 2008. *The Central African Republic and Small Arms: a regional tinderbox*. Geneva: Small Arms Survey.

Bernault, Florence. 2006. 'Body, power and sacrifice in Equatorial Africa', *Journal of African History* 47 (2): 207–39.

Bigo, Didier. 1988. *Pouvoir et Obéissance en Centrafrique*. Paris: Karthala.

Binot, Aurélie, Vincent Castel, and Alexandre Caron. 2006. 'L'interface faune-bétail en Afrique Subsaharienne', *Science et Changements Planétaires/Sécheresse* 17 (1): 349–61.

Bird, Rebecca Bliege, Brian Codding, and Douglas Bird. 2009. 'What explains differences in men's and women's production?', *Human Nature* 20 (2): 105–29.

Bjork-James, Carwil. 2015. 'Hunting Indians: globally circulating ideas and frontier practices in the Colombian Llanos', *Comparative Studies in Society and History* 57 (1): 98–129.

Boglioli, Marc. 2009. *A Matter of Life and Death: hunting in contemporary Vermont*. Amherst MA: University of Massachusetts Press.

Bohannan, Laura and Paul Bohannan. 1953. *The Tiv of Central Nigeria*. London: International African Institute.

Bohannan, Paul and Philip Curtin. 1971. *Africa and Africans*. Garden City NY: American Museum of Natural History.

Bonhomme, Julien. 2009. *Les Voleurs de Sexe: anthropologie d'une rumeur africaine*. Paris: Le Seuil.

2012. 'The dangers of anonymity: witchcraft, rumor, and modernity in Africa', *HAU: Journal of Ethnographic Theory* 2 (2): 205–33.

Bouché, Philippe, Roland Nzapa Mbeti Mange, Floride Tankalet, et al. 2012. 'Game over! Wildlife collapse in northern Central African Republic', *Environmental Monitoring and Assessment* 184 (11): 7001–11.

Boulvert, Yves. 1996. 'Le dernier grand blanc de la carte d'Afrique: premières approches de l'Oubangui-Chari ou Centrafrique à la fin du 19e siècle' in D. Locoq (ed.), *Terre à Découvrir, Terres à Parcourir*. Paris: University of Paris 7-Denis Diderot.

Brégeon, Jean-Joël. 1998. *Un Rêve d'Afrique: administrateurs en Oubangui-Chari: la Cendrillon de l'Empire*. Paris: Denoël.

Brockington, Dan. 2002. *Fortress Conservation: the preservation of the Mkomazi Game Reserve, Tanzania*. Bloomington IN: Indiana University Press.

Burnham, Philip and Thomas Christensen. 1983. 'Karnu's message and the "War of the Hoe Handle": interpreting a Central African resistance movement', *Africa* 53 (4): 3–22.

Büscher, Bram. 2013. *Transforming the Frontier: peace parks and the politics of neoliberal conservation in Southern Africa*. Durham NC: Duke University Press.

Cakaj, Ledio. 2015. 'In unclaimed land: the Lord's Resistance Army in CAR' in Tatiana Carayannis and Louisa Lombard (eds), *Making Sense of the Central African Republic*. London: Zed.

Castellani, Charles. 1898. *Vers le Nil Français, avec la Mission Marchand*. Paris: Flammarion.

Cattelino, Jessica. 2008. *High Stakes: Florida Seminole gaming and sovereignty*. Durham NC: Duke University Press.

Ceriana Mayneri, Andrea. 2014. *Sorcellerie et Prophétisme en Centrafrique: l'imaginaire de la dépossession en pays Banda*. Paris: Karthala.

Chamayou, Grégoire. 2012. *Manhunts: a philosophical history*. Princeton NJ: Princeton University Press.

2015. *A Theory of the Drone*. New York NY: New Press.

Christy, Bryan. 2012. 'Ivory worship', *National Geographic* 222: 28–61.

Clastres, Pierre. 1977. *Society against the State*. Oxford: Blackwell.

Clynes, Tom. 2009. 'They shoot poachers, don't they?', International Reporting Project, 5 June <https://internationalreportingproject.org/stories/view/they-shoot-poachers-dont-they> (accessed 9 September 2019).

Collins, Randall. 2004. *Interaction Ritual Chains*. Princeton NJ: Princeton University Press.

2009. *Violence: a micro-sociological theory*. Princeton NJ: Princeton University Press.

2013. 'Entering and leaving the tunnel of violence: micro-sociological dynamics of emotional entrainment in violent interactions', *Current Sociology* 61 (2): 132–51.

Collins, R. O. 1960. 'Ivory poaching in the Lado Enclave', *Uganda Journal* 24: 217–28.

Collyer, Rosie. 2018. 'Boko Haram huntress', *Al Jazeera*, 17 April.

Comaroff, Jean and John L. Comaroff (eds). 2006. *Law and Disorder in the Postcolony*. Chicago IL: University of Chicago Press.

Conrad, Joseph. 2002 [1897]. *Heart of Darkness and Other Tales*. Oxford: Oxford University Press.

Cooper, Frederick. 2000. 'Conditions analogous to slavery: imperialism and free labor ideology in Africa' in Frederick Cooper, Thomas C. Holt, and Rebecca J. Scott (eds), *Beyond Slavery: explorations of race, labor, and citizenship in postemancipation societies*. Chapel Hill NC: University of North Carolina Press.

Coquery-Vidrovitch, Cathérine. 1972. *Le Congo au Temps des Grandes Compagnies Concessionnaires 1898–1930*. Paris: Mouton.

2014. *Le Rapport Brazza*. Paris: Le Passager Clandestin.

Cordell, Dennis D. 1979. 'Blood partnership in theory and practice: the expansion of Muslim power in Dar Al-Kuti', *Journal of African History* 20 (3): 379–94.

1983. 'The savanna belt of North-Central Africa' in David Birmingham and Phyllis Martin (eds), *History of Central Africa*. London: Longman.

1985. *Dar Al-Kuti and the Last Years of the Trans-Saharan Slave Trade*. Madison WI: University of Wisconsin Press.

1994. 'Extracting people from precapitalist production: French Equatorial Africa from the 1890s to the 1930s' in Dennis D. Cordell and Joel W. Gregory (eds), *African Population and Capitalism: historical perspectives*. Madison WI: University of Wisconsin.

2002. 'Des 'réfugiés' dans l'Afrique précoloniale?', *Politique Africaine* 1: 16–28.

2003. 'The myth of inevitability and invincibility: resistance to slavers and the slave trade in Central Africa, 1850–1910' in Sylvaine Diouf (ed.), *Fighting the Slave Trade: West African strategies*. New York NY: Boydell and Brewer.

Dalla Bernardina, Sergio. 1991. 'Une personne pas tout à fait comme les autres: l'animal et son statut', *L'Homme* 120: 33–50.

1996. *L'Utopie de la Nature: chasseurs, écologistes et touristes*. Paris: Imago.

Danielsen, Tone. 2018. *Making Warriors in a Global Era: an ethnographic study of the Norwegian naval special operations commando*. New York NY: Lexington Books.

Das, Veena. 2007. *Life and Words: violence and the descent into the ordinary*. Berkeley CA: University of California Press.

Das, Veena and Deborah Poole (eds). 2004. *Anthropology in the Margins of the State*. Sante Fe NM: School of American Research Press.

Daspit, Lesley Lynn. 2011. 'Market women in a Central African forest reserve: engendering wildlife commerce and conservation'. PhD thesis, Purdue University.

De Dampierre, Éric. 1983. *Des Ennemis, des Arabes, des Histoires: étude*. Paris: Société d'Éthnologie.

de Heusch, Luc. 2000. *Le Roi de Kongo et les Monstres Sacrés*. Paris: Gallimard.

De Luna, Kathryn. 2015. *Collecting Food, Cultivating People: subsistence and society in Central Africa*. New Haven CT: Yale University Press.

d'Espiney, T., J. Tello, and W. Delvingt. 1993. *Le 'Programme de développement de la Région Nord' en République centrafricaine: l'expérience de la zone pilote de Sangba*. Cahier Forestier 9. Gembloux: Université de Liège, Gembloux Agro-Bio Tech, Gestion des Ressources Forestières.

de Waal, Alexander. 2009. 'Fixing the political marketplace: how can we make peace without functioning state institutions?' Fifteenth Christen Michelsen Lecture, Chr. Michelsen Institute, Bergen, 15 October.

Debos, Marielle. 2008. 'Fluid loyalties in a regional crisis: Chadian "ex-liberators" in the Central African Republic', *African Affairs* 107 (427): 225–41.

2013. *Le Métier des Armes au Tchad: le gouvernement de l'entre-guerres*. Paris: Karthala.

2016. *Living by the Gun in Chad: combatants, impunity, and state formation*. London: Zed.

Degani, Michael. 2017. 'Modal reasoning in Dar es Salaam's power network', *American Ethnologist* 44 (2): 300–14.

Deleuze, Gilles, Felix Guattari, and Brian Massumi. 1986. *Nomadology: the war machine*. New York NY: Semiotext(e).

Devine, Jennifer. 2014. 'Counterinsurgency Ecotourism in Guatemala's Maya Biosphere Reserve', *Environment and Planning D: Society and Space* 32 (6): 984–1001.

d'Huart, Jean-Pierre. 2009. *Rapport d'Expertise: bilan du système zones cynégetiques villageoises en interphase et promotion de l'autonomie de gestion des ZCV*. Bangui: PDZCV.

Dorter, Kenneth. 2013. 'The method of division in the *Sophist*: Plato's Second Deuteros Plous' in Beatriz Bossi and Thomas M. Robinson (eds), *Plato's Sophist Revisited*. Berlin: Walter de Gruyter.

Douglas, Mary. 1966. *Purity and Danger: an analysis of concepts of pollution and taboo*. London and New York NY: Routledge.

1980. *Evans-Pritchard: his life, work, writings and ideas*. New York NY: Viking.

Duffield, Mark. 2007. *Development, Security and Unending War: governing the world of peoples*. London: Polity.

Duffy, Rosaleen. 2010. *Nature Crime: how we're getting conservation wrong*. New Haven CT: Yale University Press.

2014. 'Waging a war to save biodiversity: the rise of militarized conservation', *International Affairs* 90 (4): 819–34.

Dupré, Georges. 1982. *Un Ordre et sa Destruction: anthropologie économique des Nzabi de la république populaire du Congo*. Paris: ORSTOM.

Dybowski, Jean. 1893. *La Route du Tchad: du Loango au Chari*. Paris: Firmin-Didot.

European Commission. n.d.a. *Commentaires et Suggestions pour la PF Quatrième Phase ECOFAC*. Bangui: European Commission.

n.d.b. *Note de Reflexions sur les Modalités de Mise en Oeuvre du Programme ECOFAC Phase IV*. Bangui: European Commission.

Evans-Pritchard, Edward E. 1940. *The Nuer: a description of the modes of livelihood and political institutions of Nilotic people*. Oxford: Oxford University Press.

Ewald, Janet. 1990. *Soldiers, Traders, and Slaves: state formation and economic transformation in the Greater Nile Valley, 1700–1885*. Madison WI: University of Wisconsin Press.

Faes, Géraldine and Stephen Smith. 2000. *Bokassa 1er: un empereur français*. Paris: Calmann-Lévy.

Fay, Michael J. 2007. 'Ivory wars: last stand in Zakouma', *National Geographic*, March.

Feldman, Ilana. 2008. *Governing Gaza: bureaucracy, authority, and the work of rule, 1917–1967*. Durham NC: Duke University Press.

Ferguson, James. 2006. *Global Shadows: Africa in the neoliberal world order*. Durham NC: Duke University Press.

2015. *Give a Man a Fish: reflections on the new politics of distribution*. Durham NC: Duke University Press.

Ferme, Mariane C. 2001a. *The Underneath of Things: violence, history, and the everyday in Sierra Leone*. Berkeley CA: University of California Press.

2001b. 'La figure du chasseur et les chasseurs-miliciens dans le conflit Sierra-Léonais', *Politique Africaine* 2: 119–32.

Fitzpatrick, Sheila and Robert Gellately. 1997. 'Introduction to the practices of denunciation in modern European history' in Sheila Fitzpatrick and Robert Gellately (eds), *Accusatory Practices: denunciation in modern European history, 1789–1989*. Chicago IL: University of Chicago Press.

Fleisher, Michael L. 2000. *Kuria Cattle Raiders: violence and vigilantism on the Tanzania/Kenya border*. Ann Arbor MI: University of Michigan Press.

2002. '"War is good for thieving!": The symbiosis of crime and warfare among the Kuria of Tanzania', *Africa* 72 (1): 131–49.

Fortes, Meyer. 1940. 'The political system of the Tallensi of the Northern Territories of the Coast' in E. E. Evans-Pritchard and Meyer Fortes (eds), *African Political Systems*. Oxford: Oxford University Press.

Foucault, Michel. 1977. *Discipline and Punish: the birth of the prison*. New York NY: Vintage.

Foureau, F. 1902. *D'Alger au Congo par le Tchad*. Paris: Masson et Cie.

Gaoukane, E. Kouroussou. 1986. 'La Justice Indigene en Ooubangui-Chari (1910–1945)'. PhD thesis, University of Provence.

Gary, Romain. 1956. *Les Racines du Ciel*. Paris: Gallimard.

Geertz, Clifford. 1973. *The Interpretation of Cultures: selected essays*. New York NY: Basic Books.

Gentil, Émile. 1902. *La Chute de l'Empire de Rabah*. Paris: Hachette.

Geschiere, Peter and Birgit Meyer. 1998. 'Globalization and identity, dialectics of flow and closure', *Development and Change* 29 (4): 601–15.

Geurts, Kathryn Linn. 2002. 'On rocks, walks, and talks in West Africa: cultural categories and an anthropology of the senses', *Ethos* 30 (3): 178–98.

Ghosh, Amitav. 1994. 'The global reservation: notes toward an ethnography of international peacekeeping', *Cultural Anthropology* 9 (3): 412–22.

Gide, André. 1927. *Voyage au Congo*. Paris: Gallimard.

Giles-Vernick, Tamara. 1996. 'Na lege ti guiriri (on the road of history): mapping out the past and present in M'Bres region, Central African Republic', *Ethnohistory* 43 (2): 245–75.

2002. *Cutting the Vines of the Past: environmental histories of the Central African rain forest*. Charlottesville VA: University of Virginia Press.

Girard, René. 1977. *Violence and the Sacred*. Baltimore MD: Johns Hopkins University Press.

Gluckman, Max. 1956. *Custom and Conflict in Africa*. Oxford: Blackwell.

1958. *Analysis of a Social Situation in Modern Zululand*. Manchester: Manchester University Press.

Goffman, Erving. 1959. 'The moral career of the mental patient', *Psychiatry: Journal for the Study of Interpersonal Processes* 22: 123–42.

1990 [1959]. *The Presentation of Self in Everyday Life*. New York NY: Anchor.

Goldberg, Jeffrey. 2010. 'The hunted: did American conservationists go too far?', *The New Yorker*, 5 April.

Gordon, Robert J. 1986. 'Bushman banditry in twentieth-century Namibia' in Donald Crummey (ed.), *Banditry, Rebellion, and Social Protest in Africa*. London: James Currey.

Goyémidé, Étienne. 1985. *Le Dernier Survivant de la Caravane*. Paris: Hatier.

Graeber, David. 2007. *Possibilities: essays on hierarchy, rebellion and desire*. New York NY: AK Press.

2011. 'The divine kingship of the Shilluk: on violence, utopia, and the human condition, or, elements for an archaeology of sovereignty', *HAU: Journal of Ethnographic Theory* 1 (1): 1–62.

Granier, Laurent. 2010. *Rapport d'Expertise: relecture et finalisation du projet de loi sur la faune en RCA*. Bangui: PDZCV.

Grant, Bruce. 2011. 'Shrines and sovereigns: life, death, and religion in rural Azerbaijan', *Comparative Studies in Society and History* 53 (3): 654–81.

Grasselli, Giorgio. 2007. *African Sunsets: the story of an adventurous life*. Huntington Beach CA: Safari Press.

Grinker, Roy Richard. 1994. *Houses in the Rainforest: ethnicity and inequality among farmers and foragers in central Africa*. Berkeley CA: University of California Press.

Grotius, Hugo. 2004. *The Free Sea*. Translated by Richard Hakluyt. Indianapolis IN: Liberty Fund.

Gusterson, Hugh. 2017. *Drone: remote control warfare*. Cambridge MA: MIT Press.

Guyer, Jane I. 1993. 'Wealth in people and self-realization in Equatorial Africa', *Man* 28 (2): 243–65.

1995. 'Introduction: the currency interface and its dynamics' in Jane I. Guyer (ed.), *Money Matters: instability, values, and social payments in the modern history of West African communities*. Portsmouth NH: Heinemann.

Haraway, Donna. 1984. 'Teddy bear patriarchy: taxidermy in the garden of Eden, New York City, 1908–1936', *Social Text* 11: 20–64.
2008. *When Species Meet.* Minneapolis MN: University of Minnesota.
Hardin, Rebecca Doyle. 2000. 'Translating the forest: tourism, trophy hunting, and the transformation of forest use in southwestern Central African Republic (CAR)'. PhD thesis, Yale University.
2002. 'Concessionary politics in the western Congo Basin: history and culture in forest use, environmental governance in Africa'. Working paper 6. Washington DC: World Resources Institute.
2008. 'Toward an ethic of intimacy: touring and trophy hunting for elephants in Africa' in Christen M. Wemmer and Catherine A. Christen (eds), *Elephants and Ethics: toward a morality of coexistence.* Baltimore MD: Johns Hopkins University Press.
2011. 'Concessionary politics: property, patronage, and political rivalry in Central African forest management', *Current Anthropology* 52 (S3): 113–25.
Hardin, Rebecca and Henri Zana. 2014. '"Professional death" and rebirth? History, violence, and education. Fieldsights – hot spots', *Cultural Anthropology Online*, 11 June <https://culanth.org/fieldsights/546-professional-death-and-rebirth-history-violence-and-education> (accessed 10 December 2018).
Hardin, Rebecca, Melissa Remis, and Carolyn A. Jost Robinson. 2014. 'From abundance to acute marginality: farms, arms, and forests in the Central African Republic, 1988–2014. Fieldsights – hot spots', *Cultural Anthropology Online*, 11 June <http://www.culanth.org/fieldsights/542-from-abundance-to-acute-marginality-farms-arms-and-forests-in-the-central-african-republic-1988-2014> (accessed 10 December 2018).
Harms, Robert W. 1981. *River of Wealth, River of Sorrow: the central Zaire Basin in the era of the slave and ivory trade, 1500–1891.* New Haven CT: Yale University Press.
Harrison, Simon. 2012. *Dark Trophies: hunting and the enemy body in modern war.* New York NY: Berghahn Books.
Hart, H. L. A. 1961. *The Concept of Law.* Oxford: Clarendon.
Hayden, Cori. 2003a. *When Nature Goes Public: the making and unmaking of bioprospecting in Mexico.* Princeton NJ: Princeton University Press.
2003b. 'From market to market: bioprospecting's idioms of inclusion', *American Ethnologist* 30 (3): 359–71.
Hecht, David and Abdou Maliqalim Simone. 1994. *Invisible Governance: the art of African micro-politics.* New York NY: Autonomedia.
Hellweg, Joseph. 2011. *Hunting the Ethical State: the Benkadi movement of Côte d'Ivoire.* Chicago IL: University of Chicago Press.
Hibou, Béatrice. 2004. *Privatizing the State.* New York NY: Columbia University Press.
Hobsbawm, Eric. 1969. *Bandits.* London: Weidenfeld and Nicolson.
Hoekstra, Kinch. 1997. 'Hobbes and the Foole', *Political Theory* 25 (5): 620–54.
Hoffman, Danny. 2011. *The War Machines: young men and violence in Sierra Leone and Liberia.* Durham NC: Duke University Press.

Hubbell, Andrew. 2001. 'A view of the slave trade from the margin: Souroudougou in the late nineteenth-century slave trade of the Niger bend', *Journal of African History* 42 (1): 25–47.
Huntington, Samuel P. 1957. *The Soldier and the State: the theory and politics of civil–military relations*. Cambridge MA: Harvard University Press.
ICG. 2008. 'Central African Republic: untangling the political dialogue'. Africa Briefing 55. Nairobi and Brussels: International Crisis Group (ICG).
2010. 'Dangerous little stones: diamonds in the Central African Republic'. Africa Report 167. Nairobi and Brussels: International Crisis Group (ICG).
Jepson, Paul and Robert J. Whittaker. 2002. 'Histories of protected areas: internationalisation of conservationist values and their adoption in the Netherlands Indies (Indonesia)', *Environment and History* 8 (2): 129–72.
Jusionyte, Ieva. 2015. 'States of camouflage', *Cultural Anthropology* 30 (1): 113–38.
Kalck, Pierre. 1959. *Réalités Oubanguiennes*. Paris: Berger-Levrault.
1971. *Central African Republic: a failure in de-colonisation*. New York NY: Praeger.
1974. *Histoire de la République Centrafricaine des origines préhistoriques à nos jours*. Paris: Berger-Levrault.
1993. *Un explorateur du centre de l'Afrique: Paul Crampel, 1864–1891*. Paris: L'Harmattan.
Kapferer, Bruce and Marina Gold. 2018. 'Introduction: reconceptualising the discipline' in Bruce Kapferer and Marina Gold (eds), *Moral Anthropology: a critique*. New York NY: Berghahn Books.
Keane, Webb. 2013. 'Ontologies, anthropologists, and ethical life', *HAU: Journal of Ethnographic Theory* 3 (1): 186–91.
2014. 'Affordances and reflexivity in ethical life: an ethical stance', *Anthropological Theory* 14 (1): 3–26.
2016. *Ethical Life: its natural and social histories*. Princeton NJ: Princeton University Press.
Keene, Edward. 2002. *Beyond the Anarchical Society: Grotius, colonialism and order in world politics*. New York NY: Cambridge University Press.
Kelly, Alice B. 2011. 'Conservation practice as primitive accumulation', *Journal of Peasant Studies* 38 (4): 683–701.
2015. 'The crumbling fortress: territory, access, and subjectivity production in Waza National Park, Northern Cameroon', *Antipode* 47 (3): 730–47.
Kelly, Raymond. 2000. *Warless Societies and the Origin of War*. Ann Arbor MI: University of Michigan Press.
Kohn, Eduardo. 2013. *How Forests Think: toward an anthropology beyond the human*. Berkeley CA: University of California Press.
Koolhaas, Rem. 2007. *Lagos: how it works*. Zurich: Lars Müller.
Kopytoff, Igor. 1987. 'The internal African frontier: the making of an African political culture' in Igor Kopytoff (ed.), *The African Frontier: the reproduction of traditional African societies*. Bloomington IN: Indiana University Press.
Kopytoff, Igor and Suzanne Miers (eds). 1977. *Slavery in Africa: historical and anthropological perspectives*. Madison WI: University of Wisconsin Press.
Laboureur, Matthieu. 1988. *Sans Défense*. Paris: Michel Lafon.

Laidlaw, James. 2013. *The Subject of Virtue: an anthropology of ethics and freedom*. New York NY: Cambridge University Press.
Le Noël, Christian. 1999. *On Target: history and hunting in Central Africa*. Huntington Beach CA: Trophy Room Books.
Leach, Melissa. 2000. 'New shapes to shift: war, parks and the hunting person in modern West Africa', *Journal of the Royal Anthropological Institute* 6 (4): 577–95.
2004. 'Introduction to special issue. Security, socioecology, polity: Mande hunters, civil society, and nation-states in contemporary West Africa', *Africa Today* 50 (4): vii–xvi.
Leakey, Richard with Virginia Morell. 2001. *Wildlife Wars: my fight to save Africa's natural treasures*. New York NY: Macmillan.
Lee, Richard Borshay. 1979. *The !Kung San: men, women, and work in a foraging society*. New York NY: Cambridge University Press.
Lee, Richard Borshay and Irven DeVore (eds). 1968. *Man the Hunter*. Chicago IL: Aldine Publishing Company.
Leopold, Mark. 2009. 'Crossing the line: 100 years of the North-West Uganda/South Sudan border', *Journal of Eastern African Studies* 3 (3): 464–78.
Levi, Margaret. 1988. *Of Rule and Revenue*. Berkeley CA: University of California Press.
Lindqvist, Sven. 2001. *A History of Bombing*. New York NY: The New Press.
2014 [1996]. The Dead Do Not Die: *Exterminate All the Brutes* and *Terra Nullius*. New York NY: The New Press.
Ling, Johan, Timothy Earle, and Kristian Kristiansen. 2018. 'Maritime mode of production: raiding and trading in seafaring chiefdoms', *Current Anthropology* 59 (5): 488–524.
Livingston, Julie. 2019. *Self-devouring Growth: a planetary parable as told from Southern Africa*. Durham NC: Duke University Press.
Llewellyn, Karl Nickerson and Edward Adamson Hoebel. 1941. *The Cheyenne Way: conflict and case law in primitive jurisprudence*. Norman OK: University of Oklahoma.
Lloveras, Josep M. 2002. *Réflexions sur le Programme ECOFAC en RCA (Composante ZCV) Suite à une Mission*. Bangui: European Commission.
Lombard, Louisa Nicolaysen. 2012. 'Raiding sovereignty in Central African borderlands'. PhD thesis, Duke University.
2013a. 'Navigational tools for Central African roadblocks', *PoLAR: Political and Legal Anthropology Review* 36 (1): 157–73.
2013b. 'Missing pieces', *Pacific Standard*, 6 March <https://psmag.com/social-justice/genital-theft-africa-central-african-republic-53341> (accessed 9 September 2019).
2015. 'The autonomous zone conundrum' in Tatiana Carayannis and Louisa Lombard (eds), *Making Sense of the Central African Republic*. London: Zed.
2016a. 'Threat economies and armed conservation in northeastern Central African Republic', *Geoforum* 69: 218–26.
2016b. 'Camouflage: the hunting origins of worlding in Africa', *Journal of Contemporary African Studies* 34 (1): 147–64.

2016c. 'The threat of rebellion: claiming entitled personhood in Central Africa', *Journal of the Royal Anthropological Institute* 22 (3): 552–69.

2016d. *State of Rebellion: violence and intervention in the Central African Republic*. London: Zed.

2017. 'Central African Republic: rebellion and international intervention' in Morten Bøås and Kevin C. Dunn (eds), *Africa's Insurgents: navigating an evolving landscape*. Boulder CO: Lynne Rienner.

2018a. 'General Tarzan the soccer coach: Humanitarian detours in the career of a Central African man-in-arms' in Marcia C. Inhorn and Nefissa Naguib (eds), *Reconceiving Muslim Men: Love and Marriage, Family and Care in Precarious Times*. New York: Berghahn.

2018b. 'Denouncing sovereignty: claims to liberty in northeastern Central African Republic', *Comparative Studies in Society and History* 60 (4): 1066–95.

Lombard, Louisa and Tatiana Carayannis. 2015. 'Making sense of CAR: an introduction' in Tatiana Carayannis and Louisa Lombard (eds), *Making Sense of the Central African Republic*. London: Zed.

Lombard, Louisa and Jérôme Tubiana. n.d. 'Guard-tracker trajectories in violent environments: cases from eastern Chad and northeastern Central African Republic', article under review.

Londres, Albert. 2012 [1928]. *Terre d'Ébène*. Paris: Les Éditions de Londres.

Loos, Isaac Althaus. 1899. *Studies in the Politics of Aristotle and the Republic of Plato*. Iowa City IA: University of Iowa.

Lovejoy, Paul E. 1986. *Africans in Bondage: studies in slavery and the slave trade. Essays in honor of Philip D. Curtin on the occasion of the twenty-fifth anniversary of African studies at the University of Wisconsin*. Madison WI: African Studies Program, University of Wisconsin.

Loveridge, Andrew. 2018. *Lion Hearted: the life and death of Cecil and the future of Africa's iconic cats*. New York NY: Regan Arts.

Lowy, Joan. 2002. 'Some conservationists fighting back: with guns', *Scripps Howard News Service*, 17 December.

Lucas, Colin. 1997. 'The theory and practice of denunciation in the French Revolution' in Sheila Fitzpatrick and Robert Gellately (eds), *Accusatory Practices: denunciation in modern European history, 1789–1989*. Chicago IL: University of Chicago Press.

Lundgren, Clark G. 2009. *Rapport d'Expertise: ebauche d'un schéma directeur pour l'aménagement d'un réseau des points d'eau perennes dans les zones de chasses villageoises. Rapport de la première mission (mars – avril 2009)*. Bangui: PDZCV.

Lunstrum, Elizabeth. 2014. 'Green militarization: anti-poaching efforts and the spatial contours of Kruger National Park', *Annals of the Association of American Geographers* 104 (4): 816–32.

Luxemburg, Rosa. 2003 [1951]. *The Accumulation of Capital*. New York NY: Routledge.

MacKenzie, John M. 1988. *The Empire of Nature: hunting, conservation and British imperialism*. Manchester: Manchester University Press.

Mahmood, Saba. 2004. *Politics of Piety: the Islamic revival and the feminist subject*. Princeton NJ: Princeton University Press.

Maine, Henry Sumner. 1915 [1888]. *International Law: the Whewell lectures of 1887*. London: John Murray.

Malinowski, Bronisław. 1922. *Argonauts of the Western Pacific: an account of native enterprise and adventure in the archipelagoes of Melanesian New Guinea*. London: Routledge.

1926. *Crime and Custom in Savage Society*. London: Kegan Paul, Trench, Trubner, and Co.

Mamdani, Mahmood. 1996. *Citizen and Subject: contemporary Africa and the legacy of late colonialism*. Princeton NJ: Princeton University Press.

2009. *Saviors and Survivors: Darfur, politics, and the War on Terror*. New York NY: Pantheon.

Mann, Gregory. 2009. 'What was the indigénat? The "empire of law" in French West Africa', *Journal of African History* 50 (3): 331–53.

2014. *From Empires to NGOs in the West African Sahel*. New York NY: Cambridge University Press.

Maran, René. 2012. *Batouala*. Paris: Albin Michel.

Marchal, Roland. 2009. 'Aux marges du monde, en Afrique centrale …'. Études du CERI 153–4. Paris: Centre d'Études et de Recherches Internationales (CERI).

2015. 'CAR and the regional (dis)order' in Tatiana Carayannis and Louisa Lombard (eds), *Making Sense of the Central African Republic*. London: Zed.

Marijnen, Esther. 2017. 'The "green militarisation" of development aid: the European Commission and the Virunga National Park, DR Congo', *Third World Quarterly* 38 (7): 1566–82.

2018. 'Public authority and conservation in areas of armed conflict: Virunga National Park as a "state within a state" in Eastern Congo', *Development and Change* 49 (3): 790–814.

Marijnen, Esther and Judith Verweijen. 2018. 'Pluralising political forests: unpacking "the state" by tracing Virunga's charcoal chain', *Antipode*.

Marks, Stuart A. 1991. *Southern Hunting in Black and White: nature, history, and ritual in a southern community*. Princeton NJ: Princeton University Press.

2016. *Life as a Hunt: thresholds of identities and illusions on an African landscape*. New York NY: Berghann Books.

Matfess, Hilary. 2017. *Women and the War on Boko Haram*. London: Zed.

Maurer, Bill. 2005. *Mutual Life, Limited: Islamic banking, alternative currencies, lateral reason*. Princeton NJ: Princeton University Press.

Mavhunga, Clapperton Chakanetsa. 2011. 'Vermin beings on pestiferous animals and human game', *Social Text* 29 (1): 151–76.

2014. *Transient Workspaces: technologies of everyday innovation in Zimbabwe*. Cambridge MA: MIT Press.

Mbembe, Achille. 2000. 'At the edge of the world: boundaries, territoriality, and sovereignty in Africa', translated by Steven Rendall, *Public Culture* 12 (1): 259–84.

2001. *On the Postcolony*. Berkeley CA: University of California Press.

2003. 'Necropolitics', translated by Libby Meintjes, *Public Culture* 15 (1): 11–40.

2006. 'On politics as a form of expenditure' in Jean Comaroff and John L. Comaroff (eds), *Law and Disorder in the Postcolony*. Chicago IL: University of Chicago Press.

Mbembe, Achille and Sarah Nuttall. 2004. 'Writing the world from an African metropolis', *Public Culture* 16 (3): 347–72.

McGovern, Mike. 2015. 'Liberty and moral ambivalence: postsocialist transitions, refugee hosting, and bodily comportment in the Republic of Guinea', *American Ethnologist* 42 (2): 247–61.

Metefia, Louis Bernardin. 1982. 'Evolution de la politique coloniale française dans les sultanats du Haut-Oubangui (1890–1920): des premiers contacts à la mise en place d'une administration directe'. Master's thesis, University of Provence.

Miller, Christopher L. 1998. *Nationalists and Nomads: essays on francophone African literature and culture*. Chicago IL: University of Chicago Press.

Miller, Hugh T. and Charles J. Fox. 2001. 'The epistemic community', *Administration and Society* 32 (6): 668–85.

Miller, William Ian. 2005. *An Eye for an Eye*. Cambridge: Cambridge University Press.

Mollion, Pierre. 1984. 'Étude d'une mentalité coloniale: l'image des Noirs chez les Blancs en Oubangui Chari à la fin du XIXème siècle et au début du XXème siècle' in *Recherches Centrafricaines: problèmes et perspectives de la recherché historique*. Aix-en-Provence: University of Provence.

1992. *Sur les Pistes de l'Oubangui-Chari Au Tchad, 1890–1930: le drame du portage en Afrique Centrale*. Paris: L'Harmattan.

Moreno, Eva. 1995. 'Rape in the field: reflections from a survivor' in D. Kulick and M. Wilson (eds), *Taboo: sex, identity, and erotic subjectivity in fieldwork*. London: Routledge.

Nachtigal, Gustav. 1971. *Sahara and Sudan: Kawar, Bornu, Kanem, Borku, Enned*. Volume 1. Berkeley CA: University of California Press.

Nadasdy, Paul. 2007. 'The gift in the animal: the ontology of hunting and human–animal sociality', *American Ethnologist* 34 (1): 25–43.

Naylor, R. Thomas. 2005. 'The underworld of ivory', *Crime, Law and Social Change* 42 (4): 261–95.

Nettle, John P. 1968. 'The state as a conceptual variable', *World Politics* 20 (4): 559–92.

Neumann, Roderick P. 1998. *Imposing Wilderness: struggles over livelihood and nature preservation in Africa*. Berkeley CA: University of California Press.

2001. 'Disciplining peasants in Tanzania: from state violence to self-surveillance in wildlife conservation' in Nancy Lee Peluso and Michael Watts (eds), *Violent Environments*. Ithaca NY: Cornell University Press.

2004a [1996]. 'Toward a critical theorization of conservation enclosures' in Richard Peet and Michael J. Watts (eds), *Liberation Ecologies: environment, development, social movements*. New York NY: Routledge.

2004b. 'Moral and discursive geographies in the war for biodiversity in Africa', *Political Geography* 23 (7): 813–37.

Nolutshungu, Sam C. 1996. *Limits of Anarchy: intervention and state formation in Chad*. Charlottesville VA: University of Virginia Press.

Nzabakomada-Yakoma, Raphaël. 1986. *L'Afrique Centrale Insurgée: la Guerre du Kongo-Wara (1928–1930)*. Paris: L'Harmattan.

Olin, Nathaniel. 2015. 'Pathologies of peacekeeping and peacebuilding in CAR' in Tatiana Carayannis and Louisa Lombard (eds), *Making Sense of the Central African Republic*. London: Zed.

Olson, Mancur. 1993. 'Dictatorship, democracy, and development', *American Political Science Review* 87 (3): 567–76.

2000. *Power and Prosperity: outgrowing communist and capitalist dictatorships*. New York NY: Basic Books.

Onana, Charles. 1998. *Bokassa: ascension et chute d'un empereur, 1921–1996. Une enquête qui dévoile la face cachée du pouvoir sous Giscard et Mitterrand*. Paris: Lavauzelle Graphic.

Ortner, Sherry B. 1996. *Making Gender: the politics and the erotics of culture*. Boston MA: Beacon Press.

2016. 'Dark anthropology and its others: theory since the Eighties', *HAU: Journal of Ethnographic Theory* 6 (1): 47–73.

PDRN. 1995. *Rapport d'Activités pour l'Année de Programme 1994–1995, PDRN Phase 2*. Bangui: NORCADEV (EU-DGVIII-PDRN Programme de Développement de la Région Nord).

Peluso, Nancy Lee. 1993. 'Coercing conservation?: The politics of state resource control', *Global Environmental Change* 3 (2): 199–217.

Peristiany, Jean G. 1965. *Honor and Shame: the values of Mediterranean society*. London: Weidenfeld and Nicolson.

Piermay, Jean-Luc. 1977. 'La cueillette dans l'économie villageoise centre-africaine', *Bulletin de l'Association de Géographes Français* 54 (447): 343–8.

Piot, Charles. 1999. *Remotely Global: village modernity in West Africa*. Chicago IL: University of Chicago Press.

2010. *Nostalgia for the Future: West Africa after the Cold War*. Chicago IL: University of Chicago Press.

Plato. 1961. *Plato: the collected dialogues*. Edited by Edith Hamilton and Huntington Cairns. Princeton NJ: Princeton University Press.

Porter, Doug and Michael Watts. 2017. 'Righting the resource curse: institutional politics and state capabilities in Edo State, Nigeria', *Journal of Development Studies* 53 (2): 249–63.

Pospíšil, Leopold. 1972. *The Ethnography of Law*. Reading MA: Addison-Wesley.

Poulaine, Robert. 1930. *Etapes Africaines: voyage autour du Congo*. Paris: Nouvelle Revue Critique.

Povinelli, Elizabeth A. 2002. *The Cunning of Recognition: indigenous alterities and the making of Australian multiculturalism*. Durham NC: Duke University Press.

2011. *Economies of Abandonment: social belonging and endurance in late liberalism*. Durham NC: Duke University Press.

Prins, Pierre M. 1909. 'Les troglodytes du Dar Banda et du Djebel Mela' in *Bulletin de Géographie Historique et Descriptive*. Paris: Imprimerie Nationale.

Prioul, Christian. 1981. *Entre Oubangui et Chari Vers 1890*. Paris: Société d'Ethnologie.

Radcliffe-Brown, A. R. 1940. 'Preface' in E. E. Evans-Pritchard and Meyer Fortes (eds), *African Political Systems*. Oxford: Oxford University Press.

Rentería-Valencia, Rodrigo F. 2015. 'Ethics, hunting tales, and the multispecies debate: the entextualization of nonhuman narratives', *Visual Anthropology Review* 31 (1): 94–103.

Reyna, Stephen P. 1999. 'The force of two logics: predatory and capital accumulation in the making of the Great Leviathan, 1415–1763' in Stephen P. Reyna and R. E. Downs (eds), *Deadly Developments: capitalism, states, and war*. Amsterdam: Taylor and Francis.

Richards, Paul. 1996. *Fighting for the Rainforest: war, youth, and resources in Sierra Leone*. London: James Currey.

Rid, Thomas. 2009. 'Razzia: a turning point in modern strategy', *Terrorism and Political Violence* 21 (4): 617–35.

Robinson, Carolyn A. Jost and Melissa J. Remis. 2014. 'Entangled realms: hunters and hunted in the Dzanga-Sangha Dense Forest Reserve (APDS), Central African Republic', *Anthropological Quarterly* 87 (3): 613–33.

Robinson, Carolyn A. Jost, Lesley L. Daspit, and Melissa J. Remis. 2011. 'Multifaceted approaches to understanding changes in wildlife and livelihoods in a protected area: a conservation case study from the Central African Republic', *Environmental Conservation* 38 (2): 247–55.

Rodney, Walter. 1972. *How Europe Underdeveloped Africa*. Washington DC: Howard University Press.

Roitman, Janet. 1998. 'The garrison-entrepôt (l'entrepôt-garnison)', *Cahiers d'Études Africaines* 150–2: 297–329.

2001. 'New sovereigns? Regulatory authority in the Chad Basin' in Ronald Cassimir and Thomas Callaghy (eds). *Intervention and Transnationalism in Africa: global–local networks of power*. New York NY: Cambridge University Press.

2005. *Fiscal Disobedience: an anthropology of economic regulation in Central Africa*. Princeton NJ: Princeton University Press.

2006. 'The ethics of illegality in the Chad Basin' in Jean Comaroff and John L. Comaroff (eds), *Law and Disorder in the Postcolony*. Chicago IL: University of Chicago Press.

Roulet, Pierre-Armand. 2004. '"Chasseur blanc, coeur noir? La chasse sportive en Afrique Centrale. Une analyse de son rôle dans la conservation de la faune sauvage et le développement rural au travers des programmes de gestion communautaire". Les cas du nord RCA et du sud-est Cameroun'. PhD thesis, University of Orléans.

2005. *Étude Socio-économique dans les Préfectures Vakaga et Bamingui-Bangoran, Nord-est de la République Centrafricaine*. Bangui: ECOFAC and PDZCV.

2009. *Rapport d'Expertise: bilan technique des zones cynégetiques villageoises, saison 2008–2009. Rapport de deuxième mission (15 Avril – 22 Mai 2009). Version définitive*. Bangui: ECOFAC and PDZCV.

2010. *Rapport d'Expertise: appui technique aux zones de chasse villageoises, Rapport de mission 3 (13 Décembre 2009–18 Janvier 2010)*. Bangui: ECOFAC and PDZCV.

Rupp, Stephanie Karin. 2011. *Forests of Belonging: identities, ethnicities, and stereotypes in the Congo River Basin*. Washington DC: University of Washington Press.

Rushby, George. 1965. *No More the Tusker*. London: W. H. Allen.

Rutherford, Danilyn. 2003. *Raiding the Land of the Foreigners*. Princeton NJ: Princeton University Press.

2012. *Laughing at Leviathan: sovereignty and audience in West Papua*. Chicago IL: University of Chicago Press.

2016. 'How structuralism matters', *HAU: Journal of Ethnographic Theory* 6 (3): 61–77.

Sahlins, Marshall. 1961. 'The segmentary lineage: an organization of predatory expansion', *American Anthropologist* 63: 322–45.

Santandrea, Stefano. 1957. 'Sanusi, ruler of Dar Banda and Dar Kuti, in the history of the Bahr-el-Ghazal', *Sudan Notes and Records* 38: 151–5.

1964. *A Tribal History of the Western Bahr El Ghazal*. Florence: Editrice Nigrizia.

Sassen, Saskia. 2006. *Territory, Authority, Rights: from medieval to global assemblages*. Princeton NJ: Princeton University Press.

Saulnier, Pierre. 1998. *Le Centrafrique: entre mythe et réalité*. Paris: L'Harmattan.

Schauer, Jeffrey. 2018. *Wildlife between Empire and Nation in Twentieth-century Africa*. New York NY: Palgrave.

Scheele, Judith. 2015. 'The values of "anarchy": moral autonomy among Tubu-speakers in northern Chad', *Journal of the Royal Anthropological Institute* 21 (1): 32–48.

Schlee, Günther. 2004. 'Taking sides and constructing identities: reflections on conflict theory', *Journal of the Royal Anthropological Institute* 10 (1): 135–56.

Schmitt, Carl. 2005 [1922]. *Political Theology: four chapters on the concept of sovereignty*. Chicago IL: University of Chicago Press.

Schroeder, Richard A. 2018. 'Moving targets: the "canned" hunting of captive-bred lions in South Africa', *African Studies Review* 61 (1): 8–32.

Schumaker, Lyn. 2001. *Africanizing Anthropology: fieldwork, networks, and the making of cultural knowledge in Central Africa*. Durham NC: Duke University Press.

Schweinfurth, Georg. 1873. *The Heart of Africa: three years' travels and adventures in the unexplored regions of Central Africa, from 1868 to 1871*. Translated by Ellen E. Frewer. London: Sampson Low, Marston, Low, and Searle.

Scott, James C. 1998. *Seeing Like a State: how certain schemes to improve the human condition have failed*. New Haven CT: Yale University Press.

2009. *The Art of Not Being Governed: an anarchist history of upland Southeast Asia*. New Haven CT: Yale University Press.

2017. *Against the Grain: a deep history of the earliest states*. New Haven CT: Yale University Press.

Service, Elman R. 1966. *The Hunters*. London: Prentice-Hall.

1971. *Primitive Social Organization: an evolutionary perspective*. New York NY: Random House.

Shanahan, Christopher L. 2004. '"(No) mercy" nary patrols: a controversial, last-ditch effort to salvage the Central African Republic's Chinko Basin', *Thomas Jefferson Law Review* 27: 223–54.

Siegal, Nina. 2017. 'The intimate lens of Ed van der Elsken', *New York Times*, 24 February <https://www.nytimes.com/2017/02/24/arts/design/the-intimate-lens-of-ed-van-der-elsken.html> (accessed 8 September 2019).
Sikainga, Ahmad Alawad. 1991. *The Western Bahr Al-Ghazal under British Rule, 1898–1956*. Athens OH: Ohio University Press.
Simiti, Bernard. 2013. *Le Dar-El-Kouti: Empire Oubanguien de Senoussi (1890–1911)*. Paris: L'Harmattan-Congo.
Simone, AbdouMaliq. 2001. 'On the worlding of African cities', *African Studies Review* 44 (2): 15–41.
2004a. *For the City yet to Come: changing African life in four cities*. Durham NC: Duke University Press.
2004b. 'People as infrastructure: intersecting fragments in Johannesburg', *Public Culture* 16 (3): 407–29.
Smith, Stephen. 2015a. 'CAR's history: the past of a tense present' in Tatiana Carayannis and Louisa Lombard (eds), *Making Sense of the Central African Republic*. London: Zed.
2015b. 'The elite's road to riches in a poor country' in Tatiana Carayannis and Louisa Lombard (eds), *Making Sense of the Central African Republic*. London: Zed.
Sousa Santos, Boaventura de. 1987. 'Law: a map of misreading. Toward a postmodern conception of law', *Journal of Law and Society* 14 (3): 279–302.
Steinberg, Jonny. 2013. 'Working through a paradox about sexual culture in South Africa: tough sex in the twenty-first century', *Journal of Southern African Studies* 39 (3): 497–509.
Taussig, Michael. 1992. *The Nervous System*. New York NY: Taylor and Francis.
Thompson, Edward Palmer. 1975. *Whigs and Hunters: the origin of the black act*. New York NY: Pantheon.
Tilly, Charles. 1985. 'War making and state making as organized crime' in P. B. Evans, Dietrich Rueschemeyer, and Theda Skocpol (eds), *Bringing the State Back In*. New York NY: Cambridge University Press.
2004. 'Trust and rule', *Theory and Society* 33 (1): 1–30.
Tomety, Simon Narcisse. 2009. *Analyse de la Dimension Transfrontalière des Conflits dans l'Est de la République Centrafricaine: mission d'information, d'échange, et d'étude au Tchad*. Bangui: European Commission.
Toqué, Georges. 1996 [1907]. *Les Massacres du Congo: la terre qui ment, la terre qui tue*. Paris: L'Harmattan.
Trouillot, Michel-Rolph. 2001. 'The anthropology of the state in the age of globalization: close encounters of the deceptive kind', *Current Anthropology* 42 (1): 125–38.
Tsing, Anna Lowenhaupt. 1993. *In the Realm of the Diamond Queen: marginality in an out-of-the-way place*. Princeton NJ: Princeton University Press.
2000. 'The global situation', *Cultural Anthropology* 15 (3): 327–60.
2003. 'Natural resources and capitalist frontiers', *Economic and Political Weekly* 38 (48): 5100–6.
2005. *Friction: an ethnography of global connection*. Princeton NJ: Princeton University Press.

2015. *The Mushroom at the End of the World*. Princeton NJ: Princeton University Press.
Tubiana, Jérôme. 2018. 'Mirages aux éléphants'. *Révue XXI* 42: 44–55.
van der Elsken, Ed. 1961. *Bagara: photographs of Equatorial Africa*. London: Abelard-Schuman.
Vandergeest, Peter and Nancy Lee Peluso. 2015. 'Political forests' in Raymond L. Bryant (ed.), *International Handbook of Political Ecology*. Northampton MA: Edward Elgar Publishers.
Vergès, Françoise. 2002. 'The power of words', *Public Culture* 14 (3): 607–10.
Verweijen, Judith and Esther Marijnen. 2018. 'The counterinsurgency/conservation nexus: guerrilla livelihoods and the dynamics of conflict and violence in the Virunga National Park, Democratic Republic of the Congo', *Journal of Peasant Studies* 45 (2): 300–20.
Vigh, Henrik E. 2006. *Navigating Terrains of War: youth and soldiering in Guinea-Bissau*. New York NY: Berghahn Books.
2009. 'Motion squared: a second look at the concept of social navigation', *Anthropological Theory* 9 (4): 419–38.
Watts, Michael J. 2012. 'A tale of two gulfs: life, death, and dispossession along two oil frontiers', *American Quarterly* 64 (3): 437–67.
Weber, Max. 1978 [1922]. *Economy and Society: an outline in interpretive sociology*. Edited by Guenther Roth and Claus Wittich. Berkeley CA: University of California Press.
Willerslev, Rane. 2007. *Soul Hunters: hunting, animism, and personhood among the Siberian Yukaghirs*. Berkeley CA: University of California Press.
Wonders, Karen. 2005. 'Hunting narratives of the age of empire: a gender reading of their iconography', *Environment and History* 11 (3): 269–91.
Woods, Elliott D. 2016. 'The fight for Chinko', *Virginia Quarterly* 92 (3).
Zigon, Jarrett. 2007. 'Moral breakdown and ethical demand: a theoretical framework for an anthropology of moralities', *Anthropological Theory* 7 (2): 131–50.
Zoctizoum, Yarisse. 1983. *Histoire de La Centrafrique. Tome 1: 1879–1959: violence du développement, domination et inégalités*. Paris: L'Harmattan.

Archival sources

Angoulvant, G. 1918. Letter: 'Le Gouv Gen de AEF à M. le Ministre des Colonies, Paris. Objet: AS des exodes en Territoire anglais', Dakar, 22 July. Archives Nationales d'Outre-Mer, Aix-en-Provence (ANOM), AEF/GGAEF, Carton D/4(3)/18.
Antonetti, R. n.d. [*c.* 1929]. Correspondence: No title [missing cover page]. 12 pages (unpaginated). ANOM, AEF/GGAEF, Carton D/1/4.
Bertin. 1959. Letter: 'Campagne de Birao', to Monsieur le Général de Corps d'Armée, Commandant Supérieur de la Zone d'Outre-Mer No. 2, Brazzaville. No. 255/CSC.3/S. Service Historique de la Défense, Vincennes (SHD), Carton 6/H/47.

Bordier, P. 1959. 'Note à l'attention de Monsieur le Chef du District Autonome de Birao, de l'Haut Commissariat après de la République Centrafricaine'. Cabinet Militaire, SHD, 208/CM.BE.

Boucher. 1934. 'Monographie de Birao: étude effectuée par M. 1e Administrateur des Colonies, BOUCHER, Chef de la Circonscription du DAR-KOUTI ORIENTAL. BIRAO', 31 December. SHD, Carton 6/H/124.

Cedile. 1956. Letter: '1694 A.P. 3. Direction des Affaires Politiques. A: Monsieur le Gouvereur, Chef du Territoire de l'OUBANGUI-CHARI – BANGUI. REFERENCE: Votre lettre 460 AP du 16 Mai 1956. Objet/Sujet: Passage de Frontière par les elements Soudanais', 30 May. SHD, Carton 6/H/62.

Chauvet. 1956. Letter: '12.11.56-RB/3526 AP.3. A: Monsieur le Gouverneur Chef du Territoire de l'Oubangui-Chari – Bangui. De: Directions des Affaires Politiques. Sujet/Objet: Eventualité de reflux de population soudanaise en Oubangui-Chari, référence votre lettre 1280 AP du 6 novembre 1956', 14 November. SHD, Carton 6/H/62.

Colonie du Congo. 1903. Report: 'Rapport Général Annuel, Commandant Supérieur des Troupes. Brazzaville', 20 October. SHD, Carton 6/H/2.

Commandant Militaire de l'Oubangui-Chari. 1958. Letter: 'FICHE: CAMPAGNE de BIRAO (28 Janvier au 24 Avril 1958). Brazzaville, le 17 JUIL 1958. Lettre no. 160/CM 3 du Commandant Militaire de l'Oubangui-Chari'. SHD, Carton 6/H/47.

Government of Congo Française. 1909. Report: 'Rapport Annuel 1909, Troupes du Groupe du Congo, le Commandant Supérieur. Brazzaville', 22 November. SHD, Carton 6/H/2.

Government of Oubangui-Chari. 1911. Report: 'SITUATION POLITIQUE GENERALE de L'OUBANGUI-CHARI en 1910. Signé à Bangui', 10 July. ANOM, AEF/GGAEF, Carton D/4(4)/8.

1929. 'Tarifs des permis de chasse en vigeur en AEF', 1 August. ANOM, AEF/GGAEF, Carton D/1/4.

n.d. 'Presentation Sommaire du Territoire de l'Oubangui-Chari'. Marked "très secret". SHD, Carton 6/H/127.

Governor of Oubangui-Chari. 1911. Letter: 'M le Ministre des Colonies (Cabinet. – Direction des Affaires Politiques & Administratives – Direction des Services Militaires.) A Paris le 28 Mai 1911. Objet: A.A. de l'arrestation de SENOUSSI et de la situation au Dar-Kouti', 28 May. ANOM, AEF/GGAEF, Carton D/4(4)/8.

Journal Officiel de l'Afrique Equatoriale Française. 1917. 'Arrêté fixant les conditions de la chasse dans la colonie de l'Oubangui-Chari', 15 January, p. 4. ANOM, AEF/GGAEF, Carton D/5/82.

Lavauden, M. L. 1931. Report: 'La Diminution et la protection rationnelle de la grande faune africaine. Paris. Rapport par M.L. Lavauden, Conservateur des Eaux et Forêts'. ANOM, AEF/GGAEF, Carton D/5/82.

Lieutenant Governor of Oubangui-Chari. 1911. 'Objet: HISTORIQUE Très Succinct de Nos Relations Avec Senoussi, Ayant Pour but D'expliquer Comment Nous Avons Été Amenés À Procéder À L'arrestation Du Sultan'. ANOM, AEF/GGAEF, Carton D/4(4)/8.

Lignier. 1936a. Report: 'Rapport Trimestriel de La Subdivision de NDELE. 2ème Trimestre. Trimestrial report, Ndele'. ANOM, AEF/GGAEF, Carton D/4(3)/48.

1936b. Report: 'Rapport Du 3eme Trimestre 1936. Trimestrial report, Ndele'. ANOM, AEF/GGAEF, Carton D/4(3)/48.

Mbitikon, Raymond. 2002. Report: 'Compte-Rendu de l'événement du 8 mai 2002 de Mossabio'. ECOFAC/Archives of the European Union, Bangui (AEC), Carton 8 ACP RCE 009/8 ACP CA 010.

Modat, Captain Jean. 1909. Letter no. 48 of 30 November. SHD, Carton 6/H/124.

1910a. Letter no. 14 of 3 April. SHD, Carton 6/H/124.

1910b. Letter no. 45 of 24 June. SHD, Carton 6/H/124.

1910c. Report: 'Rapport Géographique à l'appui de l'itinéraire N'Délé Kafia-Kingi Djellab N'Délé'. SHD, Carton 6/H/2.

Mordrelle. 1910. Report: 'Rapport du Colonel MORDRELLE, Commandant Supérieur des Troupes, sur l'occupation militarie de l'Afrique Equatoriale Française. Fait à Brazzaville le 28 Septembre 1910'. SHD, Carton 6/H/2.

Natalini. 1918. Report: 'Rapport de Tournée Effectuée Par Le Chef de Subdivision de Mopoi Du 23 Février Au 11 Mars 1918; BUT: Tournée de Recensement Dans Les Commandements de Selim, Degri, Bembi, Obo, et Yapassira'. ANOM, Government of French Equatorial Africa.

Pampaloni, Corrado. 2003. 'Note du dossier – Ecofac ZCV', 13 November. AEC, Carton 8 ACP RCE 009/8 ACP CA 010.

PDRN (Programme du Développement de la Région Nord). 1985. Report: 'Document de base: PDRN'. AEC, Carton P.6 ACP CA 004.

1990. Report: 'Rapport annuel au 31 Mars. PDRN 6100.37.17.004 (CA 6002). Archives of the European Commission, Bangui, Carton 31.

1998. Report: 'Rapport semestriel au 31 décembre 1997. Juillet. Norcadev. Archives of the European Commission, Bangui.

Perrien, Louis. 1936. Report: 'Rapport Politique, Subdivision Autonome de Birao'. ANOM, AEF/GGAEF, Carton D/4(3)/48.

Placet, Jean. 1949. Report by Chef du District Autonome: 'Rapport politique, année 1948, district autonome de N'Dele', 17 February. ANOM, AEF/GGAEF, Carton D/4(3)/59.

Schmoll. 1914. Report: 'Rapport de tournée du Capitaine SCHMOLL, Commandant la Circonscription du Dar-Kouti. A N'dele, le 26 Mars 1914. No. 78. Objet: Rapport de tournée Nord-Est du Dar-Kouti'. ANOM, AEF/GGAEF Carton D/2/58.

Senoussi–Gentil. 1897. Treaty of 24 August. SHD, Carton 6/H/124.

Senoussi–Fourneau. 1903. Treaty of 18 February. SHD, Carton 6/H/124.

Senoussi–Mongin. 1908. Treaty of 26 January. SHD, Carton 6/H/124.

Soulages. 1901. Report: 'Le Lac Tchad: Travail d'Hiver De Monsieur le Lieutenant Soulages', 26 February. SHD, Carton 6/H/2.

Index

Titles in the series

61. LOUISA LOMBARD *Hunting Game: Raiding Politics in the Central African Republic*
60. MARK HUNTER *Race for Education: Gender, White Tone, and Schooling in South Africa*
59. LIZ GUNNER *Radio Soundings: South Africa and the Black Modern*
58. JESSICA JOHNSON *In Search of Gender Justice: Rights and Relationships in Matrilineal Malawi*
57. JASON SUMICH *The Middle Class in Mozambique: The State and the Politics of Transformation in Southern Africa*
56. JOSÉ-MARÍA MUÑOZ *Doing Business in Cameroon: An Anatomy of Economic Governance*
55. JENNIFER DIGGINS *Coastal Sierra Leone: Materiality and the Unseen in Maritime West Africa*
54. HANNAH HOECHNER *Quranic Schools in Northern Nigeria: Everyday Experiences of Youth, Faith, and Poverty*
53. HOLLY PORTER *After Rape: Violence, Justice, and Social Harmony in Uganda*
52. ALEXANDER THURSTON *Salafism in Nigeria: Islam, Preaching, and Politics*
51. ANDREW BANK *Pioneers of the Field: South Africa's Women Anthropologists*
50. MAXIM BOLT *Zimbabwe's Migrants and South Africa's Border Farms: The Roots of Impermanence*
49. MEERA VENKATACHALAM *Slavery, Memory and Religion in Southeastern Ghana, c.1850–Present*
48. DEREK PETERSON, KODZO GAVUA, and CIRAJ RASSOOL (eds) *The Politics of Heritage in Africa: Economies, Histories, and Infrastructures*
47. ILANA VAN WYK *The Universal Church of the Kingdom of God in South Africa: A Church of Strangers*
46. JOEL CABRITA *Text and Authority in the South African Nazaretha Church*
45. MARLOES JANSON *Islam, Youth, and Modernity in the Gambia: The Tablighi Jama'at*
44. ANDREW BANK and LESLIE J. BANK (eds) *Inside African Anthropology: Monica Wilson and her Interpreters*
43. ISAK NIEHAUS *Witchcraft and a Life in the New South Africa*
42. FRASER G. MCNEILL *AIDS, Politics, and Music in South Africa*
41. KRIJN PETERS *War and the Crisis of Youth in Sierra Leone*
40. INSA NOLTE *Obafemi Awolowo and the Making of Remo: The Local Politics of a Nigerian Nationalist*
39. BEN JONES *Beyond the State in Rural Uganda*
38. RAMON SARRÓ *The Politics of Religious Change on the Upper Guinea Coast: Iconoclasm Done and Undone*
37. CHARLES GORE *Art, Performance and Ritual in Benin City*
36. FERDINAND DE JONG *Masquerades of Modernity: Power and Secrecy in Casamance, Senegal*
35. KAI KRESSE *Philosophising in Mombasa: Knowledge, Islam and Intellectual Practice on the Swahili Coast*

34. DAVID PRATTEN *The Man-Leopard Murders: History and Society in Colonial Nigeria*
33. CAROLA LENTZ *Ethnicity and the Making of History in Northern Ghana*
32. BENJAMIN F. SOARES *Islam and the Prayer Economy: History and Authority in a Malian Town*
31. COLIN MURRAY and PETER SANDERS *Medicine Murder in Colonial Lesotho: The Anatomy of a Moral Crisis*
30. R. M. DILLEY *Islamic and Caste Knowledge Practices among Haalpulaar'en in Senegal: Between Mosque and Termite Mound*
29. BELINDA BOZZOLI *Theatres of Struggle and the End of Apartheid*
28. ELISHA RENNE *Population and Progress in a Yoruba Town*
27. ANTHONY SIMPSON *'Half-London' in Zambia: Contested Identities in a Catholic Mission School*
26. HARRI ENGLUND *From War to Peace on the Mozambique–Malawi Borderland*
25. T. C. MCCASKIE *Asante Identities: History and Modernity in an African Village 1850–1950*
24. JANET BUJRA *Serving Class: Masculinity and the Feminisation of Domestic Service in Tanzania*
23. CHRISTOPHER O. DAVIS *Death in Abeyance: Illness and Therapy among the Tabwa of Central Africa*
22. DEBORAH JAMES *Songs of the Women Migrants: Performance and Identity in South Africa*
21. BIRGIT MEYER *Translating the Devil: Religion and Modernity among the Ewe in Ghana*
20. DAVID MAXWELL *Christians and Chiefs in Zimbabwe: A Social History of the Hwesa People c.1870s–1990s*
19. FIONA D. MACKENZIE *Land, Ecology and Resistance in Kenya, 1880–1952*
18. JANE I. GUYER *An African Niche Economy: Farming to Feed Ibadan, 1968–88*
17. PHILIP BURNHAM *The Politics of Cultural Difference in Northern Cameroon*
16. GRAHAM FURNISS *Poetry, Prose and Popular Culture in Hausa*
15. C. BAWA YAMBA *Permanent Pilgrims: The Role of Pilgrimage in the Lives of West African Muslims in Sudan*
14. TOM FORREST *The Advance of African Capital: The Growth of Nigerian Private Enterprise*
13. MELISSA LEACH *Rainforest Relations: Gender and Resource Use among the Mende of Gola, Sierra Leone*
12. ISAAC NCUBE MAZONDE *Ranching and Enterprise in Eastern Botswana: A Case Study of Black and White Farmers*
11. G. S. EADES *Strangers and Traders: Yoruba Migrants, Markets and the State in Northern Ghana*
10. COLIN MURRAY *Black Mountain: Land, Class and Power in the Eastern Orange Free State, 1880s to 1980s*
9. RICHARD WERBNER *Tears of the Dead: The Social Biography of an African Family*
8. RICHARD FARDON *Between God, the Dead and the Wild: Chamba Interpretations of Religion and Ritual*

7. KARIN BARBER *I Could Speak Until Tomorrow: Oriki Women and the Past in a Yoruba Town*
6. SUZETTE HEALD *Controlling Anger: The Sociology of Gisu Violence*
5. GUNTHER SCHLEE *Identities on the Move: Clanship and Pastoralism in Northern Kenya*
4. JOHAN POTTIER *Migrants No More: Settlement and Survival in Mambwe Villages, Zambia*
3. PAUL SPENCER *The Maasai of Matapato: A Study of Rituals of Rebellion*
2. JANE I. GUYER (ed.) *Feeding African Cities: Essays in Social History*
1. SANDRA T. BARNES *Patrons and Power: Creating a Political Community in Metropolitan Lagos*